Spare Time Guides, No. 9

SPARE TIME GUIDES SERIES

Ann J. Harwell, Editor

No. 1 *Automotive Repair and Maintenance.* By Robert G. Schipf.
No. 2 *Hunting and Fishing.* By Cecil F. Clotfelter.
No. 3 *Home Repair and Improvement.* By Robert G. Schipf.
No. 4 *Crafts for Today: Ceramics, Glasscrafting, Leatherworking, Candlemaking, and Other Popular Crafts.* By Rolly M. Harwell and Ann J. Harwell.
No. 5 *Stamps and Coins.* By Richard H. Rosichan.
No. 6 *Wine, Beer and Spirits.* By Dean Tudor.
No. 7 *Weaving, Spinning, and Dyeing.* By Lavonne Brady Axford.
No. 8 *Railroads.* By Paul B. Cors.
No. 9 *Outdoor Recreation.* By Robert G. Schipf.

SPARE TIME GUIDES:
Information Sources for Hobbies and Recreation, No. 9

Outdoor Recreation

ROBERT G. SCHIPF

1976
Libraries Unlimited, Inc.
Littleton, Colorado

Copyright © 1976 Libraries Unlimited, Inc.
All Rights Reserved
Printed in the United States of America

LIBRARIES UNLIMITED, INC.
P.O. Box 263
Littleton, Colorado 80120

Library of Congress Cataloging in Publication Data

Schipf, Robert G
   Outdoor recreation.

   (Spare time guides ; no. 9)
   Includes index.
   1. Outdoor recreation—Bibliography.
2. Outdoor recreation—United States—Bibliography.
3. Outdoor recreation—Canada—Bibliography.
I. Title.
Z7514.O8S33   [GV191.4]   016.796   75-30958

ISBN 0-87287-123-1

PREFACE

The Spare Time Guides series was conceived to provide librarians with selective, annotated lists of recommended books on specific hobbies and recreational activities, and also to help craftsmen and do-it-yourselfers learn more about their hobbies and crafts.

Because of the current interest in leisure time activities—and the resultant increase in the number of books concerning these activities—it has become difficult for librarians and hobbyists to determine just which books will fit their specific needs. Few selection aids on hobbies are available: the reviewing media that serve librarians devote little space to books on crafts and leisure time activities, and a search of hobby and crafts magazines reveals relatively few book reviews. In too many cases, the main source of information on crafts books is the promotional material provided by the publishers, which does not usually offer a critical evaluation of the work. The Spare Time Guides series is designed to provide sufficient information to enable librarians and hobbyists to distinguish between books of varying quality.

Although outdoor activities have always had avid supporters, several factors have recently combined to swell their ranks: more people than ever before are aware that the Great Outdoors can have a beneficial effect on the soul, particularly when used as an antidote to urban life. Another contributing factor is the current emphasis on physical fitness, which has filled the land with hikers, runners, swimmers, and skiers in unprecedented numbers.

Robert G. Schipf is the author of two earlier volumes in the Spare Time Guides series: *Automotive Repair and Maintenance* and *Home Repair and Improvement.* For the present volume he has compiled a bibliography of 739 books covering all aspects of outdoor recreation: camping and hiking; foods; identifying and collecting; vehicle, water, winter, and aerial activities; country living (including the currently popular back-to-the-land movement); and more. He brings to his task the bibliographic knowledge of a professional librarian and a lifelong interest in outdoor activities. His annotations, which reflect his first-hand knowledge of the subject, are evaluative and descriptive.

PREFACE

Following the main section of the book, which is arranged by subject, is an annotated listing of 108 pertinent periodicals, also arranged by subject. A directory of organizations and associations precedes the directory of publishers whose books are found in the bibliography. A complete author-title-subject index concludes the book. Chronologically, coverage is provided through 1974, though Mr. Schipf has also been able to include a number of books that appeared early in 1975.

Some activities have both a recreational and a competitive aspect (e.g., skiing, swimming). The recreational aspect of such activities is treated in the present bibliography, while books on the competitive aspect are covered in *Sports*, a forthcoming Spare Time Guide prepared by Marshall E. Nunn.

Ann J. Harwell
Editor, Spare Time Guides

CONTENTS

PREFACE	5
INTRODUCTION	9
CAMPING AND HIKING	15
A Word about Campground Guides	20
Camping, Campgrounds, and Travel	21
First-Choice Titles	39
Backpacking, Mountaineering, and Survival	40
First-Choice Titles	58
FOODS AND COOKING	60
IDENTIFYING AND COLLECTING	73
Identifying Animal and Plant Life	74
Identifying Rocks and Minerals; Treasure Hunting	84
VEHICLE ACTIVITIES	93
Bicycles	96
Motorcycles	103
Automobiles (Including RecVees, Four-Wheel-Drive Vehicles, Campers, and Car Travel)	110
WINTER ACTIVITIES	120
WATER ACTIVITIES	127
AERIAL ACTIVITIES	146
COUNTRY LIVING	155
ANIMAL-RELATED ACTIVITIES	172
MISCELLANEOUS	177

PERIODICALS ... 193
- General Camping and Travel ... 193
- Backpacking, Mountaineering, and Survival ... 195
- Identifying and Collecting ... 198
- Vehicle Activities ... 201
- Winter Activities ... 206
- Water Activities ... 207
- Aerial Activities ... 212
- Country Living ... 216
- Animal-Related Activities ... 219
- Miscellaneous ... 221

ORGANIZATIONS AND ASSOCIATIONS ... 225
- Camping, Campgrounds, and Travel ... 225
- Backpacking, Mountaineering, and Survival ... 226
- Identifying and Collecting ... 228
- Vehicle Activities ... 229
- Winter Activities ... 232
- Water Activities ... 233
- Aerial Activities ... 235
- Country Living ... 238
- Animal-Related Activities ... 239
- Miscellaneous ... 241

PUBLISHERS ... 244
INDEX ... 257

INTRODUCTION

A certain percentage of us have always been loafers, I suspect, but the continuing industrial revolution is probably responsible for the amazing proliferation of a species of lounger that has evolved a stunning variety of methods for avoiding physical exertion. The result of all this is the degradation of modern man (and the term encompasses those other "persons" who are so anxious to be included) into a physically weak and, often enough, mentally befuddled shell. Folks who still live active outdoor lives, whether through choice or through necessity, seem quite generally to be in better shape than the remainder of us. Since this defect in the pleasant species we know as *Homo sapiens* is now widely recognized, something is being done about it.

The "something" consists of several methods of getting people off their duffs and into physical activities not directly related to their jobs: more and better athletic facilities in schools; physical education and recreational programs through park departments, corporations, and clubs; and, of course, a plethora of publications devoted to recreation of all types. The purpose of this volume in the Spare Time Guides series is to call attention to a number of books, periodicals, and other sources of information that are thought to have some benefit both to individuals and to librarians. There are many other such publications, some rather difficult to verify or to find, but I have concentrated on the titles that were available to me in libraries, in personal collections, and from publishers.

The scope of this book may seem strange in places because of the nature of the beast we call "outdoor recreation." There are, very obviously, numerous activities that can be accomplished (or attempted) in the great outdoors. We cannot include all of them, even though some are sufficiently illegal, immoral, or exotic to attract us. We will try to include an assortment of recreational ploys that one may accomplish alone or with a minimum of companions. We will exclude "games," since for the most part these seem to require teams, much equipment, rules, and specific places. There are large numbers of books on how to play tennis, baseball, and croquet; they are not listed here. We intend, also, to exclude what is generally called "athletics"; as an example, we include books on cross-country skiing but not on alpine skiing. The intent, I

OUTDOOR RECREATION

hope, will be fairly clear. The next volume of the Spare Time Guides (*Sports*, by Marshall E. Nunn) will cover many of the sports activities excluded from this work.

At times, I had to make a choice as to where I'd place a book—a book on camping in the snow can be listed under camping or under winter sports. My rule was to choose the more specialized classification. As a result, books about canoe camping are in the section on water activities; a book about camping in snow is listed with winter activities titles; books about bicycle or motorcycle camping are in the vehicle activities chapter.

The amount of money now being expended on recreational equipment by the alert, or only affluent, citizens of the United States and Canada is truly enormous. As I drive about the country, I see large power boats being towed to lakes that did not exist a decade ago; hang gliders on every hill; mountains of garbage in every campground and roadside rest; backpacks sold in every drug store; bicyclists on every highway; rockhounds in every creek bed; motocross tracks in towns barely large enough to have post offices. Outdoor recreation, the subject of this book, takes many forms and I may have omitted some that would strike someone else as obvious inclusions. I knew a man several years ago whose outdoor hobby was the drilling of water wells. He had three complete drilling rigs and the crews to man them. He delighted in boring deep holes in the ground and, since he was sufficiently wealthy to keep going for the hell of it, he kept several good men amongst the ranks of the taxpayers. Not too many of us would regard well drilling as a "recreation," but my friend did—and it was assuredly done outdoors. Another buddy of mine would dash from his office to photograph trains as they puffed through some previously unrecorded cross-road. To each his own, if I may be permitted to coin a phrase.

There are many more books about certain recreational activities than about others. Compared to the number of books on horseback riding, the list of available titles on ballooning is pitiful. Some activities engender large and powerful organizations (motor boating), while others have difficulty attracting several hundred members. There can be a National Family Camping Week but not a National Family Shooting Week, even though the number of persons involved may be quite similar. I've celebrated National Pickle Week but not National Gold Panning Week. Even in recreation, there are powerful political forces at work; widespread prejudice against certain sports may be easily seen when looking over the list of sports in the President's Physical Fitness Program. There are legislators who would outlaw certain sports (such as shooting and football) and set up complex government bureaucracies to regulate others. Recreational activities certainly can bring out the best and the worst in folks, from the determined rescue of a stranded mountain climber to the screaming mother at a Little League baseball game.

Interest in recreational activities of all kinds is international, so it is not surprising that there is an international organization devoted to everyone's spare time. This is the World Leisure and Recreation Association, 345 East 46th

INTRODUCTION

Street, New York, New York 10017, formerly known as the International Recreation Association. Back in 1967, at a symposium on recreation held in Geneva, the IRA was asked to develop a "Charter for Leisure." A committee was formed and they completed their work in 1970. With the kind permission of Mr. William D. Cunningham, Executive Director of the WLRA, we offer the "Charter for Leisure."

CHARTER FOR LEISURE

PREFACE

Leisure time is that period of time at the complete disposal of an individual, after he has completed his work and fulfilled his other obligations. The uses of this time are of vital importance.

Leisure and recreation create a basis for compensating for many of the demands placed upon man by today's way of life. More important, they present a possibility of enriching life through participation in physical relaxation and sports, through an enjoyment of art, science, and nature. Leisure is important in all spheres of life, both urban and rural. Leisure pursuits offer man the chance of activating his essential gifts (a free development of the will, intelligence, sense of responsibility and creative faculty). Leisure hours are a period of freedom, when man is able to enhance his value as a human being and as a productive member of his society.

Recreation and leisure activities play an important part in establishing good relations between peoples and nations of the world.

Article 1

Every man has a right to leisure time. This right comprises reasonable working hours, regular paid holidays, favourable travelling conditions and suitable social planning, including reasonable access to leisure facilities, areas and equipment in order to enhance the advantages of leisure time.

Article 2

The right to enjoy leisure time with complete freedom is absolute. The prerequisites for undertaking individual leisure pursuits should be safeguarded to the same extent as those for collective enjoyment of leisure time.

OUTDOOR RECREATION

Article 3

Every man has a right to easy access to recreational facilities open to the public, and to nature reserves by lakes, seas, wooded areas, in the mountains and to open spaces in general. These areas, their fauna and flora, must be protected and conserved.

Article 4

Every man has a right to participate in and be introduced to all types of recreation during leisure time, such as sports and games, open-air living, travel, theatre, dancing, pictorial art, music, science and handicrafts, irrespective of age, sex, or level of education.

Article 5

Leisure time should be unorganized in the sense that official authorities, urban planners, architects and private groups of individuals do not decide how others are to use their leisure time. The above-mentioned should create or assist in the planning of the leisure opportunities, aesthetic environments and recreation facilities required to enable man to exercise individual choice in the use of his leisure, according to his personal tastes and under his own responsibility.

Article 6

Every man has a right to the opportunity for learning how to enjoy his leisure time. Family, school, and community should instruct him in the art of exploiting his leisure time in the most sensible fashion. In schools, classes, and courses of instruction, children, adolescents, and adults must be given the opportunity to develop the skills, attitudes, and understandings essential for leisure literacy.

Article 7

The responsibility for education for leisure is still divided among a large number of disciplines and institutions. In the interests of everyone and in order to utilize purposefully all the funds and assistance available in the various administrative levels, this responsibility should be fully coordinated among all public and private bodies concerned with leisure. The goal should be for a community of leisure. In countries, where feasible, special schools for recreational studies should be established. These schools would train leaders to help promote

INTRODUCTION

recreational programs and assist individuals and groups during their leisure hours, insofar as they can without restricting freedom of choice. Such service is worthy of the finest creative efforts of man.

Robert G. Schipf
March 1975

CAMPING AND HIKING

... tenting tonight on the old campground

Camping is one of the most popular outdoor activities with which we are concerned here. The statistics tell us this, and a visit to almost any campground during the summer months will verify it. Some campgrounds are fairly elaborate and some are spartan. I'm happy with a pure water supply and a pit toilet, but some of us need electrical and sewer hook-ups, amphitheaters, and slide shows. I've done the sleeping-bag-under-a-piece-of-canvas thing, the tent thing, and the truck camper bit, and I try to keep everything as simple as I can. In most camps, there is just not enough good firewood to make even a good cooking effort and too many campsites are either muddy or dusty. And one must stay in an established site in most campgrounds. I went to the truck camper to avoid pitching my tent in the mud where officialdom made me put it. Without having to spend an hour to find wood for heating a can of baked beans, I have time for other things such as hiking, girl watching, and teaching the kids all sorts of outdoorsy stuff. Sometimes it's hard to sleep with all those motorhome generators going, so I may stay up late and look for the Pleiades or Jupiter.

Roaming around is good fun and good exercise at anytime of the year. Even when it's freezing outside, a good walk will do wonders for the old bod and it's so nice to get back indoors for a toddy. Hiking about in the woods during a snowstorm gives me a good feeling, for some weird reason, but I head for the truck when the wind comes up. And you really can see so many more stars when you're far from town and all the lights are out. I think that only the outdoorsman really comprehends the immensity of Mother Nature's domain.

Kids generally love camping. My older son was about six months old when he was first carried into Colorado's higher and colder parts. He's off to college as I write this, but I can still see him sitting on a camp table, turning blue, with a smile on his face and a backside encased in ice. My younger son, my Vice-President in Charge of Backpacking, began at three months. So far, his only really bad experience came at about the age of one year, when he was stung on the lip by a wasp. My daughter has long believed that camping out is for the peasantry, so she hasn't had so many chances to confound Mother

15

OUTDOOR RECREATION

Nature. Whether tenting or truck camping or motorhoming, kids are all over the place and I hope they're learning something. Too many parents, though, allow their children to run through campsites, yelling like monkeys, while other folk are trying to eat or sleep. But kids are good campers, on the whole, and they take the bad better than the oldsters can.

This paragraph was written in a campground in British Columbia. We had been to an air show in Abbottsford and returned to our campsite in Cultus Lake Provincial Park to find that someone had stolen the tablecloth we had left as an indication of occupancy. This tablecloth, strangely enough, is the only thing we have had taken from us in a campground in all our years of camping out. I say "strangely enough" because campground theft has become one of the common forms of criminal activity. Vandalism, robbery, and murder are not unknown these days, much to the chagrin of the old-timers in the camping game. All this reminds me of the more disagreeable aspects of camping out. Rain and bugs are natural and we expect them, but the human population offers a number of challenges to understanding.

Vandalism, of course, is widespread in our nation; one doesn't have to visit a campground to see it. Over the years, I've seen letters to editors of outdoor magazines complaining of the out-of-state people who come to "our campgrounds" and destroy them. Over the years, though, I've noticed that most of the destruction and most of the garbage dumping is done by local folks out for a picnic or a short weekend near home. Just look around a campground and spot a dirty site. You'll probably find that the vehicle there has very local license plates. The filthiest campground I've ever seen was in Missouri at a Corps of Engineers site. It was a popular place for the local fishermen, and the refuse showed it. Fish remains and other garbage were strewn all over the place—almost every vehicle came from within a few miles of the reservoir.

And speaking of personal danger reminds me that I've had to "flourish" a firearm to prevent an attack on my family in a Forest Service campground near Ogden, Utah. This sort of thing is, luckily, still rather rare but the newspapers have told us of campers killed by robbers. Just a week or two before I sat down to write this, two rangers asked a couple of young punks to quiet down and stop raising hell in a campground near Missoula, Montana. The rangers were attacked and thrown into the river. Within a week, these two hoodlums were in a serious traffic accident and their lives were saved by the quick action of—you guessed it—the same two rangers. And that's the truth!

Throwing garbage on the ground is bad enough, but I've been rather fascinated at what happens in campground restrooms. In the summer of 1974, I noticed that mirrors and electric hand dryers had been removed from some of the restrooms in Glacier National Park, probably because of theft and damage. I sort of have a minor in physical anthropology so I have a professional interest in discovering the variety of *Homo sapiens* which is able to defecate on the underside of a toilet seat. Whenever we've experienced loud parties or other boisterous behavior in campgrounds, we have also encountered dirty people. There may be a connection.

Occasionally, one reads something about outdoor recreation that is so silly or untrue that one wonders at the amount of mutual copying that goes on among authors. As an example, few camping books have anything good to say about pack baskets. I am sure that most camping writers have never even seen a pack basket, much less used one. But the new book will repeat the old story. I was led to write this paragraph after putting down a brand-new book in which the author states categorically that one cannot use a rucksack on an overnight hike because a rucksack is too small to hold a sleeping bag. Now, aside from the fact that one may sleep without a sleeping bag, we wonder about the number of rucksacks the author has seen. I have seen only a few, but I have used one that would hold not only a sleeping bag but an air mattress, a mess kit, C-rations, and a host of miscellaneous junk. Such bags are available almost everywhere. And to top this story off—in the very next paragraph, the author recommends using a tapered mountain climber's bag on overnight hikes! These are quite a bit smaller than any true rucksack I've ever discovered. I'm sure that both paragraphs were copied and that the author didn't understand either of them. I decided not to list this particular book, so you won't even know about it.

Backpacking has become a cult. It has its gurus and its bibles and its propaganda machine and its hates. Years ago, the outing writers could tell of month-long hiking trips with nary a word of complaint about their neighbors. Now, however, a backpacker will write an article about his week-end struggle over Dum-Dum Pass and condemn every other person he met along the way. They were using the wrong kind of pack frame, the wrong kind of sleeping bag, or the wrong shoes. Perhaps, God forbid, our hero heard a motorcycle and swooned away in the 1898 style of dear old Aunt Minnie. Times have changed. We need down jackets to survive the beastly winds and nylon tents to shelter us from the foggy, foggy dew. Our ancestors, as late as World War II, got along just fine, thank you, with a pair of woolen long johns, old work shoes, a supply of matches, and a cast iron frying pan. The modern devotee of hiking can scarcely believe that grand-dad existed for months in the wilderness without freeze-dried pork chops and instant beans.

As an example of backpacker hates, let me regale you with this tale which I read in a backpacker journal. A group of hikers were wending their way along a public road and were passed by a couple of girls riding a motorcycle. Our happy hikers couldn't bear the thought of someone else sharing the outdoors with them, so they whacked over some trees and placed them across the road. When the cyclists returned, they had to remove one tree after another. To top it off, the hikers thought it horrid that the motorized girls used rather strong language. I'm sure that these pack-framed idiots had a ball, but they're not my kind of people.

During the last couple of years, an argument about the relative merits of the so-called "wrap-around" packframe has been taking up a great deal of

17

space in the backpacking journals. With all the advertising and the pro and con evidence, one would think that the device was something new and startling. Actually, the very same idea was illustrated in *Outing* magazine back around 1905. The books and periodicals change emphasis every now and then, so that new editions may be published with a clear conscience. About 15 years ago, almost everyone began to condemn the rucksack and praise the aluminum pack frame. Within the past two or three years, the old rucksack has been re-designed and re-named and is making a comeback.

Packbaskets were deemed barbaric by the camping writers quite a few years ago, but they are still sold in fairly large numbers to country folks who didn't get the word. Things that work continue to work for the people who need things that work. Knives are another item that seem to attract controversy for some odd reason. Some writers state categorically that anyone who carries a sheath knife with a blade longer than 4½ inches is a dude or a fool or both—or even a Republican. Sometimes it's rather difficult to slice a loaf of bread with a short blade, but that, I presume, is beside the point. I like to have a good long knife handy, though, because my wife hasn't figured out how to bake sliced bread. When I make a grand appearance with my machete, I'm no doubt thought a nut; but it works just as well as a small axe, is lighter, and, besides, I may stumble into a sugar cane field someday. Be prepared!

I like to read old-time camping books. They are fascinating and generally well written. It is rather difficult to find camping books from the happy years before 1900—there are a couple of titles I've been trying to obtain on interlibrary loan for years but no library seems to have them. I have a few newer ones, though, and I take them from the bookcase every now and then and wonder if we really have it better now. Back in 1903, Stewart Edward White published a novel called *The Forest*. It contains some excellent camping lore mixed in with the story (but don't wait for the movie). Warren H. Miller was an editor of *Field and Stream* magazine back around 1915 when he published a book called *Camp Craft*. Horace Kephart was a librarian, if you don't mind, but he is better known as the author of numerous articles on camping, outdoor lore, muzzle-loading rifles, and *Our Southern Highlanders*. Back in 1905, Kephart published the first edition of *The Book of Camping and Woodcraft* and it is still in print in a later edition.

I must not forget Nessmuk. Nessmuk was the pen name of George Washington Sears, a Pennsylvania shoemaker. Born in 1821, Sears grew up loving the wilds and learning all about its secrets. He wrote letters to the outing magazines of the time and even published a few poems; in 1884 his *Woodcraft* appeared as the first modern attempt to explain lightweight backpacking. The book is a gem, now in reprint. My own favorite edition is that of 1936, but you can't have it. Nessmuk also became famous for his extremely lightweight canoes. Nessmuk and Kephart and the other old-timers are condemned, now, because they made fires and burned wood and built lean-to shelters. But I love them.

CAMPING AND HIKING

Every now and then, a compilation of camping and outdoor information is published. Back in 1942, Grosset and Dunlap issued the *Outdoor Life Cyclopedia*; in 1957, A. S. Barnes published *The Outdoor Encyclopedia*, with articles by people such as Townsend Whelen and Ellsworth Jaeger. I have copies of these marvelous works and I won't part with them. Modern "encyclopedias" are better illustrated and the content is vastly different and they may even be as interesting; but we have too many gimmicks now and not as much understanding. I have even encountered people who have taken up backpacking solely for political purposes! They have no interest whatever in the outdoors but they want to impress the local commissar *cum* guru!

A few of the modern backpacking authors have become cult figures. Harvey Manning and Colin Fletcher and, to a lesser degree, Albert Saijo are worshiped by many hikers. I'll admit that they have good ideas about backpacking equipment and methods, but I'd rather butter up Mother Nature. I can't fool her but she fools me every hunting season.

In this chapter we'll have a look at a number of available books on backpacking and climbing and survival. A few trail guides are included here, too, with the warning that many—perhaps most—trail guides are published locally and in small shops. They hardly ever enter the trade bibliographies and are, therefore, hard to find. I have dozens of titles for which I can find no publisher. In areas where backpacking is a popular activity, the better shops will have guides to local trails and information about clubs and group outings.

Mountaineering is not a recreation. That is the word I have from the American Alpine Club, and you had better believe it. I like to scramble around on the rocks and look down on the earthlings below but "mountaineering" is something else, with its pitons and ropes and hanging in mid-air and—and I think I'm getting sick. I have included several publications on mountaineering just to get someone started, but I'm not about to join the McKinley and Everest crowd. My feelings about mountaineering are apparently the same as those expressed by Paul Niedieck in 1909. In his book *With Rifle in Five Continents*, Niedieck says, "I do not understand how anybody can be bitten with the mania for mountaineering. Personally I can imagine no more painful situation in the world than standing glued to a rock, like a stamp stuck on a letter tilted up on end, and looking in vain for the next foothold."

Even though the American Alpine Club states that mountaineering is not a recreational pursuit, I have found numerous climbers practicing the art. Even in Southern Illinois. Some years ago, I was giving a lecture about the geology of Giant City State Park in Illinois. I had my back toward a cliff of sandstone when two neophyte climbers flew down on their ropes to land at my feet. They thought they were having fun, but the American Alpine Club says that fun is not involved. So there.

Survival books are fairly common even though there is not an obvious need for so many of them. I attended a survival school many years ago while in the Navy and it must have been effective. I've survived several campus disturbances and years of highway driving. Almost all camping books have a chapter on survival, and survival kits are sold everywhere. Most folks are not wandering around in the woods in winter or in the desert in summer, but a few hunters and hikers do get lost so it doesn't hurt to read one of the manuals we will list. A friend of mine almost list his life in the summer of 1974 when he lost his way in the mountains. He was no more than a few miles from his cabin, but he took a wrong turn and spent a couple of days getting back. We lose a few wanderers every year here in Montana, but it does help the population problem.

When all is said and done, backpacking can't be learned from a book. You just have to get out and walk with all the junk on your back. Even an old-timer, though, ought to have a book or two handy with equipment checklists, first aid hints, and a bit about edible wild plants. Strangely enough, many backpackers report that they become starved for reading material, especially when day is done and they are sitting in camp with nothing to do. My younger son and his friend had no paperbacks on one trip and were reduced to reading the labels in their clothing and on all the food containers they picked up along the trail. I must be some kind of a nut—I can sit down and do absolutely nothing for long periods of time.

A WORD ABOUT CAMPGROUND GUIDES

Campground guides come in many shapes and sizes and prices. Almost all of them have maps that locate campgrounds, at least approximately. Some guides have no maps but they are fairly easy to use with a standard road map. Most guides use a number or other symbol to indicate the location of a campground. These symbols are only generally accurate because of printing problems, but some are rather fanciful. My first guide had no maps but we muddled through. My present guides (I always carry two of them) have maps and I find them a bit easier to use. Actually, the traveller can get along without the usual guide because every state publishes a map or other guide to the public camps within its borders, and private camps are listed in similar booklets. Most chambers of commerce have such listings, which are free, as are the state maps.

I encountered a problem with one guide which must be quite rare. Several years ago, while zipping along the Pennsylvania Turnpike, I directed the navigator to get out the campground guide to pick a few likely places near the highway in eastern Pennsylvania. The report came rather quickly, "Dad, there are no campgrounds in the eastern half of the state!" This horrible state of affairs was quickly verified with a glance at the map so, rather than sweat out the problem, we chose a state park in Maryland and found a quiet and attractive camp. The Pennsylvania fiasco, of course, occurred because the campground location overlay had not registered on the base map during

CAMPING AND HIKING

printing. I don't know whether my copy was unique or the entire run was defective, but I carry two campground guides now, wherever I go.

Sometimes the campground on the map is not on the ground. Way back in the summer of 19 and 69, we were cruising through Manitoba when the urge to settle down came on. The guide showed a campground just off the highway near a small lake. Everyone agreed that the place sounded fine and off we went. We found the lake easily enough, but there was no camp in sight. Knowing that my navigation is faultless at all times, we decided to drive off the road through several fields to a nearby farm. Surely the answer was a simple one. Indeed, the farmer had the solution. The campground owner had financial troubles and sold the site to the adjoining Hutterite colony. These folk removed all the buildings and let the place revert to a more natural condition.

Unfortunately, every campground guide is incomplete. Most are pretty well done, but there are always more campgrounds available than the guides show. In August of 1974, as an example, we drove along a highway west from Port Angeles, Washington. The campground guide indicated a few camps, but we actually found at least 20 unlisted ones within a 30- or 40-mile route. These places, mostly private but one a state park, were in neither of my guidebooks. We settled into the unlisted state park and spent a pleasant and quiet night. And there was no fee!

In listing the books, periodicals, and organizations for this section on camping, I thought it best to divide the effort into two main parts. One part is devoted to general camping or family camping titles and the campground guides that most travellers need. The second section is about some of the more demanding or more specialized activities: backpacking, mountaineering, and survival information and some of the currently available books from a bygone camping era, the old-timers in reprint.

CAMPING, CAMPGROUNDS, AND TRAVEL

1. **Adventure Trip Guide: 1000 Selected Vacation Ideas.** New York, Adventure Guides (distr.: Berkshire Traveller), 1974. 224p. illus. index. $3.50pa. LC 72-81137. ISBN 0-913216-01-1.

This is a guide to hiking, riding, bicycling, jeep, boat, covered wagon, canoe, floatboat, scuba diving, skiing, snowmobiling, and aerial activities throughout the United States. For each ranch, cruise agent, school, etc., there is information about location, facilities, cost, season, etc. An excellent source of ideas and hard-to-find data.

OUTDOOR RECREATION

2. Albright, Rodney, and Priscilla Albright. **Short Walks on Long Island.** Chester, CT, Pequot Press, 1974. 121p. maps. $2.95pa. LC 74-75075. ISBN 0-87106-143-0.

From Jamaica Bay in the West to Montauk State Park on the eastern tip, the walks described here pretty well cover New York's southeastern extension. The walks are on beaches, in towns, in woods and swamps, estates, marshes, and other places. Very handy and informative.

3. Angier, Bradford. **Wilderness Gear You Can Make Yourself.** New York, Collier Books, 1973. 115p. illus. $2.95pa. LC 72-93626.

Illustrated with numerous drawings, this guide gives suggestions on making dozens of useful items for the outdoorsman. Among the many items of "gear" are these: a packboard, animal crate, camp chest, mosquito bar, cattail basket, natural dyes, rawhide, moccasins, sunglasses, a grill, fish hooks, a bola, knife and sheath, a raft, and snowshoes. Lots of good hints in a book that most youngsters would appreciate, too.

4. Barton, Kent O. **Tourist Tips and Hints.** San Antonio, TX, Naylor, 1964. 110p. index. $3.95. LC 64-18680. ISBN 0-8111-0157-6.

This guide to vacation travel contains hints on proper driving habits and safety, what to do in case of accident, games to play along the way, etc. Travel by bus, train, plane, ship, and auto are included. Foreign travel is also described.

5. Bauer, Erwin, and Peggy Bauer, eds. **Camper's Digest.** 2nd ed. Northfield, IL, Digest Books, 1974. 288p. illus. $5.95pa. LC 73-102640. ISBN 0-695-80452-9.

This is a good general introduction to camping activities. There are hints on living in a camp, cooking and choosing food, sleeping gear, tents, taking the kids, first aid, photography, backpacking, recreational vehicles, bicycles, boat camping, and camping in various parts of the world. A good, inexpensive, and well-illustrated guide for the beginner.

6. **Bicentennial Tourguide Celebrating Our Country's 200th Birthday.** San Jose, CA, Gousha (distr.: Crown), 1973. 80p. maps. $1.00pa.

Consisting mostly of rather general state and city road maps, this guide suggests places to visit (battlefields, homes, craft centers, etc.), with hints on regional dining opportunities. It is not limited to Revolutionary War locales. Because no great detail is possible in so small a book, only the hurried or casual traveller would look for this one.

7. Boy Scouts of America. **Fieldbook for Scouts, Explorers, Scouters, Educators, Outdoorsmen.** 2nd ed. New Brunswick, NJ, Boy Scouts of America, 1967. 565p. illus. index. bibliog. $1.95pa. LC 67-14537. ISBN 0-8395-3201-6.

This is probably the largest and most inexpensive compilation of outdoor lore available. It is filled with suggestions on hiking and camping, map and compass work, use of tools and rope, fires and cooking, physical fitness, swimming and watercraft, first aid and safety, winter camping, survival, natural history, astronomy and weather lore. The detailed index makes for easy use. The emphasis is on techniques, not on equipment. "The *Fieldbook* is a guide to preparedness" and "a book of action." Buy it, you'll like it.

8. Burch, Monte. **Outdoorsman's FIX-IT Book.** New York, Harper & Row, 1971. 274p. illus. index. (An Outdoor Life Book). $6.95. LC 73-178839. ISBN 0-87468-081-6.

With drawings and photographs, this book is an aid to helpless sportsmen who have minor problems with cutting tools, boots, appliances, fishing tackle, boats and motors, guns, trailers, optical equipment, decoys, snowmobiles, archery tackle, and chainsaws. Clear instruction makes for a handy and useful book. Recommended.

9. Burton, Bill, ed. **The Sportsman's Encyclopedia.** New York, Grosset & Dunlap, 1971. 638p. illus. $9.95. ISBN 0-448-01989-2.

This is a guide to 34 sporting activities, collected from various publications that range in date from 1961 through 1970. The sports of interest to us here include: archery, canoeing, horseback riding, ice skating, motor boating, sailing, scuba diving, skin diving, surfing, swimming, target shooting, water safety, kite flying, and water skiing. This is in addition to information on numerous sports such as baseball, etc. Most of the chapters are quite good and all are written by recognized authorities. If you already have this book, you don't really need another inexpensive guide to the activities listed. *Books in Print* lists the author of this as "Ottenheimer, Inc."

10. Buryn, Ed. **Vagabonding in America: A Guidebook about Energy.** New York, Random House; Berkeley, CA, Bookworks, 1973. 354p. illus. $4.95pa. LC 72-12220. ISBN 0-394-70973-X.

Buryn states that "Vagabonding is an outlook on travel. The real definition of a vagabond is someone not entangled in travel arrangements." With "Poems, drawings and appendixes by Stephanie Mines," the book gives reasons for discovering the real America while using as little money as possible on food, lodging, fuel, etc. Buryn prefers vans as camping vehicles and talks about visiting people, travelling by motorcycle, car, bicycle, hiking, and hitchhiking. He offers tips on living and working at odd jobs, on first aid and other medical stuff (including VD), and dealing with the good old fuzz. The appendixes list information sources, books, catalogs, parks, etc. Crazy man. Lots of good, interesting material here. Read it.

11. Buryn, Ed. **Vagabonding in Europe and North Africa.** Rev. ed. Berkeley, CA, Bookworks; New York, Random House, 1973. 247p. illus. $6.95; $3.95pa. LC 73-4389. ISBN 0-394-48767-2; -70663-3pa.

This vagabond's guide to unstructured travel offers hints on driving, hitchhiking, taking a train or bus, and walking. There are good suggestions about mental conditioning, health and money matters, required documents, places to visit and how to get there, single and group travel, what to take along (sleeping bags to cameras), etc. Separate chapters are devoted to hitchhiking, plain hiking, bicycling, trains and buses, and cars and motorcycles. Among the instructions are hints on getting along with the locals, especially the police and other government types. A specific command is given NOT to fart when dealing with border guards. Crabs are called "public lice" in one place and I suppose it needn't be a misprint. Excellent reading and a good one for even the armchair traveller.

12. Cameron, Ben. **The New York Times Guide to Outdoors**, U.S.A. New York, Quadrangle, 1973. maps. indexes.

The first two volumes of this series are for the Northeast (318p. $5.95pa.) and the Southeast (224p. $4.95pa.). These are campground directories with information on facilities, dates of operation, sporting activities nearby, driving directions, etc.

13. **Camping and Caravanning Handbook 1973.** London, The Automobile Association (distr.: Harper & Row), 1972. 272p. illus. atlas. $2.95pa.

This is basically a gazetteer of campsites in England, Wales, Scotland, and all Ireland. Interesting information of all kinds is included: obtaining credit, selecting a vehicle, recipes, nature trails, etc. Apparently meant to be updated at intervals. Anyone thinking of a camping trip to the British Isles will get many good hints from this book.

14. Cardwell, Paul, Jr. **America's Camping Book.** New York, Scribner's, 1969. 591p. illus. index. $10.00. LC 68-57071. ISBN 0-684-10056-8.

Calling itself "A Comprehensive, Illustrated Guide to Camping," this volume contains much general information on camping: equipment needed, making a tent, cooking and fire-building, know-how of all sorts. Sections include material on backpacking, canoeing, bicycling, horsepacking, motor travel, photography, hunting, spelunking, etc. Also appended are lists of organizations, books, and equipment suppliers. A good, fairly well-illustrated introduction. A beginner probably ought to read this for basic facts and ideas.

15. Colby, Carroll B., and Bradford Angier. **The Art and Science of Taking to the Woods.** Harrisburg, PA, Stackpole, 1970. 288p. illus. index. $7.95. LC 71-100344. SBN 117-0109-3.

Illustrated entirely with drawings by A. J. Anderson, this book discusses trip planning (what to take, and where and how to take it) and camping techniques such as fire-making, using axes, cooking, and pitching tents. Lots of good information for the beginner.

16. Colwell, Robert. **Introduction to Foot Trails in America.** Harrisburg, PA, Stackpole, 1972. 221p. illus. index. $5.95. LC 74-179603. ISBN 0-8117-0914-0.

This is a description of foot trails in the United States. The text is divided into four parts: East, Midwest, West, and Far West. The states covered are: New England, New York, Pennsylvania, Kentucky, West Virginia, Florida, District of Columbia, Ohio, North Dakota, South Dakota, Michigan, Utah, Arizona, New Mexico, Colorado, Wyoming, Montana, Idaho and the three Pacific Coast states. Sketch maps help locate the trails. There are better trail guides.

17. Crain, Jim, and Terry Milne. **Camping Around California: The North.** New York, Random House; Berkeley, CA, Bookworks, 1973. 94p. illus. index. $3.95pa.

18. Crain, Jim, and Terry Milne. **Camping Around California: The South.** New York, Random House; Berkeley, CA, Bookworks, 1973. 94p. illus. index. $3.95pa.

These companion volumes describe camping areas with notes on location, facilities, rates, activities and natural features. There are lists of maps and organizations. The indexes are to activities and to features, and the maps are good. Recommended for anyone who wishes to camp the Golden Bear State.

19. Crain, Jim, and Terry Milne. **Camping Around New England.** New York, Random House; Berkeley, CA, Bookworks, 1973. 79p. illus. index. $3.95pa. ISBN 0-394-70799-0.

This description of camping areas in New England has notes on rates, location, facilities and activities, etc. in the same manner as the previously listed books about California. Good for someone confining himself to the northeast.

20. Darvill, Fred T., Jr. **North Cascades Highway Guide.** Mount Vernon, WA, Darvill, 1973. 47p. maps. $1.00pa.

The new highway route through the northern Cascades is well described in this handy little book. There is information on history, natural history,

25

OUTDOOR RECREATION

side trails, etc. The same publisher offers several similar books about Washington locales. Good for any traveller.

21. Dickson, Lew. **Exploring Canada by Recreational Vehicle.** Beverly Hills, CA, Trail-R-Club, 1971. 230p. illus. $3.95pa. LC 79-160193. SBN 87593-025-5.

Intended mostly for retired folks, this guide offers hints on planning a trip (maps, things to take along, etc.) but is mostly a story of the Dicksons' travels across our northern neighbor from West to East. Interesting and worthwhile for Canadian trippers.

22. Dohme, Alvin R. L. **Shenandoah: The Valley Story.** Washington, DC, Potomac Books, 1972. 248p. illus. index. $5.95; $2.95pa. LC 78-85812. ISBN 0-87107-014-6; -015-4pa.

This guide to the Shenandoah Valley in Virginia contains a history of the area, tour guides, descriptions of historic houses and other sites, notes on fishing and camping spots, etc. Photos and maps illustrate a good guide to a beautiful region.

23. Duncan, S. Blackwell. **Backpacking, Tenting & Trailering.** Chicago, Rand McNally, 1974. 192p. illus.(part col.). $3.95pa. LC 76-183965.

This is a well-illustrated guide to general outdoor activities. It covers the usual topics: why camp?, choosing a tent and other equipment, choosing a vehicle and caring for it, and suggestions on many forms of outdoor activities: bicycling, motorcycling, driving dunebuggies, canoeing and boating, snowmobiling, snowshoeing and cross-country skiing, etc. There are hints on first aid, foods, and menus and travel information of all kinds. Highly recommended for the beginner to outdoor exploration. A previous edition was titled *Camping Today*.

24. Dunlop, Richard. **Outdoor Recreation Guide.** Chicago, Rand McNally, 1974. 186p. illus.(part col.). index. $4.95pa. LC 73-14407.

This book contains general information about camping, backpacking, trail riding, hiking, bike hiking, rockhounding and spelunking, canoeing and rafting, boating and boat camping, sport diving, and conservation. Regional directories show, for each state, places to do the several activities mentioned. It is, of course, quite general. A physical map of each area shows topography, drainage, boundaries, etc. A neat package which is highly recommended for beginners. A good companion volume to Duncan's book.

25. **Explorer's Guide to the West.** San Jose, CA, Gousha (distr.: Crown), 1972. $1.95pa. each.

CAMPING AND HIKING

This is a series of six small volumes that describe various facets of Western landscape or culture. The titles are: *Deserts*; *Cities*; *Coast*; *Rivers and Lakes*; *Southern Mountains*; *Northern Mountains*. The states included are Arizona, California, Oregon, Washington, and Nevada, plus British Columbia. The information is general but useful.

26. **Farm, Ranch & Countryside Guide: 500 Selected Vacation Ideas.** 25th anniversary ed. New York, Farm and Ranch Vacations (distr.: Berkshire Traveller), 1974. 191p. illus. $3.50pa. LC 60-2113. ISBN 0-913214-00-0.

This is a directory of rural vacation spots that accept paying guests. The list of places by language spoken may be handy to many of us. The entire United States is covered, plus a few sites in Canada. An excellent little guide.

27. Frome, Michael. **National Park Guide.** 8th ed. Chicago, Rand McNally, 1974. 209p. illus.(part col.). index. $3.95pa. SBN 528-84387-3.

Each of the American National Parks, from Acadia to Zion, is described with a few maps and many photographs. Shorter sections on "Other Parklands" include historical sites and memorial, natural, and recreational areas under federal jurisdiction. Recommended as a good general guide for recreationists.

28. **The Good Sam Club's 1973 Recreational Vehicle Owner's Directory.** 7th club ed. Calabasas, CA, Trailer Life, 1973. 960p. illus. maps. $4.95pa.

This is a large, periodically updated, volume that, despite its title, is a directory of campgrounds and trailer parks. Members of the Club may receive discounts at many of the listed parks. There are articles on various aspects of camping and travelling, digests of state laws, mileage charts, and similar materials. The bulk of the book is the directory, arranged by state and city. Canada and Mexico are included. The usual information is given for each campground or park, and repair stations and disposal stations are listed. Mostly for the traveller who wishes hook-up facilities, but others can use it as well. Rather bulky but useful. *Books in Print* lists this as published by Chilton (ISBN 0-8019-5880-6) but my copy is not so marked. See: *Trailer Life's 1974 Recreational Vehicle Campground and Service Guide . . .*

29. Gregg, James R. **The Sportsman's Eye: How to Make Better Use of Your Eyes in the Outdoors.** New York, Winchester, 1971. 210p. illus. index. glossary. $6.95. LC 73-150385. ISBN 0-87691-035-5.

An optometrist, Gregg offers much valuable information on vision and visual problems, including the visual acuity of animals. He recommends methods of improving vision for several sports such as hunting and shooting, boating and

OUTDOOR RECREATION

other water sports, driving and flying, archery, skiing and golf. A rather unique book that every outdoorsman should read.

30. Gresham, Grits. **The Sportsman and His Family Outdoors.** New York, Dutton, 1969. 156p. illus. index. (An Outdoor Life Skill Book). $4.50; $1.95pa. LC 71-100360.

The activities discussed in this small book are: hunting and fishing, target shooting, camping and boating, woods walking, bird watching, photography, ice fishing, sledding, and snowmobiling. Good general information for beginners to any of the sports mentioned.

31. Grey, Hugh. **The Field & Stream Guide to Family Camping.** New York, Popular Library, 1966. 127p. illus. $1.25pa. SBN 445-08208-125.

Originally published by Holt, this little book describes a number of things the beginner should know: trip planning, using maps, animal and plant hazards, vehicle choices, food and cooking, fire-making, weather lore, first aid, and other general topics. Inexpensive, but there are several more modern and better illustrated books available.

32. **Handbook and Directory for Campers.** illus. ads. free.

Although there are articles on food and other aspects of camping, this is mostly a guide to KOA campgrounds. It may be obtained at any KOA camp.

33. Hayes, Richard L. **Trailering America's Highways and Byways: Vol. 1, The West; Vol. 2, The East.** Beverly Hills, CA, Trail-R-Club, 1965, 1970. 232p., 223p. illus. $3.95pa. each. ISBN 0-87593-008-5 (v.1); -017-4 (v.2).

This guidebook to the highways of the United States offers, for each highway, a short history of the road, mileage logs, and elevations, from end to end. Similar logs cover trips through parks and other areas. There are short notes on sundry topics scattered throughout. The information on grades would help anyone towing a trailer.

34. Hilts, Len. **Explore Canada.** Chicago, Rand McNally, 1973. 186p. illus. (part col.). index. $3.95pa. SBN 528-84150-5.

With provincial road maps and city maps, this is a description of places to visit and things to do (parks, theaters, rodeos, museums, etc.). There are lists of campgrounds with maps showing locations and information on shopping, motels, and restaurants. A handy guide, especially for the city maps.

35. Hillcourt, William. **The Golden Book of Camping: Tents and Tarpaulins, Packs and Sleeping Bags; Building a Camp; Firemaking and Outdoor Cooking; Canoe Trips, Hikes, and Indian Camping.** Rev. ed. New

York, Golden Press, 1971. 104p. illus.(col.). index. $3.95. LC 76-135478. ISBN 0-307-13568-3.

This is intended for the young camper, particularly in organized camping, but many an older reader has picked up a hint or two from it. The title tells most of the story. The material is useful and interesting.

36. Jaeger, Ellsworth. **Wildwood Wisdom**. New York, Macmillan, 1945. 491p. illus. index. $8.95.

This is mostly about how to make many items of practical value to campers and outdoorsmen. If you wish to try your hand at making a blanket coat, pack saddle, Mexican sandals, a lean-to, tinder pouch, latrine, or bark lamp shades, this is the book for you. Among the skills are such things as paddling a canoe, cooking on hot stones, flipping flapjacks, gathering wild foods, stalking animals, and predicting the weather. An excellent handbook copiously illustrated with drawings.

37. Jobson, John. **The Complete Book of Practical Camping**. New York, Winchester, 1974. 275p. illus. index. $10.00. LC 73-88874. ISBN 0-87691-147-5.

Jobson is camping editor of *Sports Afield Magazine*. In this book, he covers the usual camping themes: selecting and using tents, trailers and campers, sleeping bags and mattresses, clothing, packs, axes and knives, cooking gear, and the other things that a camper accumulates. There are many excellent suggestions on cooking, camping techniques, vehicular and horse travel, and getting out of trouble. An authoritative book for novice campers.

38. Johnson, L. W., *et al.* **Outdoor Tips**. New York, Benjamin, 1972. 190p. illus. index. $2.95pa. LC 76-121738. ISBN 0-87502-905-1.

The tips include many for hiking and camping, snowmobiling, cooking, canoeing and boating, fishing and hunting, archery and bow hunting, shooting and gun care, and conservation. Illustrated with drawings. A good little book.

39. Jones, Charles, and Klaus Knab. **American Wilderness: Where to Go in the Nation's Wilderness, on the Wild and Scenic Rivers and along the Scenic Trails**. San Jose, CA, Gousha (distr.: Crown), 1973. 212p. illus. index. maps. (A Gousha Weekend Guide). $4.95pa. LC 72-98729. ISBN 0-913040-21-5.

This attractive volume is concerned with the federally administered areas mentioned in the title. For each such area, river, or trail, the authors provide information on size, location and access, address, camping facilities, best season for a visit, etc. The maps are small but generally adequate. A handy book for the vacationer.

40. Kennedy, Mopsy Strange, and Steven D. Stark. **Let's Go: The Student Guide to the United States and Canada, 1972-73**. New York, Dutton, 1972. 704p. maps. $3.95pa. ISBN 0-525-03875-2.

This is a compilation of travel suggestions from the experience of some 40 college students. It is a fairly complete guide to many of our cities with information about accommodation, places to eat, things to see and do, the drug scene, and night life. Reasonably accurate for the places that I know about. Needs updating, of course, since even a place such as Missoula, Montana, has a few new wild spots.

41. Keyarts, Eugene. **Short Walks in Connecticut, Vol. 1**. Chester, CT, Pequot, 1968. 85p. maps. $2.50pa. LC 68-24038.

42. Keyarts, Eugene. **42 More Short Walks in Connecticut**. Chester, CT, Pequot, 1972. 87p. maps. $2.50pa. LC 74-187173.

43. Keyarts, Eugene. **Short Walks in Connecticut, Vol. 3**. Chester, CT, Pequot, 1973. 87p. maps. $2.50pa. LC 68-24038.

These volumes (the second is not marked as Volume 2) are uniform in format and pocket size. The walks are everywhere in the state and the information consists of maps, access directions, natural history, and other tidbits. Very good.

44. Kirk, Ruth. **Exploring Mount Rainier.** Corrected ed. Seattle, WA, University of Washington Press, 1973. 104p. illus. $3.95pa. LC 68-11047. ISBN 0-295-73850-2.

This guidebook, illustrated with drawings and photographs, covers the natural history and people history of the Park area. There are suggestions for auto and hiking trips, with directories of lodgings, campgrounds, transportation, and activities. Sketch maps. Good for any traveller to the scene.

45. Kirk, Ruth. **Exploring the Olympic Peninsula.** Rev. ed. Seattle, WA, University of Washington Press, 1967. 120p. illus. index. $2.50pa. ISBN 0-295-97882-1.

Similar to the Kirk book on *Exploring Mount Rainier.*

46. Kirk, Ruth. **Exploring Yellowstone.** Seattle, WA, University of Washington Press, 1972. 120p. illus. $5.95; $2.95pa. LC 78-178702. ISBN 0-295-95174-5; -95188-5pa.

Similar to Kirk's *Exploring Mount Rainier.*

CAMPING AND HIKING

47. Knobel, Bruno. **101 Camping-Out Ideas & Activities**. 1975 ed. North Hollywood, CA, Wilshire Book Co., 1974. 128p. illus. index. $2.00pa. LC 61-10408. ISBN 0-87980-290-1.

This little book, originally published in Switzerland, has quite a few good hints for outdoor activities. Any youngster will be happy trying his hand at using a lasso, making things of wood, learning about animal tracks and stars, and building a shelter or a raft. Older folk will learn something, too. If you want to find Aquarius, make a boomerang, wave semaphore flags, or even make a secret code, this book will tell you how. An interesting little pot-pourri.

48. Knox, Bob, and Wilma Knox. **All About Camping in Alaska and the Yukon**. Grass Valley, CA, Rajo, 1973. 196p. illus. $4.95pa.

The locale includes the Alaska Highway and the coastal areas, including the ferry route. Information covers planning the trip, suggestions on what to take, a fishing guide, lists of public and commercial camps, suggested travel routes, and maps. A very good and useful volume illustrated with many photos.

49. McNally, Tom. **Camping**. 2nd ed. Chicago, Follett, 1972. 128p. illus. $3.95. LC 78-125026. ISBN 0-695-80199-6.

This is a basic introduction to camping with suggestions about tents, sleeping bags, trailers and campers, cooking gear, clothing, backpacking equipment, and accessories. The beginner will be happier with a newer and better illustrated book.

50. Merrill, William K. **All About Camping**. Harrisburg, PA, Stackpole, 1970. 399p. illus. index. bibliog. (A Stackpole Rubicon Book). $2.95pa.

Originally published in 1962, this is a guide to general camping and related outdoor activities. There are suggestions about areas for camping in the United States, Canada, and Mexico, vehicle camping, boat and desert camping, animal packing, backpacking and mountain climbing, snow travel, map and compass use, food and cooking, safety and first aid, etc. Illustrated with drawings, the book has a good bibliography and many miscellaneous outdoor hints. A pretty fair guide for beginners.

51. Miller, Mike. **Off the Beaten Path in Alaska**. Juneau, AK, Alaskabooks, 1970. 116p. illus. (Alaskabook No. 101). $1.50pa.

A small guide to a number of "uncrowded, economical, out-of-the-way places to see and stay" in our largest state. Among the topics are: National Forest camps, ferry trips, Esquimo villages, etc. Very good information.

52. Miracle, Leonard. **Sportsman's Camping Guide**. New York, Dutton, 1965. 160p. illus. index. (An Outdoor Life Skill Book). $1.95pa. LC 65-14984.

OUTDOOR RECREATION

An introduction to camping for beginners, this volume contains good information on guns and ammunition, vehicles, trip planning, horseback trips, fishing needs, boat trips of several kinds, auto camping, backpacking, cold-weather camping, compass work, food and cooking, and other general camping dope. Nicely illustrated.

53. **Mobil Travel Guide**. New York, Simon & Schuster, annual. $2.95pa.

This is a series of seven volumes that contain historical and geographical facts, travel information of all kinds (highest elevations, state birds, liquor laws, etc.), and several discount coupons. Vacation suggestions abound. For each city, arranged alphabetically by state, there are lists of hotels, motels, restaurants, and what-to-do-and-see. These are NOT campground guides. The volumes are *California and the West* (includes Utah, Nevada, and Arizona); *Great Lakes Area* (Illinois, Indiana, Michigan, Ohio, Wisconsin); *Middle Atlantic States* (Delaware, D.C., Maryland, New Jersey, North Carolina, South Carolina, Pennsylvania, Virginia, West Virginia); *Northeastern States* (New England, New York); *Northwest and Great Plains* (Idaho, Oregon, Washington, Wyoming, Montana, Iowa, Minnesota, Nebraska, North and South Dakota); *Southeastern States* (Alabama, Florida, Georgia, Kentucky, Mississippi, Tennessee); *Southwest and South Central Area* (Arkansas, Colorado, Kansas, Louisiana, Missouri, New Mexico, Oklahoma, Texas).

54. Mole, Michaela M. **Away We Go! A Guidebook of Family Trips to Places of Interest in New Jersey, Nearby Pennsylvania, and New York**. 3rd ed. New Brunswick, NJ, Rutgers University Press, 1971. 203p. illus. index. $6.00; $2.75pa. LC 63-23450. ISBN 0-8135-0694-8; -0696-4pa.

With several guide maps, many photographs, and descriptions of hundreds of museums, breweries, parks, airports, villages, churches, and other places of historic or cultural interest, this guide to New Jersey and its nearby neighbors should tempt almost anyone into the outdoors for a week-end cruise.

55. Newberry, Lida. **One-Day Adventures by Car with Full Road Directions for Drives out of New York City**. New York, Hastings House, 1971. 261p. maps. index. $6.95; $4.95pa. LC 77-150020. ISBN 0-8038-5363-7; -5369-6pa.

The area covered includes New Jersey, Connecticut, the Hudson River Valley, Staten Island, Long Island, and, of course, the city itself. The information on parks, museums, villages, etc., should get anyone outdoors at least for a day.

56. Newman, James, and Barbara Newman. **Family Camping Guide**. New York, Grosset & Dunlap, 1972. 244p. illus. index. $1.25pa. ISBN 0-448-02174-9.

This is a general introduction to camping for beginners. There is instruction on choosing equipment and using things from home, on backyard camping to learn the ropes, fires and cooking, weather problems, animal hazards, games, etc. Information on types of campgrounds, care of equipment, tents and sleeping bags and what to do when lost is illustrated with drawings and photographs. Not a bad little book at all.

57. Ormond, Clyde. **Outdoorsman's Handbook.** New York, Dutton, 1970. 336p. illus. index. $5.95. LC 76-134237. ISBN 0-525-17330-7.

A handy-to-carry manual, this contains information, illustrated with drawings, on hunting and fishing methods, camping, cooking, hiking, photography, horses and their handling, rockhounding, and other outdoor skills. A very good guide for any outdoor person.

58. Patterson, Jerry G. **Campground Guide for Tent & Trailer Tourists, 1973-74.** 12th ed. Wakefield, KS, Campgrounds Unlimited, 1973. $1.95pa.

This guide to campgrounds is revised every two years so the pagination varies. It covers the United States and Canada and gives the name and location of campgrounds by state or province. There are no maps in this guide, but it is small and handy. My first campground guide was the second edition of this one. If you can get by without maps (it isn't hard to do), you might take this one along with you.

59. Patty, Thomas F., and W. R. C. Shedenhelm, eds. **Complete Book of Camping and Backpacking.** Los Angeles, Petersen, 1973. 192p. illus. $2.95pa. LC 73-75212. ISBN 0-8227-0002-6.

This is a large, magazine-format guide, generously illustrated. Most kinds of camping or outdoor activities are covered: motor and motorcycle camping, bicycling, backpacking, rock and mountain climbing, river running, cave exploration, shooting, fishing, collecting, survival, cooking, etc. There are lists of clubs, national parks and forests, and a buyer's guide to equipment. Quite general but nicely done.

60. Pepper, Choral. **Guidebook to the Colorado Desert of California.** Los Angeles, Ward Ritchie, 1972. 128p. illus. index. $1.95pa. LC 78-180603. ISBN 0-378-03762-5.

This handy guide, illustrated with photographs, contains information about the history, legends, climate, ghost towns, prehistoric sites, etc., in the vicinity of Palm Springs, Blythe, and the Salton Sea. Any traveller to the area will need this.

OUTDOOR RECREATION

61. Power, John. **The Camper's Handbook: A Complete Guide to Wilderness and Family Camping in North America**. Toronto, Modern Canadian (distr.: Hippocrene), 1974. 159p. illus. $2.95pa. LC 72-12169. ISBN 0-919364-30-6.

Intended for youngsters and other raw beginners, this little book is an introduction to general camping with hints about tents, sleeping bags, picking a campsite, cooking, fighting bugs, canoeing, hiking, snowshoeing, skiing, and snowmobiling. Lots of miscellaneous stuff. The users of kerosene stoves and heaters will be surprised to know that kerosene is "virtually non-combustible." A few drawings are included. Other guides are as inexpensive and better illustrated.

62. **Rand McNally Campground & Trailer Park Guide: United States/Canada/Mexico**. Chicago, Rand McNally, 1974. 536p. illus.(part col.). $4.95pa.

Although there is some general information about camping and travelling (mileage charts, driving laws, food suggestions, etc.), most of this book is a listing of campgrounds by state or province. A map with numbered locations is accompanied by a directory of campgrounds with information on number of sites, elevation, fees, season, facilities and activities, telephone number, and mailing address. The advertising matter does not intrude. There is a list of disposal stations and some coupons for discounts at selected camps. A widely used guide, recommended for every camper.

63. **Rand McNally Road Atlas of Europe**. Chicago, Rand McNally, 1974. 104p. maps. $2.95pa. ISBN 0-528-89359-9.

For anyone contemplating a trip to Europe (the book covers Eastern Europe and the USSR, too), this atlas is just the thing. The maps show principal and some connecting highways, there are maps of 18 cities, an index of towns, and some general suggestions about things such as passports, driver licenses, and official sources of information. There is also a *Rand McNally Guide to European Campgrounds* ($4.95pa.), which I've not seen.

64. **Rand McNally Road Atlas, United States/Canada/Mexico**. Golden anniversary ed. Chicago, Rand McNally, 1974. 132p. illus. $2.95pa. LC 75-654428.

This large atlas contains standard state/province road maps with city and metropolitan area maps, an index and gazetteer, and information on toll roads and speed limits. I've found the city maps to be quite good, and the atlas goes everywhere with me. Also published with a leatherette cover at $3.95.

65. **Rand McNally Western Campgrounds & Trailer Parks, 1974**. Chicago, Rand McNally, 1974. 342p. illus. $2.95pa.

For anyone who camps exclusively in the 13 Western states and western Canada, this standard campground guide will suffice.

66. Richmond, Doug. **Central America: How to Get There and Back in One Piece with a Minimum of Hassle.** Tucson, AZ, H. P. Books, 1974. 176p. $5.95pa. LC 72-91684.

    The title should suffice to show the coverage. Richmond's guidebooks are very good, being both readable and informative. Recommended.

67. **Road Atlas Canada.** Chicago, Rand McNally, 1974. 65p. illus.(col.). index. $2.95pa.

    This large atlas contains road maps of the Canadian provinces plus maps of the principal cities. The text describes the several provinces and points of interest. It is 15" high and 11" wide. The city maps are especially useful.

68. Ruth, Kent. **Touring the Old West.** Brattleboro, VT, Stephen Greene, 1971. 218p. illus. index. $6.95. LC 71-148620. ISBN 0-8189-0129-5.

    Devoted mostly to what's west of Kansas City, this guide lists old forts, trading posts, mining camps, ghost towns, mountain passes and rivers, back roads, and small towns. Photos and drawings illustrate a very good little guide for the traveller.

69. Rutstrum, Calvin. **The New Way of the Wilderness.** New York, Macmillan, 1958. 276p. illus. index. $4.95. LC 58-5912.

    There are a great many old-timer hints in this book. Rutstrum discusses canoeing, pack-horse travel, backpacking, auto camping, and travel in winter with dogs or hand-pulled toboggans. In addition to several itemized lists of recommended gear, there are numerous suggestions about finding one's way, choosing clothing and other equipment, choosing and preparing food, survival in emergencies, and hunting and fishing. Highly recommended for the outdoor enthusiast. There are many new items of equipment, these days, but good, basic knowledge is never outdated.

70. Safran, Rose, ed. **Very Special Resorts.** Stockbridge, MA, Berkshire Traveller, 1973. 222p. illus. index. $3.50pa. LC 73-83796. ISBN 0-912944-10-2.

    This is about resorts of various kinds, all over the United States and Canada, which can be reached by public transportation. The "special" refers to the special activities index, which will enable the vacationer to select his activity and go to it (badminton, work weekends, etc.).

71. Schell, Hal. **All about Camping in Europe.** Grass Valley, CA, Rajo, 1973. 200p. illus. $4.95pa.

OUTDOOR RECREATION

    This is an excellent introduction to European camping with its discussion of the advantages of camping in Europe, the various kinds of campgrounds found there, and all the odds and ends the traveller must know: passports and permits, student rates, rental vs. purchase, money matters, shopping differences, information of all kinds. Anyone thinking of a camping tour of Europe should have this book handy. Israel is also included, thereby confounding my geographic education.

  72. Schwartz, Alvin. **Going Camping: A Complete Guide for the Uncertain Beginner in Family Camping.** Rev. ed. New York, Macmillan, 1972. illus. index. $5.95. LC 74-185144.

    I have not seen the new edition of this book. The 1969 edition had 244 pages of basic information for campers: trip planning, equipment and clothing needs, hints on cooking, taking pets, towing a trailer, living through rain and bug invasions, etc. There are several check lists and, if you don't mind, hints on having sexual relations in tents—please be advised to stay five or six feet from other campers (and leave your horse outside, Valentino!).

  73. Shosteck, Robert. **Weekender's Guide: Places of Historic, Scenic and Recreational Interest within 200 Miles of the Washington-Baltimore Area.** Rev. ed. Washington, DC, Potomac Books, 1973. 400p. illus. index. $2.90pa. LC 71-85813. ISBN 0-87107-024-8.

    Museums, canals, fine arts things, mills, military sites, parks and nature areas, etc., are located and described. There are small drawings and a map. Good for the casual traveller near the nation's capital.

  74. Simpson, Norman T. **Country Inns and Back Roads.** Stockbridge, MA, Berkshire Traveller, 1974. 303p. illus. $3.95pa. LC 70-615664. ISBN 0-912944-16-1.

    This is an entertaining look at country inns and their environs with directions, sketch maps and notes on facilities, activities, telephone numbers, dates of operation, etc. Pleasantly illustrated with drawings, this is obviously not "outdoor" recreation but I thought it would interest most travellers anyway.

  75. Smallman, Robert E. **The Golden Guide to Camping.** New York, Golden Press, 1965. 160p. illus.(part col.). (A Golden Handbook). $1.50pa. LC 65-12446. ISBN 0-307-24343-5.

    A very small guide to family or general camping with hints on tents and other equipment, clothing, food and cooking, axe and knife skills, packs, canoeing (not enough to matter), first aid and safety, map work and survival. There is a list of information sources and a short booklist. Not a bad little book.

CAMPING AND HIKING

76. Sparano, Vin T. **Complete Outdoors Encyclopedia**. New York, Harper & Row, 1973. 622p. illus.(part col.). index. (An Outdoor Life Book). $13.95. LC 72-90934. ISBN 0-06-013955-2.

This nicely illustrated book contains a great deal of information for the outdoor recreationist. Almost a third of the text is about fishing equipment and techniques, with color plates of fish. Other topics include shooting and hunting, game animals and their habits, firearms, etc., for another third of the book, and camping, boating, archery, dogs, and first aid. There are lists of information sources, shooting preserves, and a good bibliography of recent books. A good book to have around.

77. Strung, Norman, and Sil Strung. **Camping in Comfort: A Guide to Modern Outdoor Vacations**. Philadelphia, Lippincott, 1971. 262p. illus. $7.50. LC 70-146670. ISBN 0-397-00693-4.

Although *Books in Print* calls this a "new ed." there is nothing to indicate it in the copy at hand. There is general camping information for beginners: planning a trip, choosing tents and other gear, vehicles and their care, basic camping lore. The use of recreational vehicles and boats gets quite a bit of attention.

78. Sunset Books and Sunset Magazine, Editors of. **California National Parks**. 3rd ed. Menlo Park, CA, Lane, 1969. 80p. illus. index. $1.95pa. LC 69-14225. SBN 376-06493-5.

This is a well-illustrated guide to the several national parks in California.

79. Sunset Books and Sunset Magazine, Editors of. **California State Parks**. New ed. Menlo Park, CA, Lane, 1972. 128p. illus. index. (A Sunset Book). $2.95pa. LC 79-180519. SBN 376-06773-X.

The generally crowded California state parks are described with quite a bit of general information of historical and recreational interest.

80. Sunset Books and Sunset Magazine, Editors of. **Sunset Camping Handbook**. 3rd ed. Menlo Park, CA, Lane, 1970. 96p. illus. index. $1.95pa. LC 72-100895. SBN 376-06203-7.

The usual, well-illustrated Sunset style is used to convey a great deal of general information to new campers. There are sections on basic equipment, cooking, camping on beaches and in deserts (and near bears!), hints about babies and pets in camps, renting equipment, carrying a boat, and recreational vehicles. Lots of good reading.

81. Sunset Editorial Staff. **Baja California**. Menlo Park, CA, Lane, 1971. 80p. illus. index. $1.95pa. LC 72-140160. SBN 376-06091-3.

OUTDOOR RECREATION

This contains many hints on regulations, camping and other accommodations, and fishing and hunting information, but it is mostly a guide to the roads, towns, and sights on the peninsula. The main highway is now complete, so a new edition is probably on the way.

82. Sunset Magazine, Editorial Staff of. **Sunset Beachcombers' Guide to the Pacific Coast.** Menlo Park, CA, Lane, 1966. 112p. illus. index. $1.95pa. LC 66-15333.

Covering California, Oregon, and Washington, this book discusses whale watching, fishing, crabbing and clamming, surfing, agate hunting, shell collecting, etc. My wife manages to do a lot of crabbing even when there is no beach within a thousand miles. If you are a coastal traveller, you may need this book and I'll clam up. Many photos.

83. Tanguay, Peter E., and Margaret Fife Tanguay. **Travel Adventure in Europe with Tent, Van, or Motorhome.** Beverly Hills, CA, Trail-R-Club, 1970. 271p. illus. (Book No. 98). $7.95pa. LC 71-100596. SBN 87593-098-0.

For anyone planning a camping trip to Europe this book is a must. There are hints on travelling with children and on getting along in general (customs, cameras, money, etc.), and renting a vehicle. Most of the book is devoted to descriptions of the several countries with suggestions on what to visit, highway conditions, guidebooks to buy, and campground locations. All the European countries are included except Albania (whose government hates everyone else in the world except Red China). For completely non-geographic reasons, Morocco is included, too. Photographs and maps complete an interesting book.

84. Thollander, Earl. **Back Roads of New England.** New York, Clarkson Potter (distr.: Crown), 1974. 224p. illus. $8.95. LC 73-89086. ISBN 0-517-51422-2.

This "hand-written" book was printed and drawn by Thollander. It covers most of New England, with maps and all sorts of information, both historical and practical. A pleasant book for any traveller.

85. Thomas, Bill. **Tripping in America: Off the Beaten Track.** Radnor, PA, Chilton Book Co., 1974. 223p. illus. $3.95pa. LC 74-1076. ISBN 0-8019-5970-5.

This is a good guide, arranged by state, to all kinds of odd things to do and see: the National Coon Dog Cemetery in Alabama, the Esquimo Olympics in Alaska, fishworm judging contests and the Swamp Cabbage Festival, Presley's Cross in Southern Illinois (which is one of the ugliest things I have ever seen; I

CAMPING AND HIKING

watched them build it), and the Aerial Fire Depot in Missoula, Montana. I wonder why Louisiana's Domino Championships were omitted. Oh, well, the book is illustrated with photographs and is highly recommended.

86. **Trailer Life's 1974 Recreational Vehicle Campground and Service Guide: The Official Directory for the Good Sam Club.** 8th ed. Calabasas, CA, Trailer Life (distr.: Chilton), 1974. 944p. illus.(part col.). $5.95pa.

This directory of over 15,000 places where the traveller may park his rig is a newer edition of the book I have listed as *The Good Sam Club's Recreational Vehicle Owner's Directory*. The editions fit the dates, and this one has a more logical title. The campground guide is the same. I hope that the title isn't alternated each year but you, dear reader, are forewarned.

87. Wells, George S. **Guide to Family Camping.** Harrisburg, PA, Stackpole, 1973. 188p. illus. (A Rubicon Book). $2.95pa. LC 67-22992.

Originally published as the *Modern ABC's of Family Camping*, this is a general guide to planning and equipping a family vacation trip in summer or winter. There are hints on camping in Europe, Latin America, North Africa, the Middle East, Australia, and New Zealand. But the book is rather old for this exotic stuff, and better books are available for family campers.

88. Williams, Herb. **Outdoor Adventures.** San Jose, CA, Gousha (distr.: Crown), 1973. 79p. illus. $1.95pa. LC 73-80660. ISBN 0-913040-24-X.

The subtitle is "Hundreds of ideas to add more pleasure to your family's adventures in camping, exploring, hunting, and fishing in both fresh and salt water." Most of this material was originally published in a newspaper column and it is about such things as uses for plastic jugs, estimating range when duck hunting, deodorizing a dog, etc. Good reading.

89. **Woodall's Trailering Parks and Campgrounds.** annual. Highland Park, IL, Woodall. illus. maps. $5.95pa. (1974 ed.).

This is primarily a state-by-state listing of trailer parks and other camps with information on repair stations and rental agencies and with many general camping and travel suggestions. The latest edition, which has some 1,200 pages, is a valuable handbook for any trailer or motorhome vacationer.

FIRST-CHOICE TITLES

If I had to choose a few titles on general camping and outdoor skills for the beginner and the family, I'd probably pick: The Boy Scout's *Fieldbook* ($1.95), Merrill's *All About Camping* ($2.95), and the *Sunset Camping Handbook* ($1.95). These titles will give almost anyone a good look at camping, but, if a more expensive volume is needed, preferably for you to receive as a gift, you might try for Cardwell's *America's Camping Book* ($10.00) and Colby and Angier's *The Art and Science of Taking to the Woods* ($7.95).

Add to this a couple of campground guides (they are all inexpensive) and you'll be ready for the road.

BACKPACKING, MOUNTAINEERING, AND SURVIVAL

90. Abel, Michael. **Backpacking Made Easy.** Healdsburg, CA, Naturegraph, 1972. 128p. illus. index. $5.50; $2.50pa. ISBN 0-87961-009-3; -008-5pa.

Illustrated with drawings, this introduction to backpacking contains many suggestions on clothing, packs, sleeping bags, tents and other equipment. There are sections on food and cooking, stoves and fires, maps and compass work, first aid, and thoughts on ecology.

91. Angier, Bradford. **Home in Your Pack: The Modern Handbook of Backpacking.** New York, Collier Books (Macmillan), 1972. 211p. illus. index. $1.50pa. LC 70-187069.

Originally published in 1965, this book is rather outdated so far as equipment is concerned. It contains suggestions about choosing packs, sleeping bags and other equipment, clothing, first aid kits, and wilderness living.

92. Angier, Bradford. **How to Stay Alive in the Woods.** New York, Collier Books, 1962. 285p. illus. $0.95pa.

With illustrations by Vena Angier, this is a guide to getting along in the wilderness if lost or stranded. In four main sections, Angier discusses gathering and cooking wild foods, both animal and plant (how about scaring a bear away from his kill so you can have a feast? Or, better, how about making a fish trap?), making fires and shelters and otherwise keeping warm, finding one's way and getting out of dangerous country, and basic safety and survival precautions. Lots of outdoorsman's savvy in a recommended book, which was first published by Stackpole (1956) as *Living Off the Country: How to Stay Alive in the Woods.*

93. Angier, Bradford. **Skills for Taming the Wilds: A Handbook of Woodcraft Wisdom.** Harrisburg, PA, Stackpole, 1967. 280p. illus. $6.95. LC 67-13935. ISBN 0-8117-1550-7. (Pocketbooks edition, $1.25pa. ISBN 0-671-78151-0).

CAMPING AND HIKING

Illustrated throughout with drawings, this is a guide to any number of outdoor topics and skills: finding hiking areas, weather lore, dressing for comfort, backpacks and how to use them, building fires, using a compass, axe, saw and knife, ropes and their uses, handling pack animals and canoes, making shelters, finding wild foods and water, cooking, building a cabin, first aid. This sort of information is always useful to outdoorsmen.

94. Berglund, Berndt. **Wilderness Survival: A Complete Handbook and Guide for Survival in the North American Wilds.** New York, Scribner's, 1972. 175p. illus. index. $7.95; $2.95pa. LC 72-2767. ISBN 0-684-13073-4; -13841-Xpa.

Stressing the importance of psychology in the will to survive, this manual offers many facts about climate and general natural history, wilderness travel and the use of the compass, fire-making, signals, shelter and first aid, trapping, hunting and fishing, butchering game for the pot, cooking methods, finding water and edible plants, clothing requirements, basic equipment, and much other information. Illustrated with drawings.

95. Blackshaw, Alan. **Mountaineering: From Hill Walking to Alpine Climbing.** Rev. ed. Baltimore, Penguin, 1970. 552p. illus. index. bibliog. $4.95pa. ISBN 0-14-046103-5.

This is mostly about walking and climbing in Britain and mountaineering in the Alps, so the place names and clubs will seem out of the way. There is, however, good information on the use of maps and compass, knot tying, equipment and its use, and climbing techniques.

96. Bleything, Dennis, and Ron Dawson. **Primitive Medical Aid in the Wilderness.** See: **Wilderness Pocket n' Pak Library.**

97. Boudreau, Eugene. **Trails of the Sierra Madre.** San Francisco, Scrimshaw; Santa Barbara, Capra, 1973. 77p. illus. $3.75pa. ISBN 0-912264-68-3.

This is a general description of the Sierra Madre Occidental in northwestern Mexico, with notes on geology, fauna and flora, climate and people. There are directions to trail heads, notes about food and equipment, and much other interesting material.

98. Brandner, Gary. **Living Off the Land.** Los Angeles, Nash, 1971. 179p. illus. $1.95pa. LC 77-167507. SBN 8402-8002-5.

Intended for the inexperienced visitor to the great outdoors, this book outlines the desired equipment for a wilderness trip (tent, bedding, tools, clothing, etc.) and the several techniques of signaling, travelling, finding food, making shelter, locating drinking water, fire-making, outdoor hazards, and first aid. Good reading.

OUTDOOR RECREATION

99. Bridge, Raymond. **America's Backpacking Book**. New York, Scribner's, 1973. 417p. illus. index. bibliog. $12.50. LC 73-1342. SBN 684-13370-9.

This lengthy book contains hints on the "art and folklore of backpacking," hints on walking skills, basic ideas about foods and equipment. The equipment sections are quite good and cover packs, tents, clothing, sleeping bags, cooking gear, and other items. Other chapters are devoted to map reading, first aid, hiking with children, physical conditioning, travelling light, hiking in deserts or mountains or in winter. A few more illustrations would be helpful (e.g., "how to build a snow cave" could use a drawing of a snow cave) and some new equipment is not mentioned. An excellent handbook.

100. Brower, David, ed. **Going Light with Backpack or Burro**. San Francisco, Sierra Club.

I still see this title listed in many books, but it is out of print.

101. Brower, David, ed. **The Sierra Club Wilderness Handbook**. New York, Ballantine.

This is a slightly updated edition of *Going Light with Backpack or Burro.* It is also out of print.

102. Burt, Calvin P., Ronald L. Dawson, and Frank G. Heyl. **Survival in the Wilderness**. See: **Wilderness Pocket n' Pak Library**.

103. Cheney, Theodore A. **Camping by Backpack and Canoe**. New York, Funk & Wagnalls, 1970. 210p. index. $7.95. LC 69-19649.

Intended for the camper out for two or three days, this book discusses packs and their contents, hiking and navigation techniques, and other aspects of the walker's art. The canoeing section discusses the types of canoe, handling and paddling, travel in streams and on open water. General camping instructions are included, too. There are no illustrations except for a small drawing of stars used as chapter headings. Good ideas.

104. Colwell, Robert. **Introduction to Backpacking**. Harrisburg, PA, Stackpole, 1970. 191p. illus. index. $5.95.

This is about the why and how of backpacking. There are sections devoted to choosing a pack, footwear, clothing, and other gear. Cooking methods, sleeping gear and shelter, and planning a long trip are discussed. Also included are lists of places to hike, suppliers, clubs, and books for further reading.

105. Craighead, Frank C., Jr., and John J. Craighead. **How to Survive on Land & Sea.** 3rd ed. Annapolis, MD, Naval Institute, 1956. 366p. illus. index. glossary. $5.50pa. LC 57-21769. ISBN 0-87021-277-X.

This book was used as the text for World War II Navy pilot training survival courses. The several sections offer detailed instruction in basic survival actions: orientation and foot travel, finding drinking water, using wild foods, shelter, fire-making and cooking, ocean and seashore survival, tropical and arctic survival, and various hazards such as sunstroke, snakebite, and exposure. This edition has a section on nuclear, biological, and chemical warfare that was not in the edition your reviewer studied during the war. Excellent.

106. Cunningham, Gerry, and Margaret Hansson. **Light Weight Camping Equipment and How to Make It.** 2nd ed. New York, Scribner's, 1975. illus. $8.95; $4.95pa.

The previous paperback edition had 115p. and was illustrated with drawings. The instructions covered quite a few things, from packboards and fire thongs to cattail baskets and arrowheads. A very worthy book for all outdoorsmen.

107. Cutter, Robert K. **Light Weight Outing Equipment with Check List.** San Francisco, Sierra Club, 1973. 12p. $0.25pa.

This is a pocket-sized pamphlet with hints on equipment. Very good supplement to any other book—or use it as your only text on what to buy.

108. Dalrymple, Byron. **Survival in the Outdoors.** New York, Dutton, 1972. 309p. illus. index. (An Outdoor Life Book). $6.95. LC 71-167606.

This basic guide to wilderness survival has hints on clothing and equipment most likely to be needed in an emergency, map and compass use, finding water, following trails, building fire and shelter, signalling, and weather lore. Illustrated with drawings. Excellent.

109. Disley, John. **Orienteering.** Harrisburg, PA, Stackpole, 1967. 168p. illus. index. $4.95; $2.95pa.

A good description of a growing sport. The emphasis is on the sporting aspects of wilderness route-finding rather than on practical work. The chapters cover history, needed equipment, types of competition, training games, fitness, etc. A good introduction. Illustrated with few photos but many maps and drawings.

110. Doan, Daniel. **Fifty Hikes: Walks, Day Hikes, and Backpacking Trips in New Hampshire's White Mountains.** Somersworth, NH, New Hampshire Publishing, 1973. 165p. illus. $5.95pa. LC 73-76396. ISBN 0-912274-23-9.

Illustrated with photographs, this is a fine guide to New Hampshire's best-known hiking grounds. There are general hints on equipment and weather, but the bulk of the book consists of trail descriptions.

111. **Down But Not Out.** Ottawa, Ontario, The Queen's Printer, 1965. 185p. illus. $3.00pa.

This is the survival manual of the Canadian forces. It contains excellent notes on the psychology of survival, on geography, parachuting, first aid, shelters, signalling, fire, hunting and fishing, finding plant foods and water, caring for equipment, overland travel, and ocean survival.

112. Explorers Ltd. **The Explorers Ltd. Source Book.** New York, Harper & Row, 1973. 384p. illus. index. $4.95pa. LC 72-9115. ISBN 0-06-011221-2.

Explorers Ltd. is a clearinghouse for information on all types of outdoor, adventurous, or exploring activities. This is a variant of the *Last Whole Earth Catalog* theme; it is filled with commentary, lists of books, sources of equipment, and information on backpacking, maps, cycling, the weather, motorcycling, animal packing, water and winter activities, living off the land, falconry, soaring, ballooning, parachuting, survival, caving, photography, first aid, etc. Generously illustrated. Although similar to the *Last Whole Earth Catalog*, this is more to the point and doesn't have the venereal rot that infested the other work. Highly recommended.

113. Fear, Daniel E., and Eugene H. Fear, eds. **Surviving the Unexpected: A Curriculum Guide for Wilderness Survival and Survival from Natural and Man-Made Disasters.** Tacoma, WA, Outdoor Education, 1971. 75p. illus. bibliog. $2.50pa.

This is a teacher's guide dealing with the need for survival education, the concept of survival education, general theory, wilderness survival, natural disasters, and more common emergencies. Items for a survival kit are suggested, and there are lists of books, brochures, and films. Very good manual.

114. Fear, Eugene H., *et al.* **Outdoor Living: Problems, Solutions, Guidelines.** Tacoma, WA, Tacoma Mountain Rescue, n.d. c.130p. illus.

Designed to educate outdoorsmen in the hazards of short-time emergency survival situations, the book contains excellent material on psychological preparedness, energy requirements, cold and hot climate problems, leadership, and organization. Appendices list suggestions on various kinds of survival and survival kits. These appendices are also published separately as brochures for seminar use. An excellent book.

CAMPING AND HIKING

115. Fear, Eugene H. **Surviving the Unexpected Wilderness Emergency.** 3rd ed. Tacoma, WA, Survival Education, 1973. 196p. illus. index. $6.75; $3.95pa. LC 73-78035. ISBN 0-913724-02-5.

Based on Fear's experiences as a teacher and outdoorsman, this book concentrates on how environmental stress affects the body. There are discussions of proper planning, general survival problems, effects of cold and heat, finding water and food, starting fires and building shelters, map reading, and emergency kits. Excellent material. Concise and comprehensive.

116. Fletcher, Colin. **The New Complete Walker: The Joys and Techniques of Hiking and Backpacking.** 2nd ed. New York, Knopf, 1974. 485p. illus. index. $8.95. LC 73-20763. ISBN 0-394-48099-6.

The original edition of this work, published in 1968, became a classic of its genre and generated a cult of sorts. Illustrated with drawings, this updated edition covers the same topics with newer information about the selection and use of backpacking equipment and supplies: packs, clothing, shelters, sleeping bags, food, and the rest. Suggestions about techniques abound and there are lists of suppliers and of organizations. Although "brand names" are often mentioned, the idea is on "what-to-look-for" when buying equipment and "what-to-do" when using it. Opinionated, of course, but good reading. Most hikers will want to read this excellent book.

117. Garvey, Edward B. **Appalachian Hiker: Adventure of a Lifetime.** Oakton, VA, Appalachian Books, 1971. 397p. illus. $4.50pa. LC 70-146063. ISBN 0-912660-01-5.

This is Garvey's story of his six-month hike along the entire Appalachian Trail in 1970. In addition to general information about the Trail and its history, there are suggestions on equipment, food, and other aspects of hiking. Most of the book is a guide to the Trail and to what Garvey saw and did. Natural history notes are inserted when appropriate. An excellent handbook for any Trail hiker.

118. Gearing, Catherine. **A Field Guide to Wilderness Living.** Nashville, TN, Southern Publishing, 1973. 222p. illus. index. $3.95pa. LC 72-97849. SBN 8127-0057-0.

This is an elementary survival manual for those who may find themselves in the wilderness or who are victims of a disaster. Among the topics covered are: orientation and signalling, finding water, using wild plant foods, recipes, identifying poisonous plants and pests, building fires and shelters, outdoor health, all kinds of survival hints. Illustrated with drawings, the book is based on training courses of the Seventh-Day Adventist Church. Not as complete as some other survival books, but it is a good starting point.

OUTDOOR RECREATION

119. Graves, Richard. **Bushcraft: A Serious Guide to Survival and Camping.** New York, Schocken Books, 1972. 344p. illus. index. $3.95pa. LC 74-185329.

Based on a survival course for military pilots in the Pacific, this is really not a book for the North American camper. The suggestions and information are excellent, but they are all about jungle marching, making things of tropical materials, etc. Originally published in the 1950s as several pamphlets called *The Bushcraft Handbooks*, in Sydney, Australia.

120. Greenbank, Anthony. **The Book of Survival: Everyman's Guide to Staying Alive and Handling Emergencies in the City, the Suburbs and the Wild Lands Beyond.** New York, New American Library, 1970. 256p. illus. index. $0.95pa. LC 67-28832.

Originally published in England, this book has been rather popular for its hints on various kinds of survival. It is arranged by hazard: e.g., too dry (thirsty), too wet (down at sea), too cold (making snow caves), too low (climbing trees for food). It is both entertaining and instructive with its suggestions on averting suicide, and avoiding mobs, starvation, drowning and falling from cliffs. Highly recommended.

121. Gregory, Mark (pseud.). **The Good Earth Almanac Survival Handbook.** New York, Sheed and Ward, 1973. 94p. illus. $1.95pa. LC 73-9102. ISBN 0-8362-0553-9.

Monte Burch offers many hints on survival from his "Good Earth Almanac" newspaper column. There are hints on water finding, using plant foods, hunting animals, orientation, safety, and first aid, plus ideas for city dwellers faced with auto breakdowns or electrical blackouts. Lots of good information.

122. Henderson, Luis M. **Camper's Guide to Woodcraft and Outdoor Life.** New York, Dover, 1972. 351p. illus. index. $3.00pa. LC 71-189973. ISBN 0-486-21147-9.

This is an unabridged reprint of *The Outdoor Guide* of 1950. It is one of the old-style camping books, with sections on animal tracks, trails and portages, clothing and equipment, camp living, food and cookery, canoeing, and first aid. There are instructions for making a number of articles such as a knife sheath and food bags. Illustrated with drawings. Excellent reading.

123. Herter, George Leonard, and Jacques P. Herter. **Professional Guides Manual.** Rev. 11th ed. Waseca, MN, Herter's, 1971. 456p. illus. $3.99. Cat. No. AE7C2.

CAMPING AND HIKING

Formerly published in two volumes, this work is filled with hints about most aspects of outdoor life: fishing, hunting, cooking, removing porcupine quills from dogs, using an axe, cold weather survival, etc. Lots of good reading.

124. Herz, Jerry. **The Compleat Backpacker.** New York, Popular Library, 1973. 343p. illus. $1.50pa.

This small book covers physical conditioning, care of feet and boots, navigation and weather lore, shelter, clothing and personal equipment, first aid and survival gear, food, sleeping gear, packs, how to hike, basic camping techniques, animal hazards, etc.

125. **High Sierra Hiking Guides** (series). Berkeley, CA, Wilderness Press, various dates. 96p. illus. maps.

These are guidebooks to several U.S. Geological Survey quadrangle maps. They cover the flora and fauna, fishing sites and other goodies. 21 guides are planned. The prices are either $1.95 or $2.95 for these paperback manuals. The popular hiking areas are included. Write to the publisher for a complete and up-to-date list of these excellent guides.

126. Jansen, Charles L. **Lightweight Backpacking: 2 Cups, 2 Spoons, 2 Pots.** New York, Bantam, 1974. 182p. illus. $1.50pa.

"The system . . . is based primarily on a two-person backpacking team." There are hints on boots and foot care, clothing and sleeping gear, tents (Jansen thinks that "pima cotton" means a polyester and cotton mix), packs, food and cooking, first aid, and camp procedures and sanitation. Lots of miscellaneous information is included in this interesting and lightweight book.

127. Kelsey, Robert J. **Walking in the Wild: The Complete Guide to Hiking and Backpacking.** New York, Funk and Wagnalls, 1973. 362p. illus. index. bibliog. $6.95. LC 73-8907. ISBN 0-308-10083-2.

This is an interesting and complete introduction by an avid hiker. There are many suggestions about clothing, shelters, foods, sleeping gear, packs, and other equipment. Other chapters are devoted to general camping duties from fire-making to map reading. There are lists of suppliers and much other information. Kelsey hasn't filled his book with the "hate progress and other people" thoughts that infect several other hiking manuals. A pleasant and easy-to-read book, this is highly recommended.

128. Kephart, Horace. **Camping and Woodcraft: A Handbook for Vacation Travellers in the Wilderness.** New York, Macmillan, 1948. 2v. in 1. 405p.; 479p. illus. indices. $6.95.

An old-time camper and librarian, Kephart wrote several books and many magazine articles on outdoor topics until his death in 1931. Some of the

47

OUTDOOR RECREATION

modern "environmentalist" backpackers hate books such as this one because they contain hints on cutting down good firewood, making shelters of boughs, etc. Actually, this book is a good one for any outdoorsman, with its information on clothing, equipment, recipes, and other interesting outdoor topics. Old-fashioned? You bet!

129. Kjellstrom, Bjorn. **Be Expert with Map and Compass: The Orienteering Handbook.** New rev. ed. New York, Scribner's, 1967. 136p. illus. index. map. $3.50pa. LC 72-7879. SBN 684-13091-2.

This introduction to orienteering offers many good suggestions about map reading and compass work. A topographic map section is included with a paper protractor and a practice compass. A good training manual with a glossary and answers to test questions.

130. Knap, Jerome J. **The Complete Outdoorsman's Handbook: A Guide to Outdoor Living and Wilderness Survival.** Toronto, Pagurian Press (distr.: Arco), 1974. 192p. illus. $8.95. LC 74-79519. ISBN 0-919364-62-4.

This is not the usual sort of "camping" book. It covers some of the usual things (such as choosing and using a knife, an axe, and a compass), but there is much more. Knap has much to say about observing nature and learning to use one's senses more effectively. He covers the dangers from animals and plants, from poison ivy to porcupines and bears. Among the other topics are: choosing binoculars, canoes, chainsaws, snowshoes, cross-country skis, and firearms. The use of all these things is well covered and there are suggestions about proper firewood, cooking, cleaning fish, butchering animals, wilderness survival techniques, and making sure that one has the most useful gear with him. All in all, this is an excellent book for outdoor rovers. Highly recommended as an adjunct to other, more general, titles.

131. Kodet, E. Russell, and Bradford Angier. **Being Your Own Wilderness Doctor: The Outdoorsman's Emergency Manual.** Harrisburg, PA, Stackpole, 1968. 127p. illus. index. $3.95. LC 68-15440. ISBN 0-8117-0214-6. Also available in paperback from Pocket Books (1972; $1.50pa.).

This is much more than a first aid manual, being concerned with everything from sprains and bug bites to attacks of kidney stones and snakes. Drawings are used where needed and instructions cover bandaging, setting fractures, suturing, and treating a "felon." Recommended.

132. Kreps, Elmer Harry. **Camp and Trail Methods: Interesting Information for All Lovers of Nature; What to Take and What to Do.** Columbus, OH, A. R. Harding, 1950. 273p. illus. $1.50pa.

This is an oldie but it's interesting. There are hints on clothing and equipment for woods travel, suggestions on foods, firearms, canoes and boats, snowshoes, skis, and toboggans. Lots of drawings illustrate the many instructions on preserving game, tanning hides, and other outdoor skills. Recommended for the camper who wants to know about the good old days.

133. Langer, Richard W. **The Joy of Camping: The Complete Four-Seasons, Five-Senses Practical Guide to Enjoying the Great Outdoors (without Destroying It).** New York, Saturday Review, 1973. 320p. illus. index. $8.95. LC 78-154274. ISBN 0-8415-0237-4. Also: Penguin, $2.50pa.

This is a very entertaining book about camping and backpacking, canoeing, kayaking, snowshoeing, ski touring, getting about with a baby, making a comfortable camp, etc. Written in a casual style, the book is filled with excellent suggestions on tents, sleeping bags, packs, fishing, making plaster casts of paw-prints, and a host of other skills. Nothing about campground camping. Excellent, highly recommended.

134. Learn, C. R., and Annie S. Tallman. **Backpacker's Digest.** Northfield, IL, Digest Books, 1973. 288p. illus. $5.95pa. LC 72-97509. ISBN 0-695-80386-7.

Containing general information for beginning backpackers, this book offers many suggestions on clothing, sleeping bags, tents and other equipment, map reading, food and cooking, using CB radio, photography, fishing and hunting, hiking in the mountains and on snow, and many other useful skills. There are lists of hiking areas and a guide to many of the available backpacks. Some of the advice is rather silly, but the book, on the whole, is a good one for beginners.

135. Leslie, Robert Franklin. **High Trails West.** New York, Crown, 1967. 278p. illus. index. bibliog. glossary. $4.95. LC 67-27031.

In addition to some general information on camping and equipment, this book is a guide to many of the well-known trails of the West: the Sierras, Cascades and Coast Ranges, Bitterroots, Uintas, etc. The information is general and useful to anyone planning a western trip.

136. Lindblad, Robert L. **You Can Survive: A Guide to Survival.** Saugus, CA, Barnard, 1962. 70p. illus. price not reported.

A small, pocket-sized book, this covers the four basic needs for survival: warmth, water, food, and navigation. The instruction is about fire-making, shelter-building, clothing needs, finding water and food, cooking, finding direction, using improvised materials, and first aid. The many drawings illustrate such things as fire drills, snow caves, snares, snow goggles, knots, and pressure points to stop bleeding. A very good manual.

OUTDOOR RECREATION

137. Mandolf, Henry J., ed. **Basic Mountaineering.** 3rd ed. San Diego, CA, San Diego Chapter of the Sierra Club, 1972. 136p. illus. price not reported.

This is a handy and authoritative guide to mountaineering. It covers equipment, camping and cooking, weather problems, orientation and mountain travel, alpine rescue methods, winter and desert travel, and climbing on snow. Drawings are used throughout. The ordinary hiker may get some good suggestions from this book, too, with its equipment checklists, instructions on sewing tent fabrics, cooking hints, etc. An excellent manual.

138. Manning, Harvey. **Backpacking One Step at a Time.** New York, Random House, 1973. 357p. illus. index. bibliog. $2.95pa. LC 72-11503. ISBN 0-394-71917-4.

Manning covers the basics of walking and carrying a pack. There are many good suggestions about clothing, packs, sleeping bags and shelter, food and cooking, finding one's way, taking children along, winter hiking, and the ethics of wilderness travel. Illustrated with photos and drawings, this book has become somewhat of a bible for many backpackers. It is an excellent book, but I see no reason for worship. "Pioneers (in the modern setting they are called "slobs") still walk and ride the trails . . ." Such rot!

139. Maricopa County (Arizona). Dept. of Civil Defense and Emergency Services. **Desert Survival: Information for Anyone Traveling in the Desert Southwest.** Phoenix, AZ, Author, n.d. 28p. free but send postage for a couple of ounces.

Any desert traveller should carry this booklet with him. There are many suggestions on terrain features, direction finding, navigating, signalling, clothing and equipment, finding water, and hazards of all sorts. Excellent material.

140. Mason, Bernard S. **Woodcraft and Camping.** New York, Dover, 1974. 580p. illus. index. $3.95pa. LC 73-90205. ISBN 0-486-21951-8.

Originally published in 1939 as *Woodcraft*, this is a good, though old, introduction to campcraft and woodcraft. There are many suggestions on choosing shelters, making teepees and wigwams, beds, personal gear, building fires and cutting wood (horrors!), making things of wood, storing food and equipment in caches, and making knives, rope, peace pipes, and totem poles. Lots of good, woodsy stuff. Recommended.

141. Maxwell, Lawrence. **MV Pathfinder Field Guide.** Rev. ed. Washington, DC, Review and Herald, 1970. 356p. illus. index. $2.95pa.

MV means Missionary Volunteer, and the Pathfinders are a club associated with the Seventh Day Adventist Church. This book is rather like the Boy Scouts' *Fieldbook*, with its instructions on hiking, mapping and compass work, signalling, use of knives and axes, cooking, swimming and boating, tenting, backpacking, winter and survival camping, first aid, geology, astronomy, and weather lore. Natural history of animals and plants is included, too. An excellent book, but the Boy Scout book is larger and cheaper.

142. Mendenhall, Ruth, and John Mendenhall. **Introduction to Rock & Mountain Climbing.** Harrisburg, PA, Stackpole, 1969. 192p. illus. $5.95. LC 69-16148. SBN 8117-0922-1.

The Mendenhalls introduce the beginner to climbing, providing many suggestions on equipment and technique. There are sections on snow climbing, high mountain climbs, using technical equipment such as pitons, and safety. An excellent general manual.

143. Merrill, William K. **The Hiker's and Backpacker's Handbook.** New York, Arco, 1972. 320p. illus. index. (An Arc Book). $2.95pa. LC 72-395. ISBN 0-668-02625-1. Also in hardcover, Winchester (1971; $5.95).

After 36 years as a park ranger, Merrill should know something. This book is filled with suggestions on where to hike, hiking with children, safety, clothing, sleeping bags, tents and other equipment, and food. Also mentioned are hiking with a burro, desert travel, first aid (an especially good chapter), and lists of suppliers and of books. Good reading.

144. Merrill, William K. **The Survival Handbook.** New York, Winchester, 1972. 312p. illus. index. $5.95. LC 76-188594. ISBN 0-87691-068-1. Also in paperback by Arco ($1.95).

This is a handy little book with many suggestions on direction finding, signalling, making shelters, cooking, finding wild foods, first aid, general woodcraft, mountaineering, and surviving in cold, wet, or hot climates. Shipwrecks and aircraft disasters are included. A very good manual for any outdoorsman.

145. Mitchell, Jim. **Hiking: A Teaching Guide.** Tacoma, WA, Survival Education, n.d. c.40p. illus. $2.50pa.

This book contains lesson plans and suggestions for a course about hiking techniques. Several "mini-texts" are stapled in. Interesting and informative.

146. Mooers, Robert L., Jr. **Finding Your Way in the Outdoors: Compass Navigation, Map Reading, Route Finding, Weather Forecasting.** New York, Dutton, 1972. 275p. illus. index. glossary. (An Outdoor Life Book). $5.95. LC 78-167605.

The author is a cartographer. He gives excellent instruction in how to use a compass, read maps, and make sketch maps. The weather section is a good one for the average outdoorsman. A good little book.

147. Murlless, Dick, and Constance Stallings. **Hiker's Guide to the Smokies.** San Francisco, Sierra Club, 1973. 375p. folded map. index. (Sierra Club Totebook). $7.95pa. LC 72-83981. SBN 87156-068-2.

This is an inch-thick resume of the trails in one of the nation's most popular parks. For each trail, the information given includes length, access, start and finish locations, connections with other trails, etc. There is general information about flora and fauna, Park regulations, and living with bears. Joyce Kilmer Memorial Forest and the Slickrock Creek area are also included even though they are outside the Park boundaries. Complete and authoritative.

148. Nelson, Richard K. **Hunters of the Northern Forest: Designs for Survival among the Alaskan Kutchin.** Chicago, University of Chicago Press, 1973. 339p. illus. index. bibliog. $10.50. LC 72-97941. ISBN 0-226-57177-7.

Anyone contemplating a move to the forests of northern Alaska or Canada ought to read this review of an Indian tribe's adaptation to a harsh environment. Their skills include hunting, fishing, winter travel, use of trees and other vegetation, snaring bears, ice fishing, etc. Diverse methods for obtaining food and shelter are described.

149. Nesbitt, Paul H., Alonzo W. Pond, and William H. Allen. **The Survival Book.** New York, Funk & Wagnalls, 1959. 338p. illus. index. $1.95pa. LC 59-14619.

Intended as a guide for survivors of aircraft emergencies, this is a good guide to survival methods in the Arctic, desert, rain forest, seashore, sea, and other environments. There are instructions on water finding, keeping warm, nutrition, and other aspects of getting along with little. Highly recommended.

Nessmuk. See: Sears, George Washington.

150. Olsen, Larry Dean. **Outdoor Survival Skills.** 4th ed. Provo, UT, Brigham Young University, 1973. 188p. illus.(part col.). index. $4.95; $2.95pa. LC 72-94938. ISBN 0-8425-0001-4; -0002-2pa.

Illustrated with drawings and photographs, this is an excellent manual of survival methods. It discusses shelter building, finding water, using animal and plant foods, and making stone knives and bows and arrows. Color plates show many useful plants. When things get rough, the many "caveman" skills described by Olsen will come in handy. Highly recommended.

151. **1,000,000 Miles of Canoe and Hiking Routes.** Sheffield Lake, OH, Ohio Canoe Adventures, n.d. $1.00pa.

This publication was not examined. It is a listing of numerous booklets and maps that show routes for boaters or hikers. Sounds very worthwhile.

152. Petzoldt, Paul. **The Wilderness Handbook.** New York, Norton, 1974. 286p. illus. index. $7.95. LC 74-2058. ISBN 0-393-08691-7.

The author is director of the National Outdoor Leadership School in Lander, Wyoming. Much of this book is devoted to steering the outdoorsman into safe methods of equipping himself and preparing for outdoor travel. There are excellent discussions about insulation of clothing and sleeping bags, protection from rain and wind, food and equipment, loading and carrying a pack, building fires, latrines and bathing, horse packing, and correct walking technique. Additional topics include basic rock climbing, travel on snow, medical emergencies, and educating outdoor leaders. There are equipment and food lists, recipes, and a good bibliography. Highly recommended.

153. Reidel, Arthur, ed. **Fundamental Rock Climbing.** Cambridge, MA, The M.I.T. Outing Club, 1973. 58p. illus. $1.00pa.

This fine little guide to rock climbing includes instructions on face climbing, stemming, rappelling, using pitons and carabiners, etc. The drawings are by Pearl Jusem. I'll bet that this is all the serious beginner really needs.

154. Rethmel, R. C. **Backpacking.** 5th ed. Minneapolis, Burgess, 1974. 185p. illus. index. $3.50pa. LC 74-82231. SBN 8087-1824-X.

First published in 1965, this book has become a standard text. There are good hints about selecting a pack, clothing, and sleeping gear. Notes on the use of foods and cooking equipment, safety, campmaking, map and compass use, cold weather camping, travel with children, and many other topics fill a rather large volume. Highly recommended.

155. Robinson, Donald H. **Camper's and Hiker's Guide to the Blue Ridge Parkway.** Riverside, CT, Chatham Press (distr.: Viking), 1971. 80p. illus. $1.95pa. LC 72-148579. SBN 86599-022-1.

A popular eastern hiking area is described with sketch maps of trails and numerous notes and photographs.

156. Robinson, John W. **San Bernardino Mountain Trails: 100 Hikes in Southern California.** Berkeley, CA, Wilderness Press, 1972. 240p. illus. maps. index. $4.95pa. LC 74-186760. SBN 911824-18-9.

Includes the San Jacinto Mountains.

157. Robinson, John W. **Trails of the Angeles: 100 Hikes in the San Gabriels.** Berkeley, CA, Wilderness Press, 1971. 260p. illus. maps. index. $4.95pa. LC 74-154360. SBN 911824-17-0.

OUTDOOR RECREATION

158. Rutstrum, Calvin. **Once Upon a Wilderness.** New York, Macmillan, 1973. 181p. illus. $6.95. LC 72-91260.

This little book consists of Rutstrum's thoughts after a long lifetime of wilderness living. There are comparisons of camping and cooking "then and now," stories of animals and birds, of equipment, and of the wilderness itself. Rutstrum sees hope for the future of the back country and for the people who need wilderness. Good reading for the dyed-in-the-wool outdoorsman.

159. Rutstrum, Calvin. **The Wilderness Route Finder.** New York, Macmillan, 1967. 214p. illus. index. $4.95. LC 67-12801.

Rutstrum has prepared a good, pocket-sized guide to maps and map reading, finding one's way, and determining position. The many drawings by Les Kouba and the several photographs illustrate the text very well. Probably the most complete wilderness navigation handbook available.

160. Saijo, Albert. **The Backpacker.** San Francisco, 101 Productions (distr.: Scribner's), 1972. 96p. illus. index. $1.95pa. LC 75-182417. SBN 912238-15-1.

This interesting little introduction to backpacking provides many suggestions on clothing, packs, tents, and other equipment. There are hints on ecology, trail conduct, cooking, and foods, plus a directory of mail order stores and a book list. The writing seems rather odd at times, probably for effect.

161. Schaffer, Jeff, Ben Hartline, and Fred Hartline. **The Pacific Crest Trail, Vol. 2: Oregon and Washington.** Berkeley, CA, Wilderness Press, 1974. 346p. illus. index. maps. $5.95pa. LC 72-96122. ISBN 0-911824-33-2.

Volume 1 is entered under Winnett, Thomas.

162. Sears, George Washington. **Woodcraft and Camping.** New York, Dover, 1963. 105p. illus. index. $1.25pa.

Originally published as *Woodcraft* in 1887; the present version is slightly different from the 1920 edition. It is an old-fashioned introduction to camping in the woods, with hints on what to take, cooking, fishing, canoeing, and just wandering around. A famous book among campers.

163. Sheridan, Michael F. **Superstition Wilderness Guidebook: An Introduction to the Geology and Trails, including a Roadlog of the Apache Trail and Trails from First Water and Dons Camp.** 2nd ed. Phoenix, AZ, Author, 1972. 52p. illus. glossary. bibliog. $2.95pa.

Also included are brief notes on history and natural history.

164. Shosteck, Robert. **Potomac Trail Book.** Rev. ed. Washington, DC, Potomac Books, 1971. 175p. maps. index. $2.50pa. LC 68-31585. ISBN 0-87107-030-6.

This trail guide includes notes on geology, local history, and animals and plants.

165. Survival Education Association.

This organization publishes a number of books and pamphlets which they call "mini-texts." These are on such topics as: *Wilderness Travel—Summer*, *Fatique and Exhaustion*, and *High Country Safety*. These are intended to be classroom handouts and are sold in bulk. Write to the Association for further information. (See the list of publishers for the address.)

166. Tappan, Mel. **Survival Guns.** Los Angeles, Janus, 1975.

A resume of suitable firearms and accessories for anyone in a survival situation. To be published in August 1975.

167. Tappan, Mel. **Tools for Survival and Self-Sufficient Living.** Los Angeles, Janus, 1975.

Scheduled for publication in the Fall of 1975. This publisher is planning several other titles on similar topics.

168. Tate, Grover Ted. **Survive!** Dallas, TX, Real Enterprises, 1974. 144p. illus. $5.95pa.

Written primarily for aircraft survival, this little book discusses survival psychology, survival kits, parachuting and emergency flight procedures, first aid, compass use, and survival in special places (deserts, at sea, etc.). Edible plants are noted in each section. An excellent handbook.

169. Troebst, Cord Christian. **The Art of Survival.** Garden City, NY, Doubleday, 1965. 312p. illus. $5.95. LC 65-12366.

Translated from the German, this is a record of survival methods as actually used in various accidents in the desert, on ice and snow, at sea, and in the tropics. A good resume of survival psychology and technique.

170. Tucker, John. **A Jungle Handbook.** Singapore, Asia Pacific (distr.: Cellar Book Shop), 1970. 120p. illus. $3.50pa.

Most of the material here is developed from experiences in the Malayan jungles. The book is of limited use to most Americans, but the information is interesting and nicely written. Among the topics are: pathfinding, campcraft, first aid, water and food, and clothing.

OUTDOOR RECREATION

171. Van Lear, Denise. **The Best about Backpacking.** San Francisco, Sierra Club, 1974. 384p. illus. (A Sierra Club Totebook). $6.95pa. LC 74-76312. ISBN 0-87156-009-2.

This is a selection of material from several books by several authors: Robert S. Wood on preparation for hiking and foods and cooking; Colin Fletcher on walking technique and footwear; Albert Saijo on clothing and setting up a camp; Harvey Manning on packs and bedding; Richard Langer on shelter and camping with children; Raymond Bridge on winter backpacking; Bjorn Kjellstrom on map and compass work; Robert L. Mooers on basic meteorology; Alan E. Nourse on the problems of cold and heat. There are also lists of organizations, wilderness areas and Sierra Club offices. Highly recommended, although it is expensive for a pocket manual.

172. Voge, Hervey H., and A. J. Smatko, eds. **Mountaineer's Guide to the High Sierra.** San Francisco, Sierra Club, 1972. 356p. maps. index. (A Sierra Club Totebook). $7.95pa. LC 72-83983. ISBN 0-87156-064-X.

Omitting those trails that require technical climbing equipment, this guidebook covers peaks between Bond Pass in the North and New Army and Franklin Passes in the South. Not for the casual hiker.

173. Wallace, Arthur Fuller. **Land Cruising and Prospecting: A Book of Valuable Information for Hunters, Trappers, Land Cruisers, Prospectors and Men of the Trail—Tells How to Locate One's Self on the Map, etc.** Columbus, OH, A. R. Harding, 1933. 175p. illus. $2.00pa.

An old book but an interesting one, originally published in 1908. There are hints on building a cabin, tanning skins, prospecting for furs and freshwater pearls, and other woodsy information. For anyone wishing to see how the old-timers did it.

174. Watters, Jim, ed. **Knapsacking Equipment.** Rev. ed. San Francisco, Sierra Club, 1969. 28p. illus. index. $0.75pa.

This is a guide to sleeping bags, clothing, cooking gear, personal items, and backpacks.

175. Welch, Mary Scott. **The Family Wilderness Book.** New York, Ballantine, 1973. 333p. index. $1.65pa. SBN 345-03253-5-165.

This is a beginner's guide to backpacking, bicycling, horseback riding, canoeing and ski-touring. There are sections on equipment, skills, wilderness hazards, ecology, taking the kids, and finding places to go. A very good little book.

CAMPING AND HIKING

176. Wilderness Pocket n' Pak Library. 5 vols. Manning, OR, Life Support Technology, 1974. $1.00ea.; $4.95 for the set, paper bound in a plastic envelope. 64p. each.

The booklets are:

Burt, Calvin P., Ronald L. Dawson, and Frank G. Heyl. *Survival in the Wilderness.* This has information on first aid, fires, shelter, food, orientation and travel. Drawings of snares, etc.

Bleything, Dennis, and Ron Dawson. *Edible Plants in the Wilderness, Vol. 1.*

Bleything, Dennis, and Ron Dawson. *Edible Plants in the Wilderness, Vol. 2.*

Bleything, Dennis, and Ron Dawson. *Poisonous Plants in the Wilderness.* Each volume describes about 30 plants.

Bleything, Dennis, and Ron Dawson. *Primitive Medical Aid in the Wilderness.* Covers basic first aid, fractures, cold and heat problems, contact poisons, internal disorders, medicinal plants, bites, and snowblindness, etc.

These are all very practical, handy books; all are highly recommended.

177. Winnett, Thomas. **Backpacking for Fun: A Beginner's How-to-do-it with Special Suggestions for Families.** Berkeley, CA, Wilderness Press, 1972. 143p. illus. index. $2.95pa. LC 72-89917. ISBN 0-911824-22-7.

This elementary introduction to backpacking covers equipment and clothing, food and how to cook it, general hiking hints, use of map and compass, children on the trail, first aid, and caring for one's gear. The illustrations include photos and drawings, and there are suggested readings, equipment checklists, and addresses of food and equipment suppliers. Nothing about where to hike, since Winnett assumes that the would-be hiker already knows where he's going. The bare essentials are here.

178. Winnett, Thomas. **The Comstock Backpacking Guide to California.** New York, Ballantine, 1972. 180p. illus. $1.50pa. SBN 345-02587-3-150.

There is some general backpacking information (food, packs, clothing, etc.), but most of the book is devoted to a description of 33 trips, all south of Lake Tahoe.

179. Winnett, Thomas. **The Comstock Backpacking Guide to the Pacific Northwest.** New York, Ballantine, 1972. 184p. illus. $1.50pa. SBN 345-02649-7-150.

OUTDOOR RECREATION

Although there are suggestions about equipment and camping methods (identical to those in the previous work), most of this book is a description of trails in Oregon and Washington.

180. Winnett, Thomas, and others. **The Pacific Crest Trail, Vol. 1: California.**
Berkeley, CA, Wilderness Press, 1973. 256p. illus. maps, index. $4.95pa. LC 72-96122. SBN 911824-27-8.

Volume 2, covering Oregon and Washington, is entered under Schaffer, Jeff.

181. Wood, Robert S. **Pleasure Packing: How to Backpack in Comfort.**
Berkeley, CA, Condor Books, 1972. 215p. illus. index. $3.95pa. LC 79-188894.

This is an excellent introduction to the art of carrying bags full of stuff through the wilderness or even through the woods close to home. The several chapters discuss packs, cooking gear, clothing, shelter and bedding, how to walk, first aid, survival, taking the family, trout fishing, and general camping procedures. There are explanations of why things are done as well as how they are done. A list of suppliers is appended. Illustrated with drawings by Warren Dayton. Highly recommended.

FIRST-CHOICE TITLES

If I were asked to pick out a few titles from those listed in this section, I'd probably choose the following:

Low-cost paperbacks: you can swing a couple of these and have change back from a ten-dollar bill. Rethmel's *Backpacking* is large (at 8½ x 11") so check your backpack pockets ($4.50). Wood's *Pleasure Packing* is probably your best bet for a one-volume library ($3.95). Saijo's *The Backpacker* is worthy and sort of different ($1.95). Jansen's *Lightweight Backpacking* ($1.50) may be the one you'll find most easily, since it is sold in almost every variety store book rack. Abel's *Backpacking Made Easy* was easy to read and likeable ($2.50). Langer's *The Joy of Camping* ($2.50) is especially good if you want the sections on snowshoeing, ski-touring, and canoeing.

If you want a more expensive volume you are pretty much limited to Kelsey's *Walking in the Wild* ($6.95), which I liked very much and Bridge's *America's Backpacking Book* ($12.50) which is quite good, too. Van Lear's *The Best about Backpacking* ($6.95) would also fit in here.

For possible survival use, I'd suggest getting Olsen's *Outdoor Survival Skills* ($2.95) for close study, the Wilderness Pocket n' Pak Library ($4.95) for the side pocket of your pack, and one of the Plant Decks, depending on where you are hiking, which are mentioned in the section on foods.

Remember, though, that the book is only the beginning. You have to put on the old leathers and pick 'em up and put 'em down. And don't forget a couple of the old-time books I've mentioned—on a rainy night, they'll bring nostalgia and a good feeling. And, finally, buy the *Explorers Ltd. Source Book*—there is nothing else like it.

FOODS AND COOKING

... to eat or not to eat, that is the question!

The outdoorsman cannot live on scenery alone. He must somehow carry his food along with him or pick it up as he goes along—and then he has to cook it. This section lists a few books about wild foods and about poisonous plants that must be avoided, with a selection of cookbooks that should appeal to the traveller. A few titles will be more appropriate to the homesteader, perhaps, but they are listed here because they deal primarily with food. A study of possible wild foods will repay any serious outer. There are several wild food plants that closely resemble poisonous ones and sometimes (e.g., rhubarb) some of the plant is poisonous while the remainder is quite delicious. In any event, the titles included here seemed interesting to me and valuable. Recipes and other food suggestions will be found, of course, in most camping books and in many of the country living books we mention elsewhere.

182. Allen, Jana, and Margaret Gin. **Innards and Other Variety Meats**. San Francisco, 101 Productions, 1974. 144p. illus. index. $7.95; $3.95pa. LC 73-91942. ISBN 0-912238-49-6; -48-8pa.

This is all about cooking brains, tongues, hearts, livers, kidneys, tripe, heads and tails, feet, "other offal," and whatever doesn't fall into the regular classification of meat. The excellent recipes are the heart of the book, which is illustrated with woodcuts. How about "sheep trotters with lemon sauce" or "liver knishes"? The innards and other such parts of animals are quite flavorful and generally more nutritious than the "meat," so we thought that this title should be included for the benefit of our homesteader or hunter who is faced with an animal to butcher. Actually, the 262 recipes are a bit more than the average countryman could handle on short notice, but the basic instruction is good and hard to find elsewhere. Highly recommended. Now, for the "escalopes of sweetbreads & asparagus"!

FOODS AND COOKING

183. Angier, Bradford. **Food-from-the-Woods Cooking.** New York, Collier Books, 1973. 179p. illus. index. $1.50pa. LC 72-100347.

Originally published in 1970 as *Gourmet Cooking for Free* (Stackpole), this is a handy guide to preparing the many foods available from the wilds. Large and small game, birds and fish, and plants are included. Spitted grouse, simmered heart, quail in sour cream, grilled frog legs, and braised Scotch lovage are among the suggestions for the successful hunter. An excellent little handbook for the cook.

184. Ashbrook, Frank G. **Butchering, Processing and Preservation of Meat.** New York, Van Nostrand, 1955. 318p. illus. index. $4.95pa. LC 55-5633. ISBN 0-442-20377-2.

Ashbrook presents many facts about meat eating, planning for family food needs, and federal meat inspection, but the bulk of the book is devoted to getting the meat into the pot or freezer. The several chapters cover planning the slaughter; actual butchering of hogs, cattle, sheep, wild game, poultry and fish; handling the hides and skins; preservation by freezing, chemicals, drying, pickling, etc. The use of by-products is introduced (sausages, lard, etc.) and there is a long list of reference and information sources. Illustrated with photos and drawings. An excellent manual.

185. Banks, James E. **Alferd Packer's Wilderness Cookbook.** Palmer Lake, CO, Filter, 1969. 32p. illus. $3.50; $1.00pa. SBN 910584-09-5.

Following a short history of Alferd Packer's cannibalistic exploits, we find the food lists and cooking hints of an old-timer. A very small book but an interesting one, illustrated with old woodcuts.

186. Banks, James E. **Uncle Jim's Book of Pancakes.** Palmer Lake, CO, Filter, 1967. 24p. illus. $1.00pa. ISBN 0-910584-03-6.

From plain old pancakes to buttermilk or sourdough flapjacks, this covers many variations that sound scrumptious. Illustrated with old woodcuts.

187. Bartmess, Marilyn A., ed. **Woodall's Campsite Cookbook.** New York, Simon & Schuster, 1970. 268p. index. $2.95pa. LC 77-135375. SBN 671-20753-9.

There are suggestions on nutrition, equipment for the campsite, fire building and other skills, and recipes galore: all kinds of foods cooked in foil, reflectors, Dutch ovens, and regular camping utensils.

188. Benoliel, Doug. **Northwest Foraging.** Lynnwood, WA, Signpost, 1974. 171p. illus. index. glossary. $4.50pa. ISBN 0-913140-13-9.

OUTDOOR RECREATION

Illustrated with drawings by Mark Olsen, this guide describes each plant, giving information on leaves, flowers, fruit, habitat, and edibility. There is also some information on poisonous plants and on cooking and storing wild foods.

189. Berglundt, Berndt, and Clare E. Bolsby. **Wilderness Cooking: A Unique Illustrated Cookbook and Guide for Outdoor Enthusiasts.** New York, Scribner's, 1973. 192p. illus. index. $7.95. LC 72-12158. SBN 684-13335-0.

This book describes some hunting and fishing methods, field dressing of wild game, butchering and curing meat, Indian ways of cooking (e.g., baking in mud or boiling with hot stones), preparing fish, breads, corn, beverages, sweet stuff (including desserts), and cooking wild meats. The drawings in this excellent book are by E. B. Sanders.

Bleything, Dennis, and Ron Dawson. *Edible Plants in the Wilderness.*

Bleything, Dennis, and Ron Dawson. *Poisonous Plants in the Wilderness.*

See: Wilderness Pocket n' Pak Library (entry 176).

190. Brown, Edward Espe. **The Tassajara Bread Book.** Berkeley, CA, Shambhala, 1970. 146p. illus. $5.95; $2.95pa. LC 75-143877. ISBN 0-87773-019-9; -025-3pa.

Assuming that bread is good for you (and some nutritionists know that it is not—the human race has had its medical problems ever since we began to eat grains), you need a good bread cookbook. This *is* a good one, with its recipes for basic breads, rolls, fruit-filled loaves, pastries, sourdough breads of all kinds, breads made from barley, oatmeal, millet and other grains, muffins, bagels, quick breads, and desserts. Illustrated with drawings. There are also many good hints on tools and utensils as well as baking methods. Highly recommended.

191. Brown, Edward Espe. **Tassajara Cooking.** Berkeley, CA, Shambhala, 1973. 245p. illus. index. (A Zen Center Book). $6.95; $3.95pa. ISBN 0-87773-046-6; -047-4pa.

This is as good an introduction to Buddhist vegetarian cookery as any. There are suggestions about utensils, basic ideas about cooking methods, and meal planning. The recipes are for dishes of vegetables, fruits, beans, nuts and seeds, grains, dairy products and eggs (for the modified vegetarian diet), salads, soups, sauces and main dishes. Illustrated with drawings. An excellent book.

FOODS AND COOKING

192. Bunnelle, Hasse, with Shirley Sarvis. **Cooking for Camp and Trail.** San Francisco, Sierra Club, 1972. 194p. index. (A Sierra Club Totebook). $3.95pa. LC 77-189535. ISBN 0-87156-066-6.

Several sections of this book are devoted to the planning and packaging of foods, to the building of fires or selection of stoves and other equipment, and to a glossary of terms. Most of the text, however, is a compilation of recipes: granola, stews, pasties (you don't have to be from Butte, Montana, to know what a pastie is, but it helps!), breads, and even more esoteric delights. A handy book that most outers will appreciate. This book is designed to complement the same author's *Food for Knapsackers and Other Trail Travelers* (next entry), which is mostly about lightweight foods for backpackers.

193. Bunnelle, Hasse, and Winnie Thomas. **Food for Knapsackers and Other Trail Travellers.** San Francisco, Sierra Club, 1971. 144p. illus. (A Sierra Club Totebook). $1.95pa. LC 74-162395. SBN 87156-049-6.

This pocket manual covers food planning and menu building, cooking equipment (pots, stoves, etc.), and other incidentals. A master food list gives weight-volume comparisons and number of calories per serving. Recipes and hints of all kinds. For all backpackers.

194. Burt, Calvin P., and Frank G. Heyl. **Edible and Poisonous Plants of the Eastern States.** Lake Oswego, OR, Plant Deck, Inc., 1973. $4.50.

195. Burt, Calvin P., and Frank G. Heyl. **Edible and Poisonous Plants of the Western States.** Lake Oswego, OR, Plant Deck, Inc., 1970. $4.50.

These plant decks are unique little items for the outdoorsman. A set contains 52 cards, each of which illustrates a plant and describes its habitat and uses. The illustrations are excellent color photographs. Poisonous plants are described in red print. An excellent and useful idea for every woods traveller.

196. Christensen, Clyde M. **Common Edible Mushrooms.** Minneapolis, University of Minnesota Press, 1943. 124p. illus.(part col.). index. $6.95; $2.95pa. LC 43-52551. ISBN 0-8166-0509-2; -0510-6pa.

This introduction features the "foolproof four"—Morels, puffballs, shaggymanes, and sulphur polypores. Mushrooms with and without gills are described, there are recipes for mushroom cookery, and the illustrations consist of many photographs and color drawings.

197. Conrotto, Eugene L., comp. **Game Cookery: 96 XIXth Century Recipes.** Palmer Lake, CO, Filter, 1971. 46p. illus. $1.50pa. ISBN 0-910584-17-7.

OUTDOOR RECREATION

The title continues: " . . . from bear to woodcock, and including venison, wild duck, boar, quail, hare, snipe, and all other provender from field, forest and sky along with those SAUCES necessary to the CULINARY ART." The recipes sound great, and they ought to—they are from Delmonico's! No, you won't be able to handle all this on the open fire in the woods but I thought I'd throw it in anyway.

198. Cross, Margaret, and Jean Fiske. **Backpacker's Cookbook.** Berkeley, CA, Ten Speed Press, 1974. 142p. illus. $3.00pa. ISBN 0-913668-15-X.

This is a good introduction to the nutritional needs of hikers. There are sample menus, notes on suitable foods and how to cook them, information on stoves and pots and other needed gear, and suggestions on packaging the whole lot. The recipes include those for logan bread, chicken curry, gorp, and apricot squash. Sounds great! The illustrations consist of drawings by Linda Bennett, who even shows us how to make pot and food bags. A neat little book, highly recommended.

199. Dahlem, Ted. **How to Smoke Seafood Florida Cracker Style.** St. Petersburg, FL, Great Outdoors, 1971. 44p. illus. $1.00pa. SBN 8200-0803-6.

This contains not only methods for smoking seafoods but also instructions for building and using a smoker. A handy book for any country dweller near the sea.

200. Dickey, Esther. **Passport to Survival: Four Foods and More to Use and Store.** New York, Random House, 1974. 180p. illus. index. $4.95. LC 73-20565. ISBN 0-394-49228-5.

The four foods are: wheat, powdered milk, honey, and salt. These foods are storable indefinitely and will sustain life should an emergency arise. Other foods are suggested as adjuncts. There are recipes and menus, hints on food storage and preservation and general survival methods: getting water, storing soap, first aid supplies, clothing, etc. Something about wild foods is also included. It's amazing what one can do with just four basic ingredients.

201. Ewald, Ellen Buchman. **Recipes for a Small Planet: The Art and Science of High Protein Vegetarian Cookery.** New York, Ballantine, 1973. 356p. illus. index. $1.50pa.

This book on "high protein meatless cooking" is intended to complement the ideas outlined in Lappé's *Diet for a Small Planet* (entry 218). Ewald offers many more recipes and further instruction in basic cooking methods. If vegetarianism is your bag of seeds, you need this little book.

FOODS AND COOKING

202. Furlong, Marjorie, and Virginia Pill. **Edible? Incredible!** Tacoma, WA, ERCO, 1973. 63p. illus.(col.). index. $2.50pa.

This is a guide to edible marine life, principally in U.S. West Coast waters. If you need recipes for fried moon snails, frittered keyhole limpet, raw sea-urchin eggs, or smoked grunt, this book is a must. Good photographs are used throughout. Interesting.

203. Gorton, Audrey Alley. **The Venison Book: How to Dress, Cut Up and Cook Your Deer.** Brattleboro, VT, Stephen Greene, 1957. 78p. illus. index. $2.95pa. LC 57-13401. ISBN 0-8289-0001-9.

From bagging the deer and "hog dressing" it, to getting it on the table, Gorton describes all the steps: easy ways to tell the age of the animal, how to skin it, how to butcher, package, and preserve the meat. She disapproves of hanging the meat, suggesting instead that it be used or frozen immediately.

204. Haard, Karen, and Richard Haard. **Foraging for Edible Wild Mushrooms.** Brackendale, British Columbia, Cloudburst, 1975. 94p. illus.(part col.). index. $7.95; $3.95pa.

Both authors are mycologists, so this little handbook is authoritative. The drawings adequately show the shapes and parts of mushrooms for easy identification of 36 species. There are hints on preserving and cooking the fungal delights, several color plates, and lots of good material in this highly recommended work. Probably the best for beginners.

205. Hall, Alan. **The Wild Food Trailguide.** New York, Holt, 1973. 195p. illus. index. glossary. $3.45pa. LC 72-91562. ISBN 0-03-007701-X.

Hall describes how to find and identify wild food plants. He gives suggestions about their uses (e.g., as salads, cereals, potato substitutes, etc.) and a guide to poisonous plants. Most of the book consists of the descriptions of plants, with drawings, arranged by families.

206. Hamilton, Donna Miller, and Beverly Anderson Nemiro. **The Complete Book of High Altitude Baking.** Chicago, Sage Books (Swallow Press), 1961. 370p. index. $6.95. LC 61-18656.

The greater the altitude, the lower the air pressure. This affects people's breathing and the bubbles in bread dough. The general information in this book is about baking, freezer charts, tables of equivalents, types of baking powder, etc. Most of the book consists of recipes for breads, cakes, cookies, frostings, fillings, pies, and desserts. There is also a collection of recipes for "junior bakers" and a complete index.

207. Harrington, H. D. **Edible Native Plants of the Rocky Mountains.** Albuquerque, NM, University of New Mexico Press, 1967. 392p. illus. index. bibliog. $10.00. LC 67-29685.

OUTDOOR RECREATION

The area covered includes the Rocky Mountains and foothills between the longitudes of western Nebraska and central Utah. Harrington describes the fruits, leaves, shoots, roots, and other edible parts of plants and those that can be smoked ("smoked" à la tobacco, that is!). There is also a chapter on poisonous plants and an extensive bibliography. Some 144 species or genera are indexed. This is more detailed than Harrington's *Western Edible Wild Plants*, but it is not as extensive geographically. Excellent book.

208. Harrington, H. D. **Western Edible Wild Plants.** Albuquerque, NM, University of New Mexico Press, 1972. 156p. illus. index. $2.95pa. LC 77-190061. ISBN 0-8263-0050-2.

The area covered includes the West from western Nebraska to the Pacific Coast. The book is divided into several sections: the use of underground parts, use of leaves and shoots, and use of seeds, fruits, etc. In each case, the edible part is identified and cooking instructions are provided. Poisonous plants are described, too, so we have everything from the common cattail to poison ivy. Some 42 genera are indexed as to common and generic name. Excellent book.

209. Harris, Gertrude. **Manna: Foods of the Frontier.** San Francisco, 101 Productions, 1972. 192p. illus. index. $3.95pa. LC 72-77565. SBN 912238-25-9.

This is a resume of many of the foods and recipes used by the early settlers in the United States. Among the foods are: beverages, breads, soups, meat dishes of all kinds, dairy products, eggs, vegetables, grains, sauces, preserves, and desserts. The making of candles, soap, and yeast is also described. This is where to find recipes for pickled carp, corn pones, kidney soup, hare loaf, mincemeat, miner's beans (no, they're not like Rocky Mountain oysters!), English monkey, and salpicon. The drawings in this excellent book are by Heidi Palmer.

210. Herter, George Leonard, and Berthe E. Herter. **Bull Cook and Authentic Historical Recipes and Practices.** 3 vols. (v.1, 5th ed.; v.2, 2nd ed.; v.3, 1st ed.). Waseca, MN, Herter's, 1962, 1968, 1971. 208p., 752p., 288p. illus. indices. $2.79; $3.99; $3.49.

These books are not particularly for the outdoorsman but they are filled with excellent hints on cooking a variety of foods. I know of no other source for the favorite recipes of Ghengis Khan, Saint Patrick, or Saint James the Apostle. In addition, there are all sorts of odd facts about history, restaurants, wild foods, and you name it. Fascinating reading. A "bull cook," incidentally, is the male cook in a lumber camp.

FOODS AND COOKING

211. Hertzberg, Ruth, Beatrice Vaughn, and Janet Greene. **Putting Food By.** Brattleboro, VT, Stephen Greene, 1974. 371p. illus. index. $6.95; $4.50pa. LC 71-188897. ISBN 0-8289-0164-3; -0165-5pa.

This is a guide to preserving and cooking foods. The chapters include material on canning, freezing, using the preserving kettle for jams and pickles, drying, root-cellaring, curing by salting and smoking, rendering lard, making cheese, stuffing sausage, and making soap. The emphasis is on keeping foods from spoiling without using non-food additives. There are many photos, drawings, charts, and tables. This is probably the best single source for this kind of information.

212. Horton, Lucy. **Country Commune Cookbook.** New York, Coward, McCann & Geoghegan, 1972. 240p. illus. index. $4.95pa. LC 72-76673. SBN 698-10456-0.

The author spent many months travelling from one commune to another in her search for good recipes. This book contains over 150 recipes for soups, vegetable dishes, meats (only a few), eggs, grains, salads, breads, sauces, desserts, beverages, and spicy stuff. Drawings by Judith St. Soliel and odd bits of information at every turn. I'm not too sure about the banana halvah but I'll go the rest of the way.

213. Johnson, L. W., ed. **Wild Game Cookbook.** New York, Benjamin, 1972. 174p. illus. index. (A Remington Sportsmen's Library Book). $2.95pa. LC 70-114972. ISBN 0-87502-907-8.

"Hundreds of savory ways to prepare all kinds of game." Upland game birds, small game, waterfowl, and big game are all included. Fish are excluded. A handy little book.

214. Kingsbury, John M. **Deadly Harvest: A Guide to Common Poisonous Plants.** New York, Holt, 1965. 128p. illus. $4.95. LC 65-14441. SBN 03-051160-7.

Besides explaining why some plants are deadly, this guide identifies different poisons and tells how different plants are toxic. There is a section on plants that are common enough to be potentially dangerous to almost everyone, one example being the ordinary privet so often used as a hedge plant. A very interesting book.

215. Kirk, Donald R. **Wild Edible Plants of the Western United States including also Most of Southwestern Canada and Northwestern Mexico.** Healdsburg, CA, Naturegraph, 1970. 326p. illus. index. $6.95; $3.95pa. ISBN 0-911010-85-8; -84-Xpa.

Kirk covers the major plant areas of the West, describing universal plants that are found everywhere (horsetails to junipers), plants of the

OUTDOOR RECREATION

Northwest (hemlocks to crowberries), plants of the Southwest (pinon pines to Johnny-Jump-Ups), and the Rocky Mountain states (Loveroot to Puccoon). Illustrated with drawings of flower and leaf types. A handy, pocket-sized manual.

216. Kluger, Marilyn. **The Wild Flavor.** New York, Coward, McCann & Geoghegan, 1973. 284p. illus. index. $8.95. LC 72-94117. SBN 698-10526-5.

Illustrated with drawings by Mary Azarian, this book is about gathering wild plant foods by season: springtime for sassafras tea, sugar, morels and spring greens; summer for small fruits; autumn for the larger fruits, etc. Lots of recipes and general country living philosophy. Delicious reading.

217. Krieger, Louis C. C. **The Mushroom Handbook.** New York, Dover, 1967. 560p. illus.(part col.). index. bibliog. glossary. $3.95pa. LC 67-28792. SBN 486-21861-9.

This is more of a scientific listing of mushrooms than a guide to "eaters." The excellent descriptions and drawings in this 1935 title have been brought up to date by R. L. Shaffer of the University of Michigan. The bibliography is quite long.

218. Lappé, Frances Moore. **Diet for a Small Planet.** New York, Ballantine, 1971. 301p. illus. index. $3.95pa. ISBN 0-345-02387-0.

Devoted to "high protein meatless cooking," about half the book consists of "complementary protein recipes" together with menus, basic cooking instruction, and other information. The first half of the text is about the need for protein and how one must mix vegetable proteins to get a good, complete diet. There seems to be a lot of claptrap here, so you'll just have to endure. If you're stuck with beans, this book will help.

219. McCready, Jack. **Furred and Feathered Wild Game from Bullet to Table.** Asheville, NC, Powell, 1973. 71p. illus. $2.95pa. (plus $0.30 postage).

The cover subtitle sums it up: "The comprehensive guide for handling and preparing the world's finest meat." Much game is wasted through poor handling and processing. This little book will set things straight even for the novice. There are sections on field care, skinning, butchering, aging, preserving and cooking. An excellent manual.

220. McKenny, Margaret, and Daniel E. Stuntz. **The Savory Wild Mushroom.** Seattle, University of Washington Press, 1971. 274p. illus.(part col.). index. $8.95; $4.95pa. LC 78-160288. ISBN 0-295-95155-9; -95156-7pa.

FOODS AND COOKING

Covering the Pacific Northwest and nearby areas, this book describes the many boletes, chantarelles, gilled mushrooms, puffballs, polypores, spine, coral, jelly, and cup fungi, helvellas, and morels. There is a chapter on mushroom poisons by V. E. Tyler and one called "The Hunt, the Quarry, and the Skillet" by A. M. Pellegrini. There are recipes and a bibliography. An excellent book.

221. MacManiman, Gen. **Dry It—You'll Like It!** Fall City, WA, Living Foods, 1974. 74p. illus. $3.95pa.

This little book is all about dehydrating fruit, grains, vegetables, meat, fish, and herbs. There are plans for building a dehydrator and a number of recipes. A good book.

222. MacMillan, Diane D. **The Portable Feast.** San Francisco, 101 Productions, 1973. 192p. illus. $3.95pa. LC 72-94896. SBN 912238-35-6.

This is all about "Picnic, Lunch Box and Knapsack Fare." Beginning with the needed gear (baskets, knives, forks, etc.), we proceed to breads, recipes for all sorts of salads, spreads, and cookies, suggestions for stocking the kitchen so as to be always ready to go for quick or elegant picnics. "The Pathfinder's Knapsack" has hints on what foods to carry on a hike and how to use them. Other sections are concerned with foods on boats or in campers. The drawings, by Erni Young, are appropriate, if fanciful. A good gift book as well as a good use book.

223. Melville, Betty. **The Hunter's Cookbook.** Austin, TX, Heidelberg Publishers, 1972. 141p. illus. index. glossary. $7.95. LC 72-89047. ISBN 0-913206-00-8.

An experienced home economist, Melville has prepared an excellent guide to the field dressing and processing of wild game of all kinds common to the United States. There is a chapter on seasonings, as well, but most of the book is devoted to recipes and details for handling game birds, small game, and large game. There are a few drawings of animals and of how the standard "cuts" are made on carcasses. The recipes sound delicious. The title page indicates that the publisher is Little House Press.

224. Orton, Vrest. **The Homemade Beer Book.** Rutland, VT, Tuttle, 1973. 159p. illus. $2.95pa. LC 72-89742. ISBN 0-8048-1086-9.

Privately issued in 1932 for the benefit of prohibition haters, the original edition was titled "Proceedings of the Company of Amateur Brewers." The present subtitle is "In Which are included General Principles and Recipes for Making Beer in the Home, History of Beer, Drinking Customs of Old New England, Brewing of the Olden Times, Curious Lore of Oldtime Brewing, Etc., Etc." The only change has been the updating of the recipes with modern ingredients and sources. Ginger beer is included, too, for the teetotallers.

OUTDOOR RECREATION

225. Raup, Lucy G. **The Camper's Cookbook: Equipment, Recipes, Menus.** Rutland, VT, Tuttle, 1967. 199p. illus. $3.30pa. LC 67-15139. SBN 8048-0079-0.

Raup offers basic information on camp kitchens, fires, utensils, selection and packing of supplies, methods of cooking, and several ration lists to suit various kinds of camping. She distinguishes several types of camping situations; permanent camps, light camping, very light camping, and lightest possible camping. Take your choice. There are many recipes for breads and cereals, soups, meat-fish-egg dishes, salads, vegetables, and desserts. This handy little book concludes with lists of camping gear and sources of foods (dated, of course).

226. Schubert, Ruth L. **The Camper's Cookbook.** Boston, Little, Brown, 1974. 196p. index. $3.50pa. LC 74-2177. ISBN 0-316-77496-0.

This is a compilation of 380 recipes suitable for cooking with camping equipment and a small number of ingredients. There are notes on cooking utensils, basic food supplies, and methods of cooking. Some of the chapter titles are: Baked Beans, Canned Chili, Bologna, Canned Crab, Eggs, Soups.

227. Smith, Alexander H. **The Mushroom Hunter's Field Guide.** Rev. & enl. ed. Ann Arbor, University of Michigan Press, 1963. 303p. illus.(part col.). index. glossary. $9.95. LC 63-14007. ISBN 0-472-85609-X.

Smith begins with information on the biology of mushrooms and how to use the book. There are descriptions of the various classes, information on how to find mushrooms, and an introduction to the edible species. Each species described has a note on edibility and a note on probable location. Some species are illustrated with color photographs. Well reproduced.

228. Sturdivant, E. N., and Edith Sturdivant. **Game Cookery.** New York, Dutton, 1967. 166p. illus. index. (An Outdoor Life Skill Book). $1.95pa. LC 67-13724.

With drawings and photographs, this little book illustrates how to dress, skin, freeze, preserve, and cook game animals, including birds and fish.

229. Sweet, Muriel. **Common Edible and Useful Plants of the West.** Healdsburg, CA, Naturegraph, 1962. 64p. illus. index. $1.50pa. ISBN 0-911010-54-8.

The plants include ferns and water plants, vines, trees, shrubs, and herbs. For each plant, Sweet gives the size, color, other characteristics, and notes on use. One can also find plants by an index to the color of flowers, seeds, and fruit.

FOODS AND COOKING

230. Thomas, Dian. **Roughing It Easy: A Unique Ideabook for Camping and Cooking.** Provo, UT, Brigham Young University, 1974. 203p. illus. (part col.). index. $7.95; $4.95pa. ISBN 0-8425-0887-2; -0892-9pa.

   This book contains some general advice on camping equipment, fire building, campsite selection, and related things, but it is mostly devoted to food planning and cookery. The several cooking methods (e.g., baking, boiling, frying, roasting) are described, as are the uses of aluminum foil, Dutch ovens, and other gear. There are shopping lists, tables of substitutes, and first aid information. A number of impromptu methods for fire-making (bow and drill, etc.) and using homemade stoves are described. The recipes include all sorts of goodies, such as bacon on a stick, cinnamon toast, stuffed zucchini, crepes, and sourdough hotcakes. Excellent and highly recommended.

231. Tomikell, John. **Edible Wild Plants of Pennsylvania.** California, PA, Allegheny Press, 1973. 88p. illus. index. $5.00; $2.50pa. LC 72-89403. ISBN 0-910042-14-4; -13-6pa.

   This fine little book describes many of the useful plants that can be eaten and gives cooking instructions for them. Water plants, shrubs and trees, fungi and lichens, and other plants are included. Poisonous plants are mentioned for safety. Please *do* eat the daisies (if you can stand the smell). Useful elsewhere, of course, since the plants are not restricted to the Keystone State.

232. U.S. Dept. of Agriculture. **Complete Guide to Home Canning, Preserving and Freezing.** New York, Dover, 1973. 214p. illus. index. $2.50pa. ISBN 0-486-22911-4.

   This one-volume Dover reprint is the easiest way to obtain the information from seven government manuals. There are instructions for making jams and other preserves, making pickles and relishes, home canning of fruits and vegetables, canning of meats, and freezing meats and vegetable products. Certainly a best buy.

233. Van Atta, Marian. **Living Off the Land: A Handbook for Living in the Subtropics.** Melbourne, FL, Van Atta, 1973. 59p. illus. index. $2.75pa.

   Based on the author's newspaper column, this is essentially a compilation of recipes that utilize the common plants and animals that occur in Florida. There are various bits of information on using compost, preserving foods, cooking rattlesnakes, and raising earthworms. This is not a "survival" book, as the title may imply. A good book for anyone living in an appropriate climatic zone. Van Atta also publishes a tropical-living newsletter.

234. Wickstrom, Lois. **The Food Conspiracy Cookbook: How to Start a Neighborhood Buying Club and Eat Cheaply.** San Francisco, 101 Productions, 1974. 144p. illus. index. $3.95pa. LC 73-91940. ISBN 0-912238-45-3.

OUTDOOR RECREATION

Excellent recipes and suggestions for preparing all kinds of foods including meats, grains, beans, eggs, nuts, fruits, whether canned or fresh. This is based on the experience of the Berkeley Food Conspiracies and contains chapters on the business aspects of this sort of buying cooperative. An excellent little tome.

IDENTIFYING AND COLLECTING

... seek and ye shall find. Maybe!

The outdoor recreationist may be drawn to many activities concerned with identifying things, collecting things, or hoping to find things. Among the many such activities are: bird watching, rock and mineral collecting, treasure hunting, beachcombing, or digging on old Indian sites. There are many books about these activities and I have tried to include a few that are either new or easy to find. Treasure hunting, especially, has a tremendously large number of available titles, and keeping track of them all would be a task for a lifetime. In any event, this guide is meant to suggest a few basic works and the rest is up to the reader.

Throughout this section, I have listed many titles from Golden Press. These little books are often deemed to be simply children's books but they are good basic texts, are well illustrated, and are available in many places. Among the publishers of treasure-hunting books, there seem to be at least three that specialize in how-to books, so I've noted a number of titles from Exanimo, Carson, and Ram. Naylor publishes many tales of treasure hunting, but I noted only a few to whet the appetite.

When one is afield, one must remember that private property should be respected and potential sites should not be destroyed. Many gem localities are open to the public but many are not. I've hunted for gems in many places but never allowed the practice to become a mania. I had a school chum who could not resist a piece of pyrites (fool's gold), and he would carry home a hundred pounds of it every time we found it. I once had a room full of amethysts from a New Jersey quarry. One day, my mother announced that either the minerals or I had to go. I stayed. Identifying and collecting things is a grand outdoor hobby and I hope that a few of the books listed here will lead the reader on to long bird lists or to a cellar full of junk.

I have divided this section into two parts. One deals with the identification of living things, the other with the bringing back of things. When bird watching or plant finding, the identification is the big thing (unless one is after food, of course) and one may use only a pair of binoculars in addition to a book. When after rocks and minerals or when treasure hunting, one often

OUTDOOR RECREATION

needs equipment such as metal detectors and a good deal of detailed information. There seemed to be a natural division here, so I kept it.

IDENTIFYING ANIMAL AND PLANT LIFE

235. Abbott, R. Tucker. **Seashells of North America: A Guide to Field Identification.** New York, Golden Press, 1968. 280p. illus.(col.). index. (A Golden Field Guide). $3.95pa. LC 68-10083.

This book consists of descriptions of many types of molluscs with illustrations by George F. Sandstrom. For most American collectors, this is preferable to Abbott's *Seashells of the World*, because it is more complete and detailed. A reading list is included.

236. Abbott, R. Tucker. **Seashells of the World: A Guide to the Better-Known Species.** New York, Golden Press, 1962. 160p. illus.(col.). index. (A Golden Nature Guide). $1.50pa. LC 62-9852.

Hints on collecting and identifying molluscs are illustrated with drawings by George and Marita Sandstrom. Tourists who look for shells in shops might need this along.

237. Alden, Peter. **Finding the Birds in Western Mexico: A Guide to the States of Sonora, Sinaloa, and Nayarit.** Tucson, AZ, University of Arizona Press, 1969. 138p. illus.(part col.). $5.95pa.

This book contains descriptions of the country and road directions to good localities together with bird lists and maps. The color paintings are by John O'Neill. Includes a complete list of species, a bibliography, and the San Blas Christmas bird counts for 1964 to 1967.

238. Alexander, Taylor R., and George S. Fichter. **Ecology.** New York, Golden Press, 1973. 160p. illus.(part col.). index. (A Golden Science Guide). $1.95pa. LC 72-95538.

A good introduction for the layman, this little book should adequately serve the casual outdoor recreationist on a camping trip or picnic. The text includes information on: habitats, plant succession, wildlife management, food chains, ecological techniques and other material. Photos and drawings are mostly in color; the drawings are by Raymond Perlman.

239. Austin, Oliver L., Jr. **Families of Birds.** New York, Golden Press, 1971. 200p. illus.(part col.). index. (A Golden Science Guide). $1.95pa. LC 77-149206.

Intended for birders who already know quite a few birds, this volume is more concerned with the layer concept of classification and the way families are related. There is a short glossary and a reading list; illustrations are by Arthur Singer.

240. Brockman, C. Frank. **Trees of North America: A Field Guide to the Major Native and Introduced Species North of Mexico.** New York, Golden Press, 1968. 280p. illus.(col.). index. (A Golden Field Guide). $3.95pa. LC 68-23523.

The illustrations are by Rebecca Merrilees in this guide to 730 species.

241. Brown, Vinson. **Knowing the Outdoors in the Dark.** Harrisburg, PA, Stackpole, 1972. 191p. illus. $6.95.

This is a guide to the many sounds and other aspects of the night life in the great outdoors. A good book for any camper who wonders what's going on out there.

242. Brown, Vinson. **Reading the Woods.** Harrisburg, PA, Stackpole, 1969. 160p. illus. index. $5.95. LC 70-85652. ISBN 0-8117-1397-0.

Copiously illustrated notes on the effects on the "woods" of climate and weather, information on soil types, fire, and the actions of animals and men, and an explanation of plant succession and climax forests. The serious outdoorsman will enjoy this book.

243. Brown, Vinson. **Reptiles & Amphibians of the West.** Healdsburg, CA, Naturegraph, 1974. 79p. illus.(part col.). index. $3.50pa. LC 74-3204. ISBN 0-87961-028-X.

Illustrated with many color and black and white drawings, this pocket handbook covers most Western species of snakes, salamanders, frogs, toads, and lizards. There are suggestions on catching the rascals and keeping them as pets, how to identify them, and what their real names are. Brown is an authority on this variety of animal, and the book will be useful on most outdoor excursions. It is now obvious that I was contesting the right of way, some years ago in Nebraska, with one *Crotalus viridis*, the Western Rattlesnake. An excellent book.

244. Case, Marshal T. **Look What I Found!** Riverside, CT, Chatham Press, 1971. 95p. illus. index. $4.95. LC 79-148578. SBN 85699-023-X.

The jacket subtitle is "The young conservationist's guide to the care and feeding of small wildlife," the wildlife being everything from insects and crabs to squirrels, skunks, and gerbils. There are many photographs plus drawings by Mary Lee Herbster. Most of the activities described may be "indoors" stuff, but the process begins in the natural world. An excellent little handbook for the kids.

245. Edwards, Ernest P. **A Field Guide to the Birds of Mexico Including All Birds from the Northern Border of Mexico to the Southern Border of Nicaragua.** Sweet Briar, VA, Author, 1972. 300p. illus.(col.). $8.50pa. LC 78-185930. ISBN 0-911882-03-0.

About 500 species not found in the U.S. are illustrated in color with information on range, behavior, voice, color, shapes, etc., for an additional 500 species. There is a Spanish description for each bird.

246. Lempfert, O. C. **Paw Prints: How to Identify Rare and Common Mammals by Their Tracks.** New York, Exposition Press, 1972. 71p. illus.(part col.). $7.50. LC 73-171708. ISBN 0-682-47371-5.

This consists of illustrations and descriptions of paw prints of quite a few American mammals: foxes, rabbits, squirrels, possums, bears, mice, etc. Lempfert's classification of tracks (single-line, double-diagonal, multiple) seems rather good. The prints are drawn full size and were made from actual paws. A good manual.

247. Levi, Hubert W., and Lorna R. Levi. **A Guide to Spiders and Their Kin.** New York, Golden Press, 1968. 160p. illus.(col.). index. (A Golden Nature Guide). $1.50pa. LC 68-23522.

All those rascals with four pairs of legs are described here, in addition to ticks, several myriapods, and crustaceans. Illustrations are by Nicholas Strekalovsky.

248. McElroy, Thomas P., Jr. **The Habitat Guide to Birding.** New York, Knopf, 1974. 269p. illus. index. $8.95. LC 73-9945. ISBN 0-394-47492-9.

Covering the Eastern half of the United States and Canada, this book describes the several habitats (evergreen forests, seashore, meadows, etc.), and notes the birds to be found in each. Not really a bird book but a finding guide. Drawings by Matthew Kalmenoff are excellent. All bird watchers should have this book.

249. Elliott, Charles. **The Outdoor Observer: How to See, Hear and Interpret in the Natural World.** New York, Dutton, 1969. 119p. illus. index. (An Outdoor Life Skill Book), $4.50; $1.95pa. LC 73-100358.

This book contains suggestions on how the outdoorsman may develop his senses of seeing, hearing, and smelling, and tells how and where to look. For example, one should not look for a whole deer but for an ear or a tail. Fishermen receive advice on how to read a stream, and there are hints on reading tracks and other animal signs and on how to use binoculars.

250. Fichter, George S. **Insect Pests.** New York, Golden Press, 1966. 160p. illus.(col.). index. (A Golden Nature Guide). $1.50pa. LC 66-22595.

This is "A guide to more than 350 pests of home, field, and forest," including those that are harmful to crops, other vegetation, and food stores. There are notes on control methods, a list of scientific names, and illustrations by Nicholas Strekalovsky.

251. Furlong, Marjorie, and Virginia Pill. **Starfish: Guides to Identification and Methods of Preserving.** 2nd ed. Tacoma, WA, ERCO, 1972. 104p. illus.(col.). index. $2.95pa.

This introduction to the biology of starfish includes identification guides to species on the United States West Coast. Excellent illustrations.

252. Gjersvik, Maryanne. **Green Fun.** Chatham, MA, Chatham Press, 1974. 80p. illus. $1.95pa.

The cover subtitle tells most of it: "Instant Toys, Tricks and Amusements Anyone Can Make from Common Weeds, Seeds, Leaves and Flowering Things." The kids will love this one. I still may try to stick a maple seed on my nose when no one's looking.

253. Jaeger, Ellsworth. **Tracks and Trailcraft.** New York, Macmillan, 1948. 381p. illus. index. $5.95.

The cover subtitle explains it well: "A Fully Illustrated Guide to the Identification of Animal Tracks in Forest and Field, Barnyard and Back Yard." Drawings are used throughout the book to illustrate tracks and trails of walking and running animals, including humans. A very fascinating book for every outdoorsman.

254. McKay, Frances Peabody. **Let's Go Shelling: A Handbook on How, When, and Where to Find Florida Shells.** St. Petersburg, FL, Great Outdoors, 1968. 104p. illus. $1.00pa.

A guide to the collecting and preservation of shells, mostly those of molluscs. Illustrated with black and white photographs. A good guide to a major collecting area.

255. Martin, Alexander C. **Weeds.** New York, Golden Press, 1972. 160p. illus.(col.). index. (A Golden Nature Guide). $1.95pa. LC 72-78574.

This introduction to weeds and their habitats considers some of the benefits and problems associated with them. The illustrations are by Jean Zallinger.

256. Melvin, A. Gordon. **Sea Shells of the World.** Rutland, VT, Tuttle, 1966. 167p. illus.(part col.). index. $8.25. LC 66-18967. ISBN 0-8048-0512-1.

This guide for shell collectors has many illustrations (about half in color), descriptions of the shells, and a dealer price list, which will have changed considerably by now.

257. Mitchell, Robert T., and Herbert S. Zim. **Butterflies and Moths: A Guide to the More Common American Species.** New York, Golden Press, 1964. 160p. illus.(col.). index. (A Golden Nature Guide). $1.50pa. LC 64-24907.

This is a guide to those often beautiful animals that smear on our windshields. There are hints on collecting and identification, a list of scientific names, and distribution maps. Illustrations are by André Durenceau.

258. Murie, Olaus J. **A Field Guide to Animal Tracks.** 2nd ed. Boston, Houghton Mifflin, 1975. 375p. illus. bibliog. index. (The Peterson Field Guide Series). $4.95pa. LC 74-6294. ISBN 0-395-18323-5.

Updated from the 1954 edition, this handbook is the classic treatment of tracks and other signs of most of our wildlife species: opossums, armadillos, moles and shrews, bats and bears, raccoons, weasels, dogs and cats, seals, rodents, rabbits, ungulates, birds, amphibians and reptiles, insects, and even the markings one may find chewed into leaves or bones. Illustrated throughout with drawings, the book is highly recommended.

259. Murray, Sonia Bennett. **Shell Life and Shell Collecting.** New York, Sterling, 1969. 96p. illus.(part col.). index. $4.95. LC 70-90799. SBN 8-69-3032-2.

This is an elementary guide to the life of molluscs and to the collecting and preservation of their shells. The drawings make anatomical features quite clear and the numerous photographs (about half are in color) make identification easy.

260. Peterson Field Guide Series.

Published by Houghton-Mifflin, the books in this series are well-known guides to various outdoor "things." Each of them is illustrated, including color plates, and the text is always authoritative. Some of the titles are available in paperback, all in hardcover. These are fine books for the casual outdoor recreationist, but the price may be too high for some. For carrying around in a pocket or bag, and for most of the outdoor identification I've had to do, the several guides published in the Golden Nature Guides and other series by Golden Press seem adequate and they are much less expensive. This list is offered, however, for the benefit of those wishing to spend a bit more. It is complete as of late 1974.

Borror, Donald J., and Richard E. White. **A Field Guide to the Insects of America North of Mexico.** 1970. $5.95.

Burt, W. H., and R. P. Grossenheider. **A Field Guide to the Mammals.** 2nd ed., 1964. $5.95.

Cobb, Boughton. **A Field Guide to the Ferns and Their Related Families.** 1956. $5.95.

Conant, Roger. **A Field Guide to Reptiles and Amphibians.** 1958. $5.95.

Craighead, John J., *et al.* **A Field Guide to Rocky Mountain Wildflowers.** 1963. $5.95.

Klots, Alexander B. **A Field Guide to the Butterflies.** 1951. $5.95.

Menzel, Donald H. **A Field Guide to the Stars and Planets.** 1964. $5.95.

Morris, Percy A. **A Field Guide to the Shells of Our Atlantic and Gulf Coasts.** 3rd ed., 1973. $7.95; $4.95pa.

Morris, Percy A. **A Field Guide to Shells of the Pacific Coast and Hawaii.** New ed., 1966. $5.95.

Murie, Olaus. **A Field Guide to Animal Tracks.** 1954. $5.95.

Peterson, Roger Tory. **A Field Guide to the Birds.** 2nd ed., 1947. $5.95; $3.95pa.

Peterson, Roger Tory. **A Field Guide to Western Birds.** 2nd ed., 1961. $6.95; $4.95pa.

Peterson, Roger Tory. **A Field Guide to the Birds of Texas and Adjacent States.** 1963. $6.95.

Peterson, Roger Tory, and Margaret McKenny. **A Field Guide to Wildflowers of Northeastern and North-Central North America.** 1968. $5.95.

Peterson, Roger Tory. **A Field Guide to Mexican Birds.** 1973. $7.95.

Petrides, George A. **A Field Guide to Trees and Shrubs.** 2nd ed., 1972. $5.95; $3.95pa.

Pough, Frederick H. **A Field Guide to Rocks and Minerals.** 1953. $6.95.

Stebbins, Robert C. **A Field Guide to Western Reptiles and Amphibians.** 1966. $5.95.

261. Reid, George K. **Pond Life: A Guide to Common Plants and Animals of North American Ponds and Lakes.** New York, Golden Press, 1967. 160p. illus.(col.). index. (A Golden Nature Guide). $1.50pa. LC 67-16477.

This guide covers both the lower and higher orders of plants and all kinds of animals from single-celled monsters to birds, insects, and mammals. Ever see a water bear? Neither have I but I'd rather see than be one. The illustrations are by Sally D. Kaicher and Tom Dolen.

262. Rice, Tom. **Marine Shells of the Pacific Coast.** Tacoma, WA, ERCO, 1972. 102p. illus.(col.). $2.95pa.

From British Columbia to Northern California, the several species of chitons, snails, tusk shells, and clams are described and pictured with excellent color photographs.

263. Rice, Tom. **What Is a Shell?** Tacoma, WA, ERCO, 1973. 64p. illus.(col.). $2.50pa.

This introduction to molluscs describes many chitons, tusk shells, cephalopods, limpets, snails, and clams from around the world. The many color photographs illustrate an interesting book about shells from far-away places.

264. Robbins, Chandler S., Bertel Bruun, and Herbert S. Zim. **Birds of North America: A Guide to Field Identification.** New York, Golden Press, 1966. 340p. illus.(part col.). index. (A Golden Field Guide). $3.95pa.

In addition to some general information about birds, this book, arranged by order, illustrates most of the birds one is likely to find on a trip or around home. Paintings are by Arthur Singer. There are distribution maps and lists of recordings, books, and periodicals. I have had one of these for years and think it excellent.

265. Robinson, Ellis H., and Gayle D. Robinson. **Wild Flowers of the Pacific Northwest Photographed in Their Natural Environment.** Tacoma, WA, ERCO, 1969. 63p. illus.(col.). $2.50pa.

Good, clear photographs illustrate a guide to flowers found in the state of Washington. There are occasional short verses by Gayle Robinson. Excellent.

266. Seton, Ernest Thompson. **Animal Tracks and Hunter Signs.** Garden City, NY, Doubleday, 1958. 160p. illus. index. $5.95. LC 58-7366.

The artist and naturalist has created drawings of tracks and their stories. Mostly about the smaller North American animals such as weasels, squirrels, shrews, foxes, turtles and raccoons, the book does include some of the larger mammals from horses and cows to moose and buffalo and *Homo sapiens*. A good book for woods wanderers.

267. Shuttleworth, Floyd S., and Herbert S. Zim. **Non-Flowering Plants: Over 400 Species in Full Color.** New York, Golden Press, 1967. 160p. illus.(col.). index. (A Golden Nature Guide). $1.50pa. LC 67-16476.

The plants covered include algae, lichens, mosses, fungi, liverworts, ferns, and some gymnosperms. There is a list of readings and a guide to scientific names.

268. Sprunt, Alexander, IV, and Herbert S. Zim. **Gamebirds: A Guide to North American Species and Their Habits.** New York, Golden Press, 1961. 160p. illus.(part col.). index. (A Golden Nature Guide). $1.50pa. LC 61-8316.

With illustrations by James G. Irving, this book covers the waterfowl, rails and other shorebirds, pigeons and doves, the gallinaceous birds, including foreign importations, and information on improving habitats. There are distribution maps and a short list of readings.

269. U.S. Dept. of Agriculture. Agricultural Research Service. **Common Weeds of the United States.** New York, Dover, 1971. 463p. illus. index. glossary. $4.50pa. LC 70-152417. ISBN 0-486-20504-5.

Well illustrated with drawings, this is a guide to 224 species of American weeds. The outdoor recreationist will trip over many of these plants and he might as well know what he's cussing. A very handy book.

270. Vilas, Curtis N., and Naomi R. Vilas. **Florida Marine Shells: A Guide for Collectors of Shells of the Southeastern Atlantic Coast and Gulf Coast.** Rutland, VT, Tuttle, 1970. 170p. illus.(part col.). $6.00.

Revised and enlarged from a privately printed edition of 1945, this covers most species of molluscs from our Southeastern coast.

271. Vosburgh, John. **Living with Your Land.** New York, Scribner's, 1968. 191p. illus. index. bibliog. $2.65pa. LC 68-37453. SBN 684-13058-0.

Intended for suburbanites, this is an introduction to ecology, with information on ponds, vegetation, animals, underground water, utilities, landscaping, pollution and many other aspects of near city living. Not recreation but an interesting book.

272. Watts, May. **Desert Tree Finder.** Berkeley, CA, Nature Study Guild, n.d. $0.75pa.

Covers the deserts of Arizona, New Mexico, and California. Not seen.

OUTDOOR RECREATION

273. Watts, May. **Flower Finder: A Key to Spring Wild Flowers and Flower Families East of the Rockies and North of the Smokies, Exclusive of Trees and Shrubs.** Berkeley, CA, Nature Study Guild, 1955. 62p. illus. index. $0.75pa.

   Illustrated with drawings. Easy to use and pocket-size.

274. Watts, May. **Master Tree Finder: A Manual for the Identification of Trees by Their Leaves.** Berkeley, CA, Nature Study Guild, 1963. 61p. illus. index. $0.75pa.

   The area covered includes the United States and Canada east of the Rocky Mountains. Illustrated with numerous drawings. Pocket-size.

275. Watts, May. **Tree Finder: A Pocket Manual for Identification of Trees by Their Leaves.** Berkeley, CA, Nature Study Guild, 1963. 39p. illus. index. $0.25pa.

   This little manual covers the East and Midwest of the United States and is a good guide to the evergreen and deciduous species.

276. Watts, May, and Tom Watts. **Winter Tree Finder: A Manual for Identifying Deciduous Trees in Winter.** Berkeley, CA, Nature Study Guild, 1970. 61p. illus. index. $0.75pa. ISBN 0-912550-03-1.

   Covers trees of the United States and Canada east of the Rocky Mountains.

277. Watts, Tom. **Pacific Coast Tree Finder: A Pocket Manual for Identifying Pacific Coast Trees.** Berkeley, CA, Nature Study Guild, 1973. 61p. illus. index. $0.75pa.

   Includes the western half of Oregon, Washington, and British Columbia, most of California (exclusive of the southeastern deserts), and the extreme west of Nevada.

278. Watts, Tom. **Rocky Mountain Tree Finder: A Pocket Manual for Identifying Rocky Mountain Trees.** Berkeley, CA, Nature Study Guild, 1972. 61p. illus. index. $0.75pa. ISBN 0-912550-05-8.

   Covers the area from British Columbia and Alberta south to the Mexican border, including the Black Hills and the Great Plains west from western Nebraska and South Dakota.

279. Zim, Herbert S., and Ira N. Gabrielson. **Birds: A Guide to the Most Familiar American Birds.** New York, Golden Press, 1956. 160p. illus.(col.). index. (A Golden Nature Guide). $1.50pa. LC 61-8323.

This is a good introduction to bird life and classification, with its distribution maps and illustrations by James G. Irving. There are lists of scientific names and of museums and zoos. Not as complete as Robbins' *Birds of North America*, but a youngster would love it.

280. Zim, Herbert S., and Hurst H. Shoemaker. **Fishes: A Guide to Fresh- and Salt-Water Species.** New York, Golden Press, 1955. 160p. illus.(col.). index. (A Golden Nature Guide). $1.50pa. LC 61-8322.

This handy guide will identify most of the watery things you are likely to catch. The drawings are by James G. Irving. There are lists of books and of scientific names.

281. Zim, Herbert S., and Alexander C. Martin. **Flowers: A Guide to Familiar American Wildflowers.** New York, Golden Press, 1950. 157p. illus.(col.). index. (A Golden Nature Guide). $1.50pa. LC 61-8319.

This book, arranged by the color of the flower, describes about 200 different species. The illustrations are by Rudolf Freund.

282. Zim, Herbert S., and Clarence Cottam. **Insects: A Guide to Familiar American Species.** New York, Golden Press, 1961. 160p. illus.(col.). index. (A Golden Nature Guide). $1.50pa. LC 61-8325.

This book, with its key to basic groups, is a good one for budding bug finders. Distribution maps, a list of scientific names, and a short reading list are included. The illustrations are by James G. Irving.

283. Zim, Herbert S., and Donald F. Hoffmeister. **Mammals: A Guide to Familiar American Species.** New York, Golden Press, 1955. 160p. illus.(col.). index. (A Golden Nature Guide). $1.50pa. LC 61-8320.

With illustrations by James G. Irving, this book has general information on mammals, distribution maps, a list of scientific names, and a list of zoos and museums. The pictures will enable us to identify all those critters that run around the campgrounds and all those bigger ones, too.

284. Zim, Herbert S., and Hobart M. Smith. **Reptiles and Amphibians: A Guide to Familiar American Species.** New York, Golden Press, 1956. 160p. illus.(col.). index. (A Golden Nature Guide). $1.50pa. LC 61-8324.

This guide contains general information about those slithery creatures we find in the woods and elsewhere. Distribution maps and illustrations by James G. Irving make for easy recognition.

OUTDOOR RECREATION

285. Zim, Herbert S. **Seashores: A Guide to Animals and Plants along the Beaches.** New York, Golden Press, 1955. 160p. illus.(col.). index. (A Golden Nature Guide). $1.50pa. LC 61-8318.

The illustrations by Dorothea and Sy Barlowe will enable anyone to identify the many plants and animals he finds on the beach. There are lists of scientific names and of further readings.

286. Zim, Herbert S., and Alexander C. Martin. **Trees: A Guide to Familiar American Trees.** New York, Golden Press, 1952. 160p. illus.(col.). index. (A Golden Nature Guide). $1.50pa. LC 61-8317.

Covering some 143 species, this book, illustrated by Dorothea and Sy Marlowe, will suffice for the most common trees. There are lists of parks, museums, botanical gardens, and scientific names. Obviously not as complete as Brockman's *Trees of North America*.

287. Zinn, Donald J. **The Beach Strollers Handbook from Maine to Cape Hatteras.** Chester, CT, Pequot Press, 1975. 128p. illus. $3.50pa. LC 75-1921. ISBN 0-87106-055-8.

For the benefit of Eastern-shore beachcombers, a retired university zoologist has compiled a good deal of interesting information about sponges, jellyfish, lobsters, sand-dollars, oysters, squids, quahogs, and other delicacies (and not-so-delicacies!) that might wind up in the pot or otherwise be sought out. There are a couple of photos and several drawings in this highly recommended guide.

IDENTIFYING ROCKS AND MINERALS; TREASURE HUNTING

288. Adams, George F., and Jerome Wyckoff. **Landforms.** New York, Golden Press, 1971. 160p. illus.(part col.). (A Golden Science Guide). $1.50pa. LC 77-141074.

This is a very general introduction to landforms and their origins. There is a section on "basic concepts and terms" plus photographs and drawings, the latter by Enid Kotschnig. A very good book.

289. Albano, Charles M. **Beachcombing for Treasure.** Tacoma, WA, ERCO, 1973. c.56p. illus. $1.95pa.

This little book contains hints on how and where to look for coins, floats, rings, relics, and whatever else turns up on beaches. There are directions for making a treasure scoop. Several photographs are included.

IDENTIFYING AND COLLECTING

290. Albano, Charles M. **Hidden Riches (Searching Old Abandoned and Deserted Houses for Treasures and Antiques).** Tacoma, WA, ERCO, 1972. 62p. illus. $1.95pa.

Suggestions on where to look and how to do it, with examples of the kind of luck some people have had. Illustrated with photographs.

291. Arem, Joel. **Rocks and Minerals.** New York, Bantam, 1973. 159p. illus.(col.). index. (Knowledge Through Color Series). $1.95pa. LC 72-90792.

This introduction to the study of rocks and minerals discusses basic chemistry and crystallography, the classification of minerals, gems, and rock types. Many photographs and drawings are included. Not for identifying unknown specimens.

292. Carlisle, Norman, and David Michelsohn. **The Complete Guide to Treasure Hunting.** Chicago, Regnery, 1973. 280p. illus. index. $8.95. LC 73-6452.

A general introduction to treasure hunting, this contains hints on where to look for clues, how to use metal detectors, underwater work, gem and mineral finds, lost mines, and gold panning. There are tales of treasure lost and found, information on pertinent laws, and lists of historical societies, government offices, museums, and books and journals. Illustrated with photographs.

293. Carson, H. Glenn. **Coinshooting: How and Where to Do It.** Rev. ed. Boulder, CO, Carson, 1973. 64p. illus. $2.50pa.

Hunting for coins and other small objects with a metal detector is a fascinating hobby. The title tells all and gives lists of dealers, newsletters, and books.

294. Carson, H. Glenn. **THing, a Modern Search for Adventure.** Boulder, CO, Carson, 1973. 82p. illus. $3.50pa.

THing is short, of course, for Treasure Hunting, and this is a good introduction for novices. Carson covers everything from researching in the county courthouse to exploring outhouses and ghost towns.

295. Casanova, Richard. **An Illustrated Guide to Fossil Collecting.** Rev. ed. Healdsburg, CA, Naturegraph, 1970. 128p. illus. index. $2.95pa. ISBN 0-911010-78-5.

This is a description of how fossils are formed, an introduction to the geologic time scale and to the classification of the animal and plant kingdoms. There are general rules on where and how to collect fossils but no really good directions to collecting localities.

296. Cox, Jack R. **A Gem Cutter's Handbook: Cabochon Cutting.** Mentone, CA, Gembooks, 1970. 64p. illus. $2.00pa. SBN 910652-12-0.

Listed as being a good instruction book for the collector who is lucky.

297. Cox, Jack R. **A Gem Cutter's Handbook: Specialized Gem Cutting.** Mentone, CA, Gembooks, 1970. 64p. illus. $2.00pa. SBN 910652-13-9.

What to do after you get home with the big find.

298. Dwyer, John N. **Summer Gold: A Camper's Guide to Amateur Metal Prospecting.** St. Cloud, MN, North Star, 1971. 72p. illus. $1.95pa. LC 70-163364. ISBN 0-87839-006-5.

This pleasant little book gives a short history of gold mining in the United States, a very generalized idea of where to look for it, a brief but good introduction to the use of a gold pan and other tools, some hints on using a metal detector, staking a claim, where to buy equipment, and a list of books for further reading.

299. **Family Fun with Rocks: A Guide to the Wide World of Pleasure That Can Be Found with Some Rocks, a Few Simple Tools and Inexpensive Supplies.** Mentone, CA, Gembooks, 1972. 31p. illus. $1.00pa. SBN 910652-16-3.

Written by several folks who contribute to *Gems and Minerals Magazine*, this is intended as an interest arousing pamphlet. The projects, which can be done with a minimum of equipment, look very easy.

300. Fay, Gordon S. **The Rockhound's Manual.** New York, Harper & Row, 1972. 290p. illus.(part col.). index. $7.95. LC 77-157080. ISBN 0-06-011218-2.

This excellent guide to rockhounding has hints on equipment, sources of information, where to look (with lists of counties by state), how to find and identify rocks and minerals, and how to display them. Better for how-to-do-it than for where to find minerals.

301. Faulk, Terry R. **Simple Methods of Mining Gold.** Palmer Lake, CO, Filter, 1969. 35p. illus. $1.00pa. ISBN 0-910584-08-7.

This is a nice little introduction to locating and mining placer gold. Faulk covers panning in streams, using a sluice box and rocker, filing a claim, and getting gold concentrated with mercury and retorting. Illustrated with old woodcuts.

IDENTIFYING AND COLLECTING

302. Gladson, Deek. **Sudden Wealth: An Introduction to Successful Treasure Hunting.** Rev. ed. Dallas, TX, Ram, 1974. 105p. illus. $4.00pa. LC 64-8542.

This introduction to treasure finding has suggestions on where to look and how to go about it, including the use of metal detectors. Lots of stories of successful hunters.

303. Henrichsen, Harold, and Winifred Henrichsen. **Rocks and What to Do with Them.** Rev. ed. Tacoma, WA, ERCO, 1972. 64p. illus.(col.). $2.50pa.

This contains a number of photos of gemstones with suggestions about tumbling and mounting them.

304. Lagal, Roy. **Detector How to Test Field Guide.** Dallas, TX, Ram, 1973. 60p. illus. $3.00pa. LC 73-87118.

For the detector owner who wishes to know an instrument completely and check its accuracy and reliability. All kinds of detectors (BFO, TR, etc.) are covered and a series of tests is outlined. Illustrated with drawings. Highly recommended for all detector users.

305. Lagal, Roy. **Detector How to Use Field Guide.** Dallas, TX, Ram, 1973. 49p. illus. $3.00pa. LC 73-87119.

This companion volume to the volume on testing gives complete instruction on how to use the several kinds of metal detectors while searching mine dumps, under water, ghost towns, for coins, etc. Illustrated with drawings. Highly recommended.

306. MacFall, Russell P., and Jay C. Wollin. **Fossils for Amateurs: A Handbook for Collectors.** New York, Van Nostrand, 1972. 341p. illus. bibliog. index. $10.95. LC 74-149259.

This is a well-illustrated guide to how invertebrate fossils are formed, collected, named, and displayed. There are many hints on where to look for fossils and how to dig them out. State maps and regulations are included. Highly recommended for all serious fossil hunters.

307. McGowen, Al. **The Extraction of Free Gold.** Boulder, CO, Carson, 1973. 61p. illus.(part col.). $3.50pa.

Concerned with mining from placer deposits, this is a bit more than outdoor recreation but I've included it for the serious convert.

308. Marquiss, Ken. **The Gold Hex.** Boulder, CO, Carson, 1972. 146p. illus. $4.00pa.

OUTDOOR RECREATION

This is a story about a lifetime of hunting for lost gold mines. I've included it for the benefit of those who'd like to try the activity and would appreciate knowing how someone else did it. Illustrated with photos and drawings. Very interesting little book.

309. Oles, Floyd, and Helga Oles. **Eastern Gem Trails**. Mentone, CA, Gembooks, 1967. $2.00pa. ISBN 0-910652-03-1.

Not seen. It is undoubtedly as good as the other titles published by Mentone.

310. Pearl, Richard M. **Handbook for Prospectors**. 5th ed. New York, McGraw-Hill, 1973. 472p. illus. index. glossary. $14.50. LC 72-11749. ISBN 0-07-049025-2.

This is a revision of a classic work, *Handbook for Prospectors and Operators of Small Mines*, by Max von Bernewitz. The contents include prospecting principles, staking a claim, equipment, procedures, safety, elementary geology, and mineralogy (with descriptions of minerals, opening a mine, and processing minerals). Illustrated with photos and drawings, this is highly recommended for all serious prospectors.

311. Pearl, Richard M. **How to Know the Minerals and Rocks**. New York, New American Library, 1955. 192p. illus.(part col.). index. $1.25pa.

General information on identifying rocks and minerals with some basic geology and explanations of the physical and other properties of minerals used for identification,

312. Penfield, Thomas. **Dig Here!** Rev. ed. San Antonio, TX, Naylor, 1966. 240p. illus. index. $4.95. LC 66-24362.

This consists of tales about lost mines in Arizona, New Mexico, Texas, Nevada, and California. Approximate locations are given, supposed values are listed, and a long bibliography will lead the interested treasure hunter to many other sources.

313. Powell, Guy E. **Latest Aztec Discoveries: Origin and Untold Riches**. Rev. ed. San Antonio, TX, Naylor, 1970. 79p. illus. bibliog. $4.95. LC 66-23253.

This is a resume of evidence that the Aztecs originally lived in East Texas, near Trinity. An intriguing book. Listed as an example of the many books on treasure history that the outdoor recreationist may be led to.

314. **Prospecting Hints, Vol. 1**. San Jose, CA, United Prospectors, 1971. 102p. illus. $2.50pa.

Compiled from 24 years of articles in *Panning Gold* and *Locating Gold*, two magazines published by the United Prospectors. There is much good information on locating a claim, using equipment of various kinds, panning gold, building gold catchers for streams, and so on. There's even a recipe for sourdough bread and pancakes. We presume that there will be a Volume 2, some day.

315. Rhodes, Frank H. T. **Geology.** New York, Golden Press, 1972. 160p. illus.(col.). index. (A Golden Science Guide). $1.95pa. LC 72-150741.

This is a very nice introduction to general geology, with photographs and drawings. There is basic information on erosion and deposition, crustal movements and other topics that should interest the traveller as he observes the hills and valleys around him. The drawings are by Raymond Perlman.

316. Rhodes, Frank H. T., Herbert S. Zim, and Paul R. Shaffer. **Fossils: A Guide to Prehistoric Life.** New York, Golden Press, 1962. 160p. illus.(col.). index. (A Golden Nature Guide). $1.50pa. LC 62-21640.

This is a handy little introduction to paleontology and how to collect fossils. A review of the commonly found fossil groups and genera is illustrated by Raymond Pearlman.

317. Robbins, Maurice, with Mary B. Irving. **The Amateur Archaeologist's Handbook.** 2nd ed. New York, Crowell, 1973. 288p. illus. index. glossary. bibliog. $7.95. LC 73-245. ISBN 0-690-05569-2.

This is a brief resume of North American archeology by the Massachusetts State Archaeologist. He discusses the lives of prehistoric peoples with hints on where to dig, planning an excavation, recording the data, preserving and restoring artifacts, etc. There are suggestions on how to write site reports and an introduction to historical archeology. Appendices list sites open to the public, societies and museums, colleges with archeology courses, and antiquities laws. An excellent book for the serious amateur.

318. Rynerson, Fred. **Exploring and Mining for Gems and Gold in the West: 54 Years of Prospecting, Digging and Gem-Cutting.** Healdsburg, CA, Naturegraph, 1967. 204p. illus. $3.95pa. ISBN 0-911010-60-2.

This biography of an old-time gem and gold hunter who died in 1960 contains many hints on gem finding. Recommended for newcomers.

319. Ryerson, Kathleen H. **Rock Hound's Guide to Connecticut.** Rev. ed. Chester, CT, Pequot, 1972. 60p. maps. $2.50pa. LC 68-24037.

I've listed this title as being a good example of the type of book a gem hunter needs. This one has hints on collecting, needed equipment, a list of

OUTDOOR RECREATION

books, and directions to collecting locales. I used to have lots of fun looking for garnets near Roxbury, Connecticut, but I didn't have this book to guide me.

320. Santschi, Roy J. **Doodlebug Edition of Treasure Trails with Extracts from Mysteries of Treasure Hunting.** Segundo, CO, Exanimo, 1973. 117p. illus. $6.00; $4.00pa.

321. Santschi, Roy J. **Doodlebugs and Mysteries of Treasure Hunting Illustrated.** Segundo, CO, Exanimo, 1974. 160p. illus. $7.00; $5.00pa.

These books are reprints of editions of 1938 and 1941. Doodlebugs are divining rods, and the books tell how to use these rods and pendula to find treasure and other objects. Lots of folks are interested in trying their hand at using divining rods so this book is listed for their benefit. There are also hints on the occult, conjuring the dead, and using talismans! One never knows what one will encounter in the great outdoors—it pays to be prepared for everything.

322. Smith, Alan. **Introduction to Treasure Hunting.** Harrisburg, PA, Stackpole, 1971. 192p. illus. index. bibliog. $5.95. LC 78-140743. ISBN 0-8117-0924-8.

This book contains many stories about hidden or lost treasures and artifacts with hints on looking for treasure on beaches, in lakes, and in the sea. Smith also covers the use of metal detectors, describes how to make one, and includes suggestions on finding coins, prospecting for gold and gems, obtaining permission, and keeping legal. There is a list of equipment suppliers and of books.

323. Strong, Mary Frances. **Desert Gem Trails: A Field Guide to the Gem and Mineral Localities of the Mojave and Colorado Deserts in California and Adjacent Areas of Nevada.** 2nd ed. Mentone, CA, Gembooks, 1971. 80p. maps. $2.00pa. SBN 910652-15-5.

This book gives locations and descriptions of hundreds of localities with notes on road conditions, camping facilities, sources of supplies, points of interest, what to collect, and whether or not an area is open.

324. Tanner, Hans, ed. **The Complete Guide to Rocks, Gems & Minerals.** Los Angeles, Petersen, 1970. 97p. illus.(part col.). $2.00pa. LC 74-118980.

This magazine-format publication has articles on many topics of interest to rockhounds, including moon rocks. The section on identification is good and includes methods that use physical properties, some chemical tests, and the use of goniometers. Don MacLachlan has a section called "Mineral

IDENTIFYING AND COLLECTING

Recognition by the Five-Digit System," which uses five mineral characteristics to construct an index for identification. It works for me. Many color photographs and interesting articles. A good book.

325. Von Mueller, Karl. **Gold Dredger's Handbook.** Segundo, CO, Exanimo, 1972. 84p. illus. $4.00pa. LC 73-80391.

This is a good introduction to mining gold from placers with dredges and sluiceboxes.

326. Von Mueller, Karl. **The Master Hunter Manual.** 1st revision. Dallas, TX, Ram, 1973. 88p. illus. $4.00pa. LC 72-166399.

This is a good introduction to the use of metal detectors. "Master Hunter" is a trade name, but the information is useful generally.

327. Von Mueller, Karl. **Treasure Hunter's Manual #6.** 3rd rev. ed. Dallas, TX, Ram, 1973. 369p. illus. $6.50pa. LC 73-88545.

This contains lots of information on hunting buried treasure and minerals. It covers the use of instruments and tools, maps and photos, laws and regulations, taxes, how to research possible locations, and disposing of finds. There are suggestions about clothing, food, money needs, first aid and safety, organizations and historical societies, something about the many myths and legends of lost treasure, etc. An excellent and fascinating book.

328. Von Mueller, Karl. **Treasure Hunter's Manual #7.** Dallas, TX, Ram, 1972. 293p. illus. $6.50pa. LC 70-166133.

Another good manual for treasure hunters with hints on where to look and how to do it. Although many of the topics included are similar to those in No. 6, the content of each is essentially different. Both volumes are highly recommended to all potential seekers of the grail.

329. Wertz, Ed, and Leola Wertz. **Handbook of Gemstone Carving: A Complete Guide to the Materials, Equipment and Techniques for Carving Gemstones.** Mentone, CA, Gembooks, 1968. 48p. illus. $2.00pa.

Listed for those who have found pretty minerals and wish to carve them.

330. Wilson, James. **Apache Jim: Stories from His Private Files on Unfound Treasures.** Boulder, CO, Carson, 1973. 107p. illus. c.$3.50pa.

Some of these tales are pretty wild and fascinating, so I've included this book for its interest-arousing value. Should get almost any treasure hunter into the outdoors.

331. Zeitner, June Culp. **Midwest Gem Trails: A Field Guide for the Gem Hunter, the Mineral Collector and the Tourist; Includes South Dakota, Michigan, Illinois, Iowa, Wisconsin, Ohio, Kansas, North Dakota, Nebraska, Indiana, Missouri, Minnesota.** 3rd ed. Mentone, CA, Gembooks, 1964. 80p. illus. $2.00pa.

Contains narrative descriptions of localities, not all with maps. Much good information for the collector.

332. Zim, Herbert S., and Paul R. Shaffer. **Rocks and Minerals: A Guide to Familiar Minerals, Gems, Ores and Rocks.** New York, Golden Press, 1957. 160p. illus.(col.). index. (A Golden Nature Guide). $1.50pa. LC 61-8326.

Contains several tests to identify samples. The illustrations are by Raymond Perlman and there is a list of readings and of museums. A good one for youngsters to start with.

VEHICLE ACTIVITIES

. . . big wheels move by faith

There are several popular vehicular sports and I have no hesitation grouping them together here. I realize that bicyclists often hate not only motorcycles but just about every wheel-type vehicle that isn't a bicycle, but the wheel was not invented for the benefit of only one variety of the species. For those who may disagree with my remark about bicyclists' hates, I offer this sentence, found in a pamphlet on bicycling: "No good environmentalist should be caught dead in a car." This is nothing short of blatant stupidity but it is, unfortunately, the sort of stupidity I find in numerous letters to editors.

I find it extraordinarily odd that "environmentalists" are quick to tell us how the automobile pollutes our air but they *never* tell us how much pollution is required to produce a bicycle: how much steel and aluminum is dug from open pits, how much power, often from coal or oil, is needed to generate the electricity needed in steel and, especially, aluminum plants, how many trees are cut down to give us the crates in which bikes are shipped. Yes, there is a great deal of pollution in the world and we're all responsible. And, yes, I like to ride my ancient single-speed, balloon-tired bicycle. But I'm not a bigot.

Bicycling is an excellent sport and it is very good exercise. The variety of bikes on our streets and roads is rather amazing and their cost is staggering. A bicycle will cost somewhere between $50.00 and $500.00 or more. Most of the ten-speeds we see so frequently these days will be priced at $90.00 to $150.00, which ain't hay; but it is not too great a price to pay for a means of keeping fit and of keeping up with the Joneses. Bicycle lanes are being established in many cities in response to political pressure.

Motorcycling is also a great sport, even though the bicyclists claim otherwise. A local professor writes many letters to the newspaper decrying the motorcyclist who rides about the countryside. He calls motorcyclists weak and unfit, among other things. I'm sure that his mind is closed tightly enough that no one could convince him that riding a motorcycle through one of the motocross or enduro runs, for example, is a great deal more demanding, physically

OUTDOOR RECREATION

and mentally, than riding a bicycle down the highway. Motorcycles are also very cheap transportation when one must go farther than a bicycle can reasonably carry him. After all, if you have ten minutes to get to work and you are two miles from work, the bicycle is a total failure. I know all about it.

The use of four-wheel-drive vehicles is quite necessary in some places and I often wish I had such a machine, especially when I'm up to the bumpers in snow and twenty miles off the blacktop. I was once shown a house that had a driveway so steep that the realtor had to use a Jeep to get to it. In the summer! Public lands are sometimes closed to recreational activities on the excuse that four-wheel-drive vehicles have destroyed the environment, etc. Most of these accusations are pure rot, but the ignorant applaud and leave the land to some rich rancher who merely wants to have Forest Service land all to himself and his cows. It happens.

Off-road racing, whether in autos or trucks or on motorcycles, is a fascinating pastime. I'd like to have the time and loot to run the Baja 500, at least. The little Japanese pickup trucks are very commonly used in this sort of race and they really do get one out into the great outdoors. And you get to *stay* in the great outdoors when you break your axle! So far as I'm concerned, there is room for all sorts of outdoor recreational activity. We should not tolerate appeals for the prohibition of one or another of them.

Rallying and other forms of automobile competition are not so common as motorcycle races or bicycle tours, but there is enough interest to sustain a national organization and at least one magazine. I have seen a number of sports car fans assembling for a day at the races but have never had the chance to join them. Sometimes these folks merely have skill competitions around obstacles in a large parking lot. At other times, and more commonly, they have road races. As the sport gains a following, more books and journals will emerge.

I managed to find a couple of publications about landsailing. Most everyone has seen a picture of an ice-boat. Well, landsailors use a similar craft but it is, of course, on wheels rather than skids. I'm told that this form of zipping across the flats is quite popular in Europe, especially in Holland. I suppose that if there is sufficient wind for windmills there is enough for a landsailing boat. In the United States, the sport is mostly a Southern California thing, since large expanses of fairly level land are needed. The sport is touted as a very safe, family sport.

No matter what you like to do with a vehicle in the outdoors, there is ample chance to do it so far. I like to bicycle and motorcycle and see no reason for one trying to prohibit the other. I also like to drive about the country just to see new places. I'm a dirt road type and a shunpiker who is happier doing 40mph on a backroad than 70mph on a freeway (or even 55mph!). Getting out in the open is the excuse for all these activities, and that's good.

There seems to be a good deal of anti-RecVee propaganda going through the media. I've seen articles in bicycling and hiking journals, for example, which are obviously intended to drum up a "ban the motor vehicle" sentiment among readers. The government, too, has entered the fray. As an example, I'll mention a study of recreational vehicle safety that was done by the National Transportation Safety Board. Among other things, this report states that accident risk increases with driver unfamiliarity. This is obviously true with any vehicle or other device, whether it is a hammer or a bicycle. The blast, intentional or otherwise, tends to show the uninformed that RecVees are unsafe even though the cause is not within the vehicle itself. Absurdity is not foreign to this tax-supported study—parked recreational vehicles are dangerous because, when they are parked somewhere, they are exposed to forest fires and floods! I wonder at the sanity or the honesty of the civil servant who writes that sort of rot. The same could be said of log cabins, picnic benches, and sleeping tourists, but the blast is at the vehicle and the sole intent of the remark is to "prove" that recreational vehicles are unsafe and must, therefore, be the object of massive governmental supervision. One of my neighbors has a small house trailer which he keeps on a piece of land out in the country. Sometime during the several months when the trailer was unoccupied, a bear broke into it, tearing off curtains, windows, and doors. The government bureaucrats would immediately blame the trailer and urge intensive federal supervision of recreational vehicles. If any reader thinks that I'm exaggerating, I will only urge him to read what is coming from the federal and state agencies. It is rather frightening.

This is as good a time as any to say a few words about repair manuals. I've stated elsewhere that repair manuals (I was writing of automotive manuals at the time) are generally good and quite authoritative, since they are based on factory repair manuals. This is probably not so true with bicycle repair manuals, but there cannot be much difference among even these, since the basis (the bicycle) is pretty well standardized. When my vice-president in charge of fixing things acquired his first ten-speed (he was ten years old at the time), he decided that the best thing to do was to tear it down and really learn how it works. He learned well, on his own, and periodically reduces the bike to its essentials, cleans everything up, and puts it back together again, it being easier to do this with bicycles than with large eggs. He has seen many repair manuals since that time but he remains unimpressed by them. He apparently can understand the mechanism and see how it works without being told.

During the three weeks before this paragraph was written, my motorcycle was giving us fits. My vice president did flips over it for reasons such as this: several troubleshooting guides tell us that Symptom A is caused by too lean a mixture; Symtom B is caused by too rich a mixture. Because the motorcycle exhibits both Symptoms A and B, something is radically wrong. Obviously, the carburetor cannot be giving too lean *and* too rich a mixture at the same time. The solution seems to be clear now—the valves were out of adjustment. Now, this doesn't negate the value of repair manuals, but it points out that a bit of knowledge, a bit of luck, and a good deal of work may be the only answer. I'll list a couple of repair manuals as a service, but with the suggestion that you refer to something like *Automotive Repair and Maintenance* (No. 1 in the Spare Time Guides series) for further edification.

BICYCLES

333. Aigner, Hal, and others. **The Clear Creek Bike Book**. New York, New American Library, 1972. 184p. illus. (A Plume Book). $2.95pa.

Based on several articles that originally appeared in *Clear Creek* magazine (now defunct), this compilation of articles contains a bit of biking philosophy, the history and lore of cycling, hints on buying and riding, and information on health and safety (avoiding cars and heart attacks, for example), legislation about bike ways, racing and touring, dealing with politicians, and touring in Great Britain. The section on repairing and maintaining a bicycle is quite good. Any cyclist, especially the newcomer to the sport, will enjoy this book and it will get him through almost any bicycling problem. Highly recommended.

334. Ald, Roy. **Cycling**. New York, Grosset & Dunlap, 1968. 96p. illus. $1.25pa. LC 68-21294. ISBN 0-448-00824-6.

This is a very general introduction to cycling with advice on choosing a bicycle, learning to ride it, taking day trips and longer ones, racing, and keeping fit with exercises. There is also something about why one should use a bicycle and how to go about it.

335. **All About Bicycling**. Chicago, Rand McNally, 1974. 194p. illus. $3.95pa.

A large, well-illustrated introduction to bicycling, this book contains a history of cycling, hints on getting the proper size bike and appropriate accessories, reasons for cycling (health, fun, ecology, cheap transportation, etc.), safety, camping and touring, racing, bicycle polo, and repair and maintenance. This latter section has instruction on checking alignment, steering, chains, gears, and other components. There are lists of bicycle clubs, manufacturers, and a glossary of terms. On the whole, a very good and readable guide.

336. Alth, Max. **All About Bikes and Bicycling: Care, Repair, and Safety**. New York, Hawthorn, 1972. 198p. illus. index. $5.95. LC 75-39250.

VEHICLE ACTIVITIES

Illustrated with drawings by Ed Epstein, this is a good manual for beginners. There are chapters on selecting a bicycle, learning to ride, development of safe riding habits, and bicycle camping and touring, together with lists of cycle dealers and organizations, periodicals, camping supply dealers, and American Youth Hostel offices. Most of the book is devoted to the care and repair of the bike, with information on frame sizes, gear ratios, tools, tire care and repair, etc.

337. Asa, Warren. **American Youth Hostels' North American Bicycle Atlas.** 3rd ed. Delaplane, VA, AYH (distr.: Crown), 1973. 192p. illus. $5.95.

This atlas's basic information about bicycle touring is supplemented with suggestions on equipment, food, cooking, and safety. The tour section lists "88 Bicycle Trips Arranged Geographically from WEST to EAST," including Canada, Mexico and Hawaii. Additional sections have information on biking in Europe, Asia, Africa, South America, and Australia and New Zealand. Illustrated with photographs and maps plus incidental information on AYH.

338. Ballantine, Richard. **Richard's Bicycle Book.** New York, Ballantine, 1972. 249p. illus. index. $1.95pa. SBN 345-22813-8-195.

Richard offers information on why one should ride a bicycle, how to choose a good one (construction features, proper size, seat and handlebar fitting, etc.), gear tables, proper riding habits, touring, and burglar-proofing a bike. About two-thirds of the book is about repair and maintenance work, with clear drawings and excellent instruction. The fine drawings are by John Batchelor. Excellent for beginners and oldtimers, too. All a cyclist will ever need. Highly recommended.

339. **Bicentennial Bike Tours: Recycle the Past with 200 Historical Rides and 100 Maps Prompted by the 200th Birthday Celebration of the United States.** San Jose, CA, Gousha (distr.: Crown), 1973. 223p. illus. index. maps. $3.95pa. LC 72-97827. ISBN 0-913040-20-7.

This guide for bicyclists divides the nation into several regions: New England, New York-Pennsylvania, Mid-Atlantic, Southeast, Midwest, Plains-Rockies, Southwest, and Far West. For each region, a series of tours is outlined with maps and information about mileage, terrain, traffic conditions, historical sites, and best time to make the trip. Nothing about camping techniques or about cycling. The guide could, of course, be used by any traveller.

340. Blish, Jeffrey. **The Pedaler's Handbook: A Guide for Bicyclists.** Los Angeles, Nash, 1972. 206p. illus. index. $2.95pa. LC 70-186917. SBN 8402-8033-5.

OUTDOOR RECREATION

Emphasizing the health and easy sightseeing aspects of bicycling, Blish offers tips on selecting a bike (proper frame size, quality, lights, etc.), getting in shape, learning to ride, safety, rules of the road, checking used bikes, making repairs, and doing general maintenance work. There are sections on first aid, racing, handling dogs, avoiding theft, transporting the bike on cars, trains, etc. Short checklists cover bike features to look for while shopping, what to take on a trip, and what to check before making a trip. Appendixes list AYH offices and cycling organizations.

341. Carrell, Al. **The Super Handyman's Big Bike Book.** Englewood Cliffs, NJ, Prentice-Hall, 1974. $5.95.

Not seen. I imagine it is much like Carrell's similarly titled book on household hints, which is an alphabetically arranged selection of hints sent in to a newspaper column.

342. **Coaster & 3-Speed Bicycle Repair.** Canoga Park, XYZYX Information, 1974. illus. $4.95pa.

Not seen. It must be quite like their *Derailleur . . . Repair* book (entry 346).

343. Coles, Clarence W., and Harold T. Glenn. **Glenn's Complete Bicycle Manual: Selection, Maintenance, Repair.** New York, Crown, 1973. 339p. illus. $7.95; $5.95pa. LC 70-185100. ISBN 0-517-50092-2; -50093-0pa.

This is a large-format book with remarks about selecting a bicycle for particular needs, the history of bicycles, and other general topics. Most of the book is about maintenance and repair, beginning with taking the bike out of the crate. The several chapters are concerned with troubleshooting, working on the front-wheel hubs, rear-wheel hubs, free-wheel body and sprocket clusters, derailleurs (front and rear), hangar sets and pedals, brakes and headsets. American, Japanese, and European cycles are covered. The drawings and photographs are clear and complete. An excellent manual.

344. Cuthbertson, Tom. **Anybody's Bike Book: An Original Manual of Bicycle Repairs.** Berkeley, CA, Ten Speed, 1971. 177p. illus. index. $6.95; $3.00pa. LC 76-29188.

Illustrated with drawings by Rick Morrall, this handy guide has suggestions on tools, repairing brakes, handlebars and stems, headsets, forks, wheels and tires, frames and seats, cranks, sprockets, and gears. There is a list of parts suppliers, too. An interesting and practical manual. Highly recommended.

345. Cuthbertson, Tom. **Bike Tripping.** Berkeley, CA, Ten Speed (distr.: Random House), 1972. 177p. illus. index. $6.95; $3.00pa. LC 72-475. SBN 394-48150-X; -70775-3pa.

All about bicycle riding. Contains hints on selecting the right bike, learning to ride it safely, taking short and long trips, carrying a bike on planes, trains, etc., traffic problems, dog problems, rain and wind as adversaries. The drawings are by Rick Morrall and there is a chapter on bike frames by Albert Eisentraut. This is a companion volume to *Anybody's Bike Book* (previous entry). Highly recommended.

346. **Derailleur 5, 10 & 15-Speed Bicycle Repair.** 2nd ed. Canoga Park, CA, XYZYX Information (distr.: Crown), 1972. 132p. illus. $3.95pa. ISBN 0-914514-01-6.

Labelled "Another Xyzyx Consumer Aid," this manual covers maintenance, cleaning, lubrication, adjustment of frames, brakes, wheels, tires, etc. Illustrated with photographs and drawings. A very good handbook.

347. Draughton, Guy. **Complete Bicycle Book.** Los Angeles, Petersen, 1972. 240p. illus. $3.95pa. LC 76-185813.

This is a copiously illustrated, magazine-format guide to all aspects of bicycling: history, the manufacture and assembly of bicycles, safety and riding techniques, touring and camping (with lists of hostels and groups and suggestions about specific tours in various parts of the United States), fitting, adjusting, and maintaining the bike. There is a buying guide to the commonly available 1972 models. An excellent resume for all bicyclists.

348. Ewers, William. **Sincere's Bicycle Service Book.** Phoenix, AZ, Sincere, 1970. 88p. illus. $6.95. LC 72-20654. ISBN 0-912534-02-8.

Illustrated mostly with drawings, this is a good guide to maintaining bicycles: assembly, wheels and related components, frames, forks, handlebars, chains, brakes, axles, and gears. There are troubleshooting and safety hints.

349. Fichter, George S., and Keith Kingbay. **Bicycling.** New York, Golden Press, 1972. 120p. illus.(part col.). index. bibliog. (A Golden Guide). $1.50pa. LC 77-184015.

This is a shirt-pocket manual for beginning bicyclists. It has hints on types of bikes, selecting the proper size and type, accessories, elementary care, safe riding habits, suggestions for safety checks, touring, and racing. There are lists of organizations, suggestions for games and club work and a list of things to take on a camping trip. Very small, but it may be all the average rider needs.

350. Frankel, Lillian, and Godfrey Frankel. **The Bicycle Book (Bike-Ways).** New rev. ed. New York, Cornerstone (distr.: Simon & Schuster), 1972. 126p. illus. $1.50. LC 61-15857.

This is the paperback edition of *Bike-Ways* (see next entry).

OUTDOOR RECREATION

351. Frankel, Lillian, and Godfrey Frankel. **Bike-Ways (101 Things to Do with a Bike).** New rev. ed. New York, Sterling, 1972. 128p. illus. index. $3.50. LC 61-15857. ISBN 0-8069-4004-2.

Intended for youngsters and originally published in 1950, this is filled with suggestions about club activities, games (bicycle polo, etc.), taking trips, photography, camping, selecting a bike and learning how to ride it, safety, and elementary repair and maintenance. The text hasn't been changed since first published, apparently, as the authors recommend woolen or kapok sleeping bags!

352. Hawkins, Karen, and Gary Hawkins. **Bicycle Touring in Europe.** New York, Pantheon (distr.: Random House), 1973. 184p. illus. $8.95; $2.95pa. LC 72-12381. ISBN 0-394-48471-1; -70961-6pa.

Among the topics discussed here are: the economics of bike touring, choosing a proper bike, selecting clothing, packs and equipment, buying food and cooking it. The authors outline nine favorite tours and offer good, solid information on expenses, climate, money, European clothing sizes, and lists of organizations and supply sources. There are a few drawings. Lots of good reading with good hints.

353. Henkel, Stephen C. **Bikes: A How-to-Do-It Guide to Selection, Care, Repair, Maintenance, Decoration, Safety, and Fun on Your Bicycle.** New York, Bantam, 1972. 189p. illus. index. $1.25pa. LC 73-172354.

Also published in hardback by Chatham Press ($4.95), this book contains, in addition to what is listed in the title (!), some history of the bike, how bikes are built, nomenclature, and choosing the proper size. Completing the work are hints on adjusting, riding skills, and needed tools, and a good bibliography. The illustrations by Henkel include drawings of gear systems and of "exploded" bikes. There are charts of recommended tire pressures, frame sizes, average parts prices, and other handy information. A nice little book.

354. Humphrey, Clifford C. **Back to the Bike.** San Francisco, 101 Productions, 1972. 96p. illus. index. $2.95pa. LC 72-77563. ISBN 0-912238-22-4.

Printed, appropriately enough, on recycled paper, this book is illustrated with drawings by Keith Halonen and has many suggestions on selecting a bike and its accessories, maintaining both the bike and its rider (proper clothing, safety, good riding positions, etc.), and using the bike as an alternate to the auto. There are suggestions, too, on transporting a bike on trains and buses and getting action on such things as cycle paths. *Books in Print* lists a

VEHICLE ACTIVITIES

subtitle for this ("How to Buy, Maintain & Use the Bicycle As an Alternative Means of Transportation") that does not appear on the title page or cover. Highly recommended.

355. Jorgensen, Eric, and Joe G. Bergman. **Fix Your Bicycle: All Speeds—All Major Makes—Simplified—Step-by-Step.** Los Angeles, Clymer, 1972. 117p. illus. index. $3.95pa.

There are hints on selecting a bike, but most of the book is devoted to the repair and maintenance of all sorts of bicycles. Illustrated with many photos and drawings, there are chapters on the basic tools needed for repair work; maintenance and lubrication; repair of tires, tubes and wheels; working on brakes, gears, cranks, and chains; repairing the frame; and accessories. A table of gear ratios is included. This is a very clear and handy manual.

356. Luther, Kenneth E. **Bicycling for Fun and Good Health.** 1973 ed. North Hollywood, CA, Wilshire, 1973. 146p. illus. $2.00pa. LC 72-79304. ISBN 0-87980-214-6.

Illustrated with photographs and drawings, this introduction to bicycling tells you why to do it, which bike to choose, how to ride alone and with groups, how to prevent theft, and other such "what-to-do" things. Nothing about maintenance or repair.

357. Macfarlan, Allan A. **The Boy's Book of Biking.** Harrisburg, PA, Stackpole, 1968. 160p. illus. index. (World of Boyhood Library). $4.50. LC 68-29592.

Elementary information for bikers: why ride a cycle, how to select a bike, proper riding technique, games and bike events, club activities, camping and touring, care of a bike. Good reading for youngsters. Illustrated with drawings.

358. McFarlane, John W. **It's Easy to Fix Your Bike.** 3rd ed. Chicago, Follett, 1972. 128p. illus. $2.95pa. LC 73-185890. ISBN 0-695-80343-6.

This manual covers all sorts of "fixing," from adjusting the seat to overhauling a derailleur. The many photographs (and some drawings) are clear and the text is simple but comprehensive. There are suggestions about tools, adjustments, and further reading. Small, concise, and useful.

359. **Schwinn Bicycle Service Manual.** Chicago, Schwinn, 1972. 2v. 956p.(total). illus. index. $20.00 set.

These volumes, intended for the cycle shop owner and repairman, have complete information about Schwinn bicycles. Copiously illustrated with photographs and drawings, this guide is clearly written with hints on troubleshooting, tools, materials, and how to fix all components of the cycle. Very good.

360. Shaw, Reginald C. **Cycling.** 2nd ed. New York, Dover, 1971. 160p. illus. index. $2.50. ISBN 0-340-05559-6.

This is a volume in the Teach Yourself Books series, published originally in England. A good introduction to cycling from the British point of view, with suggestions on: good riding habits, rules of the road, gearing, types of bicycle, maintenance, touring and camping, club travel, racing, and other aspects of the game. A very good book with eight charming drawings by Frank Patterson.

361. Sloane, Eugene A. **The New Complete Book of Bicycling.** New York, Simon & Schuster, 1974. 531p. illus. index. bibliog. $12.50. LC 73-9362. SBN 671-27119-9.

Sloane, who writes a bicycle column in *Popular Mechanics* magazine, presents excellent information for beginning riders. There are hints on the health aspects of riding, safety and good riding habits, choosing and fitting a bike and its accessories, touring and camping, racing, and maintaining the machine. In addition to a short history of cycling and a glossary of terms, there are also lists of organizations, supply sources, books, and magazines. This is the "big book" on bicycling and it's the one to get if you've got the cash. Highly recommended.

362. Steward, Chuck. **Bicycling in Seattle.** Seattle, Recreation Consultants, 1971. 31p. maps. $1.50pa.

Listed as an example of the type of riding guide that a cyclist will find in his local shop. Usually published by small presses, most of these books are never listed in national book trade sources but they are filled with good information and will make any trip more enjoyable.

363. Thiffault, Mark. **Bicycle Digest.** Northfield, IL, Digest Books, 1973. 287p. illus. $5.95pa. LC 72-97510. ISBN 0-695-80398-0.

There is a good history of cycles in this book about the why and the how of bicycling. There are chapters on learning to ride safely, foiling thieves, using bike-ways, first aid, cycle camping and touring, choosing a cycle from among the many available models, information on cycling organizations, and on maintenance and repair. A photo-catalog shows easily purchased cycles and some equipment. There is even a short note on the Israeli bicycle industry. Good reading.

364. Wagenvoord, James. **Bikes and Riders.** New York, Van Nostrand, 1972. 160p. illus. index. (VNR Sports & Leisure Series). $7.95; $3.95pa. (Avon). LC 71-184820.

For the most part, this is designed to get the reader to ride a bicycle. There is a history of cycling (with cuts from old magazines and ads) and notes on equipment and racing. Fine reading.

365. Whiter, Robert. **The Bicycle Manual on Maintenance and Repair.** Hollywood, CA, Laurida, 1972. 272p. illus. glossary. $2.95pa. LC 73-187067.

Illustrated with drawings, this is a complete guide to the bicycle, with information on frames, seats, handlebars, wheels, gears, brakes, pedals, tires, tubes, etc. A good book for any cyclist.

MOTORCYCLES

366. Arctander, Erik. **The Book of Motorcycles, Trail Bikes & Scooters.** New York, Arco, 1965. 96p. illus. $3.50. LC 65-22856. SBN 668-01311-7.

The publication date indicates that this book is outdated in its photos and price lists of available models, but there is good information on engines, travelling on cycles, etc. Good reading.

367. Arctander, Erik. **The New Book of Motorcycles.** New York, Arco, 1968. 112p. illus. $3.50. LC 68-54470. ISBN 0-668-01813-5.

Rather outdated if you need current information about cycles, but the material is good and interesting. There are articles on safety, a "dream" collection, competition, testing a used cycle, engine types, and older American motorcycles. Good reading.

368. Bailey, Gary, and Carl Shipman. **How to Win Motocross.** Tucson, AZ, H. P. Books, 1974. 190p. illus. $5.95pa. LC 73-92958. ISBN 0-912656-16-6.

All about motocross racing on a track with numerous curves, banks, soft spots, and other goodies. There is good information about the available bikes and equipment, the care and tuning of a cycle, and, mostly, about how to ride through turns, mud, etc. Excellent and clearly presented material.

369. Behme, Bob, and Malcolm Jaderquist. **The Motorcycle & Trail Bike Handbook.** New York, Pyramid, 1971. 188p. illus. $0.95pa.

This is a good introduction for youngsters or parents. It is about the different kinds of cycles and learning to ride them, forming a club, tools and maintenance, cycle camping, racing. There is a "roundup" of 1971 models with some photographs. Not too much meat here but enough for the rank beginner. I obtained a copy free, at a local cycle dealer's open house.

370. Boswell, Cliff, and George Hays. **Two-Wheel Touring & Camping.** 1st rev. ed. Lake Arrowhead, CA, Bagnall, 1970. 110p. illus. $3.50pa.

This large-format book is about *motorcycle* travel. There is good information about selecting a proper machine and equipping it, preparing the bike and planning a trip, camping equipment and how to pack it, driving and safety hints, photography, trail bike touring and camping, carrying small cycles on trucks or trailers, navigation, and survival. Travel in the United States, Canada, and Mexico is discussed. There are also addresses of youth hostels, equipment dealers, government offices, federal recreation areas, and where to write for further information. A very good resume for motorcycle tourists. There are photographs and a few advertisements.

371. Davis, Jim, and Bob Jackson. **The Complete Book of Moto-Cross.** Lake Arrowhead, CA, Bagnall, 1972. 112p. illus. $5.95pa.

In large magazine-type format and with photographs and maps of race courses, this guide discusses rules, choice of a cycle, its preparation and maintenance, clothing (mostly for protection), physical conditioning, beginning in competition, riding techniques, and an imaginary "day at the races." The few advertisements do not detract. An excellent text for a very popular sport.

372. Davis, Pedr, and Mike McCarthy. **Ride . . . and Stay Alive.** Los Angeles, Clymer, 1973. 120p. illus. glossary. $2.95pa.

This is all about motorcycle riding with an introduction to cycling and safety. There is information about clothing and helmets, the machine and its preparation, riding in town and country, day and night, wet and dry, on and off the road. The authors stress the importance of riding defensively and of being visible. Troubleshooting and maintenance hints and a few words about carrying passengers are included. An excellent guide. Highly recommended.

373. Dempsey, Paul. **The Complete Mini-Bike Handbook.** Blue Ridge Summit, PA, TAB Books, 1973. 320p. illus. index. (TAB Book No. 651). $8.95; $5.95pa. LC 72-97221. ISBN 908386-3651-X; -2651-4pa.

This is a guide to the maintenance and repair of those squat little machines with the fat wheels. There is information about selection, riding, safety, and other aspects of the sport. Recommended as the book for mini-bike owners who do lots of repair work.

VEHICLE ACTIVITIES

374. Driscoll, Joe. **California Trailbike Guide.** San Leandro, CA, Driscoll/ Hough (distr.: Ten Speed), 1973. 124p. illus. map. $5.95pa. LC 73-81372.

This is a large (15" high by 9½" wide) view of the problems of off-road vehicle owners in the Golden State: the legal aspects of noise, trespass, environmental damage, etc. Various alternatives are suggested. The guide includes county maps showing open riding areas and a large folded map. Although it is aimed at California problems, the suggestions could be useful to groups of riders elsewhere. There are cartoons of the adventures of Joel DeBear, an ursine cycle rider. Excellent and recommended.

375. Edmonds, I. G. **Motorcycling for Beginners: A Manual for Safe Riding.** Philadelphia, Macrae Smith, 1972. 156p. illus. index. glossary. $4.95. LC 74-183864. ISBN 0-8255-3006. Also published by Wilshire ($2.00pa.).

This elementary guide has a cursory history of motorcycles and an introduction to the operation of two- and four-stroke engines, information on operation and riding techniques (off- and on-road and in races) and some hints on cycle care. A good book for beginners.

376. Greene, Bob. **Motorcycle Repair Manual.** Rev. ed. Los Angeles, Petersen, 1973. 288p. illus. $3.95pa. LC 72-85366.

In the usual Petersen magazine format, this contains good, clear and handy information for the motorcycle recreationist. There are hints on troubleshooting, maintenance, repair, and rebuilding. The tuning instructions should bring out the best in your machine. Many photographs and drawings. Highly recommended.

377. Griffin, Al. **Motorcycles: A Buyer's and Rider's Guide.** 2nd ed. Chicago, Regnery, 1974. 317p. illus. index. $10.00; $4.95pa. LC 73-20682. ISBN 0-8092-8996-2; -8995-4pa.

An interesting introduction to motorcycles and their use: history, organizations and gangs, economics of riding, insurance coverage, legislation, types of bikes, and how to choose the proper one. There are many lists of books, periodicals, motorcycle distributors, and other odds and ends. A good, easy book for beginners. More photos would help.

378. Gutkind, Lee. **Bike Fever.** Chicago, Follett, 1973. 234p. $6.95. LC 72-94778. ISBN 0-695-80380-8.

This is basically a journal of motorcycle trips through the United States with information on cycle gangs and daredevils. It is essentially literary rather than practical, although the suggestions on buying a bike, learning how to ride it, and safety are informative. Very well done—reads like a series of magazine articles.

OUTDOOR RECREATION

379. **How to Ride Motorcycles.** Los Angeles, Coronado Book Corp., 1971. 82p. illus. $1.00pa.

In magazine-type format, this guide is elementary but effective. There are hints on street riding, physical fitness, noise problems, motocross, trials, and trail riding. Illustrated with photographs. Good, basic stuff for novices. From this one, proceed to *Off Road Cycling* (entry 383).

380. Jones, Thomas Firth. **Enduro.** Radnor, PA, Chilton, 1970. 155p. illus. $5.50; $2.95pa. LC 79-138557. ISBN 0-8019-5593-9; -5597-1pa.

This is a good description of an enduro, which is an endurance run on a motorcycle. There are suggestions about selecting the right cycle and modifying it, maintenance, clothing and tools, riding techniques, organizing an enduro, and how a enduro course is designed. Good reading for the beginner.

381. Koch, Don. **Chilton's Complete Guide to Motorcycles and Motorcycling.** Radnor, PA, Chilton, 1974. 197p. illus. index. glossary. $7.95; $5.59pa. LC 74-17365. ISBN 0-8019-6069-X; -6089-4pa.

The basics of motorcycling are covered in this book: choosing a machine for road or for the trail, the economics of cycling (taxes, insurance, financing, etc.), the engineering features of a motorcycle, safe riding techniques, simple maintenance procedures, taking a trip (planning, assembling a proper tool and spare parts kit, etc.), competition riding (in enduros, motocross, etc.), choosing accessories such as helmets, fairings and modified ports, and the impact of motorcycling on the environment (noise levels, land use, etc.). The book is well written and adequately illustrated, mostly with photographs. Excellent reading for any novice rider.

382. Lovin, Roger. **The Complete Motorcycle Nomad: A Guide to Machines, Equipment, People and Places.** Boston, Little, Brown, 1974. 308p. illus. $7.95; $3.95pa. LC 73-17057. ISBN 0-316-53355-6; -53356-4pa.

This is an excellent guide to motorcycle touring. Lovin uses "Speed, carrying capacity, and terrain" as his three vectors when choosing a proper cycle. The book is filled with suggestions about power requirements, suspension, brakes, safety, riding comfort, clothing needs, camping gear, cookery, finding a job, loading all the stuff on the cycle, riding in traffic, handling the police, etc. The instructions for laying a bike down (sliding it on the pavement and getting off it!) are the best yet. Highly recommended as an interesting and authoritative book.

383. **Off Road Cycling.** Mount Morris, IL, Cycle Guide, 1972. 98p. illus. $1.25pa.

In large magazine format, this manual offers many hints on how to ride a motorcycle: enduros, motocross, specialty races, and just plain dirt riding.

VEHICLE ACTIVITIES

There are suggestions on buying a used bike, tuning a bike, understanding ignition systems, handling factors, and making the bike more reliable. Among the other aspects of off-road riding covered here are: fixing flats, transporting cycles safely, stocking a good tool kit, and choosing accessories. A catalog section shows many accessories and special parts. Good for novices and a bit more advanced than *How to Ride Motorcycles*. Read 'em both. This should be on your local newsstand.

384. Perry, Robin. **Road Rider: A Guide to On-the-Road Motorcycling.** New York, Crown, 1974. 152p. illus. $4.95; $2.95pa. LC 73-91519. ISBN 0-517-51501-6; -515024pa.

For economical transportation, a motorcycle can hardly be bettered. Perry discusses the types of cycle and accessories needed for road travel, offers hints on learning to ride safely, riding with a passenger, and travelling at night, in mountains, and in deserts. A short section on maintenance is included but the emphasis is on the proper technique for highway motorcycling. An excellent book for beginners and those who have some experience on dirt bikes. Highly recommended.

385. Perry, Robin. **The Woods Rider: A Guide to Off-the-Road Motorcycling.** New York, Crown, 1973. 144p. illus. $4.95; $2.95pa. LC 72-96666. ISBN 0-517-50369-7; -50377-8pa.

This is an excellent introduction to trail riding. Nicely illustrated with photographs, it covers the techniques of cycle control, crossing logs and streams, riding in sand and snow (not at the same time, please!), and other seemingly odd procedures. There is some attention to maintenance; safety and protective clothing are emphasized. Intended for the novice who isn't going too far off the road. Graduate from this one to Richmond's *How to Select, Ride and Maintain Your Trail Bike* (entry 388) and then to *The Boonie Book* by Shipman ($2.95pa., published by The Dirt Rider, P.O. Box 14422, Albuquerque, NM 87111).

386. Radlauer, Ed. **Motorcyclopedia.** Glendale, CA, Bowmar, 1973. 79p. illus.(col.). (A Pix Dix Book). $4.24; $2.95pa. LC 72-92678. ISBN 0-8372-0298-1; -0885-8pa.

This is a small dictionary of many of the terms used by motorcyclists. Illustrated entirely with color photographs. Handy for beginners.

387. Richmond, Doug. **All about Minibikes.** Tucson, AZ, H. P. Books, 1970. 89p. illus. $5.00pa.

All about the little rascals you can put into your auto trunk. Suggestions for buying a minibike, learning to ride and what to wear, off-road travel and what to take along (tools, etc.), repairing flats, improving the bike, camping, riding in rough country, and maintenance. Excellent for beginners.

OUTDOOR RECREATION

388. Richmond, Doug. **How to Select, Ride and Maintain Your Trail Bike.** Tucson, AZ, H. P. Books, 1972. 160p. illus. $5.00pa. LC 72-91687. SBN 91256-08-5.

This excellent guide tells all about trail bikes, with hints on selection, learning to ride, choosing equipment for the trail, maintenance, preparation, camping, and safety. Illustrated with many photographs, the book is a must for any trail rider. Highly recommended.

389. Salinger, Peter H. **Motorcycling and the New Enthusiast.** New York, Grosset & Dunlap, 1973. 95p. illus.(part col.). glossary. $4.95. LC 73-825. ISBN 0-448-11500-4.

The topics covered in this book include explanations of how motorcycles work (two- and four-cycle engines, etc.), and why there are different kinds of bikes, how to ride, how to choose the proper cycle for the rider's purpose, maintenance and tools, organizations, courtesy, and racing. Photographs and drawings are used throughout. The glossary is of many of the words used by cycle makers or suppliers. Intended, I'm sure, for youngsters. Good reading.

390. Sanford, Robert. **Riding the Dirt.** Newport Beach, CA, Bond/Parkhurst, 1972. 221p. illus. glossary. $6.95. LC 72-83608. ISBN 0-87880-012-3.

This is a guide to dirt riding for beginners and more advanced cyclists. There are suggestions on clothing, physical conditioning, and mental attitude; transporting the machine; technical notes on trail cycles (frame geometry, suspensions, engines, etc.); choosing a bike and preparing it for off-road use, for motocross racing, enduros, and trials; and suggestions on techniques for all these uses. Several well-known competitors offer personal advice. Safety, ecology, and courtesy are part of it, too. An excellent handbook.

391. Shipman, Carl. **How to Ride Observed Trials for Fun!** Tucson, AZ, H. P. Books, 1973. 158p. illus. $5.95pa. LC 73-82436. ISBN 0-912656-14-X.

Riding through a series of traps while being observed and scored by a judge is the big thing with trials riders. This manual covers types of cycle, setting up a course, official rules of both the Rocky Mountain and the American Trials Associations, and expert advice, well illustrated with photographs, on the theory and practice of riding a cycle through it all. An excellent book for anyone who wishes to learn precise handling. Highly recommended.

392. Smith, LeRoi. **Fixing Up Motorcycles.** New York, Dodd, Mead, 1974. 202p. illus. index. $6.95. LC 73-5838. ISBN 0-396-06519-8.

Smith offers good advice on buying and repairing a used motorcycle and basic information on engines and tuning, transmissions and drive trains,

VEHICLE ACTIVITIES

and brakes, tires, and wheels. There are also suggestions on using trail bikes, mini-bikes, street bikes and choppers. More illustrations would help.

393. Streano, Vince. **Touching America with Two Wheels.** New York, Random House, 1974. 145p. illus. $3.95pa. LC 73-20564. ISBN 0-394-71053-3.

This is the log of a trip on a Honda 750 motorcycle. Throughout the book, there are suggestions on choosing a bike for long trips, safety, first aid, getting along with the police, equipment, combating fatigue and theft, and a resume of cycle laws. The author travelled through the South, Navajoland, Amish country and Canada. Good reading for any motorcycle buff who already knows what he's doing.

394. Wallach, Theresa. **Easy Motorcycle Riding.** New York, Sterling, 1970. 144p. illus. index. $3.95; $0.95pa. (Bantam). LC 75-126853. ISBN 0-8069-4038-7; -4039-5pa.

Illustrated with drawings, this is a good book for beginning riders with its hints on riding techniques and information about the cycle itself. There is advice on buying new or used motorcycles. An English cyclist, Ms. Wallach has operated a motorcycle riding school in Chicago.

395. Watson, Jack B. **How to Buy a Used Motorcycle.** Saugus, CA, Barnard, 1971. 35p. illus. $1.95pa.

I should have had this little book when I bought my first cycle—it was a dog but it wasn't barking so I was bitten. Watson recommends buying from an individual rather than a dealer and he gives an excellent price guide for use with any make or model of cycle. Highly recommended.

396. Watson, Jack B. **How to Ride in Sand.** Saugus, CA, Barnard, 1972. 24p. illus. $1.00pa.

It's hard enough to walk in sand, so a cyclist had better do the right thing. With several photographs and canny hints, this little text is a valuable one for any cyclist. Starting, steering, and using the berm—it's here and very clearly stated.

397. Watson, Jack B. **How to Use the Front Brake.** Saugus, CA, Barnard, 1972. 26p. illus. $1.00pa.

A motorcycle's front brake is more effective than the rear one, so the rider must learn how to use it properly. The little tricks are clearly explained and Watson even covers "how to use the rear brake" for good measure.

OUTDOOR RECREATION

398. Watson, Jack B. **Learn to Hill Climb!** Saugus, CA, Barnard, 1971. 34p. illus. $3.49pa.

Whether for competition or for getting around in the boonies, climbing steep slopes is something every rider should be able to do safely. If you want to look like a pro, read this book and study the photographs.

399. Watson, Jack B. **Learn to Wheelie!** 4th ed. Saugus, CA, Barnard, 1971. 35p. illus. $3.49pa.

Tooling along on only the rear wheel of a motorcycle takes a good bit of finesse. My son has it but I do not! This little book tells all and shows you how with photos and drawings. The technique works with almost any cycle, even a bicycle.

400. Yerkow, Charles. **Here Is Your Hobby ... Motorcycling.** New York, Putnam's, 1973. 126p. illus. index. $4.19. LC 72-76740. SBN GB-399-60477-4.

This guide for beginners will assist in selecting and buying a first motorcycle. There are chapters on riding in traffic, development of technique, maintenance and troubleshooting, and a history of motorcycles. Illustrated with photographs. Another good book for youngsters.

AUTOMOBILES
(Including RecVees, Four-Wheel-Drive Vehicles, Campers, and Car Travel)

401. Ash, David, ed. **1973 Automobile Almanac.** 6th ed. Nyack, NY, Automobile Almanac, 1973. 230p. illus. index. $4.95. LC 67-7349.

This is an annual resume of automobile racing results and other data of interest to auto fans. Each edition contains a pictorial record of available cars, speed records, a list of American auto makers from early days to the present, details of many racing courses, a glossary of auto terms, and incidental material. Sports car buffs probably know this one already.

402. Bauer, Erwin. **The Sportsman on Wheels.** New York, Dutton, 1969. 146p. illus. index. (An Outdoor Life Skill Book). $1.95pa. LC 77-100359.

The wheels included here are on station wagons, truck campers and motor homes, four-wheel-drive vehicles, all kinds of trailers, all-terrain-vehicles (ATVs), motorcycles and trail bikes, and snowmobiles. The text is a general

VEHICLE ACTIVITIES

discussion of the many uses of these vehicles. Good reading for the novice to outdoor recreational vehicles.

403. Bean, Richard. **Basic Automotive Troubleshooting.** Los Angeles, Petersen, 1974. 144p. illus. $2.95pa. LC 74-76521. ISBN 0-8227-0051-4.

With a minimum of equipment, the traveller should be able to find out what's wrong with his vehicle. This manual describes how an engine works and how to troubleshoot, and it has numerous checklists to follow. Listed here rather briefly as being a good book to carry on a trip.

404. **The Best of Europe.** Mill Valley, CA, Rajo, 1970. 54p. illus. $3.00pa.

This looks like a magazine because it consists of reprints of articles from *Camping Guide*, *Motor Coach Travel*, and *Trailer Guide* magazines. The information is about trailering and motor camping in Russia, Spain, and other places in Europe.

405. Brittan, Nick. **Safari Fever: The Story of a Car Rally They Said No European Could Win.** Croydon, England Motor Racing (distr.: Motorbooks International), 1972. 160p. illus. index. $9.95. ISBN 0-900549-16-5.

This is about the East Africa Safari Rally, especially the 1972 race. Illustrated with photographs. After reading the book, I still don't understand why they said . . . .

406. Browning, Peter, ed. **Castrol Rally Manual 2: A Further Outstanding Collection of Practical, Informative Articles and Reference Material for Rally Drivers, Navigators, Organizers & Enthusiasts.** London, Patrick Stephens (distr.: Motorbooks International), 1972. 128p. illus. $5.95. ISBN 0-85059-105-8.

So there, too! There are ten articles in all, with good basic information for beginners to rallying. Some of the information is good only for Britishers but it's interesting. Good reading.

407. Crow, James T., and Cameron A. Warren. **Four Wheel Drive Handbook.** 4th ed. Newport Beach, CA, Bond/Parkhurst, 1973. 96p. illus. $2.95pa.

Originally published in 1970, this little handbook is an excellent introduction to the use of four-wheel-drive vehicles. Explaining why this sort of vehicle is needed in certain places (i.e., rough, off-road country, etc.), the authors compare the available vehicles (Jeep, International, Land Rover, Range Rover, Toyota, Datsun, Ford, Chevrolet, and Dodge). They discuss desirable options and accessories, tools, driving techniques, tire problems, etc.

OUTDOOR RECREATION

Filled with excellent hints of all kinds. The Suzuki is not mentioned. All 4WD buffs, especially novices, should have this book.

408. Crow, James T. **New Baja Handbook for the Off-Pavement Motorist in Lower California.** Newport Beach, CA, Bond/Parkhurst, 1973. 95p. illus. $3.95pa. LC 73-81325. ISBN 0-87880-020-4.

This is a guide to travel in Mexico's western-most state, with information on border crossing, required permits and insurance, maps, etc. Contains suggestions on suitable vehicles and equipment, camping gear, travel conditions, places to visit and what to buy, when to travel, safety and survival, local plants, and sources of books, supplies, and maps. The general information would be useful to any traveller who ventures off the road in a desert climate.

409. Davidson, Sharon, and Gary Davidson. **Europe with Two Kids and a Van.** San Francisco, 101 Productions (distr.: Scribner's), 1973. 192p. illus. index. $3.95pa. LC 72-94895.

An entertaining little book about a trip through Europe in a Volkswagen van. There are suggestions about a proper vehicle, purchasing or renting, what to take or buy, passports and other documents, where to write for additional information, tools for the car, clothing, and camping gear. The areas covered are Scandinavia, England, France, Germany, Spain, Switzerland, the Riviera and northern Italy. For each country, the Davidson's offer travel routes, places to visit, things to do (especially with kids), addresses of camp grounds and of places to buy food and do laundry. Drawings by Bill Oetinger add a great deal to a delightful guide.

410. Day, Dick. **The Complete Book of Karting.** Englewood Cliffs, NJ, Prentice-Hall, 1961. 179p. illus. index. $7.95. LC 61-8967. SBN 13-157487-6.

Although rather old, this book has many suggestions about proper machines and the history of karting. Racing rules, engines and maintenance, how to drive, and building a kart are some of the topics covered.

411. Dunn, William J. **Enjoy Europe by Car.** New ed. New York, Scribner's, 1973. 284p. illus. index. (Emblem Editions). $4.95pa. LC 72-7940. SBN 684-13256-7.

This book contains suggestions on planning a trip, choosing a car, and on fly-drive tours from the United States. Among the many topics covered are: European road systems, police regulations, traffic conditions, customs, international road markings, fuel and repair problems, changing money, and handling hitchhikers. There is a list of road maps and hotel guides in the Western European countries. For hints on driving in mountains and across the Channel, auto clubs, and food along the way, this is the book for the tourist.

VEHICLE ACTIVITIES

Appendices list passport regulations, comparisons of auto and fuel prices, mileage charts, currency regulations, clothing sizes, and other useful information.

412. Dunne, Jim, ed. **Motorcamping Handbook 1973.** New York, Popular Science, 1973. 144p. illus. $1.50pa.

Using the format of its parent magazine, this well-illustrated review covers the available types of camping vehicles: vans, motorhomes, trailers, four-wheel-drive vehicles, and pickup campers. There is additional information about driving techniques, repairs, and equipment, and several tours are outlined. A good book for the prospective buyer.

413. Engel, Lyle Kenyon. **The Complete Book of Mobile Home Living.** New York, Arco, 1973. 143p. illus. $5.95. LC 73-85274. ISBN 0-668-02896-3.

This is a well-illustrated look at the world of mobile homes: choosing and buying, construction and building codes, floor plans, decor, other aspects of livability, warranties, and buying a used home. Further information is given about finding a suitable park, taxes, and maintaining the unit. A good resume.

414. Engel, Lyle Kenyon. **The Complete Book of Motor Camping.** Rev. ed. New York, Arco, 1973. 191p. illus. $2.95pa. LC 75-103075.

Intended for beginning campers, this is an elementary view of the available automobiles, trucks, vans, and motor homes. Information on finding a campground, towing boats, things to take, basic maintenance, and safety rules are mentioned. Dodge products are prominent throughout the book, since this is also meant to be a handout at your local Good Guys dealership (where I got my copy). Easy to read and filled with valuable material for the novice.

415. Engel, Lyle Kenyon. **The Complete Book of Trailering.** New York, Arco, 1973. 192p. illus. $5.95; $2.95pa. LC 72-85679. ISBN 0-668-02716-9; -02715-0pa.

In this guidebook for beginners to the trailer camping set, Engel discusses automotive towing requirements, the various kinds of trailers, and their features (including accessories and appliances). There are hints on safe driving, planning a trip, storing trailers, and handling trailer boats. A good book.

416. Gartner, John. **All about Pickup Campers, Van Conversions and Motor Homes.** Beverly Hills, CA, Trail-R-Club, 1969. 224p. illus. $4.50pa. LC 72-83767. ISBN 0-87593-016-6.

This is an explanation of the different types of self-propelled recreational vehicles, the advantages and disadvantages of each, and their construction features. About half the book is a catalog of the units available in 1969. Still has a good bit of pertinent material.

417. Griffin, Al. **A Buyer's & User's Guide to Recreational Vehicles.** Chicago, Regnery, 1973. 269p. illus. index. $1.00. LC 73-6459.

Griffin discusses the relative merits (and demerits!) of the many kinds of recvees: vans, motor homes, pickup campers, and trailers. The book has much good information about renting versus buying, buying a used vehicle, and towing laws. All novice prospective buyers of recreational vehicles should read this one.

418. Howes, Connie B. **Recreational Vehicle Handbook.** Chicago, Rand McNally, 1974. 104p. illus. index. $1.95pa. LC 73-14406.

A general introduction to all types of recvees. There are many suggestions about choosing the right vehicle for specific needs, financing and insuring, driving or towing, planning a trip, finding a campsite, packing all the nooks and crannies, cleaning and maintenance work, camping in cold weather, deserts or mountains, and in Canada, Mexico, and Europe. Many photographs illustrate this good, well-written guide to all those little things a new or prospective owner must think about: fires, construction standards, safety features, furnaces and stoves, electrical systems, water supplies, and sewage.

419. Hudson-Evans, Richard. **The Rally Handbook.** London, Batsford (distr.: Motorbooks International), 1972. 206p. illus. index. $7.95. ISBN 0-7134-0469-8.

Intended for the English driver, this contains some good material on preparing the person and the car for an exciting sport. There are hints on the art of driving, the role of the navigator with his maps and timepiece, the service crew, the organizers, and officials. There is a glossary and other information of use primarily to drivers in Great Britain.

420. Hull, Clinton R. **Motor Home Manual.** Beverly Hills, CA, Trail-R-Club, 1973. 266p. illus. (Book 64). $4.95pa. LC 73-6827. ISBN 0-87593-064-6.

Motor homes are the most expensive types of recvees, so it is wise for a buyer to know as much as possible about them. Hull's book tells what to look for: chassis design, framework, furnishings, utilities, and layout. There are also suggestions on trip planning, storage problems, and other items of interest. Van conversions and mini-motor homes are also discussed.

421. Hull, Clinton R. **Pickup Camper Manual.** Beverly Hills, CA, Trail-R-Club, 1974. 245p. illus. (Book 83). $4.95pa. LC 73-19696. SBN 87593-083-2.

VEHICLE ACTIVITIES

Anyone contemplating the purchase of a truck/camper combination will find this to be required reading. Hull offers many suggestions about what to look for while shopping (beds, stoves, etc.), possible problems (from freezing water lines to not being allowed to park your truck in your own driveway!), choosing and maintaining the truck and accessories, and general hints on how to live in a camper. Many photos and drawings illustrate a useful book.

422. **Kings of the Open Road.** Highland Park, IL, Woodall, 1969. 32p. illus. $1.00pa.

This is a small pamphlet intended for new owners of pickup-campers. There are hints on safe driving, preparing for a trip, maintaining the camper, and getting it on and off the truck. It has good hints, but many other titles offer more information.

423. Kneass, Jack. **How to Buy Recreational Vehicles.** Beverly Hills, CA, Trail-R-Club, 1969. 164p. illus. (Book 94). $2.95pa. LC 79-83766. SBN 87593-094-8.

A well-known recvee writer discusses primarily trailers (truck campers and motor homes are treated only briefly) with chapters on water systems, windows, sanitation systems, stoves and furnaces, insulation, batteries, and air conditioners. Rather dated in regard to available models but a trip to the library will let you get some good information.

424. Kneass, Jack. **How to Select a Car or Truck for Trailer Towing.** Beverly Hills, CA, Trail-R-Club, 1969. 144p. illus. (Book 93). $2.95pa. LC 73-75471. SBN 87593-093-X.

Outdated in many ways but still useful for its information on gear ratios, engines, and transmissions.

425. Lahue, Kalton C., *et al.* **Basic Auto Repair Manual.** 6th ed. Ed. by Spencer Murray. Los Angeles, Petersen, 1973. 384p. illus. $3.95pa. LC 74-83025. ISBN 0-8227-0008-5.

This best buy in auto repair manuals is listed for the traveller who wants to carry such a book with him. It is generously illustrated with photographs and drawings and its large size (8½" x 11") allows for rather extensive instruction. There is much more in this book than could possibly be done on the road but you can't beat it. Volkswagens are included, too.

426. Lockwood, Tim. **Recreational Vehicle Maintenance: All Sizes of Campers, Trailers, Motor Homes.** Los Angeles, Clymer, 1973. 219p. illus. index. $7.95pa.

Intended for the recreational vehicle owner, this manual covers LPG systems, electrical systems, hitches and towing aids, wheels and tires, trailer

OUTDOOR RECREATION

brakes, the water system, appliances, pickup campers, body maintenance, tools and techniques, and emergencies. There is also a chapter on selecting a proper vehicle for one's needs. Illustrated with photos and drawings, this is a very handy book to have around.

427. McFarland, Kenton D., and James C. Sparks, Jr. **Midget Motoring and Karting.** New York, Dutton, 1961. 159p. illus. $4.50. LC 61-12462.

This introduction to karting covers the selection of engines and accessories, the chassis, and wheels and brakes. The book is old, so some things are outdated. Nevertheless, the suggestions are still good; karting hasn't changed that much.

428. **The Milepost: All-the-North-Travel Guide.** Anchorage, AK, Alaska Northwest, annual. (25th ed., dated 1973, has 546p.). illus. index. $3.95pa.

This is the bible for travellers on the Alaska Highway. Mile by mile highway logs from the lower U.S. border, through Canada, to Alaska. Information on road conditions, gasoline supplies, places to visit, churches, parks, campgrounds, etc. Small maps throughout and many advertisements. Everything the flat-land tourister needs to know!

429. Miller, Mike. **Camping and Trailering in Alaska: The Complete Guide.** Juneau, AK, Alaskabooks, 1971. 111p. illus. (Alaskabook No. 103). $2.00pa.

If you make it to Alaska over the Alaska Highway or take the coastal ferry, you'll need this little book, which describes the southeastern quarter of the state. Most of the text is a guide to camping facilities along each of the major highways.

430. Norris, Monty, and Lyle Kenyon Engel. **Off-Road Racing.** New York, Dodd, Mead, 1974. 148p. illus. index. $5.95. LC 73-11553. ISBN 0-396-06867-7.

This is all about auto, truck, and motorcycle racing away from regular tracks. Most of this action takes place in the southwestern United States and Baja California, with the Baja 1000 the big prize event. The book is a good introduction to the thrills and defeats of a rugged sport. Good reading, especially for the kids.

431. O'Shea, Paul. **Guide to Competition Driving.** New York, Sports Car (distr.: Crown), 1957. $2.95.

Outdated and not seen for many years, but still available.

432. Pritchard, Anthony. **The Motor Racing Year No. 3.** New York, Norton, 1972. 271p. illus. $8.95. LC 71-28136. ISBN 0-393-08536-3.

Intended to give a comprehensive account of a season's results in Formula 1 and Sports Car Championship racing. This is apparently an annual publication (at least it should be). It contains information on most of the races such as the Sebring, LeMans, and Indianapolis 500. Interesting but rather expensive.

433. **Recreation Rental Guide.** Calabasas, CA, Trailer Life, 1973. 204p. illus. $1.00pa.

The cover subtitle sums it up: "Where and how to rent houseboats, motorhomes, travel trailers, camping trailers, pickup campers, anywhere in the U.S., Canada, and overseas."

434. Richmond, Doug. **Baja.** Lake Arrowhead, CA, Bagnall, 1970. 112p. illus. $4.00pa.

Written by a long-time Baja-buff who fell in love with the country, this little book includes some general introductory remarks and then gets into the nitty-gritty: personal equipment needed for safety or survival or only convenience (clothing, camping gear, cameras, etc.), equipment needed for the motorcycle (tools, spare parts, flat fixing kit, etc.), suggestions on choice of a bike and its preparation and maintenance, and a description of the country, especially the roads and places to stop. Intended for cyclists but the information is good for any desert traveller. Excellent.

435. Siebert, Alan H. **To Hell on Wheels: The Illustrated Manual of Desert Survival.** 2nd ed. Pasadena, CA, Brown Burro, 1974. 64p. illus. $2.95pa. LC 74-75051.

Heat and a lack of water can easily kill the unwary visitor to our desert regions. Siebert's compact book gives many first-class suggestions about coping with the desert environment: preparing a vehicle, driving techniques, emergency supplies, poisonous animals, surviving afoot, finding water, navigating, keeping warm at night, finding food. The sections on needed gear and on first aid are especially good. Recommended for all off-road travellers.

436. Siposs, George C. **Landsailing: From RC Models to the Big Ones.** Blue Ridge Summit, PA, TAB Books, 1973. 192p. illus. index. (TAB Book No. 659). $7.95; $4.95pa. LC 73-78196. ISBN 0-8306-3659-5; -2659-Xpa.

Landsailing is sailing a "boat" on wheels rather in the manner of ice boating. Rather old in concept and execution but only recently the subject of mass-produced vehicles and national organization. Photos and drawings illustrate this guide to the theory and practice of the sport. The book notes

OUTDOOR RECREATION

available models, clubs, required equipment, maintenance, and scale model boats. In addition to a glossary, the rules of the North American Land Sailing Association are included. This is the only book on landsailing that I've found.

437. Smith, LeRoi. **Karting.** New York, Arco, 1971. 215p. illus. $4.95. LC 70-77893. ISBN 0-668-01939-5.

This is mostly a description of karts and the several classes they race in, with rules for competition and information on the chassis, engine, wheels, tuning, safety, and driving skills. A chapter on "Mathematics for the Karts" has formulas, decimal equivalents, and similar material. Many illustrations.

438. Trail-R-Club of America, Box 1376, Beverly Hills, CA 90213.

Over many years, now, this publisher has issued many good handbooks on all kinds of recreational vehicles. Some of these books have been noted in this volume. There are many others, so any prospective buyer or user of a trailer, pickup camper, etc., should write for a complete catalog.

439. Trout, Perry. **Alaska! By Pickup Camper.** Beverly Hills, CA, Trail-R-Club, 1972. 138p. illus. (Book No. 26). $2.95pa. LC 72-160194. SBN 87593-026-3.

There are two ways to "drive" to Alaska—on a ferry boat or on the Alaska Highway. Travelling over the Highway can be quite an adventure, and this book is a record of how to do it. It gives advice of all sorts about the problems of driving on gravel roads, about side trips, and about camping and equipment needs. Good reading.

440. Turner, Stuart. **Rallying: Preparation—Navigation—Organisation.** Rev. 4th ed. Minneapolis, Motorbooks International, 1971. 120p. illus. index. $5.95. ISBN 0-85429-085-0.

Good advice on preparing both the crew and the car, with information about navigation, driving, and other aspects of a sport that hasn't really taken the United States by storm, yet.

441. Waar, Robert. **Off Road Handbook with Back Country Travel Tips.** Tucson, AZ, H. P. Books, 1975. 193p. illus. $5.95pa. LC 74-83546. ISBN 0-912656-15-8.

This is a general introduction to equipping and handling an off-road vehicle, mostly four-wheel-drive types. Illustrated with many drawings and photographs, this manual contains much useful information on transmissions, jacks and winches, tires and wheels, factory and after-market options, good driving habits, technical data and practical hints of all kinds. Recommended for all boondockers.

442. Weiers, Ronald M. **Chilton's More Miles Per Gallon Guide**. Radnor, PA, Chilton, 1974. 131p. illus. index. $5.50; $2.95pa. LC 74-2958. ISBN 0-8019-6120-3; -6121-1pa.

This book covers many aspects of more economical driving: air resistance, road and engine friction, car size, axle ratios, air conditioning, disc brakes, power accessories, and the many other things that affect fuel consumption. Trucks, recreational vehicles, and motorcycles are included. There are 125 hints for economical driving, illustrated with drawings and photographs. Highly recommended.

443. Wolters, Richard A. **Living on Wheels**. New York, Dutton, 1973. 237p. illus. index. (A Sunrise Book). $4.95pa. LC 72-94701. ISBN 0-87690-107-0.

Beginning with a VW camper, Wolters has lived in several homes on wheels. In this book, he discusses van conversions, trailers, motor homes, and pickup campers. Among the many sections are those on engineering features, stoves and refrigerators, extra batteries, water tanks, toilets, and beds. Drawings and photos illustrate a book which is filled with good suggestions and "know how" by one who has lived through it.

WINTER ACTIVITIES

...abominable snowpersons

I can well imagine that the skiers and snowshoers will be after me with sharpened poles for my putting them in the same chapter with those horrid snowmobilers. Before being impaled on the good old bamboo, however, I'll hasten to explain that because all these wintry folk must operate on the same messy white stuff, they are all in this together. A great many cross-country skiers wish to outlaw snowmobiles altogether, and they may yet have their way; people who can shout very loudly about their hates have an easy time in some legislatures. I like to sneak around in the snow, too, but I have no skis or snowmobile. My snowshoes are made of plastic, which makes me a frozen low-brow but I generally wander around in my regular hunting shoes getting wet and cold.

I sympathize with some of the anti-snowmobile arguments. These machines are very noisy because most of them use two-stroke engines and too many snowmobilers cruise around the back country vandalizing cabins. Some folk, apparently, get very brazen during the winter months when so few people are in the woods. The snowmobile industry has recently taken steps to silence their machines, and it is about time. I've ridden a snowmobile and it is fun, so I hope that quiet and good sense will prevail. I don't like prohibitionists.

444. **All About Snowmobiles.** Los Angeles, Argus Publishing Corp., 1972. 138p. illus. (An Argus Special). $1.75pa.

This is a magazine-format publication that offers a good look at snowmobiles and their uses. There are articles on driving techniques, engine fundamentals, and a directory of machines available in 1973. I presume that this will be updated someday.

445. Arctic Enterprises, Inc. **Snowmobile Operator Responsibility Training: Student Manual.** Thief River Falls, MN, Arctic Enterprises, 1972. 46p. illus.

The snowmobile manufacturer has prepared a good manual designed for use in grade and high schools. The guide covers the elements of snowmobile history, construction and use, proper clothing and safety, the theory of engines, electrical systems, and drive trains. Includes a glossary, a troubleshooting guide, and a list of clubs. A student workbook comes with the manual. We presume that the price of the set will vary with the number of copies ordered.

446. Auran, John Henry. **Skiing Is a Family Sport!** New York, Association Press, 1970. 144p. illus. glossary. $4.95. LC 68-31329. SBN 8-96-1691-2.

This is almost entirely about alpine skiing, but there is one 12-page chapter devoted to ski touring. Almost any other book listed here would be more useful.

447. Baldwin, Edward R. **The Cross-Country Skiing Handbook: A Detailed Instruction Book on Cross-Country Ski Touring for Both Beginners and Experts.** 2nd ed. New York, Scribner's, 1973. 159p. illus. glossary. $3.50pa. LC 73-2115. SBN 684-13420-9.

This is an introduction to the sport with chapters on history, equipment and clothing, techniques, waxing, and physical conditioning. There are lists of ski areas, photographs and drawings, and a glossary (which is not completely alphabetical).

448. Bennett, Margaret. **Cross-Country Skiing for the Fun of It.** New York, Dodd, Mead, 1973. 206p. illus. $5.95. LC 73-9269. ISBN 0-396-06860-X.

This introduction is written by June Biermann and Barbara Toohey, who write under the pseudonym Margaret Bennett. There are sections devoted to equipment, waxing, clothing, survival in cold and wind, skiing techniques. Waxing guides, a list of places to ski, boot size conversion tables and lists of equipment suppliers, touring organizations, resorts, and races complete the book.

449. Bridge, Raymond. **The Complete Snow Campers Guide.** New York, Scribner's, 1973. 390p. illus. index. $10.00; $4.95pa. LC 72-37223. SBN 684-12769-5; -13130-7pa.

This is a general introduction to winter camping. The sections include good discussions of heat loss and wind chill and resultant insulation needs, clothing, sleeping gear, shelter and campsite needs, travelling in snow (snowshoeing, skiing, direction finding), cooking and food needs, making clothing and other gear, and special conditions such as avalanches, snow slopes, winter weather, and other emergencies. There is a bibliography, a list of suppliers, and an equipment checklist. Highly recommended.

450. Brunner, Hans, and Alois Kalin. **Cross-Country Skiing.** New York, McGraw-Hill, 1972. 79p. illus. $4.95. LC 72-9533. ISBN 0-07-077478-1.

Published in Switzerland in 1969, this translation is concerned primarily with technique and waxing. In the technique discussions, suggestions for advanced skiers are printed in blue. There are shorter sections devoted to conditioning, competition, and equipment.

451. Caldwell, John. **The New Cross-Country Ski Book.** 4th ed. Brattleboro, VT, Stephen Greene, 1973. 144p. illus. $7.95; $3.95pa. LC 73-82743. ISBN 0-8289-0235-6; -0187-2pa.

A good introduction to the sport, with chapters on equipment and its care, clothing, skiing techniques, waxing, training, and other aspects. I've found this title in more shops than any other skiing book. Highly recommended.

452. **Chilton's Repair and Tune-Up Guide for Snowmobiles.** Radnor, PA, Chilton Book Co., 1972. 243p. illus. $6.95; $4.95pa. LC 72-5957. ISBN 0-8019-5742-7; -5805-9pa.

Covers maintenance procedures for several snowmobiles: Arctic Cat, Evinrude, Mercury, Polaris, Rupp, and Yamaha.

453. Colwell, Robert. **Robert Colwell's Guide to Snow Trails.** Harrisburg, PA, Stackpole, 1973. 185p. illus. index. $2.95pa. LC 73-11147. ISBN 0-8177-2015-2.

Illustrated with numerous photographs, this is a listing and evaluation of organized places to ski in the United States: the East (New England, New York, Pennsylvania, and Virginia), the Midwest (Iowa, Michigan, Minnesota, and Wisconsin), the West (Arizona, Colorado, Idaho, Montana, New Mexico, Utah, and Wyoming), and the Far West (California, Oregon, and Washington).

454. Danielsen, John A. **Winter Hiking and Camping.** Glens Falls, NY, Adirondack Mountain Club, 1972. 192p. illus. index. $4.50pa.

This pocket-size book is intended for beginners and emphasizes the physiological aspects of cold weather travel and the needed safety precautions. Good sections on bodily response to cold, clothing selection, food, packs, sleeping bags, snowshoes, skis, and other equipment. There are notes on ski travel, survival, map and compass use, mountain weather, and selecting places to camp. This is not a skiing or snowshoeing instruction manual. Highly recommended.

WINTER ACTIVITIES

455. Helmker, Judith. **A Manual of Snowmobiling.** 2nd ed. New York, A. S. Barnes, 1975. 240p. illus. $8.95. LC 75-146757. ISBN 0-498-07794-2.

This is an interesting introduction to the history of snowmobiles, the industry, the machine itself, legal problems, insurance, racing and clubs, safety and first aid, and places to go. Appendices list organizations and sources of snowmobiles and equipment; some mention is made of the ethics of the sport.

456. Hollatz, Thomas. **The White Earth Snowshoe Guide Book.** Saint Cloud, MN, North Star Press, 1975. 106p. illus. $4.00; $2.95pa. ISBN 0-87839-010-3.

This is an excellent guide to the basics of snowshoes and of snowshoeing. There is information on types of shoes and bindings, clothing, winter survival, games (e.g., snowshoe racing), the history of snowshoes, and the identification of animal tracks. A bit better on the types of snowshoes than *The Snowshoe Book* by Osgood and Hurley, but devotees of the sport will want both titles.

457. Lederer, William J., and Joe Pete Wilson. **Complete Cross-Country Skiing and Ski Touring.** 2nd ed. New York, Norton, 1972. 189p. illus. $6.95. ISBN 0-393-08551-1.

This is a complete manual of instruction from beginner to advanced skier. Illustrated with drawings.

458. Liebers, Arthur. **The Complete Book of Cross-Country Skiing and Ski Touring.** New York, Coward, McCann & Geoghegan, 1974. 285p. illus. index. bibliog. $8.95. LC 73-78759. ISBN 0-698-10533-8.

After a short introduction to the history of skiing, the emphasis shifts to equipment, techniques, and physical conditioning, including weight training. Competition is described, with the complete Olympic Biathlon rules. Almost half the book is a listing of ski touring areas in the United States and Canada. Not for rank beginners.

459. Liebers, Arthur. **The Complete Book of Winter Sports.** New York, Coward, McCann & Geoghegan, 1971. 246p. illus. index. bibliog. $6.95. LC 70-166594.

A number of the winter sports are described in this book: alpine skiing, ice skating, ice hockey, ice boating, sled dog racing, bobsled and luge racing, snowshoeing, curling, and snowmobiling. Rather a survey than a book of instruction.

460. Lund, Morten. **The Pleasures of Cross-Country Skiing.** New York, Dutton, 1972. 195p. illus. $6.95. LC 72-84103. ISBN 0-87690-077-5. Also published by Avon ($2.95pa.).

A good introduction to the history of skiing is followed by elementary instruction illustrated with photographs. Waxing, notes on clothing and gear, racing, overnight camping, and "fun" skiing are considered. There are also lists of organizations and of places to ski in the East and Midwest.

461. Newman, Doug, and Sally Sharrard. **Oregon Ski Tours (65 Cross-Country Ski Trails).** Beaverton, OR, Touchstone, 1973. 160p. illus. $4.95pa. ISBN 0-911518-18-5.

Most of this book is devoted to descriptions of ski touring routes in various parts of Oregon. The illustrations include maps and photographs.

462. Osgood, William E., and Leslie J. Hurley. **Ski Touring: An Introductory Guide.** Rutland, VT, Charles E. Tuttle, 1969. 148p. illus. bibliog. $5.80. LC 78-83073. ISBN 0-8048-0531-8.

Illustrated entirely with drawings, this guide covers equipment needs, preliminary conditioning, skiing techniques, safety and winter camping. Among the topics are igloo building, food preparation, emergency signaling, and first aid. Highly recommended.

463. Osgood, William E., and Leslie J. Hurley. **The Snowshoe Book.** 2nd ed. Brattleboro, VT, Stephen Greene, 1975. 164p. illus. (An Environmental Sports Book). $7.95; $4.50pa. LC 75-4769. ISBN 0-8289-0222-4; -0221-6pa.

All kinds of snowshoes are described so that the reader can make a proper selection. Also covers bindings, clothing, equipment (from longies to an ice axe), and a list of makers. There is instruction on the technique of snowshoeing, racing, and other sorts of fun. The drawings are very good on the whole and there are some photographs too. The definitive book on the subject, so it has to be highly recommended!

464. Pedersen, Tage. **Getting in Shape to Ski.** New York, Association Press, 1970. 95p. illus. bibliog. $3.95. LC 73-129423. SBN 8096-1793-5.

The material here, taken mostly from 1968-69 issues of *Skiing* magazine, is illustrated with drawings. The exercises, which are good for any outdoor activity, include jogging, bicycling, circuit training, tension relieving, and treating minor ski injuries.

465. Rossit, Edward A. **Snow Camping and Mountaineering.** New York, Funk & Wagnalls, 1970. 276p. illus. index. $10.00. LC 76-90054. ISBN 0-308-70374-X.

This good introduction to winter and high altitude activities contains sections on cold weather physiology, clothing, other equipment, snow camping, glacier mountaineering, snow and ice travel, cooking, hunting, and arctic survival. Safety is emphasized. The author has never heard of foam pads, so some updating may be needed. Recommended.

466. Rutstrum, Calvin. **Paradise Below Zero.** New York, Macmillan, 1968. 244p. illus. index. $5.95. LC 68-23643.

Written by a man who obviously loves cold weather and who has lived in Canadian climes, this is a very good book. Rutstrum discusses the beauties and rewards of wintry living and how people react to such weather. His more technical sections deal with clothing and equipment for winter living and travel. There are drawings by Les Kouba and numerous photos. Interesting and authoritative information with equipment lists and many survival hints. Highly recommended.

467. Tejada-Flores, Lito, and Allen Steck. **Wilderness Skiing.** San Francisco, Sierra Club, 1972. 310p. illus. (A Sierra Club Totebook). $6.95pa. LC 72-89120. SBN 87156-069-0.

Basic nordic or cross-country skiing techniques are outlined, together with suggestions on clothing and equipment, sleeping gear, shelter, food, and cooking. The sections on technique include alpine touring. There is a bibliography and check lists of food, first aid needs, and equipment. Illustrated with drawings and photographs.

468. Thomas, James L. **Safe Snowmobiling: Fun without Damage.** New York, Cornerstone Library, 1972. 124p. illus. index. $1.50.

This basic guide discusses the many uses of snowmobiles and how to operate them. Thomas includes notes on accessories such as trailers and sleds, the history of snowmobiles, and legal and ethical matters.

469. Tokle, Art, and Martin Luray. **The Complete Guide to Cross-Country Skiing and Touring.** New York, Holt, 1973. 168p. illus. $6.95; $2.45pa. (Random House/Vintage). LC 72-78119. ISBN 0-03-001056-X.

It's a fact—"If you can walk, you can ski." Well, you can try. This short text is a good one, with instruction on techniques, waxing, conditioning, and ski touring. The skiing areas listed are in the Northeast. Highly recommended.

470. Wallace, Clarke. **The Complete Snowmobiler.** New York, Scribner's, 1971. 180p. illus. index. glossary. $2.95pa. LC 72-178233. SBN 684-12696-6.

OUTDOOR RECREATION

An excellent guide with hints on selecting a machine, learning how they run, how to use them and how to keep them in good repair. Safety and emergency procedures, racing and club activities are included.

471. Wimer, Sally. **The Snowmobiler's Companion.** New York, Scribner's, 1973. 236p. illus. index. $9.95. LC 72-1235. SBN 684-13080-7.

This very good guide covers many aspects of snowmobiling: history, buying suggestions, engines and running gear, maintenance, riding and handling problems, clothing, and winter camping. The section on cold weather survival is very good, there are many miscellaneous tables, and the chapter on ethics is excellent. Recommended as a better choice than the book by Helmker (entry 455).

WATER ACTIVITIES

... but don't go near the water

Water sports are increasingly popular. Almost every lake has not only its share of motorboats but an abundance of water skiers. Recently, near my home, a speedy boat towing a skier ran over and decapitated a swimmer. I'm not sure which of the two activities should be banned because of this incident, but I'm sure that there is at least one legislator who would prohibit water. Canoeists condemn the operators of motorboats. Swimmers condemn the water skiers. Kayakers look down their wet noses at everyone else in or on the water, so I am left in the middle of the pile trying to keep a taut ship and a happy crew. On the whole, boat owners seem to have good lobbying success. They have large and powerful organizations and more than one government agency looking out for them.

I cannot always sympathize with those who cry about our supposed economic crises while large automobiles race by towing even larger cabin cruisers. I've seen boats bouncing up and down on very flimsy trailers but I have yet to see one fall off. Truly, God is not dead! The advent of the boat trailer has been a boon to the boating industry. Quite large boats are sold in towns that are several hundred miles from a body of water large enough to float anything that can accommodate an outboard motor. Boats are now made in towns so far from water that one may wonder if Noah has been reincarnated and given some private intelligence concerning an imminent aqueous disaster.

Kayaks have come a long way since the Esquimos gave them to a grateful world. I presume that some diehard on the floes is still making these simple and seemingly frail craft from walrus ribs and seal hides, but the technicians among us are using canvas, plastics, fiberglass, and rubberized nylon. While shooting rapids in one of these paddled speedboats, one generally wears a protective helmet to avoid deep headaches. The ability to right oneself after capsizing is very important to the lungs, so there is much practice in doing liquid slow rolls. I'm not too sure that I'd like to go downstream under water, but more power to those who do.

Canoes are more my style and if this book sells like hotcakes, I'll be able to afford one. I'd like a folding one, please, so it will fit into a vehicle.

Skin boats are very strong because they are able to bend as stress is applied to them. Folding canoes seem the nearest cousin to the primitive craft with their flexible structure and covering.

Rubber rafts are fun, too, but you can't get very far in one unless you're going downstream. They are hard to paddle and the wind catches them in its clutches every time. They make excellent swimming pools for little kids or bathtubs for older folk. Rowboats are good, clean fun if you have someone to row them. Of if you have an outboard motor. There are so many of these heavy craft around that launching areas are very common. On a nice warm sunny day, an aluminum boat will be very hot until you put it in the water. Then it is very cold. You just can't win.

Most of us don't realize it, but motorboating is fairly dangerous. The people who own large boats operate them in adequately deep water, but the fishermen and others who use the smaller boats with outboard motors often do not pay attention to where they are going. Apparently, quite a few boaters are killed or injured when they run into submerged logs and rocks or onto shoals. The problem must be widespread, because I've seen two articles on the subject during the summer of 1974. New regulations that require life jackets or other flotation devices in almost all water craft should help, but the fool who insists on speed in shallow water will always have accidents.

Readers who like book clubs will be happy to know that there is one designed to please the nautically minded. I'm sure that a postcard will bring quick results in case you haven't seen the advertisements in magazines. Write to: The Dolphin Book Club, Book-of-the-Month Club, Inc., Camp Hill, PA 17011.

472. Adkins, Jan. **The Craft of Sail**. New York, Walker, 1973. 64p. illus. index. $5.95. LC 72-87347. ISBN 0-8027-0401-8.

Described as "written, designed and illustrated" by "the scourge of Buzzard's Bay," this is a beautifully executed guide to the handling of small sailboats. Adkins covers the theory of wind and water phenomena on the craft, including airfoil and vector effects; reaching, running, and beating (sounds rather violent, but sailors speak in strange tongues); nomenclature of boats and gear; boat handling; knots and line handling (there are no "ropes" on a boat!); weather; and elementary navigation. This is a "handwritten" book but it is easy to read and attractive. Highly recommended.

473. Arighi, Scott, and Margaret S. Arighi. **Wildwater Touring: Techniques and Tours**. New York, Macmillan, 1974. 334p. illus. index. $8.95. LC 73-21708. ISBN 0-02-503150-3.

This is an excellent guide to the sport of shooting the rapids in canoes, kayaks, drift boats, or rafts. Half the book is a general discussion of rivers, boats, equipment, and techniques. There is good material on food, safety, and stream judging. The remainder is a guide to the Rogue, Grande Ronde, John Day, Salmon, and Owyhee Rivers in Oregon and Washington. Relative difficulty is clearly stated and the mileage logs are very useful. There are also lists of food and equipment suppliers, of books and organizations, a glossary, and a method of estimating flow and gradient from topographic maps. Highly recommended.

474. Aymar, Gordon C. **1973-1977 Yacht Racing Rules and Tactics.** 7th ed. New York, Van Nostrand Reinhold, 1974. 146p. illus. glossary. $9.95. LC 73-110056. ISBN 0-442-20388-8.

Illustrated with photographs (mostly of boat models) and drawings, this handbook describes and explains the Rules of the North American Yacht Racing Union and then offers a discussion of tactics for winning races. Every serious racing skipper needs this well-known title.

475. **The BUC Book: A Statistically Authenticated Used Boat Directory...** 25th ed. Fort Lauderdale, FL, BUC International Corp., 1974. index. $29.50pa.

This pricing guide is published annually, and the title varies from year to year. It contains listings of almost every boat or engine the prospective owner is likely to find for sale. No illustrations.

476. **BUC's 1974 New Boat Directory: Boat and Engine Manufacturer's Complete Specifications and List Prices.** 12th ed. Fort Lauderdale, FL, BUC International Corp., 1974. index. $5.95pa.

This is a guide to almost every new boat or engine available in the United States. No illustrations. Updated annually.

477. Bacon, Thorn. **Weather for Sportsmen: A New Kind of Book for Sailors and All Outdoorsmen.** New York, Motor Boating & Sailing, 1974. 115p. illus. $6.95. LC 74-21668. ISBN 0-910990-12-3.

Beginning with some record of "folklore sayings of sailors and fishermen," Bacon offers many simplified forecasting hints. He speaks of wind and clouds, storms, and the use of "nature signs" to have a safer outing. Specific suggestions are included for skin divers, fishermen, and boaters. Illustrated with drawings plus a number of color photos of clouds (from another book) on the jacket. An excellent book. Remember, now, that cold air flows downhill onto your otherwise snug campsite.

478. Bearse, Ray. **The Canoe Camper's Handbook.** New York, Winchester, 1974. 366p. illus. index. $7.95. LC 73-78836. ISBN 0-87691-094-0.

This is the most modern guide to a popular activity. There is good information on selecting and outfitting a canoe, camp clothing, equipment, and cooking. Canoeing techniques and water travel, including such topics as map and compass work, safety, and outboard motor troubleshooting, are well done. There is a glossary and directory-type information on places to canoe, canoe makers, equipment and food sources, guidebooks, map sources, and a short reading list. Illustrated with drawings and photographs, the coverage is of the United States and Canada.

479. Bottomly, Tom, comp. **Boatman's Handbook: The Keep-Aboard Almanac of Useful Boating Information.** 2nd ed. New York, Motor Boating, 1973. 308p. illus. $3.95pa. LC 76-172013. ISBN 0-910990-06-9.

Among the many topics discussed are: basic seamanship, piloting and navigation, weather, radio usage, radar gear, and general maintenance. Other chapters are devoted to racing, government regulations, information sources, hints about pets and shipboard cooking, photography, personal flags, and yachting etiquette. Safety and emergency procedures are emphasized, especially fires. Most of the material in this handy volume is directed at the salt-water sailor and those who ply the large lakes and inland waters. Highly recommended.

480. Bunker, Moss. **Damn the Garbage, Full Speed Ahead: A Handbook on the Joys and Sorrows of Pleasure Boating.** New York, McGraw-Hill, 1973. 149p. illus. index. $5.95. LC 72-10084. ISBN 0-07-007035-0.

This is entertaining information about boating, hopefully for pleasure. Bunker (a nom-de-plume) discusses boat selection, weather, the rules of the road, boat handling, cooking on the briny, basic navigation with charts and compass, water pollution, and marinas. The entire text of Chapter 10 reads: "It's the same as on land, except slightly damper." I'll leave you in the dark about that one! Several interesting charts are included: the Beaufort Scale, signals, chart symbols, and fishing suggestions. Safety and first aid receive some attention as well.

481. Burmeister, Walter F. **Appalachian Waters—The Delaware River and Its Tributaries.** Oakton, VA, Appalachian Books, 1974. $10.00; $7.50pa.

A guidebook for canoeists. Not examined.

482. Burmeister, Walter F. **Appalachian Waters—The Hudson River and Its Tributaries.** Oakton, VA, Appalachian Books, 1974. $10.00; $7.50pa.

A guidebook for canoeists. Not examined.

483. Cantin, Donald. **The Care & Maintenance of Small Boats.** New York, Manor Books, 1974. 177p. illus. $1.65pa.

WATER ACTIVITIES

Originally published in 1973 by Drake, this pocket manual covers painting and other finishing techniques, the repair of metal, wooden and fiberglass hulls, sailboat rigging and sails, engines, water, fuel and electrical systems, safety gear, trailers and personal equipment. Illustrated with photographs and drawings.

484. Cantin, Eugene. **Yukon Summer.** San Francisco, Chronicle Books, 1973. 198p. illus. $6.95. LC 73-84519. ISBN 0-97701-043-9.

Cantin rode a folding kayak down the Yukon River. He went over the mountains from Skagway to Bennett Lake in British Columbia and thence down the fifth longest river on the continent to Tanana in Alaska, a voyage of some 1,200 miles. All this in the summer of 1972. Illustrated with photographs, this tale will bring out the wanderlust in almost anyone. Nicely told.

485. Carrier, Rick, and Barbara Carrier. **Dive: The Complete Book of Skin Diving.** Rev. by Charles Berlitz. New York, Funk & Wagnalls (distr.: Crowell), 1973. 285p. illus. index. bibliog. $6.95. LC 73-4513.

A revision of the Carriers' 1963 work, this is an excellent introduction to the underwater world, with bits of history and hints of the dangers and delights of diving. Included here are discussions of the physiological aspects of diving, equipment (with suggestions for homemade gear), spearfishing and photography. Illustrated with many photographs.

486. Carter, Randy. **Canoeing Whitewater.** Rev. ed. Oakton, VA, Appalachian Books, 1974. 195p. illus. $4.75.

A guidebook, not examined, to canoeing in Virginia, West Virginia, and the Smoky Mountain streams.

487. **Chilton's Repair and Tune-Up Guide: Outboard Motors 30 Horsepower & Over.** Radnor, PA, Chilton Book Co., 1973. 284p. illus. $6.95; $4.95pa. LC 72-11533. ISBN 0-8019-5722-2; -5803-2pa.

This book contains general maintenance, troubleshooting, and repair instructions for the following engines: Chrysler, 1966-1972; Kiekhaefer Mercury, 1966-1971; Evinrude & Johnson, 1966-1972. Also included are safety and distress procedures.

488. **Chilton's Repair and Tune-Up Guide: Outboard Motors Under 30 Horsepower.** Radnor, PA, Chilton Book Co., 1973. 223p. illus. $6.95; $4.95pa. LC 72-10846. ISBN 0-8019-5723-0; -5802-4pa.

Maintenance, repair and troubleshooting information is given for these engines: Chrysler, 1966-1972; Kiekhaefer Mercury, 1966-1972; Evinrude & Johnson, 1966-1971. Safety and distress procedures are also suggested.

OUTDOOR RECREATION

489. Coles, K. Adlard. **Heavy Weather Sailing.** Tuckahoe, NY, John DeGraff, 1968. 304p. illus. index. $12.50. LC 68-26061. ISBN 0-8286-0029-5.

The sailor dreads the heavy storm at sea, especially when he's in a small craft. Hurricanes, gales, and "survival storms" are described by Coles, with suggestions for "getting through" based on his own experiences and those of many other seamen. The examples are European, but the danger and the possible solutions are universal. "The Meteorology of Depressions," by Alan Watts, is included. Drawings and photographs illuminate an excellent book for the deep-sea sailor. It's good reading for the armchair types, too.

490. Corbett, H. Roger, Jr., and Louis J. Matacia, Jr. **Blue Ridge Voyages, Vol. 1: One & Two Day River Cruises: Maryland, Virginia, West Virginia.** 3rd ed. Oakton, VA, Appalachian Books, 1972. 75p. illus. maps. price unknown (may be out of print).

This small book is a guide to canoeing on several streams in that area where the three states adjoin. In addition to the list of canoeing literature, there are hints on equipment and notes on the streams. A good guide.

491. Cotter, Edward F. **Multihull Sailboats: Sailing, Cruising, Racing.** 3rd ed. New York, Crown, 1971. 275p. illus. index. $6.95. LC 77-147323.

This is a general review of multihull craft from the native canoes of the Pacific and Indonesian peoples through outriggers, catamarans, and trimarans to the modern boats. There are suggestions on selecting a boat from the several types available, handling the craft, and cruising or racing it. A complete guide.

492. Creagh-Osborne, Richard. **This Is Sailing: A Complete Course.** Boston, Sail Books (distr.: Norton), 1973. 220p. illus.(col.). index. $12.95.

Several photographs and many color drawings by Peter Milne illustrate this "instructional course in small boat handling." Section 1 is about hull design and the basics of sail arrangement, rigging, rudders, and the other things that make up the boat. Also discussed are life jackets, clothing, handling and launching boats, and other elements of the craft. Section 2 is devoted to the actual sailing of a small boat: steering, sail handling, learning the wind, and other basic sailing skills. Section 3 gets into the advanced skills of towing, using spinnakers, sailing in poor weather, righting capsized boats, and using the trapeze. The drawings are very detailed. Sail Books also has a series of three motion pictures for classroom use with this excellent manual. Highly recommended.

493. D'Alpuget, Lou. **Successful Sailing.** New York, Sterling, 1972. 80p. illus. index. $6.95. LC 77-180469. Also available from Macmillan ($1.95pa.).

WATER ACTIVITIES

This is a large-format book illustrated with photographs and drawings. Arranged in lessons, it covers the parts of a boat, safety, sails and rigging, nautical terms, the effects of wind and water, and, mostly, boat handling. There is a glossary. The paperback edition is a good bet for beginners.

494. Devereaux, Frederick L., Jr. **Practical Navigation for the Yachtsman.** New York, Norton, 1972. 316p. illus. index. $12.00. LC 78-155984. ISBN 0-393-03171-3.

A good, basic introduction to latitude and longitude, charts, the magnetic compass, nautical time, plotting positions, electronic aids to navigation, the use of sextants for celestial navigation, and the use of almanacs. Numerous examples of the arithmetic are given with extracts from almanacs. There are several sample work forms and a list of references.

495. Duncan, Roger F., and John P. Ware. **A Cruising Guide to the New England Coast including the Hudson River, Long Island Sound, and the Coast of New Brunswick.** 7th ed. New York, Dodd, Mead, 1972. 603p. illus. index $15.00. LC 78-39650. ISBN 0-396-05599-0.

Intended to supplement the several official handbooks and charts for coastal navigation, this volume provides information on shore facilities, coastal geology, history, navigational hazards, and lively information of interest to yachtsmen. Illustrated with aerial photographs, maps and drawings, this handbook belongs in every Down East sailor's ditty bag.

496. Evans, Jay, and Robert R. Anderson. **Kayaking: The New Whitewater Sport for Everybody.** Brattleboro, VT, Stephen Greene, 1975. 192p. illus. (An Environmental Sports Book). $8.95; $4.95pa. LC 73-82750. ISBN 0-8289-0208-9; -0192-9pa.

An up-to-date book that suggests suitable boats and other equipment for a rapidly growing sport. Technique, both basic and whitewater, are described clearly and effectively. There are notes about kayak cruising, racing, and training. Drawings and photographs illustrate the book, which concludes with lists of clubs, manufacturers, and distributors. Highly recommended.

497. Furrer, Werner. **Water Trails of Washington.** Lynnwood, WA, Signpost, 1973. 31p. illus. maps. $2.50pa.

This little book outlines canoe/kayak routes in the state of Washington. There are also general suggestions and maps that indicate mileage and other features.

498. George, M. B. **Basic Sailing.** Rev. ed. New York, Motor Boating, 1971. 109p. illus. glossary. $2.50pa. LC 78-184227. ISBN 0-910990-03-4.

OUTDOOR RECREATION

This elementary guide outlines the types of sailboats, basic sailing and boat handling, emergency action, and handling lines; it includes a glossary of nautical terms. Illustrated with drawings and photographs. A good manual for beginners. Highly recommended.

499. Gibbs, Tony. **Practical Sailing.** New York, Motor Boating, 1971. 123p. illus. glossary. $5.95; $3.95pa. LC 70-172014. ISBN 0-910990-00-X; -01-8pa.

Beginning with the basics of the boat itself (hull, sails, etc.), Gibbs leads into the theory of sailing, basic boat handling, the various kinds of rigging, sailing in rough seas, and elementary line and knot work. Excellent drawings and photographs. A good handbook, more complex than the title by George.

500. Harlé, Philippe. **The Glénans Sailing Manual.** Rev. ed. Tuckahoe, NY, John deGraff, 1967. 448p. illus. index. $10.00. LC 65-21841. SBN 8286-0009-0.

This manual was first published in 1961 by the Centre Nautique des Glénans, a sailing school in Brittany. It is an excellent guide to boats, with discussions of displacement, buoyancy, trim, stability and the forces of wind and water, the sails and keel, steering, and boat handling gear. The sailing instructions include boat handling, safety in dinghies, and practical hints on hull and rigging maintenance. Copiously illustrated with excellent drawings, this has to be the best book for the sailor who has learned the basics and wants to become quite proficient. Highly recommended.

501. Harris, Thomas. **Down the Wild Rivers: A Guide to the Streams of California.** Rev. 2nd ed. San Francisco, Chronicle Books, 1973. 223p. illus. $4.95pa. LC 72-76932. ISBN 0-87701-072-04.

Harris offers hints on choosing a boat and its equipment and on classifying streams. The rivers described are: Klamath, Trinity, Eel, American, Consumnes, Merced, Mokelumne, Stanislaus, Tuolumne, Owens, Feather, Sacramento, Yuba, Cache Creek, Salmon, Scott, Big, Mad, Mattole, Navarro, Noyo, and Russian. A very good guidebook.

502. Hardman, Tom, and Bill Clifford. **Let's Go Water Skiing.** Winter Haven, FL, American Water Ski Association, 1969. $4.95pa. (Also published by Hawthorn.)

Not examined. This is the basic handbook issued by the national association.

503. Heaton, Peter. **Cruising: Sail or Power.** Baltimore, Penguin, 1970. 301p. illus. index. glossary. $1.95pa. SBN 14-046155-8.

Cruising is the art of making extended trips on the water for pleasure. Heaton gives good advice on the various sizes and kinds of boats for cruising,

WATER ACTIVITIES

using specific boats as examples. He discusses buying and berthing a boat, planning and executing a cruise, and learning the many arts and techniques of the sailor. Sea-sickness and other maladies are mentioned (and so is cooking, but not in the same chapter). Weather signs and hazards, maintenance, knotwork, and other topics are included. The glossary includes seamen's words in 10 European languages.

504. Heaton, Peter. **Sailing.** 4th ed. Baltimore, Penguin, 1970. 255p. illus. $1.45pa. ISBN 0-14-046049-7.

This beginner's guide to sailing has suggestions on choosing a proper boat, learning the nomenclature of boats and equipment, doing knotwork, moorings and anchors, learning the rigging, and handling the sails. Heaton includes the theory of sailing, elementary navigation, and weather lore. Finally, there are hints on the storage of boats and sails and the care of the hull. Drawings are used throughout and there is a selection of photographs. A handy, pocket-sized manual.

505. Henderson, Richard. **The Cruiser's Compendium: A Complete Guide to Coastal, Inland and Gunkhole Cruising.** Chicago, Regnery, 1973. 188p. illus. index. $12.50. LC 73-6473.

This is about sailboats and their use. Henderson discusses the types of boat and their construction features and layouts (cabins and storage areas), inspecting and testing a boat, learning about the instruments and mechanical things (batteries, depth sounders, etc.), fitting out, planning a trip, navigation, and many other aspects of sailing. Illustrated with photographs and drawings.

506. Henderson, Richard. **Hand, Reef and Steer.** Chicago, Regnery, 1965. 95p. illus. index. $5.95. LC 65-21488.

Illustrated with numerous drawings, this is a very good text on the art of sailing small boats. Henderson explains the various parts of a boat (the hull, sails, and rigging), the theory of sailing (including mooring and heavy weather sailing), the rules of the road, and safety and emergency actions.

507. Jenkinson, Michael. **Wild Rivers of North America.** New York, Dutton, 1973. 413p. illus. index. (A Sunrise Book). $12.95. LC 73-158604. ISBN 0-87690-099-6.

This is a very good introduction to river running. The bulk of the book is devoted to detailed descriptions and "guide notes" of several large and many smaller streams. The major rivers include: Rogue, Salmon, Rio Urique, Colorado, Suwanee, Yukon, Buffalo, Rio Grande, and the voyageurs route near Lake Superior. Streams in all parts of the United States, Canada, Mexico, and Central America are mentioned. Sketch maps and photographs complete the survey. There are appendices with lists of books, information and map

OUTDOOR RECREATION

sources, and directories of organizations, outfitters, and equipment suppliers. Well done and good reading for doer or dreamer.

508. Jones, Theodore A. **Learn to Sail.** Chicago, Rand McNally, 1971. 72p. illus. glossary. $1.95. LC 70-122888.

   This good short text covers the theory of sailing, boat handling, types of boats and rigging, emergency actions, bad weather, and capsizing.

509. Kittredge, Robert Y. **Self-Taught Navigation: Ten Easy Steps to Master Celestial Navigation.** Flagstaff, AZ, Northland Press, 1970. 81p. illus. $1.95pa. LC 73-121015. SBN 87358-049-4.

   Concise and clear, this book and an almanac will allow you to steer a straight course. The book covers: shooting the sun, moon, stars, and planets; the importance of time; and suggestions to boat owners about steering, handling, and the use of sextants.

510. Knight, Austin M. **Modern Seamanship.** 15th ed., rev. by John V. Noel, Jr. New York, Van Nostrand, 1972. 684p. illus. index. $14.95. LC 75-189513. ISBN 0-442-26047-4.

   Originally published in 1901, this is usually referred to as "Knight's Modern Seamanship" even on the jacket. It contains basic information on all types of ships and boats and their equipment, including handling, docking, towing, use in ice, rules of the road, oceanography and weather, and many other topics. Illustrated with photographs and drawings, this is probably more than the ordinary weekend boater needs, but he should know about the long-time bible for sailors.

511. Knight, David C. **How to Identify 101 Popular Sailboats Under 30 Feet.** New York, Arco, 1973. 108p. illus. $1.45pa. LC 72-86422. ISBN 0-668-2728-2.

   For each boat, there is a photograph, sail symbol, specifications, and name of manufacturer.

512. Knights, Jack. **Sailing Step by Step.** New York, Arc Books (Arco), 1963. 150p. illus. index. $0.95pa. LC 62-18283. SBN 668-00997-7.

   A member of the British Olympic Yachting Team, Knights explains sailboats and sailing in what the cover subtitle calls "A Complete Course." Nomenclature of boats and sails, how to sail, avoiding accidents, trailering a boat, and maintenance are covered.

513. Lane, Carl D. **Boatowner's Sheet Anchor: A Practical Guide to Fitting Out, Upkeep, and Alteration of the Small Wooden Yacht.** 2nd ed.

136

WATER ACTIVITIES

New York, Funk & Wagnalls, 1969. 304p. illus. index. $7.95. LC 68-31551.

Very interesting introduction to small yacht ownership. Covers the choosing of a suitable boat, paying for it, and taking care of it. Among the topics are: inspecting used boats, converting to sail or power, repairing hull and rigging, painting, interior layouts, masts and sails, dinghies, and storage. Illustrated with drawings by the author, this is a good one for a would-be or actual boat owner. Has a good feel to it.

514. Lane, Carl D. **The Cruiser's Manual: A Complete Handbook of Yacht Cruising Under Sail and Power.** 2nd ed. New York, Funk & Wagnalls, 1970. 387p. illus. index. $10.00. LC 68-18122. ISBN 0-308-70305-7.

All about the joys of cruising and what to look for on deck and below. There are notes on construction, layout, equipment, lighting, plumbing, heating, and ventilation. Cooking, social activities, kids and pets, shipboard etiquette, and the like receive attention. Further chapters are devoted to radio and radiophone operation, power plants, navigation and seamanship, insurance, and planning a cruise. Illustrated with numerous drawings.

515. Lane, Carl D. **The New Boatman's Manual: A Complete Manual of Boat Handling, Operation, Maintenance, and Seamanship.** 3rd ed. New York, Norton, 1962. 643p. illus.(part col.). index. $8.95.

Although the jacket is imprinted "YA," more than young adults will enjoy this book. It covers boat handling, regulations, use of anchors and moorings, signals, and much other sea lore. There is information about piloting and navigation, maintenance, safety, customs, and etiquette. Illustrated with drawings. Highly recommended.

516. Lee, Eric C. B., and Kenneth Lee. **Safety and Survival at Sea.** New York, Norton, 1972. 286p. illus. index. $8.25. SBN 393-03112-8.

This book is all about coping with shipwrecks, people fallen overboard, drownings, etc. The physiological aspects of exposure afloat are well described as are search and rescue procedures, treatment of survivors, safety and survival equipment, living off the sea, and getting along in general. The Lees have written a very good manual for sailors.

517. Liebers, Arthur. **The Complete Book of Water Sports: Completely Illustrated.** Rev. ed. New York, Coward, McCann & Geoghegan, 1972. 253p. illus. index. bibliog. $6.95. LC 75-189241. SBN TR698-10432-3.

The sports included are: water skiing, skin diving, scuba diving, spearfishing and underwater hunting, underwater photography, surf riding, whitewater canoeing and kayaking, swimming and water games, and competition

OUTDOOR RECREATION

diving, plus suggestions on safety. Illustrated with many photographs, this is a good, general introduction.

518. McCollam, Jim. **The Yachtsman's Weather Manual.** New York, Dodd, Mead, 1973. 190p. illus. index. glossary. $6.95. LC 72-7198. ISBN 0-396-06721-2.

Because bad weather may bring death, the sailor needs this important information. This book covers the origins of weather, winds, tides, and currents, low pressure areas, cloud forms, seasonal changes, and average off-shore weather conditions by month for both coasts of the United States. A very good resume.

519. McNair, Robert E. **Basic River Canoeing.** 2nd ed. Martinsville, IN, American Camping Association. $2.00pa.

Not examined. Although this title is widely advertised, I was unable to find a copy of it.

520. Makens, James C. **Makens' Guide to U.S. Canoe Trails.** Irving, TX, Le Voyageur, 1971. 86p. illus. $4.95pa.

Not examined. This book is widely advertised but mail to the publisher is returned as undeliverable. Good luck.

521. Malo, John W. **The Complete Guide to Houseboating.** New York, Macmillan, 1974. 182p. illus. index. $8.95. LC 73-2122. ISBN 0-02-579300-4.

This is a large, well-illustrated guide to the construction and use of a very popular type of boat. The topics include: selection of a boat, interior arrangements, insurance, nautical terms, shiphandling, rules of the road, equipment, and used boats. A variety of models are described, with specifications. There is a guide to houseboating areas and to rentals throughout the United States, plus lists of associations, publications, courses for beginners, and a few suppliers. Also discussed is the practice of living on a houseboat as a permanent home or at least for extended periods of time.

522. May, Judy Gail. **Scuba Diver's Guide to Underwater Ventures.** Harrisburg, PA, Stackpole, 1973. 222p. illus. $5.95; $2.95pa. LC 73-9949. ISBN 0-8117-1513-2; -2017-9pa.

Intended for new divers who want to know what to do with their newly learned skills. There is basic information on equipment, rules, and health problems but most of the book is concerned with hints on photography, treasure diving, ice diving, fish-watching, capturing marine life, collecting shells, and diving in caves. Careers in diving are also mentioned. Well done and interesting.

523. Mitchell, Leeds, Jr. **Introduction to Sailing.** Harrisburg, PA, Stackpole, 1971. 192p. illus. index. $5.95. LC 77-162448. ISBN 0-8117-0921-3.

Mitchell discusses the adventure of sailing, attending a school, choosing a boat, boarding safely and getting off again, basic sailing methods and boat handling, safety and traffic rules, equipment, and "what to wear." Illustrated with drawings, but not enough of them.

524. Morgan, Lael. **The Woman's Guide to Boating & Cooking.** Rev. ed. Garden City, NY, Doubleday, 1974. 254p. illus. index. bibliog. $7.95. LC 73-81444. ISBN 0-385-08072-7.

This is a general introduction to the world of boating, seamanship, social life afloat, and safety. Almost half the text covers the provisioning of a boat and using the food. There are a few drawings.

525. Nelson, William D. **Surfing: A Handbook.** New ed. Philadelphia, Auerbach, 1974. $9.95.

I've not seen this title, old edition or new, but I list it as something to check in your local library.

526. **The New Science of Skin and Scuba Diving.** 3rd rev. ed. New York, Association Press, 1968. 224p. illus. index. glossary. $2.95pa. LC 67-14583. SBN 8096-0453-1.

The Council for National Cooperation in Aquatics sponsored this guide to the basic requirements for diving, the physics of diving, medical aspects of the sport, equipment, planning, first aid, and general information on the underwater world. Illustrated with drawings. The appendix contains U.S. Navy decompression tables.

527. North, Wheeler J. **The Golden Guide to Scuba Diving: Handbook of Underwater Activities.** New York, Golden Press, 1968. 160p. illus.(part col.). index. (A Golden Handbook). $1.50pa. LC 68-22602.

This is probably all a beginner needs. It has information on the underwater environment, equipment and training, diving procedures, collecting things, photography, spearfishing, and careers. There is a short list of readings.

528. O'Keefe, M. Timothy, ed. **Erving's World Wide Skindiver's Guide.** 10th anniversary issue. Winter Park, FL, Erving Publishing Co., 1973. 231p. illus. $2.95pa.

Called "The Complete Guide to Diving Around the World," this contains several articles of general interest but is mostly a state-by-state and country-by-country directory to good diving locations. Specific locations within each area should make for easy and successful diving. There are also lists of clubs and air supply stations, recipes, and notes on shipwrecks. All peripatetic divers need this information.

OUTDOOR RECREATION

529. Perry, Ronald H. **Canoeing for Beginners.** New York, Association Press, 1967. 126p. illus. $1.75. LC 67-11069. SBN 8096-1775-7.

This is a "new, revised edition of *The Canoe and You.*" It is an introduction to the several canoe types, paddles, safety, and the art of paddling and caring for canoes. There are hints on teaching and standards at camps. Intended for class use.

530. Phillips, Norman. **All about Houseboats: Your Complete Guide to the Fabulous World of Inland and Coastal Cruising—the Evaluation, Selection, Purchase and Safe Use of Today's Houseboats.** New York, Motor Boating, 1972. 128p. illus. $3.95pa. LC 72-86443. ISBN 0-910990-05-0.

The title tells most of the story. There is also information on outfitting, trailering, handling, and engine troubleshooting. Boats from 16' to 65' are illustrated and described.

531. Pilkington, Roger. **Waterways in Europe: A Guide to Inland Cruising.** New York, Scribner's, 1974. 279p. illus. index. $8.95. LC 73-7213.

This is a good general introduction to boating in Europe. There are hints on appropriate boats and gear, needed paper work, best season, national customs and signals, getting through locks, etc. The countries included are: France, Germany, Belgium, Holland, and Scandinavia. Historical and navigational information abounds. Although it is intended for the sailor on the scene, the armchair sailor may wish to read it, too. The author has written a number of similar guides, all published in England by Macmillan.

532. Riviere, Bill. **Pole, Paddle & Portage: A Complete Guide to Canoeing.** Boston, Little, Brown, 1969. 259p. illus. index. glossary. bibliog. $3.95pa. LC 73-22726.

A former Maine guide describes the various types of canoe and their appropriate sizes. There are notes on paddling and poling, learning to read the water, using a motor, hunting and fishing along the way, safety and repairs, and suggestions on equipment for a trip. Illustrated with photographs and drawings, the book also includes a listing of possible canoeing waters by state and province with addresses of agencies and clubs and a directory of canoe makers. Published in hard cover in 1969 by Van Nostrand ($6.95). Recommended.

533. Robinson, William W. (Bill). **The Right Boat for You.** New York, Holt, 1974. 214p. illus. index. $7.95; $3.95pa. LC 73-16243. ISBN 0-03-012246-5; -088388-1pa.

Boats are being manufactured and sold in very large numbers and the investment is often considerable. The editor of our largest boating magazine

WATER ACTIVITIES

offers many suggestions: buying a used or new boat, the many types of boats (dinghies to ocean sailers), construction features, equipment, and legal matters such as insurance and registration. The appendices include U.S. Coast Guard equipment lists and offshore equipment lists. The book is illustrated with photographs and is recommended to all would-be boat owners.

534. Robinson, William W. **The Sailing Life and How to Enjoy It.** New York, Scribner's, 1974. 316p. illus. $12.50. LC 73-14403. ISBN 0-684-13642-2.

The editor of *Yachting* magazine presents a selection of his articles from that magazine and elsewhere. There is information on buying a new boat, taking that first cruise, cooking at sea and cruising with the family, racing, chartering a boat, and cruising in Europe and the South Seas. Illustrated with photographs, the book also contains a running account of the famous Gretel/Intrepid foul and protest in the 1970 America Cup Race. Very good reading.

535. Rothrock, Bill (pseud.). **A Somewhat Irreverent Look at the Design of the Long Distance Cruiser.** Costa Mesa, CA, Wilson Stone, 1974. 175p. illus. $8.95. LC 74-78744.

The author is a designer of many things, including boats. He thinks that the average ocean-going yacht, whether sail or power, is not worth the money paid for it. In this book, Rothrock blasts the boating industry, yachting magazines, designers, and the boat-buying public for producing or buying poorly designed and poorly built boats. Believing that a good cruiser must be comfortable, pleasant, and safe, he makes many excellent suggestions about size, accommodations, and type of boat (he prefers schooners and ketches). I'm not about to have a cruiser but I have thought the same things about truck campers that Bill Rothrock thinks about boats. An entertaining and useful book. This is, incidentally, a "hand written" book but it is readable. Recommended to anyone who's getting serious about an open-sea boat.

536. Ruck, Wolfgang E. **Canoeing and Kayaking.** New York, McGraw-Hill Ryerson, 1974. 95p. illus. $6.95. LC 73-21369. ISBN 0-07-077761-6.

This book is concerned with a description of canoes and kayaks and their methods of construction, the techniques of paddling the craft, touring, and tactics and training for whitewater and other races. This latter section is mostly about kayaking. The text is clear and interesting, the illustrations, both photos and drawings, very good. Canoeists have other choices, but these are the best kayaking instructions I've seen.

537. Rutstrum, Calvin. **North American Canoe Country.** New York, Macmillan, 1964. 216p. illus. $6.95. LC 64-18269.

OUTDOOR RECREATION

The best ways to handle canoes have changed very little since Indian days. Rutstrum discusses canoe travel in the wilderness, at organized camps, and with commercial outfitters. The very nice drawings by Les Kouba illustrate a book filled with hints on types of canoe, paddling/poling/portaging, needed equipment, and provisions. The chapter on notable canoe voyages has a good resume of the famous trip that Eric Sevareid, the television reporter, made from Minneapolis to Hudson's Bay as a teenager. This is one of the best books on canoeing.

538. **Sea Boating Almanac. 1974 Pacific Northwest Edition.** Costa Mesa, CA, Sea Magazine, 1974. 352p. illus.(part col.). $3.50pa. LC 65-2700. ISBN 0-88403-010-5.

This edition covers Oregon, Washington, and British Columbia coastal and river areas such as the Columbia and Willamette. In addition to many advertisements for boats and gear, there are chart catalogs, climate tables, tide tables, radio information and procedures, and just about everything a cruiser would like to know. Revised annually. The same publisher also issues these editions, which have similar material: *Sea Boating Almanac, 1974 Northern California & Nevada Edition* ($3.50pa.) and *Sea Boating Almanac, 1974 Southern California Edition* ($3.50pa.).

539. Smith, Hervey Garrett. **Boat Carpentry.** 2nd ed. New York, Van Nostrand Reinhold, 1965. 178p. illus. index. $7.50. LC 65-26467.

This good little book discusses wood and fiberglass boats and their construction and repair. Alterations, tools, adhesives, treatment and prevention of dry rot, and painting are covered. Illustrated with a few drawings.

540. Smith, Hervey Garrett. **The Marlinspike Sailor.** Tuckahoe, John deGraff, 1971. 131p. illus. index. $7.95. LC 77-143856. ISBN 0-8286-0044-9.

Marlinspike seamanship is the ability to make proper knots and lashings and to do all sorts of needle and palm work. Smith's drawings will show any landlubber how to knot, splice, make a heaving line or a turk's head, cleats, sea bags and sennits. A wonderful craft book updated from the 1960 edition by Rudder Publishing Co. Highly recommended.

541. Stensvold, Mike, ed. **Complete Book of Powerboats.** Los Angeles, Petersen, 1973. 240p. illus. $3.95pa. LC 73-75210.

This large-format, copiously illustrated book describes sport boats of all kinds: inflatables, houseboats, cruisers, and wooden, metal and fiberglass boats. Other sections cover the elements of boating, how boats are built, storing a boat, navigation, racing, and maintenance. There are also some test reports; catalogs of boats, engines, and accessories; and a glossary of terms.

WATER ACTIVITIES

542. Stephens, Kenneth. **Waterskiing.** New York, McGraw-Hill, 1974. 141p. illus. $6.95. LC 74-11780. ISBN 0-07-077762-4.

This is a concise and well-illustrated (with drawings and photos) introduction to a most popular outdoor recreation. Safety, boats and boat handling, basic instruction, conditioning, equipment care, and advanced skiing are covered. Quite a good book.

543. Steward, Robert M. **Boatbuilding Manual.** Camden, ME, International Marine, 1970. 220p. illus. index. $9.50. LC 77-133677. ISBN 0-87742-014-9.

An experienced builder, Steward has prepared a very clear introduction to the art of building a small motor or sail boat. He covers basic hull design and construction, choice of wood, use of fiberglass, choice of fastenings. The emphasis is on making a good firm boat, but there are also suggestions on planning the engine, fuel spaces, and mast attachments. Illustrated mostly with drawings. The principles could be applied to a boat of any reasonable size.

544. Street, Donald. **The Ocean Sailing Yacht.** New York, Norton, 1973. 703p. illus. index. glossary. $18.95. LC 73-8635. ISBN 0-393-03168-3.

Devoted to the specialized art of equipping and operating the deep-sea sailing yacht, the book covers construction details from hull to interior accommodations, anchors, dinghies, all the mechanical systems, navigation and seamanship, safety, and long distance sailing. There is an extensive glossary, lists of tools and supply sources, tables of materials and stores weights, line sizes and other items of interest. Illustrated with drawings and photographs and with stories and hints throughout. Highly recommended.

545. Sullivan, George. **Fell's Teen-Age Guide to Skin and Scuba Diving.** New ed. New York, Fell, 1975. $6.95.

Not examined.

546. **The Surfboard Builders' Yearbook, vol. 9.** La Mesa, CA, Transmedia, 1973. 64p. illus. $4.00pa.

The 1973 edition is a well-illustrated manual for building a surfboard from high-density foam. Transmedia also distributes full-size patterns.

547. Taylor, Zack. **101 Ways to Go Boating for under $1000.** New York, Funk & Wagnalls, 1970. 182p. $7.95. LC 79-104964. ISBN 0-308-70398-7.

Among the many ways to enjoy boating on a budget, Taylor mentions such methods as using aluminum rowboats, various small sailboats, inflatables,

OUTDOOR RECREATION

used boats, building your own or renting a boat, and using a canoe.

548. Toghill, Jeff. **The Boat Owner's Maintenance Manual.** Tuckahoe, NY, John DeGraff, 1970. 308p. illus. index. $12.50. ISBN 0-8286-0043-0.

This is all about materials and how to use them for hull maintenance, the upkeep of mast and sails, engine repair, and other general work about a boat. Illustrated mostly with photographs. Highly recommended.

549. Townsend, Sallie, and Virginia Ericson. **The Amateur Navigator's Handbook.** New York, Crowell, 1974. 226p. illus. index. $7.95. LC 73-15985. ISBN 0-690-00192-4.

Intended for beginners or other amateurs, this manual describes the types of charts and the information on them, compasses, plotting courses, determining fixes, depth sounding, using the several types of radio or radar devices; it also includes information on tides, fogs, and night cruising. There are lists of publications and a selection of other valuable hints for boaters. Celestial navigation is not included.

550. U.S. Coast Guard. Office of Boating Safety. **The Skipper's Course.** Washington, DC, Government Printing Office, 1972. 96p. illus. $1.50. Stock number S/N 5012-00050.

This is a programmed course for neophytes in the small boat game. Each section contains an illustrated text and review questions on a variety of nautical topics: pertinent regulations, safety, rules of the road, boat handling, emergencies, and trailering a boat. As I write this entry, the Government Printing Office is so slow in filling orders that it is being investigated by the General Accounting Office. Good luck.

551. Verney, Michael. **Boat Maintenance by the Amateur.** New York, Winchester, 1971. 288p. illus. index. $6.95. LC 70-16539. ISBN 0-87691-058-4.

Originally published in England, this is a good introduction to keeping a boat in operating condition. There is material on buying a boat, the tools and materials needed, the preparation and refinishing of the hull, maintenance of sails, rigging and mechanical equipment, and storing a boat either in the water or ashore. A table of British and American boating terms is included and the work is illustrated with drawings and photographs.

552. Wallace, Bill. **Sailing: A Guide to Handling, Equipping, Maintaining, and Buying the Small Sailboat.** Rev. ed. New York, Golden Press, 1966. 160p. illus.(part col.). glossary. (A Golden Handbook). $1.50pa. LC 61-8493.

WATER ACTIVITIES

This general look into sailboats and their use offers advice on the types of sailboats and rigging, on equipment and handling, and racing. Most boating books have more about handling than is given here.

553. Wynn, Peter. **Foam Sandwich Boatbuilding: A Practical Guide to Home Construction.** Camden, ME, International Marine, 1972. 128p. illus. $9.95. LC 72-87223. ISBN 0-87742-027-0.

Foam sandwich construction is a method of building something of foam between two layers of fiberglass or other material. Very clear and complete instruction is given about building the mold, applying foam over the mold, coating with fiberglass, and finishing both surfaces. There are hints and details galore, together with photographs and drawings. The method can be used to build anything from geodesic domes to dog houses.

554. Zadig, Ernest A. **The Complete Book of Boating: An Owner's Guide to Design, Construction, Piloting, Operation and Maintenance.** Englewood Cliffs, NJ, Prentice-Hall, 1972. 640p. illus. index. glossary. $12.95. LC 77-98528. ISBN 0-13-160143-1.

This rather large book covers the theory and practice of designing and building small boats and their components (hulls, engines, drive train, steering and other controls); the arrangement of spaces and of equipment; sailboats and sailing; outboard boats and motors; and the handling of boats. The latter section deals with seamanship, the rules of the road, navigation, safety and emergency procedures, and weather. There is further information on repair and maintenance work, using marinas, boating law, buying and selling a boat, and learning the game through the many courses offered nationwide. Photographs and drawings illustrate this very comprehensive book.

AERIAL ACTIVITIES

... come Josephine!

The aerial sports (no, I don't mean the martini-sippers in the 747's upstairs lounge) remain popular but the emphasis changes, with new ideas and aircraft appearing at odd intervals. When I was a kid, barnstorming was quite the thing, and folks could get airplane rides in such devices as Curtiss Jennies, Wacos, or Travelaires. I never got to do this because barnstormers never landed on my block in New York City—and I didn't have the fare even if they had. Chugging around in a Piper Cub or a Taylorcraft remains my idea of fun in the skies, but other people get a charge from soaring, parachuting, ballooning, hang gliding, and other lofty shenanigans that are either unknown to me or of such a nature that I dare not mention them in this, a family publication.

Soaring is an interesting activity that seems to be growing in popularity at a fairly good rate. Sailplanes are used in this sport, these being light-weight craft, quite streamlined, with long, narrow wings. The idea is to find thermal updrafts, aerial "waves," or whatever natural phenomena the happy Icarus can discover to keep him airborne. Most sailplanes are launched by being towed aloft with an airplane. The cost of the tow and the expense of the sailplane combine to make this as expensive as flying a powered plane. Many years ago, things called "gliders" were used for elementary flight instruction (e.g., the Luftwaffe and the Soviet forces), but these tended to come down rather quickly. Gliders were used extensively during World War II to carry troops and supplies into battle zones. The sailplanes of today are entirely different machines, even though they can be used for other than sporting purposes. Some intrepid maniacs fly heavily instrumented sailplanes into hurricanes, and a scientific bird-watcher in East Africa used a sailplane to follow the movements of vultures and other birds that soared from thermal to thermal over amazingly great areas in search of the next dead zebra. Some of the oceanic birds, too, are able to remain aloft for extended flights, utilizing the natural ways of doing things, which man has only recently learned. I expect that some nut will try to soar across the Atlantic one day. I wish him better luck than the unhappy balloonist who died in the attempt early in 1974. Over 12,000

Americans use sailplanes and, since these craft retail at $5,000 to $20,000, the economic impact must be reckoned with.

Jumping out of an airplane, with or without a parachute, is not my idea of recreation, but parachuting is a widely popular way to get downstairs in a hurry. When I first began flight training in the United States Navy, during World War II, I quickly resolved not to leave the aircraft by means of the silken canopy unless the plane was afire or breaking apart. For one thing, I was (and am) too chicken, but I also had a practical reason—I rarely had a parachute that fit. I was sure that I would have sailed right through the harness when the 'chute opened up. Of course, with my luck, the thing probably wouldn't have opened anyway. I recall one horrible moment when the seat of an airplane flew outward as I become inverted in a slow roll. I had visions of trying to disengage the seat before I could open the parachute, but happily for me and for the Navy's accident record, the last bolt in the seat assembly held everything inside. I recovered my heart and stomach later in the week. If I had been practicing outside loops, the story might have had a somewhat hilarious if deadening result. My older son has a buddy who has made a few jumps, so there has been some filial talk of attempting this, I hope, decelerating practice but nothing has come of it so far. One old friend who had been a paratrooper had a wife who disapproved of this sport, so Gene would sneak out to the airport under the pretext of having to work on Saturday mornings; he even used a fictitious name to cover his tracks.

I can look through my front window at times to see the National Guard Ranger company jumping from a large helicopter into the confines of historic old Fort Missoula. We also have, near this Montana town, the Smoke Jumper Center of the United States Forest Service. This is a school to train firefighters as parachutists, and it is also an aerial depot with large stores of firefighting equipment. The smokejumpers do a magnificent job and they are frequently called on to perform. During the Spring 1974 streaker craze, we had a vainglorious announcement that a streaker would descend upon the University of Montana campus in nothing but his parachute. The event never came off because, I suspect, the would-be descendent realized that something else might have come off, too. And it *was* pretty cold that day.

Ballooning is the oldest of the practical aerial activities, ever since the Montgolfier brothers charmed their Parisian neighbors using paper balloons and hot air, a commodity that seems to abound in the land of the Franks. A flying saucer report in Carbondale, Illinois, some years ago resulted in the discovery of several boys who had made a paper balloon with a candle held beneath to supply the needed heat and consequent lift. The craft made an eerie spectacle as it sailed through the dusk, glowing in soft orange hues. The serious devotee of this sport may purchase a somewhat sturdier and a much larger and more colorful balloon for his cross-country travel. I don't think that many modern sport balloons are held aloft with hydrogen or helium, these days (hydrogen, of course, explodes at odd times); the common method of supplying lift is through the use of a propane flame held beneath the open bottom of the generally striped globe. I should like to try this fairly silent method of heavenly transport, even though one is at the mercy of an often errant wind. I have read of complaints from nudist camps and sunbathers that balloonists cruise quite low and give no warning; but I suppose that there are folk who will complain if the Angel Gabriel appeared in a balloon blowing his mighty message with an elongate cornet.

    The most rapidly growing aerial sport is what is generally called "hang gliding." Over a hundred outfits are making these "foot launched" machines and the things appear almost everywhere. They are endemic, of course, in California (where just about anything is endemic), but I have sat me down to supper in Missoula, Montana, and glanced up to see eight hang gliders arranged in a neat and reasonably colorful formation on the hill behind the house. Some of these pilots can remain aloft (with the gliders, naturally) for quite lengthy periods. I have timed a couple of flights at 15 to 20 minutes, so there is a seat of some sort for the pilot. Hanging by his hands for that length of time would do in the hardiest calisthene. The climb back up the hill is probably worth the effort. My younger son, Jim, announced in June of 1974 that he would like to try hang gliding, so we may be afflicted with yet another kind of nut. At first glance, this remarkable recreation seems a spectacular way to accomplish the second sin of Judas Iscariot, but I am assured that deaths are not common (I've read of two in Southern California during the summer of 1974), although sprains and broken bones are not unknown. There is very little protection for our pendulous pilot but the followers of the sport (may I call them "hangers-on?") remind one that they don't achieve any great altitude. I have seen a number of these craft at heights of several hundred feet, however, and I'm sure that a fairly free-fall declination from such an altitude would break or macerate a number of parts, public and private. Some of the descents witnessed near my place have been on the lower end of the humiliation scale, involving flights of several feet. One safely executed but misdirected flight ended in a large tree on the University of Montana oval, to the applause of several hundred happy hookey players. Hang gliders are relatively cheap or easy to build, especially from kits, so a good many of them are around in the hands of incompetents. These seemingly simple aircraft are actually very tricky machines which must be, among other things, properly balanced and rigged. Proper instruction is a must in this sport just as much as in flying, ballooning, soaring, or parachuting.

    If someone says he's "going flying," he probably means in an airplane; "planes" are still the most common of the craft that cavort through the friendly skies. A goodly pride of small planes will be seen purring around almost any airport on a clear and not-too-windy day. The number of such planes manufactured in the United States and the world is rather large and names such as Cessna, Piper, and the not-so-venerable Bede are household words to many of us. Flying is expensive, commercial propaganda to the contrary, and will remain so. I learned to fly in a Taylorcraft (Mr. Taylor invented the Piper Cub, strangely enough) and I loved it. My very first "check ride" was quite an event. The engine conked out as I neared the airport after the ride, but I thought nothing of it, believing that the inspector had turned off the switch as part of the test! He was more surprised than I, as I discovered rather quickly, but he let me do what I could and I managed to land right in the middle of the circle painted on the end of the runway. I received the hearty congratulations of both the check pilot and my horror-stricken instructor, but I never again rose to similar heights of aerial glory.

But so much for hangar flying. We are concerned here with books and periodicals for the beginner in some kind of aerial recreation, so elementary texts and "how-to" titles are included. Most libraries are glutted with books about airplanes and aviation history; the devotee of the wild, blue yonder is urged to visit his local Carnegie massage parlor for further uplifting delights.

Let me emphasize again that proper instruction is imperative and that books are only an introduction. Most airport shops will have a supply of books and of aeronautical charts to supplement local tuition. Up and at 'em and good luck!

555. **Air Progress Sport Aircraft, 1973.** Los Angeles, Petersen Publishing Co., 1973. 192p. illus.(part col.). $2.95pa. LC 73-86795. ISBN 0-8227-0047-6.

Any pilot (actual, would-be, or has been) will enjoy this well-illustrated guide to homebuilt aircraft, antique and classic planes, hang gliding and soaring, acrobatics, racing, and other airy stuff. There are cut-away drawings of a number of planes, pilot reports on homebuilt and standard craft, and directories of engines, books, events, associations, navigation and other equipment, plans for homebuilts, and other goodies. Highly recommended.

556. Bowers, Peter M. **Soaring in America.** 2nd ed. Los Angeles, Soaring Society of America, 1967. 17p. illus. $0.25.

A very brief introduction to soaring—what it's like, how one begins, what it costs, etc.

557. Carrier, Rick. **Fly: The Complete Book of Sky Sailing.** New York, McGraw-Hill, 1974. 128p. illus. $7.95. LC 74-4221. ISBN 0-07-010097-7.

A copiously illustrated book about hang gliding. It describes the several types of glider now available and includes information on learning to fly the little devils. There are lists of manufacturers, publications, and clubs, plus drawings and photographs. The instructions are better than those in Poynter's *Hang Gliding.* Highly recommended.

558. Dixon, Peter L., and Jay Fionella. **Ballooning.** New York, Ballantine, 1972. 209p. illus. $1.50pa. SBN 345-02641-1.

Short of jumping off a cliff, ballooning is the oldest form of human flight. This book is primarily a history of ballooning, with some general information about the sport. Only about 50 pages are devoted to the art and technique of ballooning, but there are lists of manufacturers, schools, clubs, and societies. Recommended.

559. Doherty, William E., Jr. **After Solo.** Elmira, NY, Schweizer, 1974. c.125p. illus. $2.95pa.

The cover subtitle reminds us that this is about "Soaring Adventures in the I-26," which is made by the Schweizer firm. Illustrated with photos and drawings, this is a collection of short articles about soaring and sailplanes to whet the appetite of the novice pilot. There are tales of clubs, memorable flights, competitions, and other interesting material, including a glossary and a bibliography. Recommended.

560. **Federal Aviation Regulations for Pilots, 1974.** Fallbrook, CA, Aero, 1973. 132p. $1.95pa. LC 60-10472.

This resume of pertinent federal regulations for pilots includes parts 1, 61, 67, 71, and 91 of the Federal Aviation Regulations (FAR), which are about definitions, pilot certificates, medical standards, airway designations, and general operating rules. Also appended is Part 430 of the National Transportation and Safety Board, which pertains to aircraft accidents. A must for all pilots.

561. Flying Magazine, Editors of. **America's Flying Book.** New York, Scribner's, 1972. 365p. illus. index. bibliog. $12.95. LC 72-1213. SBN 684-13003-3.

The joys of flying are introduced in this well-illustrated work, which has an introduction by Ernest K. Gann. It is an introduction to the variety of aircraft and activities available to Americans. Chapters cover learning to fly, buying used planes, taking cross-country trips, business flying, racing, acrobatics, soaring and ballooning, and homemade planes. Information on engines, aircraft construction, controls, instruments, and the history of aviation are complemented with appendices, which list organizations and clubs, describe the Federal Aviation Administration, and give a directory of available aircraft. Highly recommended.

562. Francis, Mary. **The Beginner's Guide to Flying.** New York, Transatlantic Arts, 1969. 192p. illus. index. $9.50.

Intended for those interested in learning what flying is all about, this guide by an English pilot explains basic theory of flight, piloting, the use of instruments, navigation and the use of maps, getting a license, using the radio, safety, acrobatics, weather, and regulations (these being British regulations). Each chapter is lettered, rather than numbered, with the radio alphabet (Alpha, Bravo, etc., through Zulu), making it easy to learn. Basically a good book, but several things just do not apply in the colonies. Recommended.

563. Guerny, Gene, and Joseph A. Skiera. Rev. by L. W. Reithmaier. **Pilot's Handbook of Weather.** 2nd ed. Fallbrook, CA, Aero, 1974. 191p. illus. glossary. $7.95. LC 74-77535. ISBN 0-8168-7355-0.

Originally published in 1964, this guide discusses the importance of weather knowledge to pilots, the basics of weather, and the effects of various weather phenomena on aircraft and on flight procedures. The revision updates the information and notes the newer methods of gathering and presenting meteorological data. Highly recommended.

564. Gunby, R. A. **Sport Parachuting Handbook: The 1970's Textbook of Sport Parachuting.** 4th ed. Denver, CO, Jeppesen, 1972. 162p. illus. $3.50pa.

A well-known aviation publisher offers a good introduction to a modern sport. There are chapters about parachutes and their use and care, aircraft procedures, actual jumping methods, control of the canopy, safety and emergency measures, jumping at night, and jumping into water. The drawings and photos are good and readings are suggested wherever appropriate. Recommended.

565. **How to Get Started in Soaring: Guide to Sky Sailing.** Elmira, NY, Schweizer, 1968. 65p. illus. $1.00pa.

Basically a booklet designed to stimulate interest in soaring and in Schweizer sailplanes, this contains a history of soaring, description of the various types of plane, and information on learning to fly. There are lists of readings, of soaring records, and of clubs. Schweizer also publishes a series of Soaring School Manuals in four volumes (*Beginners*, $4.00; *Transition*, $3.50; *Commercial*, $5.00; and *Instructors*, $6.50) and several other titles of interest. All are recommended.

566. Langewiesche, Wolfgang. **Stick and Rudder: An Explanation of the Art of Flying.** New York, McGraw-Hill, 1944. 389p. illus. index. $8.95. LC 44-3302. SBN 07-036240-8.

The basic theory of flight and of piloting is well explained in this classic book. The author tells how a plane stays up, what effects the controls have, elementary maneuvers, taking off and landing. Leighton Collins has contributed a chapter on "The Dangers of the Air," which is about spins, poor techniques, etc. Illustrated with drawings, this text is very clear and easy to understand. Highly recommended.

OUTDOOR RECREATION

567. Lincoln, Joseph Colville. **On Quiet Wings: A Soaring Anthology.** Flagstaff, AZ, Northland Press, n.d. 320p. illus. $30.00. LC 70-174993. ISBN 0-87358-082-6.

An anthology of articles from *Soaring* magazine from 1937 to 1969. Recommended.

568. Misenhimer, Ted G. **Aeroscience: Basic Textbook for Aeroscience Courses.** Culver City, CA, Aero Products, 1970. 798p. illus. index. insert map. $12.98. LC 77-79613.

This is actually meant to be a high-school textbook, but I include it because it is a readily available and comprehensive introduction to theories of flight, aircraft construction and operation, meteorology, navigation, rules of flight, space flight, physiology, the history of aviation, and career opportunities. Illustrated with many drawings and photographs. Highly recommended.

569. Park, Jack. **Simplified Performance Testing for Hang Gliders.** $2.00.

This booklet was not examined. It may be obtained from the author at 15237 Lakeside, Sylmar, CA 91342.

570. Poynter, Dan. **Hang Gliding: The Basic Handbook of Skysurfing.** Rev. ed. Santa Barbara, CA, Author, 1974. 201p. illus. $9.95; $5.95pa. LC 74-77827. ISBN 0-915516-03-9; -02-0pa.

This book reviews the long and honorable history of hang gliding, but it is mostly concerned with the sport today. Poynter covers the construction, maintenance, and testing of the machines and has extensive data on the materials used. The design of hang gliders is discussed, and there is a listing of most of the available models. Other sections are about the actual flying: launching, guiding, etc. Drawings and photos. Highly recommended.

571. Poynter, Dan. **Manned Kiting: The Basic Handbook of Tow Launched Hang Gliding.** Santa Barbara, CA, Author, 1974. 98p. illus. $3.95pa. LC 74-20186.

A variant of hang gliding, manned kiting requires a boat, vehicle or winch to pull the glider into the air. This manual describes the historic background of manned kiting and gives much technical information in addition to federal regulations; there are lists of associations, publications, and sources of supplies. The glider may be tethered or free and it may actually even be a parachute. This sort of sport is often seen on television shorts about water skiing. Illustrated with drawings and photographs, the book is a complete and recommended one.

572. Reithmaier, L. W. **Private Pilot's Guide.** With **Supplement.** Fallbrook, CA, Aero, 1972. 288p. illus. index. $7.95. LC 70-188851. ISBN 0-8168-7600-2.

Illustrated mostly with drawings, this compact guide explains the many things a private pilot must know: elementary aerodynamics, aircraft systems and instruments, radio and navigational gear, aeronautical charts, weather and weather briefing, flight planning, and emergency action. Included is a sample aeronautical chart. The *Supplement* includes a sample written examination and excerpts from pertinent federal publications. Highly recommended.

573. Schweizer Aircraft Corp. **Basic Manual: A Standardized Guide to Training and Advanced Soaring.** Elmira, NY, Schweizer, 197?. c.200p. illus. $4.00pa.

In addition to something about the history and lore of soaring, this booklet contains syllabi for several levels of flight instruction. There is good information about towing, radio procedures, government regulations, and other study materials. Intended for the non-pilot and for the pilot who wishes to know how he can advance to an instructor rating. Recommended.

574. Sellick, Bud. **Parachutes and Parachuting: A Modern Guide to the Sport.** Englewood Cliffs, NJ, Prentice-Hall, 1971. 223p. illus. index. $7.95. LC 75-153950. ISBN 0-13-648535-9.

An excellent guide for the beginner. There are many facts about the history of parachuting and information about testing, safety, and professional and sport jumping. Appendices list record holders and the basic safety rules of the sport. Many illustrations. Well written and very informative. Highly recommended.

575. Simonson, Leroy. **Private Pilot Study Guide.** Glendale, CA, Aviation Book Co., 1970. c.400p. illus. $13.00; $9.00pa. LC 76-120103. ISBN 0-911720-02-2; -01-4pa.

The prospective or beginning pilot needs the basic information on ground school studies presented in this book. The many sections include those on: aircraft and engine operation, flight instruments, navigation, weather, federal regulations, radio operation, and parts of the Airman's Information Manual. Flight maneuvers are not covered. This is one of the many texts used in aviation schools, and it is listed as an excellent example of that genre. Anyone enrolling in a ground school program will use whatever text is required.

576. Tanner, Hans, ed. **Fun Flying Guide.** Los Angeles, Petersen, 1971. 192p. illus. $2.50pa.

A large magazine-type publication with information about all aspects of modern aviation: learning to fly, the cost of flying, buying a new or used plane, joining a club. There is a directory of planes available in 1971 and of plans for building a plane at home, plus "pilot impressions" of 17 fairly common planes. Quite a bit of good, well-illustrated information. Recommended.

577. Wind Drifters Balloon Club (see list of organizations).

Publishes several manuals on ballooning. These are intended for the club's training programs and I don't know whether they are available otherwise.

578. Wolters, Richard A. **The Art and Technique of Soaring**. New York, McGraw-Hill, 1971. 197p. illus. $14.95. LC 78-168460. ISBN 0-07-071560-2.

An active soaring pilot, Wolters gives a bit of history of the sport but the book is mostly concerned with concise instruction for the beginner. Among the topics covered are: flight theory, being towed, developing flying skills, finding thermals and other ways of staying in the air, landing, and cross-country flight. The drawings, by Edward Hanke, are excellent. Throughout the book, the emphasis is on good technique and safety. Highly recommended for all pilots.

COUNTRY LIVING

... how *are* you gonna keep 'em down on the farm?

This section on getting along in the country may not seem very closely related to outdoor recreation, but we think there is some good to be gotten from it. Actually, a good many recreationists spend a lot of time in the farther places; either have need for this information for incidental reasons or they may decide to try to "make it" on the land. In my excursions into Montana's off-road parts, I often imagine how I would live off the land if I were suddenly stranded. Sometimes it's rather frightening, especially when I consider that Lewis and Clark almost starved to death traversing the country near my home! In any event, I've tried to list a few books and periodicals that may give the reader a skill or a bit of information he may need. I've included a couple of "gardening" books that I have found useful, but most of the titles are of a more general nature.

I think it unfortunate that some of the media have tried to portray the "back-to-the-land" movement as something recent and something leftist and hippie and drug-related. Ever since man emerged on the earth, there have been folk who subsist on what they can gather in the wilds or grow for their own use. We have millions of people doing these things today. And most of them are not hop-heads or leftist radicals who hate the United States and its political system. Actually, the sort of life we are dealing with would be prohibited in a socialist planned economy. The point is that one doesn't have to be a leftist to enjoy country living or a clean and simple environment, and I wish that the magazine and other media outlets would at least admit it.

Admittedly, many of the newcomers to simple, country living have no obvious regard for their personal appearance or for the neatness of their surroundings. Junk may be piled up to incredible heights on the new "homestead" and the denizens of the pile may resemble a group just rescued from a coal mine disaster. This should not dissuade the public from accepting a different solution to a problem, but it is doubtful whether personal filth is a necessary complement to country living. If many of our recently moved country dwellers would clean up themselves and their surroundings, the public and the police would probably leave them alone. In my area of Montana, there

OUTDOOR RECREATION

have been cases of "hippies" trying to live off the country by raiding vegetable gardens and homes. This leads to a certain amount of opposition from the raided public. Several years ago, a "commune" was broken up near Missoula. The cries of "persecution" went up and the community was duly aroused. I think that the law enforcement people would have stayed away except for the fact that a couple of wanted criminals were involved and the commune residents didn't look like good neighbors. Some communal groups have been successful because, I think, they have tried to be good neighbors and have not attempted to entice the local kids into drug use or sexual orgies. These later considerations will really get the locals' backs up in a hurry and trouble is inevitable. But, let's get back to the books.

579. Abler, Bill. **The Sensuous Gadgeteer: Bringing Tools and Materials to Life.** Philadelphia, Running Press, 1973. 114p. illus. index. $3.95pa.

"*The Sensuous Gadgeteer* is a guide to tools, materials and procedures that are within the reach of a small basement shop." Or a shop in the garage or barn. This is an introduction to the "theory" and use of hammers, saws, hacksaws, knives, sharpening stones, soldering, metal work, using plastics, making molds and casts, etc. Fascinating bits of information for any small shop worker. Illustrated with drawings.

580. Anderson, L. O., and Harold F. Zornig. **Build Your Own Low-Cost Home.** New York, Dover, 1972. 206p. illus. $4.95pa. ISBN 0-486-21525-3.

This is a compilation of material published by the U.S. Department of Agriculture. There are working drawings, lists of materials and other needed information for the carpenter. A good, handy book for the craftsman. Dover publishes other books on similar subjects, so a look through their catalog will be rewarding.

581. Angier, Bradford. **How to Build Your Home in the Woods.** New York, Hart, 1952. 310p. illus. $2.45pa. LC 52-13865. SBN 8055-0069-3.

Intended for the woods dweller, this handbook contains instruction on choosing a site, cutting and seasoning timber, splitting and preserving wood, building a foundation, and raising the house. Furniture, stoves, and heating methods are described, and there are hints on water supplies, making fences, and other related topics.

582. Angier, Bradford. **We Like It Wild.** New York, Collier, 1973. 212p. $1.50pa.

Brad and Vena Angier took to the wilds of northwestern Canada some years ago and built a cabin, hunted their food, and otherwise became homesteaders. This book is a record of their life—what they did, how they did it, how they liked it. Anyone thinking of really living in the far-out parts of the world ought to read this little book for its cautions and its promises. Originally published in 1963.

583. Bealer, Alex. **The Art of Blacksmithing.** New York, Funk & Wagnalls, 1969. 425p. illus. index. $10.00. LC 68-564655. ISBN 0-308-70371-5.

The ancient and honorable art of the blacksmith receives its due respects in this volume. Bealer describes the trade, its tools, and its techniques. The author's drawings are used throughout. Forging, welding, decorative work, and making flint locks are among the many topics covered in a marvelous look at a trade that is apparently making a comeback.

584. Beard, Daniel Carter. **The American Boy's Handy Book: What to Do and How to Do It.** Rutland, VT, Tuttle, 1966. 391p. illus. index. $5.50. LC 66-15858. ISBN 0-8048-0006-5.

First published in 1882, with the title reversed, this book by the founder of the Boy Scouts is filled with ideas for projects: making kites, fishing, camping, making musical instruments, building snowhouses, puppetry. Lots of good ideas for youngsters in the country.

585. Beard, Daniel Carter. **Shelters, Shacks, and Shanties.** New York, Scribner's, 1972. 243p. illus. $4.95. SBN 684-12805-5.

This reprint of a 1914 title has instructions for building all sorts of shelters with an axe or hatchet: birch bark and tar paper shacks, sod houses, log cabins, etc., from simple lean-tos to rather elaborate dwellings. Good hints for cabin builders.

586. Beard, Lina, and Adelia B. Beard. **The American Girl's Handy Book: How to Amuse Yourself and Others.** Rutland, VT, Tuttle, 1969. 474p. illus. index. $6.25. LC 69-11086. ISBN 0-8048-0008-1.

The nostalgia continues with a book by Dan Beard's sisters. Aimed at the girls of yesteryear, this one provides instructions for preserving wild flowers, organizing walking clubs, modeling in wax and clay, candy making, exercises for fitness, decorating windows, etc. There are many good suggestions, illustrated with drawings by the authors. These sisters founded the "Pioneers of America" for girls and watched it grow into the Girl Scouts.

587. Belanger, Jerome D. **The Homesteader's Handbook to Raising Small Livestock.** Emmaus, PA, Rodale, 1974. 246p. illus. index. $8.50. LC 73-88254. ISBN 0-87857-075-6.

The animals included in this handbook are: rabbits, chickens, turkeys, geese, guinea fowl, ducks, pigeons, goats, sheep, and hogs. The information is about breeds, feeding, breeding, raising young, cooking the resulting food products, and hints of all kinds. Anyone intending to raise any of the listed critters should have this excellent volume—it has more good material in a neat package than any other book. Illustrated with drawings and photographs.

588. Blandford, Percy W. **Country Craft Tools.** Detroit, Gale Research, 1974. 240p. illus. index. $8.50. LC 73-22569. ISBN 0-8103-2011-8.

With the increase of interest in handcraftmanship, especially in rural settings, there is also an increase of interest in the nature of hand tools—especially old tools, which were often quite specialized. Blandford is British, so the emphasis is on tools used in his homeland, but the American names are noted and the work of the cooper and other tradesmen was similar on both sides of the water. The various chapters cover axes, knives, hammers, chisels, saws, planes, drills, agricultural and weaving tools, and the work of using all these artifacts. The many illustrations include drawings and photographs. This is a very informative book and, indeed, a charming one. Highly recommended.

589. Blandford, Percy W. **Knots & Splices.** New York, Arco, 1967. 79p. illus. $4.50; $0.95pa. LC 65-25270. ISBN 0-668-01330-3; -01331-1pa.

Whether for boating, camping, climbing, fishing, or fun, the knots and ropework described and illustrated here will tie up most any problem.

590. Boericke, Art, and Barry Shapiro. **Handmade Houses: A Guide to the Woodbutcher's Art.** San Francisco, Scrimshaw, 1973. c.90p. illus. (part col.). $12.95. LC 73-78445. ISBN 0-912020-00-8.

With text by Boericke and photos by Shapiro, this is a guide to "handmade houses" and other structures made from salvaged materials, handhewn lumber, and other such stuff. Lots of people are trying the "homemade" house route, these days, and this book may have just the right solution to a problem.

591. Bromfield, Louis. **Malabar Farm.** New York, Ballantine, 1970. 470p. illus. $1.25pa. ISBN 0-345-02054-5.

Originally published in 1947, this is the story of how a novelist moved to an Ohio farm and rebuilt it with organic methods. The book is beautifully written and is somewhat of a classic among the folks who follow the homesteading movement. It is sort of a diary with much farm lore. The drawings are by Kate Lord.

592. Canfield, D. M. **Elements of Farrier Science.** Albert Lea, MN, Enderes, 1968. 169p. illus. index. $11.95.

Anyone seriously attempting to care for horses should know something about "horseshoeing" even if he doesn't do the work himself. The Enderes Tool Company makes horseshoes, farrier's tools, and other horse gear. Their book covers equine anatomy and pathology, shoeing requirements, ordinary and corrective shoes, and the whole gamut of hoof preparation, shaping, forge work, and keeping the neighing ninnies quiet. An excellent manual.

593. Castle, Bryan, and Caralie Bryan. **The Edible, Ornamental Garden.** San Francisco, 101 Productions, 1974. 192p. illus. index. glossary. $7.95; $3.95pa. LC 73-91941. ISBN 0-912238-57-X; -46-1pa.

I've included this title for the edification of anyone who wishes to have a garden that looks pretty and is fit for the pot. About 45 plants are mentioned, including trees and shrubs, ground covers, and herbs. Recipes, too. Interesting.

594. Churchill, James E. **The Homesteader's Handbook.** Harrisburg, PA, Stackpole, 1974. 224p. illus. index. $7.95. LC 74-1333. ISBN 0-8117-0815-2.

A quite general introduction to homesteading, this book for beginners, or for those thinking of the supposedly good life, is filled with information. The several chapters are concerned with finding suitable land, using tools, repairing old houses, building cabins and obtaining water supplies, growing food or using wild foods, utilizing animals for meat or work, making such things as sugar and soap, preserving foods, and keeping healthy. There is even a chapter on spinning, knitting, and weaving. Suggestions for further reading and for finding other information are scattered throughout. Illustrated with drawings (I'd prefer to have more of them, for greater clarity), the book, being general and elementary, is a good starting place. The author doesn't really understand the occurrence of underground water and he even states that Indians had no waste (what does he think the archeologist digs up?), but this handbook is recommended for the basics.

595. **Cloudburst: A Handbook of Rural Skills & Technology.** Brackendale, B.C., Cloudburst (distr.: Book People), 1973. 128p. illus. $3.95pa.

This large manual discusses the making of dome houses, privies, poultry houses, saunas, windmills, and forges, digging water supplies, making a wood lathe and a fruit press, splitting shakes, preserving and storing foods, using a water wheel, planting by moon signs, raising bees, and doing other country things. Illustrated mostly with drawings. A good book to have around.

596. Copans, Stu, and David Osgood, eds. **The Home Health Handbook.** 3rd ed. Brattleboro, VT, Stephen Greene, 1972. 284p. illus. index. $7.95; $3.95pa. LC 72-90930. ISBN 0-8289-0177-5; -0125-9pa.

OUTDOOR RECREATION

Written by many people, this is described as "A Preliminary Guide to Self-Help and Rural Medicine." The editors are a physician and a public health worker. The topics include: first aid and common medical emergencies, poisons, water supplies and sanitation, canning and freezing food, home childbirth, psychological problems, communal and venereal diseases, home burial, using farm equipment safely, and much else of concern to country people. Illustrated with drawings. The second edition was financed by the Burlington Ecumenical Action Ministry in Vermont, and this book is sometimes listed as authored by BEAM. An excellent book for any rural dweller.

597. Cuddy, John, and Dore Cuddy. **Locating Low Cost Land.** Shevlin, MN, Sunflower Farm, 197?. 16p. price unknown.

A small pamphlet outlining a number of ways to locate land for country living: advertising, local papers, tax sales, etc. The Cuddys searched for a homestead in 1971 and this record of their methods may be useful to others.

598. Cummings, Elsie J., and Wavie J. Charlton. **Survival: Pioneer, Indian and Wilderness Lore.** 3rd ed. Hot Springs, MT, Authors (Orders to W. J. Charlton), 1972. 210p. illus. index. paper. price not reported.

Illustrated with drawings, this 8½" x 11" handbook is by two sisters. Members of an old pioneer family in western Montana, they tried to gather all they can remember of the old ways of doing things. They have lists of needed clothing, medications, foods, and other supplies for possible emergency use, with information on making comfortable camps, keeping warm, making children's clothing, etc. There is a heavy emphasis on home remedies for illness and wounds and on wild foods, teas, recipes, preserving foods, making pemmican and cheese, and other such skills. If you need to find a madstone or discover a witch, the methods are here. An excellent source of fascinating and useful intelligence.

599. Dahlem, Ted. **How to Make and Mend Cast Nets.** 2nd ed. St. Petersburg, FL, Great Outdoors, 1968. 72p. illus. glossary. $1.25pa.

Instruction on the making and use of cast nets for catching mullet. The skills are useful universally, though, and net-making isn't a commonly known talent.

600. Davis, Cindy, and Elizabeth Mabe. **Out of the Molasses Jug.** Brackendale, B.C., Cloudburst, 1974. 101p. illus. index. $8.95; $4.25pa. ISBN 0-88930-001-3; -002-Xpa.

Based on a newspaper column, this is a collection of food recipes, natural medicine advice and other home concoctions, methods of cleaning things, heating, lighting, and growing things. There are, as examples, instructions for making scarecrows, canning foods, and making sanitary napkins. Illustrated with drawings. A very good book for any country bookshelf.

601. Elder, Leon. **Hot Tubs: How to Build, Maintain & Enjoy Your Own.** Santa Barbara, CA, Capra, 1973. 80p. illus. $2.95pa. ISBN 0-912264-57-8.

This is mostly about making wooden tubs, but various other materials are suggested. There are construction details and words about heaters, pumps, and filters. Illustrated with photos and drawings. Now, if I could only afford to buy that place with the hot spring on the hill!

602. Ervin, Jonathan. **Jonathan Ervin's Leather Notebook.** Philadelphia, Running Press, 1973. 86p. illus. $3.95pa.

This is a hand-printed book about the basic tools and machines used in leather work, with instructions on making sandals, belts, and other small items of leather. Included here for the country dweller who may wind up with the outside of a side of beef. Illustrated with drawings.

603. Farnham, Albert B. **Home Tanning and Leather Making Guide.** Columbus, OH, A. R. Harding, 1950. 176p. illus. $2.00pa.

The subtitle continues: "A Book of Information for Those Who Wish to Tan and Make Leather from Cattle, Horse, Calf, Sheep, Goat, Deer and Other Hides and Skins; also Explains How to Skin, Handle, Classify and Market." Illustrated with photos and drawings, the book was originally published in 1922. Rather old, of course, but the methods are good ones and they use materials that the rural dweller may have handy.

604. Fries, Gene E. **Indian, Pioneer and Home Tanning Methods.** Cedar Rapids, IA, Buffalo Bull Press, 1973. 54p. illus. $3.00pa.

This small pamphlet has detailed tanning recipes compiled from a number of sources, based largely on Otis T. Mason's U.S. National Museum monograph from the 1880s. A good source for instructions that are not easily gotten elsewhere.

605. Gibson, Charles E. **Handbook of Knots and Splices and Other Work with Hempen and Wire Ropes.** New York, Emerson, 1963. 152p. illus. index. $4.95. LC 63-8697. ISBN 0-87523-146-2.

Illustrated with drawings, this is a good introduction to how ropes are made and handled. It describes hitches and knots of many kinds, splices, and fancy work.

OUTDOOR RECREATION

606. Gregory, Mark (pseud.). **Good Earth Almanac.** New York, Grosset & Dunlap, 1973. 111p. illus.(col.). index. $3.95pa. LC 72-90840. ISBN 0-448-02038-6.

This almanac is intended to be "a rediscovery of the natural world, with all its creatures and plants that surround us." Divided into several parts, the variety of subjects is intriguing: wild foods, natural gardening, cooking, hunting and fishing, camping, survival and safety, useful crafts, several outdoor sports, bird feeding, and using wood. A month-by-month almanac guides us through seed planting, fruit gathering, and other activities. Illustrated with color drawings, this is a useful pot-pourri for young and old.

607. Havens, David. **The Woodburner's Handbook.** Portland, ME, Media House (distr.: RPM Distributors), 1973. 107p. illus. $2.00pa.

The cover subtitle tells us that this is about "Rekindling an Old Romance." When the oil and gas and electricity gives out, what do we burn? Wood, naturally! This is a fine little book about wood as a fuel; wood stoves and how to build, buy, or install them; how to cook on them; and how to keep them going. Chimneys and fireplaces get some attention and there is much about felling, splitting, and seasoning wood. Illustrated with photos and drawings.

608. Hennessey, James, and Victor J. Papanek. **Nomadic Furniture.** New York, Pantheon, 1973. 150p. illus. $3.95pa. LC 73-3412. ISBN 0-394-47577-1.

609. Hennessey, James, and Victor J. Papanek. **Nomadic Furniture, 2.** New York, Pantheon, 1974. 151p. illus. $4.95pa. LC 73-18725. ISBN 0-394-70638-2.

These books are about making furniture or otherwise obtaining furniture that is easily portable or easily made from odds and ends. Lots of good hints for the country dweller who needs to pad his pad.

610. Herter, George Leonard, and Berthe E. Herter. **How to Get Out of the Rat Race and Live on $10 a Month.** 4th ed. Waseca, MN, Herter's, 1970. 656p. illus. index. $4.89. (Order No. AE7C14).

This is all about living in the boondocks where one can make a living by raising his own food, hunting and fishing, trapping, living off the land, home industry, building one's own log home and, generally, getting by on little. An excellent book and good reading.

611. **Hey Beatnik! This Is the Farm Book.** Summertown, TN, Book Publishing Co., 1974. 104p. illus.(part col.). $1.95pa.

COUNTRY LIVING

This is about a community of some 600 persons living on a 1,700-acre farm in Tennessee. It describes how novices became good farmers trying to grow almost all their own food. Some of the book is about the religious or philosophical motivation behind the movement, but it is mostly about how the people learned to farm, what they plant, how they work. The group is vegetarian. An interesting look at country living.

612. Holdgate, Charles. **Net Making.** Buchanan, NY, Emerson, 1972. 136p. illus. $4.95. LC 72-84056. SBN 87523-180-2.

Basic netting knots, needles, frames, and other needs are described in this handbook on a useful skill. Illustrated mostly with drawings.

613. Israel, Rich, and Reny Slay. **Homesteader's Handbook: A Guide to Raising, Growing, Preparing and Preserving Foodstuffs . . . and a Few Side Trips.** San Francisco, Author, 1973. 319p. illus. index. $3.50pa. LC 73-82562. ISBN 0-913978-01-9.

This is for folks who are trying to live in the country by raising their own food and being as self-sufficient as possible. It is concerned with growing vegetables, grain, marijuana, gathering wild foods, cooking and otherwise preparing foods, making beer and white lightning, and canning, pickling and preserving foods. The authors assume that you already have the homestead, so they concentrate on food—there is nothing about building your own shack or digging a well. Excellent.

614. Kahn, Lloyd, ed. **Shelter.** Bolinas, CA, Shelter Publications (distr.: Random House), 1973. 176p. illus.(part col.). $20.00; $6.60pa. LC 73-5415. ISBN 0-394-48829-6; -70991-8pa.

This is an interesting manual on different types of natural and man-made shelters as used throughout the world. It is about caves, tents, yurts, cottages, tipis, barns, adobe haciendas, treehouses, domes and others. There is good material about building methods and materials plus a section on energy systems, water supplies, gardening, and disposing of waste. A good book for the homeless homesteader.

615. Kains, Maurice Grenville. **Five Acres and Independence: A Practical Guide to the Selection and Management of the Small Farm.** Rev. and enl. ed. New York, Dover, 1973. 397p. illus. index. $2.50pa. LC 72-92758. ISBN 0-486-20974-1. (Also published by New American Library at $3.95pa.)

This is a reprint and up-dating of the 1940 edition. The book was originally written as a guide to farming for a profit by selling produce. Now it should suffice as a guide to country living and subsistence. Among the many topics are these: how to choose a place to farm, financing, getting a water supply, irrigating, raising food, fertilizing, fighting pests. Illustrated with drawings. Lots of good reading for potential country folk.

616. Kaysing, William. **Bill Kaysing's the Ex-Urbanite's Complete & Illustrated Easy-Does-It First Time Farmer's Guide**. Rev. ed. San Francisco, Straight Arrow, 1973. 320p. illus. index. $3.95pa. LC 77-158518. ISBN 0-87932-047-8.

Illustrated with photos and drawings, this is all about finding one's place and farming it. Good information about farming needs and sources, water and soil conditions, growing vegetables and fruits, raising livestock of all kinds, fish farming, gathering wild foods, selling farm products, obtaining power (wind, water, manure, etc.), controlling pests, and other odds and ends. An excellent guide.

617. Kaysing, William. **The Robin Hood Handbook**. New York, Links Books (distr.: Quick Fox), 1974. 276p. illus. bibliog. $9.95; $5.95pa. LC 73-80398. ISBN 0-8256-3024-X; -3017-7pa.

This is for those who wish to get along in the boonies and beat the Establishment by starting their own establishment. There is lots of "philosophy" here, but a pair of hip-boots will carry us through. The information is about finding a place to drop out to (or into, or whatever the proper word is), obtaining basic equipment for living, using wild foods and whatever tame ones you can rustle, finding or building shelters, utilizing water, wind or solar power, first aid, etc. There are notes on clothing, hiking, mountain climbing, travelling on horses or rafts, and generally getting around in the open spaces. An annotated bibliography is included. Lots of good suggestions.

618. Kern, Ken. **The Owner-Built Home**. Oakhurst, CA, Ken Kern, 1972. 4v. in 1. c.290p. illus. $7.50pa.

Describing this as a "how to think" book as well as a "how to do" one, Kern offers many hints on planning a home according to climate and site, choosing materials, building foundations, walls and floors, roofs, plumbing, and the other parts of a home. There is a list of readings with each chapter. This is an excellent manual for anyone planning to do his own home construction.

619. Kern, Ken. **The Owner-Built Homestead**. Oakhurst, CA, Ken Kern, 1974. 2v. 209p. illus. $2.50pa. each Vol.

Kern proposes a "life of self-reliance and at least partial economic self-sufficiency." In this book, he describes the many aspects of planning and building a homestead: water supplies, use of woodlands, raising fish, fencing, housing, raising animals, using manure as fuel and compost, food preservation, and nutrition. Lots of basic "philosophy" about getting back to the land. Very good reading.

COUNTRY LIVING

620. Kreps, Harry Elmer. **Science of Trapping.** Rev. ed. Columbus, OH, A. R. Harding, 1944. 229p. illus. $2.00pa.

Originally published in 1909, this is one of the old standbys for trappers of North American furbearers, including bears and cougars. Lots of hints in a little book with a long subtitle: "Describes the Fur Bearing Animals, Their Nature, Habits and Distribution, with Practical Methods for Their Capture." Good reading.

621. Laubin, Reginald, and Gladys Laubin. **The Indian Tipi: Its History, Construction, and Use.** New York, Ballantine, 1971. 270p. illus. index. bibliog. $1.65pa. LC 57-5958. SBN 345-22339-X-165.

This book describes the construction and use of tipis, including transporting them. Each tribe had a different pattern and many are shown here. There is a chapter on "The History of the Tipi" by Stanley Vestal. Interesting reading, illustrated with photos and drawings.

622. Laurel, Alicia Bay (pseud.). **Living on the Earth: Celebrations, Storm Warnings, Formulas, Recipes, Rumors, & Country Dances.** New York, Random House, 1971. 214p. illus. index. $7.95; $3.95pa. LC 72-182389. ISBN 0-394-48301-4; -71056-8pa.

This hand-written book is not very easy on my old eyes, but it has interesting notes on backpacking and camping, furniture, building shelters, making a kitchen, yoga and crafts, gardening, food preservation, cooking, making simple clothing, home childbirth, and disposing of dead bodies. Much good reading even if you're not a hippie.

623. **Log Cabin Manual.** Phoenix, AZ, Sincere, 1967. 42p. illus. $4.95.

This thin manual contains suggestions on building log cabins—details of construction, examples, and plans.

624. Logsdon, Gene. **Homesteading: How to Find New Independence on the Land.** Emmaus, PA, Rodale Press, 1973. 256p. illus. index. $7.95. LC 73-5159. ISBN 0-87857-068-3.

This general introduction to a modern form of homesteading is concerned with living fairly close to civilization and with at least a fair income from regular sources. It offers quite a bit of information on choosing the right place and then buying it, managing soil and building it up with organic methods, choosing and raising vegetables, fruits, grains and livestock, supplementing the larder with gathered wild foods, using available technology to produce power and convert waste to compost, developing water supplies, and selling surplus products. "Livestock" here includes bees and fishworms as well as larger animals. Lots of good hints and "philosophy," but for really getting down to

OUTDOOR RECREATION

earth and starting from scratch, the homesteader will need some other book, such as those by Ken Kern or Bill Kaysing.

625. Long, Sam. **Scissors Sam Says Be Sharp: An Authentic Manual on the Sharpening & Care of Scissors & Tools.** San Francisco, Scrimshaw, 1972. 52p. illus. $1.50pa. LC 72-77027. ISBN 0-912020-28-8.

This is a very good little book filled with hints on sharpening all sorts of edged household tools, including lawn and garden tools. Excellent.

626. Mackinley, Ian, and W. E. Willis. **Snow Country Design.** Oakland, CA, Mackinley/Winnacker/McNeil, 1973. 53p. illus. price not reported.

This is a short paper on the design of houses and other structures for deep snow country. Very interesting data are presented although most of us will never use the information.

627. Martin, George A. **Fences, Gates and Bridges: A Practical Manual.** Brattleboro, VT, Stephen Greene, 1974. 196p. illus. index. $5.95. ISBN 0-8289-0240-2.

This is about the various kinds of fences, gates, and bridges one can build from wood, sod, stone, barbed wire, etc. The instructions for setting posts and making stiles make for an interesting book for country folk.

628. Mewhinney, H. **A Manual for Neanderthals.** Austin, TX, University of Texas Press, 1957. 122p. illus. index. $6.00. LC 57-8821. ISBN 0-292-70067-9.

This "treatise on flint-flaking" reviews the several ways of making tools of flint and other such rocks. An engaging book on an odd topic.

629. Moral, Herbert R. **Buying Country Property.** New York, Bantam, 1972. 167p. illus. $1.75pa.

This is based on a rather old (1947) book. About a quarter of the text is devoted to the judging of old houses, and other sections deal with real estate agents, getting mortgages, and the like. There is a checklist of 25 main sources of trouble. Good reading for any one planning a move to the country.

630. **The Mother Earth News Almanac: A Guide through the Seasons.** New York, Bantam, 1973. 373p. illus. $1.95pa.

This explanation of the seasons carries the reader through the growing of crops, the roasting of turkeys, the toasting of pumpkin seeds, the making of whitewash, and a host of other homey topics. There is much of interest to country dwellers and marvelous reading for all.

631. **The Mother Earth News Handbook of Homemade Power.** New York, Bantam, 1974. 374p. illus. index. $1.95pa.

This manual carries the Mother Earth News philosophy to the use of wood as fuel, home water power, wind power, solar energy, and making methane from manure and other organic waste. Illustrated with drawings. The bibliography is especially good.

632. Needham, Walter. **A Book of Country Things.** Brattleboro, VT, Stephen Greene, 1965. 166p. illus. index. $4.50. LC 65-14693.

This book consists of Needham's recollections of his grandfather's life in southeastern Vermont through most of the last century. It is about farming, mostly, and the various skills that country people needed in those days. Some of the "recollections" about muzzle-loading rifles are strange, but the story of a self-reliant Yankee is interesting and important.

633. **The Old Farmer's Almanac.** 183rd ed. Dublin, NH, The Old Farmer's Almanac, 1974. 192p. illus. $0.75pa.

Published each year since 1792, this is the old standby for country folk throughout the United States. The weather forecasts are the most famous of the *Almanac*'s resources, but there are articles and notes on all manner of interesting, exotic, and practical things: postal laws, history, gardening, astronomy, etc. Advertisements throughout. Every country dweller should have this almanac—it is published in October of each year.

634. Prenis, John, ed. **The Dome Builder's Handbook.** Philadelphia, Running Press, 1973. 107p. illus. $4.00pa.

Several different sizes and types of domes are described and pictured in this resume of dome builders' problems. A good book for anyone about to try a dome.

635. Rodale, Robert. **The Basic Book of Organic Gardening.** New York, Ballantine, 1971. 377p. index. $1.25pa.

This is a handy guide to organic gardening by the editor of *Organic Gardening & Farming* magazine. It has many hints on homesteading, the use of compost, garden planning, bug control, and harvesting. Good reading.

636. Schuler, Stanley. **How to Grow Almost Everything.** New York, Evans (distr.: Lippincott), 1965. 256p. illus. index. $4.95; $0.75pa. (Pocket Books). LC 65-13249. ISBN 0-87131-061-9; 0-671-75429-7pa.

This is a dictionary of most of the plants that will grow in the good old 48. Alphabetically arranged with pertinent facts about plants and their culture

OUTDOOR RECREATION

and instructions on such things as transplanting and soil improvement. A good guide.

637. Severn, Bill. **Rope Roundup: The Lore and Craft of Rope and Roping.** New York, David McKay, 1960. 237p. illus. index. $3.95. LC 60-7196. ISBN 0-679-20163-7.

This book contains a history of rope and rope making, but we're mostly interested in its descriptions of rope work, both for work and for fun. Lots of excellent advice for anyone making it in the country. There is something about rope magic, too. A good book.

638. Stark, Norman H. **The Formula Manual.** 2nd ed. Cedarsburg, WI, Stark Research, 1974. 142p. illus. index. $9.95pa.

This new manual contains many formulas for making home medications, cosmetics, lotions, degreasing compounds, modeling clay, charcoal starter, and a host of other items. The formulas are designed to be made in small quantities and with common home equipment. Recommended for every farm or home bookshelf.

639. Stoner, Carol Hupping, ed. **Producing Your Own Power: How to Make Nature's Energy Sources Work for You.** Emmaus, PA, Rodale, 1974. 322p. illus. index. bibliog. glossary. $8.95. LC 74-10765. ISBN 0-87857-088-8.

Using more "natural" ways to produce small quantities of power is becoming popular; I had a request for such information about three weeks before reading this book. The methods covered here are: wind, water, wood, methane, and solar power. Excerpts from a number of sources are included, and the illustrations consist mostly of drawings. There are numerous jokes about using manure to generate gas but, let's face it, this sort of thing works. Actually, I love windmills and I'm glad they're coming back. This is a very fine compilation of data and instruction; highly recommended.

640. Sun Bear. **At Home in the Wilderness.** Healdsburg, CA, Naturegraph, 1968. 90p. illus. $3.00pa. ISBN 0-87961-004-2.

The title makes this sound like a survival manual but it is rather a guide to raising fruits and vegetables, building root cellars, preserving food, gathering wild plants, hunting, making fires and shelters, and other country skills. There is a list of equipment needed for back-country living. A good book filled with good advice.

641. Szykitka, Walter, ed. and comp. **Public Works.** New York, Links (distr.: Quick Fox), 1974. 1023p. illus. index. $24.95; $10.00pa. LC 74-78871. ISBN 0-8256-3047-9; -3041-xpa.

The title refers to the fact that the "works" reprinted here are "public," being either government documents or having expired copyrights. The cover subtitle reads: *A Handbook for Self-Reliant Living.* Of interest to us are such chapters as those on first aid (a Bureau of Mines handbook), survival (an Air Force manual), food values (USDA charts), cookery, farming, child care, home repair, construction techniques and the use of tools, motor vehicle maintenance, etc. Country dwellers will find this book a valuable source of information on a host of topics. There is also material about bus fares, social security payments, income taxes, and a final section on "consciousness-raising." The illustrations are, of course, reprinted as well. The format is rather different from that of the Whole Earth Catalog series but the idea is similar. No summary could possibly indicate the total content so everyone will have to rush out and buy the book.

642. Tangerman, E. J. **Whittling and Woodcarving.** New York, Dover, 1962. 293p. illus. index. $2.00pa. SBN 486-20965-2.

This was originally published in 1936, but the instructions are still as good as ever. There are notes on suitable woods and on useful wood projects of various kinds (whistles, puzzles, etc.). Included here because every country dweller should have a good whittling knife and know how to use it.

643. **The Trapper's Companion.** Rev. ed. Columbus, OH, A. R. Harding, 1946. 158p. illus. index. $1.00pa.

This old book, illustrated with drawings, has instructions for trapping all sorts of fur bearers, turtles, and small game. There are notes on making scents, handling pelts, boat building, bee hunting, collecting plants such as ginseng, and fur farming. Good reading.

644. **2,000 Down Home Skills & Secret Formulas for Practically Everything.** North Hollywood, CA, Gala Books, 1971. 368p. illus. index. $2.95pa. LC 76-180143. ISBN 0-912448-04-0.

This is a reprint of a late 1880s formula book. I've included it because many of the formulas will be useful and because the old-time flavor is interesting. There is something for everyone, whether trapper, farrier, cook, dairyman, home nurse, or sot.

645. Viherjuuri, H. J. **Sauna: The Finnish Bath.** Brattleboro, VT, Stephen Greene, 1972. 89p. illus. index. $2.95pa. LC 65-24620. ISBN 0-8289-0132-2.

This contains a history of the sauna and hints on building one for home use. Illustrated with photos and drawings, the guide has well-prepared plans and should do the job for anyone.

OUTDOOR RECREATION

646. Volunteers in Technical Assistance. **Automotive Operation and Maintenance.** Mt. Rainier, MD, VITA, 1973. c.200p. illus. index. $4.00pa.

Subtitled, "A manual for drivers using pioneer roads and for novice mechanics who must depend upon their own resources in areas without extensive service facilities." The book is filled with excellent advice on using vehicles under primitive conditions and on repairing them. Included here for those who wish to do much of their own work.

647. Volunteers in Technical Assistance. **Village Technology Handbook.** Mt. Rainier, MD, VITA, 1970. 387p. illus. $7.00pa.

Intended for instructors in remote foreign villages, this book will be useful to anyone contemplating a country home under primitive conditions. Among the topics are: developing water supplies and systems, building dams, sanitation, irrigation systems and earth moving devices, food processing and storage, building homes of primitive materials, making solar water heaters and washing machines, developing crafts, and other skills. A very good source of country-living information, illustrated with photos and drawings.

648. Weygers, Alexander G. **The Making of Tools.** New York, Van Nostrand, 1973. 93p. illus. glossary. $8.95; $4.95pa. LC 72-7847. ISBN 0-442-29361-5; -29360-7pa.

This is a very interesting little book about making one's own tools. Weygers discusses workbenches, basic tools (both hand and machine), and the supplies needed. There are instructions on designing, sharpening, and tempering a variety of tools such as screwdrivers, chisels, knives, cleavers, hammers, tinsnips, shears, pliers, and wire cutters. One needs a basic shop outfit: small forge, grinders, drills, etc. Illustrated with drawings. For all craftsmen. (See also entry 736.)

649. Wigginton, Brooks Eliot. **The Foxfire Book.** Garden City, NY, Doubleday, 1972. 384p. illus. $3.95pa. ISBN 0-385-07353-4.

650. Wigginton, Brooks Eliot. **Foxfire 2.** Garden City, NY, Doubleday, 1973. 410p. illus. $4.50pa. ISBN 0-385-02267-0.

Based on material collected by high school students in northern Georgia, these fascinating books contain a great deal of information for country folk. Among the topics are: hog slaughtering, building cabins, gathering wild foods, making soap, preserving meats and other foods. In addition, there are stories of moonshining, country methods of burying people, ghosts, witches and faith healing. Illustrated with many photographs. Highly recommended.

651. Wildcrafters Publications. R.R. 3, Box 118, Rockville, IN 47872.

This is a home industry, so to speak, which publishes quite a few manuals and guides for country dwellers. The topics include such things as trapping, fishing and hunting, fleshing pelts, growing and gathering ginseng, catching snakes, country remedies and formulas, and making a living in the country. These booklets vary in size and price, the main series being the *Wildcrafter Manuals*. A couple of first-class stamps will bring a complete catalog. Very interesting reading.

652. Wizansky, Richard, ed. **Home Comfort: Stories and Scenes of Life on Total Loss Farm.** New York, Saturday Review, 1973. 331p. illus. $8.95. LC 72-91186. ISBN 0-8415-0228-5.

A number of folks living on Total Loss Farm in New England have written and illustrated (with drawings) a series of stories or essays about their lives and daily routines, their thoughts, and their hopes. There are numerous hints of a practical nature (e.g., bread making, wood cutting, farm expenses, and well digging), but much of the content is philosophical. Good reading for anyone but especially for someone thinking about living on a commune.

653. Young, Jean, and Jim Young. **People's Guide to Country Real Estate.** New York, Praeger, 1973. 192p. illus. $3.95pa. LC 73-1911.

This is an excellent little guide to buying property outside the cities and suburbs. Illustrated with photographs, the book's basic philosophy is summed up in a chapter called "Real Estate Is the Best Investment." There are suggestions about using brokers, lawyers, bankers and appraisers, knowing about insurance, contracts and loans, remodeling and improving property, etc. For anyone who's "in the market."

ANIMAL-RELATED ACTIVITIES

... going to the dogs

We won't say very much about animal books. There are entirely too many books about horses and dogs and pets are beyond the scope of this volume. It seemed best, though, to include something about a few of the animals that are directly involved with man's outdoor recreational activities. Many people like to "trail ride." Others like to chase hounds which are, in turn, chasing raccoons. All this is good, healthy outdoor activity.

Working with animals is an exacting task that requires much patience. An untrained dog is an abomination and an untrained horse is useless. The movies of Walt Disney and a few other producers have, I think, done more to place animals in a ridiculous, anthropomorphic image then even the maudlin titles that infest the shelves of a public library's kiddie collection. Animals do not think as humans do and they do not have human emotions. When we forget such elementary facts, we have trouble with animals. Animals do as their instinct demands. If a knowledgeable and dedicated person is able to direct this instinctive behavior into beneficial channels (beneficial to both the animal and the person), an animal is trained and can be a companion on outdoor jaunts.

In addition to the several titles listed here, we should remember that there are not only a large number of "animal" books issued through regular trade channels but that there is much material available from government sources and from the manufacturers of animal feeds, medicines, and supplies. Some of this "commercial" information may be excellent, but it is ephemeral. It is also free or nominally priced, and advertisements in the appropriate magazines will lead us to it. County agents can be good sources of assistance, but we must remember that they are generally trained in agriculture so may not know what to do about a sick falcon.

Information about animals is also found in general books on outdoor recreation. The *Complete Outdoors Encyclopedia* has a good chapter on hunting dogs. The *Explorers Ltd. Source Book*, which has an excellent chapter on horse gear for pack trips, is also one of the few easy sources of information about dog packing. This latter activity has become quite popular recently. I

ANIMAL-RELATED ACTIVITIES

don't know how the dogs feel about it, but several manufacturers are making packs and harnesses so that Rover may carry his own biscuits into the great outback.

There is a convenient book service for horse lovers. For information, drop a line to: Horse Book Readers Service, Drawer 1709, East Lansing, MI 48823. They'll give you all the details.

654. Allen, William H., Jr. **How to Raise and Train Pigeons.** Rev. ed. New York, Sterling, 1972. 160p. illus.(part col.). $5.95. LC 58-7602. ISBN 0-8069-3706-8.

Allen discusses the various breeds, training methods, care and feeding problems, and the general management of the birds. Color photographs of many pigeon varieties.

655. Back, Joe. **Horses, Hitches and Rocky Trails.** Chicago, Swallow Press, 1959. 117p. illus. (A Sage Book). $5.00. LC 59-11063. ISBN 0-8040-0147-2.

Horse and mule packing is pretty tricky business. This book offers many excellent suggestions on the proper ways to put things on horses' backs while said horses are trying to keep clear. Joe Back has been a professional packer in Wyoming, so his book rings true. The several chapters cover horse psychology, needed equipment, proper pack saddles, packing and balancing a load, hitches and rope work, and handling the animals on the trail. Illustrated with drawings by the author, this little book also has a bit of horse history and suggestions on getting along in the wilderness. Highly recommended.

656. **Back Country Horsemen's Guidebook.** Columbia Falls, MT, Back Country Horsemen, 1973. 59p. illus. free.

This shirt-pocket manual contains many suggestions on handling horses, selecting camping spots, trail courtesy, packing, and first aid. Highly recommended. Send them some postage with your order; a half-a-buck ought to do it.

657. Beebe, Frank L., and Harold M. Webster. **North American Falconry and Hunting Hawks.** 2nd ed. Denver, CO, North American Falconry and Hunting Hawks, 1970. $25.00.

I have not seen a copy of this book, but it is widely advertised as the last word on the subject.

658. Bernstein, Susan, ed. **Dog Digest: The Total Guide to Dog Ownership.** Northfield, IL, Digest Books, 1972. 320p. illus. glossary. $5.95pa. LC 70-163107. ISBN 0-695-80271-2.

OUTDOOR RECREATION

This well-illustrated guide, in the usual Digest Book format, contains excellent information for dog lovers: choosing the right dog, feeding, caring for and training a dog, handling an "outdoor dog," and much else. General enough to please most readers.

659. Falk, John R. **The Practical Hunter's Dog Book.** New York, Winchester Press, 1971. 318p. illus. index. $7.95. LC 70-159426. ISBN 0-87691-037-1.

Falk, who has been the gun dog editor of *Guns and Hunting* magazine for many years, offers good advice on choosing a dog for hunting (will it also be a house pet? how much room will it have to live in?). There are chapters on training, health problems, and types of hunting. This book should serve the beginner well.

660. **Farnam Horse Library.** 8701 North 29th St., Omaha, NB 68112.

This is a series of paperback books that cover most aspects of horsemanship and horse care for the beginner. Each volume is written by experts and contains many illustrations, some in color. The price is $1.50 for each volume, $23.85 for a complete set. The titles are these: *Know First Aid for Your Horse, Riding the Gymkhana Winner, Know English Equitation and Training, How to Correct the Problem Horse, Know All about Tack, How to Show Your Horse and Win, Know the Anatomy of the Horse, Riding the Show-Ring Hunter, Know Practical Horse Breeding, How to Shoe Your Horse, Know the Arabian Horse, How to Buy the Right Horse, Understanding Horse Psychology, How to Become a Better Rider, Know Practical Horse Feeding, How to Break and Train the Western Horse, Know the American Quarter Horse,* and *How to Recognize Horse Health Problems.* Recommended as the best bet for any beginner, these books are inexpensive but authoritative.

661. Fishback, Mel. **Novice Sled Dog Training.** Lynnwood, WA, Raymond Thompson. $2.50 plus $0.15 postage.

Not examined.

662. Foy, Charles. **Pigeons for Pleasure and Profit.** Moline, IL, Swanson, 1972. 64p. illus. $1.50pa.

This beginner's guide tells how to purchase the birds, to care for and train them, to select proper housing and equipment, and, finally, to prepare them for the market.

663. Hapgood, Ruth. **First Horse: Basic Horse Care Illustrated.** San Francisco, Chronicle Books, 1972. 159p. illus. index. $6.95. LC 72-76929. ISBN 0-87701-072-02.

This is a good introduction to horse care: food and water, grooming, saddling, riding and leading, health problems, care in barn and field, trailering, and hints on buying a horse. Illustrated with photographs and drawings. A good choice for the beginner.

664. Jameson, E. W., Jr., and Hans J. Peeters. **An Introduction to Hawking.** Davis, CA, Authors, 1971. 42p. illus. $4.00pa.

This is the best available manual about the several kinds of hawk and where to get them, about the care and housing of hawks and the equipment required. There is a glossary, a bibliography, and a list of sources of books and supplies. Illustrated with drawings. Let me point out here that most of the hawking or falconry books available today are reprints of old titles. Highly recommended.

665. Mavrogordato, Jack. **A Hawk for the Bush: A Treatise on the Training of the Sparrow-Hawk and Other Short-Winged Hawks.** New York, Clarkson Potter (distr.: Crown), 1974. 206p. illus.(part col.). index. glossary. $12.50. LC 73-90106. ISBN 0-517-51434-6.

Originally published in England in 1960, this is a good description of the various hawks and an introduction to their capture and care. Good suggestions on equipment, diet and health, hunting methods. The legal notes pertain to Great Britain so are of no use to us, but the appendices include various items of interest such as codes of conduct, patterns for making hoods, etc. A good book.

666. Michell, E. B. **The Art and Practice of Hawking.** Newton, MA, Branford, 1959. 291p. illus. index. $7.00. SBN 8231-2009-0.

This is a good resume of hawking knowledge as originally published in 1900. There is information about the birds used, the needed equipment (called "furniture"), the training of young and adult birds, hunting, and the care of hawks through illness or accidents. The beginning hawker will enjoy this look at the sport at the turn of the century.

667. Self, Margaret Cabel. **Fun on Horseback.** 1974 ed. North Hollywood, CA, Wilshire Book Co., 1974. 271p. illus. index. $3.00pa. LC 64-20093.

A prolific "horse author" offers good basic advice about breaking and training a colt, riding (from beginning to jumping), hunting with bloodhounds, forming a military horse troop, and other items of general interest. Illustrated with photos and drawings, this is a good, inexpensive introduction.

668. **Sled Dog Bulletin.** Lynnwood, WA, Raymond Thompson.

This is an irregularly published series. The following issues are available as of early 1974: *Sled Building Plans* ($1.50pa. plus $0.15 postage); *Packing Dogs* ($1.50pa. plus $0.15 postage); *Skijoring with Dogs* ($1.00pa. plus $0.15 postage); *Line Breeding and Racing Notes* ($1.00pa. plus $0.15 postage); *History and Racing Rules* ($1.00pa. plus $0.15 postage); *Sled and Harness Styles* ($1.00pa. plus $0.15 postage).

669. Streever, Fred. **The American Trail Hound.** New York, A. S. Barnes, 1948. 202p. illus. (The Sportsman's Library).

This work is out of print but I include it because it is something of a classic and the beginner will probably wish to read it. It is typical of the older genre of sporting book—filled with information yet easy to read.

670. Thompson, Raymond. **Cart and Sled Dog Training Manual.** Lynnwood, WA, Raymond Thompson, $2.50 plus $0.15 postage.

Not examined.

671. Thompson, Raymond. **Sled Dogs Encyclopedia.** 3 vols. Lynnwood, WA, Raymond Thompson. $7.00/set plus $0.45 postage.

Not examined.

672. Wiseman, Robert F. **The Complete Horseshoeing Guide.** 2nd ed. Norman, OK, University of Oklahoma Press, 1973. 286p. illus. index. $5.95. LC 72-9279. ISBN 0-8061-1049-X.

This standard guide covers all aspects of both hot and cold shoeing. Hoof care, correct use of tools, horse psychology, diseases and other physical problems, metalwork and, of course, shoeing. There is a good glossary and bibliography and a reprint of Longfellow's "The Village Blacksmith."

MISCELLANEOUS

... at wit's end

Our miscellaneous category includes a few titles on a variety of subjects. Physical fitness should be of some concern to the outdoorsman. A number of hunters, for example, manage to drop dead each year thereby adding to the statistical abominations of government. Taking pictures is a pastime of many, so a few photography books are mentioned. In the hope that some readers may be led to sketching, we note a few books about drawing. I was going to include nudism but have had trouble getting the bare facts.

For more scientific-minded folk, we have included something about astronomy and meteorology. I love to watch thunderstorms developing over the Great Plains because you can see them for so many miles there. The ability to identify a few stars will amaze the neighborhood children and will result in a reputation for omniscience. Caving is an intriguing sport, too, so a couple of titles are listed. On all these subjects, there are many other available books, and most libraries are well stocked.

More and more people are becoming interested in the shooting sports, including archery. Archery is taught in many schools and books are to be found in most libraries. I have listed only a few titles on archery because I'm interested, in this book, in the practical aspects of the sport—bowhunting. Shooting firearms is our chief concern, and we'll mention a few of the many available titles. One of the fastest-growing aspects of the shooting sports is the shooting of muzzle-loading firearms. Because information on this activity is sometimes hard to find (books on the subject are rare in libraries), we'll try to give a representative selection of easily obtained titles.

The shooting of muzzle-loading firearms is really booming, and several ancillary activities are becoming full-fledged sports: knife throwing, tomahawk throwing, and "buckskinning." Buckskinning is the attempt to live as much as possible in the ways of our ancestors in the last century. Buckskinners shoot muzzle-loading rifles and other firearms (often made by themselves), dress in authentic clothing (again, often made by themselves), and try, generally, to recreate a bygone era in our history. Buckskinners don't do this all the time, of course, as they must make a living, too, but they get together on weekends or at regional events and live as the mountain men did. Many of these buckskinners have become experts in the regional or social history of our early days and could correct much of the misinformation we too often find in history books. Knife- and tomahawk-throwing are established events at these meetings and at other muzzle-loader shoots.

I've also included a few titles on shooting in general just to get the novice on the right track. A few other odds and ends are thrown in here, too, just because there was no better place for them.

673. Ackerman, R. O. **The Muzzle Loader's Little Library** (series). Tofield, Alberta, The Outpost. $1.50pa. each.

The titles, so far, are *Introduction to Muzzle Loading* (1966; 20p.); *Shooting the Percussion Rifle* (1966; 20p.); and *Care and Repair of Muzzle Loaders* (1966; 24p.). Although they are rather small booklets, the advice and information is valuable to any beginner in the sport.

674. Ald, Roy. **Jogging, Aerobics & Diet: One Is Not Enough—You Need All Three.** New York, New American Library, 1968. 191p. illus. $1.25pa.

The belief expressed in the title caused Ald to prepare this compact guide to aerobic exercises, human physiology, running programs, and nutrition. Recommended for anyone who needs a short manual on an important subject for outdoorsmen.

675. Amber, John T. **Gun Digest.** 28th ed. Northfield, IL, Digest Books, 1974. 480p. illus. $7.95pa. LC 44-32588. ISBN 0-695-80395-6.

"The World's Greatest Gun Book" is filled with information for sportsmen and collectors. The book is different from year to year so the articles vary in content and interest. Highly recommended to all shooters and others interested in firearms and related accessories.

676. Bauer, Erwin A. **Hunter's Digest.** Northfield, IL, Digest Books, 1973. 320p. illus. $6.95pa. LC 73-83467. ISBN 0-695-80431-6.

This copiously illustrated guide is filled with hints on hunting all kinds of game animals. It is an example of the kind of publication the country dweller may wish to read for information. Included, too, are articles on dogs, conditioning, and using horses.

MISCELLANEOUS

677. Bauer, Erwin A. **Hunting with a Camera: A World Guide to Wildlife Photography.** New York, Winchester, 1974. 324p. illus.(part col.). index. bibliog. $12.95. LC 74-78698. ISBN 0-87691-143-2.

Bauer offers many suggestions on equipment and technique (cameras, accessories, stalking animals, composition, etc.), but most of this book is devoted to descriptions of the many "camera hunting" areas of North America and the rest of the world. The information concerns places to go within each area (national parks, good game areas, etc.), required equipment (e.g., a four-wheel-drive unit may be needed), organized tours, species likely to be encountered. Generously illustrated, of course, and filled with stories. Bauer is a professional photographer and author/illustrator of many books and articles. This is a good resume of camera "safari" trips for the serious amateur.

678. Bentley, W. A., and W. D. Humphreys. **Snow Crystals.** New York, Dover, 1931. 226p. illus. $4.00pa. ISBN 0-486-20287-9.

This book consists of photomicrographs of snow crystals and hints on photography.

679. **Black Powder Basics.** Middlefield, CT, Lyman, 1973(?). 25p. illus. $1.00pa.

A small booklet with suggestions on using muzzle-loading firearms, casting bullets, types of patching material, etc. Very elementary, of course, but worthy for the beginner.

680. Blevins, Winfred. **Give Your Heart to the Hawks: A Tribute to the Mountain Men.** Los Angeles, Nash, 1973. 350p. illus. index. $8.95. LC 72-95248. ISBN 0-8402-1302-6. Also available in paperback: New York, Ballantine ($1.50pa.).

Intended to be an informal history of "the freest men our country has known," this wonderful book is an introduction to the men and their trade—Colter, Bridger, Smith, etc. The facts are here, with suggestions of fiction added to fill in the gaps. Blevins points out that the mountain men have not captured the "popular imagination" of America, perhaps because "We may, on the whole, be a little afraid of them." I think that Blevins is correct when he says that this fear may be because we, today, are afraid of "freedom, individualism, and self-reliance." Many of our citizens constantly demand "freedom" while also constantly demanding further governmental controls on all aspects of our lives. This book reads well and is illustrated with maps and several old portraits. A good appreciation of the men and their times, their travels, the dangers they faced, and the ways they died.

OUTDOOR RECREATION

681. Bridges, Toby, ed. **Black Powder Gun Digest.** Northfield, IL, Digest Books, 1972. 288p. illus. $5.95pa. LC 72-86645. ISBN 0-695-80360-3.

This is a compilation of articles by a number of well-known "shooting" authors. An introduction to black powder shooting, it tells something about the history and romance of the early types of firearms, the modern manufacture of replicas, and the loading, firing, and care of the guns. Old-time guns and modern copies are used for hunting, fun shooting, and historical representations such as the classic "North/South Skirmish." Tests on a number of currently available guns are included and there are articles on making a gun, on the growth of the National Muzzle Loading Rifle Association, and on its annual shoots at Friendship, Indiana. Good reading, even though muzzle-loader fans may disagree on some things.

682. Brummitt, Wyatt B., R. Will Burnett, and Herbert S. Zim. **Photography: The Amateur's Guide to Better Pictures.** Rev. ed. New York, Golden Press, 1964. 160p. illus.(part col.). index. (A Golden Handbook). $1.50pa. LC 64-11591.

This elementary text has good advice on the basics of a popular outdoor activity. Although some of the material is dated (types of film, for example), the notes on composition, movie making, nature photography, etc., are good.

683. Buchele, William, and George Shumway. **Recreating the American Longrifle.** 3rd ed. York, PA, Shumway, 1970. 110p. illus. $6.50pa. LC 70-105321. ISBN 0-87387-062-X.

Interest in making muzzle-loading firearms, especially rifles, is growing each year. Information on rifle-making is scattered through many journals and other publications, mostly pamphlets issued by individuals. This manual, illustrated with a few photos and many drawings, covers the entire beast—from designing the rifle, through metal and wood work, to browning the barrel. Full-size plans are included. Recommended for the library of every muzzle-loader fan.

684. Cassidy, William L., ed. **Knife Digest.** Berkeley, CA, Knife Digest (distr.: Ten Speed Press), 1974. 285p. illus. $10.00; $5.95pa. LC 73-76891. ISBN 0-913668-31-1; -30-3pa.

Called the "First Annual Edition of the First Annual Publication Ever Produced for the Cutlery Enthusiast, Collector & Maker," this pot pourri contains articles on how knives are made, sharpened and used, prominent knife makers, the etching of blades, historical knives and their uses, product reports, excerpts from old knife-makers' catalogs, book lists

MISCELLANEOUS

and reviews, and other useful data. Photos and drawings are used throughout. The book is not especially "outdoor recreation," but almost every outdoorsman uses knives and the book is recommended for its wealth of information.

685. **A Catalogue of the South.** Birmingham, AL, Oxmoor House, 1974. 343p. illus. indexes. $4.95pa. LC 74-79238.

Regional catalogs are an interesting phenomenon. This one covers the South in a variety of ways: there are sections that include recipes, history books, furniture sources, camping and gardening, buying pecans, pottery and baskets, hot sauce, etc. Most of the material consists of descriptions of products and sources, but there are a number of articles on personalities or other interesting features of the Southern heritage. Highly recommended and good reading.

686. **Celestial Wall Map.** San Francisco, Astrographics, 1973. $9.95.

This 77" x 42" map of the heavens shows some 88 constellations and 5,179 stars. Designed for wall display (it is too much for field use at night!), the chart is beautifully done and highly recommended for all serious amateur astronomers.

687. Cooper, Jeff. **Cooper on Handguns.** Los Angeles, Petersen, 1974. 257p. illus.(part col.). $4.95pa. LC 74-79226. ISBN 0-8227-0067-0.

This is an excellent modern resume of handguns and their use, written by one of the old hands in the game. Covering sporting, police, and collecting activities, the several chapters are about the various types of guns and accessories. Highly recommended for all gun buffs.

688. Davis, Don, ed. **Muzzle Loading Shooting and Winning with the Champions.** Friendship, IN, Powder, Patch & Ball Publications, 1973. 169p. illus. $7.95pa.

The several chapters are by Max Vickery, Webb Terry, Bob Butcher, Walter Grote, Bill Carmichael, Peter Allen, Warren Boughton, and Don Davis, experts all. There are general hints of all kinds, notes on match shooting, handguns, bench rest rifles, muskets, Hawken rifles, and shotguns. In addition to information on hunting with muzzle-loading guns, there are remarks on the several "primitive" games that are so important a part of matches these days: beef shoots, Seneca matches, knife- and tomahawk-throwing. Highly recommended for the serious black powder shooter.

689. **The First New England Catalogue.** Chester, CT, Pequot, 1973. 192p. illus. index. $4.95pa. LC 72-12224. ISBN 0-394-70662-5.

OUTDOOR RECREATION

This is another takeoff on the *Whole Earth Catalog* theme but it is naturally not as complete. The information about New England is very interesting and the sources are legion. If you need a sun dial, a harpsichord, a divining rod, or some kind of regional food, the addresses are here. Lots of good reading about geology, history, crafts, etc.

690. Fries, Gene. **Muzzle Loaders Almanac/Pioneer & Game Recipes/Rifle Making in the Great Smoky Mountains.** Cedar Rapids, IA, Buffalo Bull Press, 1972. 56p. illus. $2.50pa.

A small pamphlet containing three separate publications. The first two titles contain many hints for shooters and a number of old recipes. There are notes on pioneer clothing, shot sizes for game birds, stock finishing, and the like. The third title is a reprint of a National Park Service pamphlet written by Arthur I. Kendall. It is an excellent guide to old-time methods of riflemaking by hand in the Smokies. A very good little publication.

691. Gillelan, G. Howard. **Complete Book of the Bow and Arrow.** Harrisburg, PA, Stackpole, 1971. 320p. illus. index. $9.95. LC 72-140739. ISBN 0-8117-0420-3.

This introduction to the whole field of archery has chapters on history, equipment, form and technique, target archery, field archery, bowhunting and bowfishing, archery as a career, and the future of the sport. Also included are a glossary and a list of suppliers and the rules of several archery associations. Good reading for beginning archers.

692. **Guns & Ammo 1974 Annual.** Los Angeles, Petersen, 1973. 368p. illus.(part col.). $3.95pa. LC 72-1758. ISBN 0-8228-0043-3.

Guns & Ammo is one of Petersen's many magazine titles. Each year, its "annual" presents a pretty complete record of the guns available in the United States. More importantly, it contains many articles on all aspects of the shooting sports, ranging from tests of new products to historical reviews such as (in this issue) "The Arms of Abe Lincoln." Copiously illustrated, mostly photographs. Highly recommended, every year.

693. Henderson, Joe. **Long Slow Distance: The Humane Way to Train.** Los Altos, CA, Tafnews, 1969. 62p. illus. $2.50pa. LC 78-102774. ISBN 0-911520-12-0.

The idea put forth here is that distance runners should slow down but go greater distances during their training periods. The principle is illustrated through the programs of several runners. Running is one of the common outdoor recreations, these days, so this book is recommended reading.

694. Herring, William C. **Ballistics and the Muzzle Loading Rifle.** Friendship, IN, National Muzzle Loading Rifle Association, 1974. 111p. illus. $5.95pa. LC 74-19682.

With the phenomenal rise in popularity of shooting muzzle-loading firearms, the lack of easily found ballistic data became evident. Although many articles have appeared in journals and other places, the material was too scattered or too old to be useful to modern shooters. Herring's book is based on a series of actual tests with a chronograph to measure velocities. Numerous graphs are presented and the explanations are clear and concise. There are also some general observations on killing power and on muzzle-loader shooting. Highly recommended.

695. Hoagland, Clayton. **The Pleasures of Sketching Outdoors.** 2nd ed. New York, Dover, 1969. 179p. illus. $3.00pa. LC 70-95244. SBN 486-22229-2.

This includes instruction and examples of sketching things outdoors. It is a large book and it is recommended for the artistic among the outdoor clan.

696. Hochman, Louis. **The Complete Archery Book.** New York, Arco, 1957. 143p. illus. $3.50. LC 57-2516.

This basic guide to archery is rather outdated as to equipment, but the hints on bowmaking and techniques are still valid.

697. Horenstein, Henry. **Black and White Photography: A Basic Manual.** Boston, Little, Brown, 1974. 179p. illus. glossary. bibliog. $7.95; $3.95pa. LC 73-20140. ISBN 0-316-37310-9; -37311-7pa.

Illustrated, naturally enough, with many black and white photos, this is an excellent little handbook to cameras, films, accessories, proper exposure, use of filters, developing and printing, etc. Recommended.

698. Hughes, B. R., and Jack Lewis. **The Gun Digest Book of Knives.** Northfield, IL, Digest Books, 1973. 288p. illus. $5.95pa. LC 73-83465. ISBN 0-695-80429-4.

This large-format book contains much information about the history of knives (e.g., about Jim Bowie and his famous blade) and about some of the modern knife makers. Illustrated with many photographs, the book is highly recommended to all outdoorsmen who need information about knives.

699. Jacobs, Lou, Jr., *et al.* **Basic Guide to Photography.** Los Angeles, Petersen, 1973. 144p. illus.(part col.). index. $2.95pa. LC 73-79969. ISBN 0-8227-0006-9.

One of the first spin-offs from Petersen's new *Photographic Magazine*, this is a complete and appropriately well-illustrated guide for amateur photographers. There are suggestions on buying a camera, lenses, accessories, lighting and composition, films, close-ups, color photography, making a pinhole camera and a camera dolly. I especially liked the sections on outdoor lighting and composition. Highly recommended.

700. Jaeger, Ellsworth. **Nature Crafts.** New York, Macmillan, 1950. 128p. illus. (Olympic Editions). $4.50.

Craft books are a dime a dozen, but this one is concerned with making things from plants, rocks, and other natural sources. Among the objects, many being of use to outdoorsmen, are flint knives, driftwood bowls, a bow-drill fire-making set, wooden whistles, wooden dolls, snowshoes, sleds, and stone tomahawks. Illustrated with drawings. Jaeger's *Easy Crafts* (Macmillan, 1947, $4.95) is quite similar. Both books are recommended to outdoor recreationists who have the urge to create from nature.

701. LaChapelle, Edward R. **Field Guide to Snow Crystals.** Seattle, University of Washington Press, 1969. 101p. illus. $6.50; $2.95pa. LC 70-85215. ISBN 0-295-95014-5; -95040-4pa.

This consists of a classification of snow crystals, technical information on them, and a review of the various classification schemes. Numerous photos, discussions of the crystals, and hints on photography.

702. Lachuck, John, ed. **Wonderful World of the .22.** Los Angeles, Petersen, 1972. 192p. illus. $2.95pa. ISBN 0-8227-0040-9.

This is a well-illustrated guide to informal shooting with the .22 caliber firearms. There are suggestions about plinking, hunting, and target shooting, learning to shoot, care of guns, holsters, and other topics. There is a complete catalog of available guns. Lots of good reading.

703. Lahue, Kalton C. **Petersen's Guide to Pocket Camera Photography.** Los Angeles, Petersen, 1973. 80p. illus. $2.00pa. LC 73-79966. ISBN 0-8227-0009-3.

The great interest in small cameras, especially the 110 size, makes this book especially welcome. It describes the several pocket cameras now available and the films and techniques needed to get good photographs. An excellent guide for the outdoor recreationist who carries a small camera.

704. Latham, Sid. **Knives & Knifemakers.** New York, Winchester, 1973. 152p. illus.(part col.). index. $15.00. LC 73-78815. ISBN 0-87691-109-2.

There are so many custom knife-makers these days that it is difficult to keep even a list of them, much less anything more detailed. Latham has

MISCELLANEOUS

included information on how knives are made, how they are used for various purposes, and how they are sharpened. Well-illustrated (Latham is a professional photographer), basic material for outdoorsmen. Interest in knives is becoming greater all the time, so this book becomes a good start.

705. Laycock, George, and Erwin Bauer. **Hunting with Bow and Arrow.** New York, Arco, 1965. 111p. illus. glossary. $2.50. LC 65-2859. ISBN 0-668-01417-2.

This is a well-illustrated guide to archery history and to the equipment and techniques of bowhunting. Small and large game are included, as are birds and fish. Some of the information is necessarily dated, but the tyro will get some good hints.

706. Learn, C. R. **Bowhunter's Digest.** Northfield, IL, Digest Books, 1974. 288p. illus. glossary. $6.95pa. LC 73-91589. ISBN 0-695-80451-0.

This is probably the best, up-to-date guide to bowhunting. There is much information on equipment, the skills needed, women in the sport, hunting small and large game, how bows and arrows are made, crossbows, varmit calling, target practice, safety, and getting a good guide. One of the chapters is by Fred Bear, the best-known archer since Howard Hill. A list of equipment suppliers is included. Highly recommended.

707. Lehr, Paul E., R. Will Burnett, and Herbert S. Zim. **Weather: Air Masses—Clouds—Rainfall—Storms—Weather Maps—Climate.** New York, Golden Press, 1965. 160p. illus.(col.). $1.50pa. LC 61-8327.

This is a good little guide to the weather and how it happens. Outdoorsmen will like to know about fronts, cloud identification, and amateur weather forecasting. There is much new information available about the weather, but this basic guide is still suitable for beginners.

708. Lewis, Jack, ed. **Bow & Arrow Archer's Digest.** Northfield, IL, Digest Books, 1971. 320p. illus. $5.95pa. LC 77-148722. ISBN 0-695-80218-6.

Subtitled "The Encyclopedia for All Archers," this contains articles on history, basic shooting, equipment, hunting and fishing, making a bow, and much else. There are directories of the archery trade and of organizations, and there is a glossary. Lots of illustrations add interest. For every archer.

709. Lind, Ernie. **The Complete Book of Trick & Fancy Shooting.** New York, Winchester, 1972. 159p. illus. $5.95. LC 79-159431. ISBN 0-87691-045-2.

One of the last of the old professional shooters offers many excellent hints on all kinds of shooting: handguns, shotguns, and rifles. Exhibition shooting is the goal of all this, and there are stories of many of the now-dead champions. Good reading for any gun bug and good instruction for the aspiring marksman. Highly recommended.

710. **Lyman Cast Bullet Handbook.** Middlefield, CT, Lyman Products, 1974. 240p. illus. $4.95pa.

Shooting hand-cast lead bullets is an economical and fascinating activity for sportsmen. Both cartridge and muzzle-loading shooters are well served by this compilation of loading data and other suggestions. For most shooters' libraries.

711. MacLoud, David, *et al.* **Guide to Movie Making.** Los Angeles, Petersen, 1973. 80p. illus. $2.00pa. LC 73-82541. ISBN 0-8227-0024-7.

I've never been bitten by the home movie bug, but I know that I'm the exception. This book is an excellent introduction to the use of movie cameras and accessories for the amateur. Not all the photography will be "outdoor," but the book is a good one to have available.

712. McClurg, David R. **The Amateur's Guide to Caves & Caving.** Harrisburg, PA, Stackpole, 1973. 191p. illus. glossary. $5.95; $2.95pa. LC 72-14152. ISBN 0-8117-0094-1; -2003-9pa.

This is a general introduction to the sport of spelunking. McClurg gives some ideas about why people go caving, about safety and conservation, and about the scientific aspects of cave life. Primarily, however, the book is about the equipment and techniques needed for safe caving. Illustrated with drawings. The book is about caving, not caves, so there are no lists of places to go. Highly recommended.

713. McCrory, Robert H. **Drawings of Locks and Pistols.** Bellmore, NY, McCrory, 1962. 6 plans with text. illus. $3.00.

Nineteen pistols and 4 lock types are illustrated and described. The four lock styles are the match lock, wheel lock, flint lock, and percussion lock. Very good information for the muzzle-loader fan.

714. McCrory, Robert H. **Lock, Stock and Barrel: Antique Gun Repair.** Bellmore, NY, McCrory, 1966. 122p. illus. $4.00pa.

Muzzle-loader shooters are generally inveterate tinkerers, not only building their own guns but constantly adjusting and repairing them. This excellent manual will make the job a lot easier; it has hints on general metal work, wood work, welding and soldering, repairing locks and barrels, disassembly and assembly, and detecting fakes. Highly recommended.

715. McCrory, Robert H. **Make Muzzle Loader Accessories.** 2nd ed. Bellmore, NY, McCrory, 1971. 46p. illus. $2.50pa.

MISCELLANEOUS

Nicely illustrated with drawings, this manual gives instruction in making powder horns, cappers, a loading block, nipple wrench, shot measure, spring vise, adjustable powder measure, ball starter, vent shields, cleaning tools, and patch knives. A very good little book.

716. McCrory, Robert H. **The Modern Kentucky Rifle: How to Build Your Own.** 3rd ed. Bellmore, NY, McCrory, 1968. 71p. illus. plans. $4.00pa.

With photos and drawings and three separate full-scale plans for a flintlock rifle and a pistol, this is a complete guide to making a firearm in a small shop. McCrory notes the parts needed, the metal and wood work, and he gives a plan for a percussion lock as well. Highly recommended for any gun bug with the urge to create his own rifle or pistol.

717. McCrory, Robert H. **A Muzzle-Loading Pistol You Can Build for Under $10.** Bellmore, NY, McCrory, 1963. 17p. illus. $1.50pa.

This handy little manual lists the required parts (barrel, stock, etc.) and gives the directions for building a small muzzle-loading pistol. There are photos and full-size drawings. There are only 29 parts involved, of which 11 are screws and pins. Highly recommended for the craftsman.

718. McEvoy, Harry K. **Knife Throwing: A Practical Guide.** Rutland, VT, Charles E. Tuttle, 1973. 108p. illus. $3.25pa. LC 72-91550. ISBN 0-8048-1099-0.

McEvoy is an old-timer at the game of knife throwing (and knife-making, too, for that matter!) so this little book is authoritative and interesting. There is information about choosing a proper knife, throwing it, developing accuracy, and having fun in general. Tomahawk and Bowie knife throwing is also covered. To round it up, there are notes on hunting with a knife and introductions to some of the noted flingers of today. Highly recommended.

719. Nonte, George C., Jr. **Firearms Encyclopedia.** New York, Harper & Row, 1973. 341p. illus. index. (An Outdoor Life Book). $11.95. LC 73-80712. ISBN 0-06-013213-2.

From "abutment" to "zeroing in," this is an alphabetically arranged dictionary of shooting and related terms. There is a bibliography, a listing of arms associations, a directory of suppliers, and lots of other miscellaneous information. This is the best of the currently available gun dictionaries or encyclopedias for the amateur or beginner.

720. Nonte, George C., Jr. **Home Guide to Muzzle-Loading.** Harrisburg, PA, Stackpole, 1974. 219p. illus. $6.95pa. LC 74-16168. ISBN 0-8117-2101-9.

This general overview of the fast-growing muzzle-loader field has articles on the types of muzzle-loading arms and their ammunition; learning to load, shoot, and care for the arms; safety; using replica guns; making a muzzle-loader; choosing sights and accessories; hunting; modern industrial production; restoring old guns; how old-time gunsmiths worked; and other topics of interest. Edward Yard has contributed a chapter on the "Behavior of Modern Black Powder," and there are appendices with ballistic data and lists of dealers and suppliers. Muzzle-loader shooters tend to be "sot in their ways," as we say in the hills, so some may quibble with parts of this book (or any book on the subject!) but the effect, overall isn't too bad. Recommended as a source of information for the beginning shooter or for anyone needing information on the old-time arms and their use.

721. Phydeaux, Djaugh. **Trapper's Guide.** Taos, NM, Limbo Library, 1973. 56p. illus. $1.95pa.

The cover title reads: "Rocky Mountain Fur Trapper's Guide: the Use of the Mountain Man's Gear Particularly the Indian Trade Gun, Plains Rifle & Accoutrements of the Fur Trade Era." Illustrated with drawings and several photographs, this little book is great reading for the muzzle-loader shooter. There are hints on sharpening flints, setting traps, making clothing, and many more subjects of interest. Highly recommended. The author's name is a pseudonym; it reminds me of the punch line in a well-known Cajun joke.

722. Pullam, William C., and Frank T. Hanenkrat. **Position Rifle Shooting: A How-To Text for Shooters and Coaches.** New York, Winchester, 1973. 272p. illus. index. price not reported. LC 73-75665. ISBN 0-87691-097-5.

Illustrated mostly with photographs, this is the best available manual for shooters wishing to master the basic shooting positions. The athletic challenge is great in this sport, and exacting equipment and technique are required. The positions (kneeling, prone, standing, and sitting) are described for shooters and coaches. Highly recommended as the complete guide. For rank beginners who do not need advanced information, the Boy Scout's $0.45 manual on *Rifle & Shotgun Shooting* will suffice.

723. Ramage, C. Kenneth. **Lyman Black Powder Handbook.** Middlefield, CT, Lyman Products, 1975. 240p. illus. $5.95pa.

The constantly increasing interest in shooting the old-time muzzle-loading guns and modern copies of them inspired this compilation of data for those who need ballistic information. A number of handguns, rifles, and shotguns were fired under test conditions and the results tabulated. There are also several articles on the history of firearms, the methods used in these tests, hunting with muzzle-loaders, and the use of the several types of guns

MISCELLANEOUS

now being made. Especially interesting to many newcomers is the article on how black powder is made. Well illustrated, this handbook belongs in every black powder shooter's library.

724. Roberts, Ned H. **The Muzzle-Loading Cap Lock Rifle.** New York, Bonanza (Crown), 1952. 308p. illus. index. $4.98.

Ned Roberts was one of the grand old-timers who carried the love and knowledge of muzzle-loading guns into this century. He knew the guns, the shooters, and the old-time methods. This book is an excellent compendium of information for all shooters of the old-time guns.

725. Rosenbloom, Joseph. **Kits & Plans.** Willits, CA, Oliver Press, 1973. 273p. $3.95pa. LC 73-92459. ISBN 0-914400-00-2.

This is a listing of available kits and plans for the do-it-yourselfer. Among the "things" are: hi-fi equipment, hovercrafts, boats, homes, cuckoo clocks, airplanes, muzzle-loading rifles, and barbecue pits. A master list of products indexes the listings by manufacturer. Very handy.

726. Rowlands, John J. **Cache Lake Country: Life in the North Woods.** Wilderness ed. New York, Norton, 1959. 272p. illus. index. $5.95. LC 59-13370. ISBN 0-393-08468-X.

Originally published in 1947, this is the story of a man's life during a year spent in the North Woods of eastern Canada. Throughout the text, Rowlands philosophy comes through and he introduces much woods lore, natural history, recipes and other pertinent material. The delightful drawings are by Henry B. Kane. Highly recommended.

727. Rutstrum, Calvin. **The Wilderness Cabin.** Rev. ed. New York, Macmillan, 1972. 194p. illus. index. $5.95. LC 73-171992.

Illustrated with numerous photographs and with drawings by Les Kouba, this book is subtitled "How to build your own log, frame, or adobe cabin and where to build it." The history of our cabins, selecting a site, and choosing and using the several tools (including a chain saw), accompany the many suggestions for cabins of several sizes and styles. I'm for the "one-room unimproved cabin" because I doubt if I'd be able to do much more, but the more advanced builder will find more sophisticated plans. Recommended for any cabin-builder.

728. Scorer, Richard Segar. **Clouds of the World: A Complete Colour Encyclopedia.** Harrisburg, PA, Stackpole, 1972. 176p. illus.(part col.). index. bibliog. $29.95. LC 72-1112. ISBN 0-8117-1961-8.

This is a large photographic record of most of the cloud types likely to be encountered anywhere on earth. There is a short history of cloud

OUTDOOR RECREATION

classification, but most of the book consists of color photos with descriptive text. Expensive, of course, but the serious amateur will be well-served by this one.

729. Smith, Ronald. **Drawing.** New York, Dover, 1942. 189p. illus. (Teach Yourself Books). $2.00pa. ISBN 0-340-05562-6.

This is a pocket-sized text in the basic principles of drawing. Smith covers the materials, perspective, light and shade, etc. Drawing outdoor subjects is included, and pencil, pen, charcoal and other media are discussed. A good little book for the outdoor recreationist.

730. Stelle, James Parish, and William B. Harrison. **The Gunsmith's Manual.** Highland Park, NJ, Gun Room Press, 1972. 376p. illus. $9.95. LC 72-187111. ISBN 0-88227-002-8.

Originally published in 1883. The subtitle reads: "A Complete Handbook for the American Gunsmith, being a Practical Guide to All Branches of the Trade." Stelle was a watchmaker and archaeologist; Harrison wrote books about mechanics. This book is a good description of the guns in use during the 1880s, including muzzle-loaders and breech-loaders. Among the many topics are cleaning and repair, required tools and how to use them, work benches, working in steel, iron, silver and other metals, making gun stocks, barrels, and other parts. This is an excellent source of obscure information for muzzle-loader fans. Highly recommended for the serious shooter.

731. Styers, John. **Cold Steel.** Boulder, CO, Paladin, 1974. 179p. illus. $9.95. ISBN 0-87364-025-X.

This is an introduction to bayonet and knife fighting and other types of combat. There is a section on knife throwing, which is why we include it here. A very good book for knife fans.

732. Sussman, Aaron. **The Amateur Photographer's Handbook.** 8th rev. ed. New York, Crowell, 1973. 562p. illus.(part col.). index. glossary. $8.95. LC 72-8868. ISBN 0-690-05782-2.

A complete explanation of photography for the amateur: cameras, films, composition, developing and printing, filters, you name it. For the really serious camera user.

733. Townsend, Philip. **Maine Catalog.** Portland, ME, Media House (distr.: RPM Distr.), 1973. 177p. illus. $2.00pa.

This seems to be the first "state" catalog on the "Whole Earth" theme. It contains a good many facts about the state of Maine, with its rich natural and historic heritage. There are sections on such subjects as edible plants, wildfood recipes, topographic maps, canoeing, camping, bicycling and

MISCELLANEOUS

recycling, geology, farming, the dance and the theater, museums and landmarks, free schools, and cooperatives. Lots of good information and addresses for further information or products.

734. Tryon, T. B. **The Complete Rehabilitation of the Flintlock Rifle & Other Works.** Taos, NM, Limbo Library, 1972. 112p. illus. $6.95.

The material in this book was originally published in a series of articles in *The American Rifleman* of the 1930s. It is about percussion plains rifles, Colt revolvers, and other aspects of muzzle-loader shooting. Illustrated with drawings and containing a glossary, this is all about "How to load, shoot, clean, repair & enjoy muzzle loading flintlock and percussion rifles, revolvers and shotguns." T. B. Tryon is a pen name. Many excellent hints for the shooter.

735. Wambold, H. R. **Bowhunting for Deer.** Rev. ed. Harrisburg, PA, Stackpole, 1965. 160p. illus. $5.95. LC 64-21466.

This is a concise guide to bowhunting for deer. It has information on equipment, game habits, hunting methods, and getting the meat to the table. An interesting manual for the countryman.

736. Weygers, Alexander G. **The Modern Blacksmith.** New York, Van Nostrand Reinhold, 1974. 96p. illus. $8.95; $4.95pa. LC 73-14101. ISBN 0-442-29362-3; -29363-1pa.

Since blacksmithing is the basis of most metal work, a knowledge of its tools and methods will benefit anyone trying to do his own repairs around the old homestead. Weygers has been concerned mostly with making tools and other devices for his sculpturing activities, but his instructions on blacksmithing without a helper are excellent and easy to follow. Beginning with the shop and the equipment needed to furnish it, Weygers covers heating, hammering, shaping, bending, tempering, hardening, and making tools and various useful items. Illustrated mostly with drawings, this book and its companion, *The Making of Tools* (entry 648) should be available to most handy country dwellers. Highly recommended.

737. Woods, Jim, ed. **Guns & Ammo Complete Guide to Blackpowder.** Los Angeles, Petersen, 1974. 224p. illus.(part col.). $4.95pa. LC 73-92483. ISBN 0-8227-0053-0.

This is a guide to shooting blackpowder guns, mostly muzzle-loaders. Rifles, shotguns, and handguns are included. There are tests of several modern guns, articles on hunting and target shooting, and historical features about guns, people, and battles. Some of the information is odd or incorrect, but the bulk of the book is of value to shooters. Recommended.

738. Woods, Jim, ed. **Guns & Ammo Guidebook to Knives & Edged Weapons.** Los Angeles, Petersen, 1974. 192p. illus.(part col.). $4.95pa. LC 74-77029. ISBN 0-8227-0054-9.

This well-illustrated manual is all about knives and how they are made today. Commercial and custom knife-makers are covered, and there are articles on the history and use of knives. Knife throwing is described, too. A lot of good reading in this one.

739. Zim, Herbert S., and Robert H. Baker. **Stars: A Guide to the Constellations, Sun, Moon, Planets, and Other Features of the Heavens.** New York, Golden Press, 1956. 160p. illus.(col.). index. (A Golden Nature Guide). $1.50pa. LC 61-8327.

This introduction to astronomy is rather badly outdated so far as some of the facts go, but the star charts are good enough to be used by the casual observer. It is easy to carry around in the field. For planet identification, I'd want something more.

PERIODICALS

GENERAL CAMPING AND TRAVEL

Articles on all aspects of camping and recreational vehicle travel will be found in many magazines not directly concerned with camping. Among the many periodicals that may carry information of interest are these: *Holiday*, *Sunset*, *Popular Science*, *Popular Mechanics*, *Mechanix Illustrated*, and quite a few regional magazines of rather limited circulation. Some of the general periodicals on camping and the outdoors are listed here.

740. **Boys Life.** Route 1, New Brunswick, NJ 08902. monthly. illus. ads. $4.00.

This is the official Boy Scout magazine. It contains fiction, Scout news, plus articles and notes on camping equipment and techniques.

741. **Campground & RV Park Management.** P.O. Box 1014, Grass Valley, CA 95945. 8x/yr. illus. ads. $4.00.

This is a newspaper for owners of campgrounds. Listed here in case a reader wishes to explore the legislative and business aspects of campground operation.

742. **Camping.** Link House, Dingwall Ave., Croydon CR9 2TA, England. monthly. illus. ads. $8.00.

This British magazine covers most aspects of camping with news of new equipment, campgrounds, vehicles, etc. For anyone wishing to get the British viewpoint on camping, this is the magazine to get. Well illustrated.

743. **Camping and Trailering Guide: The Magazine of the Friendly Campers.** P.O. Box 1014, Grass Valley, CA 95945. monthly. illus. ads. $5.50.

Contains feature articles on many aspects of camping and vehicle travel, campground trends, nature study, and things to visit.

OUTDOOR RECREATION

744. **Camping Journal.** P.O. Box 2600, Greenwich, CT 06830. monthly. illus. ads. $8.95.

"The Magazine of Family Outdoor Recreation," this one contains articles and notes on all aspects of camping: equipment, vehicles, places to visit, campgrounds, photography, etc. Many suggestions for vacation planners. I'd choose this title as best for a family wanting interesting general camping information.

745. **Camping Magazine.** 5 Mountain Ave., North Plainfield, NJ 07060. 9x/yr. illus. ads. $9.00.

This is the "Official American Camping Association Magazine," and it is not for campers at all. Listed here so you'll know that it is primarily for the owners and operators of organized private camps.

746. **Canadian Frontier.** P.O. Box 2071, Vancouver 3, British Columbia. quarterly. illus. $3.50.

Covering all provinces, this magazine is mostly about the history of the country, but it does have articles on treasure hunting, old mines, and other things of interest to back-road rovers.

747. **Desert Magazine.** 74-109 Larrea St., Palm Desert, CA 92260. monthly. illus. ads. $5.00.

Basically about the Southwest deserts, this contains information on travel, wildlife, gem collecting, ghost towns, relics, and local history.

748. **Field and Stream.** 383 Madison Ave., New York, NY 10017. monthly. illus. ads. $5.00.

This is one of the old national outdoor magazines. It carries articles on all aspects of outdoor recreation: fishing and hunting, conservation, shooting, dogs, backpacking, etc.

749. **Four Seasons Trails.** 534 North Broadway, Milwaukee, WI 53202. bimonthly. illus. ads. $3.60.

Illustrated with many photographs, this contains travel suggestions.

750. **Leisure Trails.** P.O. Box 137, Billings, MT 59103. quarterly. illus. $1.00.

The official KOA magazine, this is free to members of the KOA Kamper Klub. There are reports of rallys, new campgrounds, places to visit, etc.

PERIODICALS

751. **Midwest Outdoors.** P.O. Box 426, Downers Grove, IL 60515. monthly. illus. ads. $3.00.

In newspaper format, this contains information on hunting, fishing, places to visit, and how-to articles.

752. **Northeast Outdoors.** 95 North Main St., Waterbury, CT 06702. monthly. illus. ads. $3.00.

Covering New England, New York, and New Jersey, this regional publication carries information on campgrounds, things to do and visit, and vacation hints.

753. **Outdoor Life.** 355 Lexington Ave., New York, NY 10017. monthly. illus. ads. $5.00.

Another of the older outdoor magazines, this contains articles on all aspects of camping, hunting, fishing, shooting, conservation, etc. It is the only general outdoor magazine that has an archery column.

754. **Southern Outdoors.** 6300 Westpark, Suite 430, Houston, TX 77027. bimonthly. illus. ads. $3.60.

A regional magazine with articles on fishing, boating, hunting, camping, and travel.

755. **Sports Afield.** 250 West 55th St., New York, NY 10019. monthly. illus. ads. $5.00.

A long-time general outdoor magazine with articles on fishing, hunting, camping, travel, dogs, etc.

756. **Western Outdoors.** P.O. Box 2027, Newport Beach, CA 92663. monthly. illus. ads. $5.50.

This is "The Monthly Magazine for the Western Sportsman." It carries articles on hunting, fishing, travel, boating, archery, cooking, etc.

BACKPACKING, MOUNTAINEERING, AND SURVIVAL

757. **American Hiker.** 2236 Mimosa Dr., Houston, TX 77019. bimonthly. illus. ads. $5.00.

OUTDOOR RECREATION

No longer in existence. The subtitle reads: "the magazine for backpackers and hikers." Contained articles on hiking technique, equipment and technical reports, trail news, conservation, and stories of hikes.

758. **Appalachia.** 5 Joy St., Boston, MA 02108. 13x/yr. illus. ads. $10.00.

This is the publication of the Appalachian Mountain Club. It carries articles about hiking, climbing, equipment, general information, and club news.

759. **Back Country.** 350 South Kellogg Ave., Suite S, Goleta, CA 93017. monthly. illus. $12.00.

Announced for publication early in 1975, this is intended to be a newsletter about equipment, techniques, new books, and other such things of interest to backpackers, ski tourers, snowshoers and similar folk. None of the travelogues and no color photos. No advertising. Looks good. In April 1975 the title was changed to *Wild Country*.

760. **Backpacker.** 28 West 44th St., New York, NY 10036. quarterly. illus. ads. $7.50.

This magazine began by stating that it would be sold only to backpackers and that it was not interested in enticing newcomers to the sport. It contains articles on all aspects of the sport: equipment tests, book reviews, stories about personalities (e.g., John Burroughs), suggestions on places to hike, etc. Many photographs, especially color.

761. **Better Camping & Hiking.** 500 Hyacinth Place, Highland Park, IL 60035. monthly. illus. ads. $6.00.

No longer in existence. Formerly called *Better Camping* or *Woodall's Better Camping*, this magazine had articles on hiking, backpacking, trailering, kayaking, vehicles, places to go, trail information, all kinds of camping and the equipment that goes with it.

762. **The Canadian Alpine Journal.** P.O. Box 1026, Banff, Alberta. annual. illus. $3.50.

This is the complete record of climbing activity in Canada, with articles about climbs, climbers, equipment and technique. Beautifully done.

763. **Climbing.** P.O. Box E, Aspen, CO 81611. bimonthly. illus. $4.50.

This is the "American Mountaineering and Rockclimbing Magazine." It has articles on climbing equipment and technique, personalities, book notes, climbing routes, safety hints, and fiction.

PERIODICALS

764. **Hiking & Ski Touring.** P.O. Box 7421, Colorado Springs, CO 80907. bimonthly (?). illus. $10.00 membership.

This is an eight-page newsletter for those interested in establishing and rebuilding America's trails. The issue I've seen has articles on shoes and ski-touring equipment plus notes on a variety of the organization's activities.

765. **Mountain Gazette.** 1801 York St., Denver, CO 80206. monthly. illus. ads. $5.00.

This newspaper-format publication carries articles on anything even remotely related to mountains: backpacking, climbing, mountain music, etc., with news stories, book reviews, and lots of interesting material.

766. **Mountain Safety Research Newsletter.** South 96th St. at 8th Ave. South, Seattle, WA 98108. irreg. illus. $0.50 per issue.

This small publication primarily carries reports of equipment tests, but there are other articles on health, safety, etc. The organization also has a manufacturing and retail business. An interesting and very informative title for almost any serious outdoorsman.

767. **National Trails Council Newsletter.** P.O. Box 236, Harpers Ferry, WV 25425.

The organization attempts to coordinate information about trails. I have not seen the newsletter.

768. **Pacific Wilderness Journal.** P.O. Box 22272, Portland, OR 97222. bimonthly. illus. ads. $3.00.

"The journal is dedicated to the re-evaluation, to the pleasure of knowing a piece of land intimately, the insights we can gain from our past, the importance of our heritage and the need to save it, to the need for clear thinking." Well, I'm for all that! The magazine carries articles on backpacking and its equipment, nature crafts, animal life, canoeing, walking, and local history. Interesting.

769. **Sierra Club Bulletin.** 1050 Mills Tower, San Francisco, CA 94104. monthly. illus. ads. $5.00 to non-members.

Contains articles on conservation, legislation, Club projects, etc. Nothing about recreational activities, as such, but I thought you should know.

770. **Signpost.** 16812 36th Ave. West, Lynnwood, WA 98036. 16x/yr. illus. ads. $7.50.

This is published in two formats: there is a quarterly magazine and a monthly newsletter, both carrying articles on backpacking and related

OUTDOOR RECREATION

subjects. Trail reports are an important concern of the organization, which also publishes several booklets about backpacking. Rather local in interest: Washington, Oregon, and British Columbia.

771. **Summit.** P.O. Box 1889, Big Bear Lake, CA 92315. 10x/yr. illus. ads. $7.00.

This is "a mountaineering magazine" with articles on climbing in the United States and the world: safety, accident reports, equipment, skiing, climbing reports, anything of interest to climbers.

772. **Trail Camping.** P.O. Box 310, Canoga Park, CA 91305. monthly. illus. ads. $9.00.

No longer published. "The complete magazine for the wilderness enthusiast" contained many color illustrations and articles on hiking and backpacking, snowshoeing and ski-touring, packing with stock animals, canoeing, and mountaineering. There was a "strong conservation theme."

773. **Wilderness Camping.** P.O. Box 1186, Scotia, NY 12302. bimonthly. illus. ads. $3.00.

Begun in 1971, this magazine contains articles on all aspects of backpacking, equipment and techniques, book reviews, ski touring and snowshoeing, etc. If I had to choose one title from this list, this would be the one.

Woodall's Better Camping. *See* **Better Camping & Hiking.**

IDENTIFYING AND COLLECTING

774. **Canadian Rockhound.** 941 Wavertree Rd., North Vancouver, B.C. V7R 1S4. bimonthly. illus. ads. $3.00 (U.S. $3.50).

This is published by The Lapidary, Rock and Mineral Society of British Columbia, but it appears to cover all of Canada with club news. Although it is mostly concerned with lapidary work, there are suggestions about collecting localities.

775. **Canadian Treasure.** P.O. Box 2071, Vancouver 3, British Columbia. quarterly. illus. ads. $3.50 Canadian.

Features true stories about buried treasures, lost mines, collecting bottles, etc.

PERIODICALS

776. **Earth Science.** P.O. Box 1815, Colorado Springs, CO 80901. bimonthly. illus. ads. $3.00.

A popular journal of geology, mostly for rock and mineral collectors, fossil and artifact hunters, all amateurs. Well-done little magazine.

777. **Gems and Gemology.** 11940 San Vicente Blvd., Los Angeles, CA 90049. quarterly. illus. ads. $3.50.

Mostly for the jewelry trade, it concerns gem testing and cutting. Published by the Gemological Institute of America, which also has several technical publications.

778. **Gems and Minerals.** P.O. Box 687, Mentone, CA 92359. monthly. illus. ads. $4.75.

This is the official magazine of the American Federation of Mineralogical Societies, which says that it is "The Leading Gem and Mineral Hobby Magazine." Features news of shows, field trips, club outings, etc. Articles on gem cutting, collecting localities. Excellent journal.

779. **Lapidary Journal.** P.O. Box 80937, San Diego, CA 92138. monthly. illus. ads. $5.75.

Carrying news of gem shows and articles about gems, localities, gem cutting and other lapidary arts, this publication says that it is "The largest gem publication for amateur hobbyists in the world."

780. **Locating Gold, Gems & Minerals.** 5665 Park Crest Drive, San Jose, CA 95118. bimonthly. illus. ads. $6.00.

The United Prospectors publishes this small newsletter, which contains club news and suggestions about prospecting anywhere in the United States. The group offers a course in the "Principles of Prospecting."

781. **The Mineralogical Record.** P.O. Box 783, Bowie, MD 20715. bimonthly. illus. ads. $6.00.

This is "affiliated with the Friends of Mineralogy." It carries articles on general mineralogy, field occurrences, and lapidary work. It is about half-way between a technical journal and the popular collectors' magazines.

782. **National Treasure Hunters League.** P.O. Box 53, Mesquite, TX 75149. quarterly. illus. ads. $5.00.

This is essentially a catalog of items available from the League. There are short articles on treasure hunting, mostly with metal detectors. Interesting stuff. An excellent source for treasure hunting books.

OUTDOOR RECREATION

783. **Popular Archaeology.** P.O. Box 18387, Wichita, KS 67218. monthly. illus. $7.00.

Devoted to news of interest to archaeologists, particularly amateurs. Articles on personalities, historical events, salvage projects, etc. Interested in getting amateurs into proper scientific techniques.

784. **Rock and Gem.** 16001 Ventura Blvd., Encino, CA 91316. monthly. illus. ads. $8.00.

Mostly about lapidary work and crafts.

785. **Rockhound.** P.O. Box 328, Conroe, TX 77301. bimonthly. illus. ads. $3.50.

"Where and how to find gems & minerals." Features maps and good directions to collecting sites. Has many ads for books and supplies.

786. **Rocks and Minerals.** P.O. Box 29, Peekskill, NY 10566. monthly. illus. ads. $4.25.

"America's Oldest and Most Versatile Magazine for the Mineralogist, Geologist, Lapidary." Official journal of the Rocks and Minerals Association. Contains articles on gems, minerals, lapidary work, collecting sites, and club news.

787. **The Treasure Hunter.** P.O. Box 188, Midway City, CA 92655. bimonthly. illus. ads. $3.00.

This small newsletter for treasure hunters has articles on lost treasure hoards, meetings, equipment, and current events. Mostly about California.

788. **Treasure Hunting Unlimited.** 406 Broadway, Truth or Consequences, NM 87901. irreg. illus. ads. $7.50.

Contains news items but is mostly a catalog of detector equipment.

789. **True Treasure.** Drawer L, Conroe, TX 77301. bimonthly. illus. ads. $3.50.

Contains true stories about lost mines and buried or sunken treasure. Many advertisements for equipment and books.

VEHICLE ACTIVITIES

In addition to the periodicals listed here, there are many general "outdoor" magazines that carry articles of interest to vehicle users. Too, there are many magazines devoted to specific autos or cycles.

790. **AMA News.** P.O. Box 141, Westerville, OH 43081. monthly. illus. ads. $3.00.

A subscription to this magazine is included with membership in the American Motorcycle Association. The publication carries articles on various aspects of motorcycling, including news of races, legislation, and uses for motorcycles.

791. **American Bicyclist & Motorcyclist.** Cycling Press, Inc., 461 Eighth Ave., New York, NY 10001. monthly. illus. ads. $4.00.

This is a trade publication only. Not for recreationists.

792. **The Bicycle Paper.** P.O. Box 842, Seattle, WA 98111. 7x/yr. illus. ads. $2.25.

This small newspaper contains biking news of interest to those in Seattle and the immediate Northwest. It was formerly called "The Great Bicycle Conspiracy" and is mostly about touring.

793. **Bicycle Spokesman.** 119 East Palatine Rd., Palatine, IL 60067. monthly. illus. ads. $8.00.

"Devoted to recreation, camping, safety and touring--family style." Contains articles about tours and touring, legislation, racing events, and new equipment.

794. **Bicycling!** P.O. Box 3330, San Rafael, CA 94901. monthly. illus. ads. $8.00.

This is about "The Pleasure & Excitement of Cycling." It carries road tests, racing news, vacation suggestions, fiction, and articles about equipment, technique, health, and general bicycling news. It incorporates the former publication *Two Wheel Trip.*

795. **biker/hiker.** P.O. Box 919, Kermit, TX 79745. monthly. illus. ads. $5.00.

A small newspaper, this carries news of interest to both the bicyclist and the hiker: bike tripping, racing, legislation, backpacking, news of equipment.

OUTDOOR RECREATION

796. **Bike World.** P.O. Box 366, Mountain View, CA 94040. monthly. illus. ads. $7.00.

All aspects of bicycling are covered in this excellent magazine: selection and care of bikes, cross-country touring, personalities, racing, etc. If you want only one periodical, this is the one. Highly recommended.

797. **Camper Coachman.** 23945 Craftsman Rd., Calabasas, CA 91302. monthly. illus. ads. $5.00.

"America's First & Only Publication Devoted Exclusively to Truck Campers." Contains articles of general interest plus technical information about trucks, campers, and accessories.

798. **Competitive Cycling.** P.O. Box 1256, Pacific Palisades, CA 90272. 10x/yr. (April-January). $5.00.

Devoted to racing. No issues were examined.

799. **Cycle.** P.O. Box 2776, Boulder, CO 80302. monthly. illus. ads. $6.00.

This is about motorcycles; it carries road tests and articles on touring and competition.

800. **Cycle CMA.** 20 Jarvis St., Hamilton, Ontario L8R 1M2. monthly. illus. ads. $7.00.

This is the "Official National Publication of the Canadian Motorcycle Association," covering club news, racing, personalities, legislation, and notices of new products.

801. **Cycle Guide.** P.O. Box 267, Mount Morris, IL 61054. monthly. illus. ads. $6.00.

A general motorcycling magazine covering such things as road tests and races, with articles on a variety of topics.

802. **Cycle Illustrated.** 222 Park Ave. South, New York, NY 10003. 8x/yr. illus. ads. $5.00.

Carries general articles about motorcycles and motorcycling.

803. **Cycle News West.** P.O. Box 498, Long Beach, CA 90801. weekly. illus. ads. $12.50.

This is the best newspaper for motorcyclists. It carries all sorts of news of interest—about racing, new products, legislation, etc. Also published in editions for the *East* and *South*.

804. **Cycle World.** P.O. Box 2324, FDR Station, New York, NY 10022. monthly. illus. ads. $7.00.

"America's Leading Motorcycle Enthusiasts' Publication." Carries articles about races, road tests of new cycles, and general material of all kinds. Best for the average motorcycle fan.

805. **Cyclenews: A Journal of Bicycle Racing.** 12 Cherry St., Brattleboro, VT 05301. 10x/yr. (Feb.-Nov.). illus. ads. $2.00.

A newspaper carrying news of racing, personalities, and equipment.

806. **Dirt Bike.** P.O. Box 317, Encino, CA 91316. monthly. illus. ads. $7.50.

This is the best magazine for dirt bike fans. It contains articles on riding techniques, racing, personalities, technical stuff, and tests of motorcycles and accessories. Highly recommended.

807. **Dirt Cycle.** 222 Park Ave. South, New York, NY 10003. bimonthly. illus. ads. $6.00.

Contains road tests and articles about techniques and competitive events. Intended for the off-road motorcyclist.

808. **Dune Buggies & Hot VWs.** P.O. Box 2260, Costa Mesa, CA 92626. bimonthly. illus. ads. $4.00.

Contains articles of interest to racers and dune buggy fans, mostly owners of VWs and Porsches. A good little magazine.

809. **Family Motor Coaching.** P.O. Box 44144, Cincinnati, OH 45244. 7x/yr. illus. ads. $5.00.

This is the "Official Publication of the Family Motor Coach Association" and it has articles about living in and driving motor homes. Articles on places, people, problems, clubs, and hints of all sorts.

810. **Four Wheeler.** P.O. Box 978, North Hollywood, CA 91601. monthly (except May). illus. ads. $7.00.

"Everyone's Off Road Magazine" has articles on vehicles, racing, and technical information about vehicles and accessories. Mostly for competition drivers.

The Great Bicycle Conspiracy. *See* **The Bicycle Paper.**

811. **Mini Cycle.** P.O. Box 978, North Hollywood, CA 91601. monthly. illus. ads. $7.50.

OUTDOOR RECREATION

"America's First Mini-Cycle Magazine" carries articles on road tests, racing, riding techniques, etc. Probably the best magazine for riders of the small cycles.

812. **Mobile Living: The Magazine of Recreational Living.** 1323 Main St., Sarasota, FL 33578. monthly. illus. ads. $3.00.

Intended for owners of mobile homes, this contains articles about trailers and equipment, trailer problems, etc. Formerly called the *Mobile Home Owner Magazine.*

813. **Motorcycle World.** 222 Park Ave. South, New York, NY 10003. bimonthly. illus. ads. $4.50.

Contains road tests and other general information.

814. **Motorcyclist.** P.O. Box 3296, Los Angeles, CA 90028. monthly. illus. ads. $6.00.

Contains road tests and other general material of interest to motorcyclists. An old publication taken over in 1972 by Petersen Publishing Co. The title was formerly spelled as two words. One of the best.

815. **Motorhome Life.** 23945 Craftsman Rd., Calabasas, CA 91302. bimonthly. illus. ads. $5.00.

All about motorhomes, van conversions and mini-motorhomes. Has articles about vehicles, accessories, technical information, road tests, travel suggestions, and much general material.

816. **New Directions in Bicycle Safety.** c/o Bicycle Institute of America, Inc., 122 East 42nd St., New York, NY 10017. free.

This is a small resume of safety information for bicyclists, carrying news of new booklets, films, and programs.

817. **The ORV Monitor.** Environmental Defense Fund, 2728 Durant Ave., Berkeley, CA 94704. bimonthly. illus. $6.00.

The source of this newsletter should alert the reader to the fact that this is an anti-vehicle propaganda sheet. The letter which came with what I presume was a sample issue announced that "Snowmobiles, dune buggies, trail bikes and other off-road vehicles (ORVs) have become a major threat to our environment." The hordes of backpackers are a major threat, too, but who cares, huh? The title of this publication does not indicate its content, hence this note.

PERIODICALS

818. **Off-Road Advertiser.** P.O. Box 340, Lakewood, CA 90714. monthly. illus. ads. $3.00.

A small magazine that is mostly about racing in Southern California. It does, however, carry many advertisements for dune buggy parts, so it is useful to drivers anywhere.

819. **Off Road Vehicles.** 131 South Barrington Place, Los Angeles, CA 90049. irreg. illus. ads. $0.75 per copy.

This is a very good magazine about off-road racing. It carries articles on vehicles and equipment, road tests, and travel notes. Includes motorcycles, too.

820. **PV4, Pickup, Van & 4WD.** P.O. Box 2324, FDR Station, New York, NY 10022. bimonthly. illus. ads. $4.00.

Contains feature articles on all aspects of the vehicles mentioned in the title: road tests, accessories evaluations, technical information of all kinds. Very good.

821. **Popular Cycling.** 131 South Barrington Place, Los Angeles, CA 90049. monthly. illus. ads. $6.00.

A general motorcycling magazine with articles on racing, road tests, personalities, etc. A good magazine.

822. **RV World.** 16200 Ventura Blvd., Encino, CA 91316. monthly. illus. ads. $7.50.

"The Family Camping Guide" carries articles on recvees and their use, including travel suggestions and other general information.

823. **Road Rider.** P.O. Box 678, South Laguna, CA 92677. monthly. illus. ads. $7.50.

Intended for touring motorcyclists, this great magazine has articles on the large bikes, side cars, trip narratives, rallies, camping, and road tests.

824. **Sailing Wheels.** 7305 Van Nuys Blvd., Van Nuys, CA 91405.

This is the official publication of the National Sand Sailing Association. I think it appears bimonthly. In mimeograph format, it costs $10.00 for full members and $5.00 for non-owners. News of the Association.

825. **Sport Car.** P.O. Box 32, Nyack, NY 10960. monthly. illus. ads. $0.75 per issue.

The journal of the Sports Car Club of America, this carries news mostly of race results.

826. **Trail Bike Quarterly.** 131 South Barrington Place, Los Angeles, CA 90049. quarterly. illus. $1.00 per issue.

This is intended for dirt bike owners. It contains road tests of new motorcycles, practical technical articles, and other items of interest. This may no longer be available as of late 1974; I have not been able to find a copy or get an answer from the publisher.

827. **Trailer Life.** 23945 Craftsman Rd., Calabasas, CA 91302. monthly. illus. ads. $6.50.

This is the official publication of the International Travel and Trailer Clubs of America, Inc. It has articles of general interest to trailer owners, including road tests, travel suggestions, etc.

Trailer Travel. *See* **Woodall's Trailer Travel.**

Two Wheel Trip. *See* **Bicycling!** (entry 794).

828. **Wheels Afield.**

"The Complete Camping Magazine" ceased publication and merged into *Motor Trend* magazine early in 1975.

829. **Woodall's Trailer Travel.** 500 Hyacinth Place, Highland Park, IL 60035. monthly. illus. ads. $6.50.

Contains news of interest to travel trailer owners, primarily, with articles on places to go, new vehicles, and technical material.

WINTER ACTIVITIES

Please note that articles on any of the wintry activities will be found in almost any "camping" magazine.

830. **Nordic World.** P.O. Box 366, Mountain View, CA 94040. bimonthly. illus. ads. $4.00.

This is apparently the only magazine devoted to ski touring or cross country skiing and, indeed, it calls itself the "Cross-country skiers' magazine."

PERIODICALS

There are travel suggestions and reports, news of personalities, history of ski touring, backpacking, technical articles about snow and skiing equipment, and health and safety hints.

831. **Popular Snowmobiling.** 131 South Barrington Place, Los Angeles, CA 90049. 4x/yr. (Sept.-Dec.). illus. ads. $4.00.

Contains feature articles on the use of snowmobiles, tests of new machines, technical features on rebuilding engines, general snowmobile repair, competition news, etc.

832. **Sno Mobile Times.** 3000 France Ave. South, Minneapolis, MN 55416. 6x/yr. (Sept.-Feb.).

I have not been able to find a copy of this magazine, but I believe it is intended for snowmobile dealers.

SnoTrack. *See* **USSA SnoTrack.**

833. **Snow Goer.** P.O. Box 3566, St. Paul, MN 55165. 6x/yr. (Sept.-Feb.). illus. ads. $4.00.

"The International Snowmobile Magazine." Publishes test reports, technical information, and feature articles on all aspects of the sport. A supplement is called the *Racing Annual* ($1.25).

834. **USSA SnoTrack.** 534 North Broadway, Milwaukee, WI 53202. 6x/yr. illus. ads. $3.00.

Contains general interest articles about snowmobiling, but racing is the chief interest.

WATER ACTIVITIES

835. **Amateur Boat Building.** 3183 Merrill, Royal Oak, MI 48072. bimonthly. illus. ads. $6.00.

The official publication of the "International Amateur Boat Building Society" carries articles on the building of larger boats, both power and sail. The guy who wants to build a canoe or rowboat must go elsewhere.

836. **American Boating.** 13920 Mt. McClellan, Reno, NV 89506. monthly. illus. ads. $5.00.

OUTDOOR RECREATION

"The Journal of Western Waterways" is a newspaper that carries news of interest to boaters, principally in the Western states: boating, racing, new boats and other products, stories of cruises, etc. Many illustrations. There are editions for: Northern California, Southern California, and the Northwest.

American Canoeist. *See* **Canoe.**

837. **American Whitewater.** P.O. Box 1584, San Bruno, CA 94066. quarterly. illus. ads. $3.50.

This is "The Journal of the American Whitewater Affiliation." It is "dedicated to the sport and adventure of whitewater paddling and to the saving of wild, free-running rivers." There are articles on boats and equipment, techniques, racing, and club activities.

838. **Aquatic World.** P.O. Box 366, Mountain View, CA 94040. bimonthly. illus. ads. $3.50.

"The Swimmers' Magazine" is mostly about competitive swimming, training, and personalities.

839. **Boat Owners Buyers Guide.** Yachting Pub. Corp., 50 West 44th St., New York, NY 10036. annual. illus. ads. $2.00.

This is a directory of all kinds of boating equipment and accessories.

840. **Boating.** P.O. Box 1090, Flushing, NY 11352. monthly. illus. ads. $7.00.

This magazine contains much interesting information for the owners of small boats.

841. **Canadian Boating.** Arthurs Publications Ltd., 5200 Dixie Rd., Mississauga, Ontario. 10x/yr. illus. ads. $4.00.

"Canada's National Magazine of Boating and Yachting since 1925." Contains general boating news, stories of cruises, and information about safety, piloting, technical gear, and new products. Covers both sail and powerboats. The same company also publishes a quarterly for boat dealers called *Marine & Outdoor Trades.*

842. **Canoe.** P.O. Box 1888, St. Paul, MN 55111. bimonthly. illus. ads. $5.00.

The official publication of the American Canoe Association, this is a continuation of *American Canoeist.* It is devoted to canoeing and associated activities: kayaking, racing, camping, safety, and equipment.

PERIODICALS

843. **Dive: The Prestige Magazine of Sport Diving and Oceanology.** P.O. Box 7765, Long Beach, CA 90807. bimonthly. illus. ads. $5.00.

With lots of color photography, this large magazine contains articles on travel, spearfishing, treasure hunting, marine life, boats, diving equipment, and techniques.

844. **Down River.** P.O. Box 366, Mountain View, CA 94040. bimonthly. illus. ads. $4.00.

This is all about kayaking, canoeing, rafting, wilderness camping, river racing, techniques, and equipment. First issue in July 1974. It looks better than *Canoe* and *American Whitewater* and covers more types of action.

845. **Family Houseboating.** 23945 Craftsman Rd., Calabasas, CA 91302. bimonthly. illus. ads. $4.00.

"America's first magazine devoted exclusively to houseboats." Articles about buying and using houseboats, travel information, and news about boats, motors, and accessories.

846. **International Surfing.** 27635 Forbes Rd., Laguna Naguel, CA 92677. bimonthly. illus. ads. $5.00.

Contains articles and shorter items about surfing news, personalities, equipment, and techniques. Many illustrations, including color photos.

847. **Motor Boating & Sailing.** P.O. Box 544, New York, NY 10019. monthly. illus. ads. $10.00.

Contains feature articles on seamanship, boats, places to visit, design and building of boats, plus shorter news items on new products, laws and regulations, etc. Many advertisements for boats and equipment.

848. **Multihull Sailing.** P.O. Box 57218, Los Angeles, CA 90057. quarterly. illus. ads. $5.00.

Contains articles about new boats and accessories, races, building plans, and other items of interest to owners and users of catamarans and trimarans. Now containing fewer than 30 pages, the magazine will probably grow with interest in this type of sailing craft.

849. **Powerboat: The World's Leading Performance Boating Magazine.** P.O. Box 3842, Van Nuys, CA 91407. monthly. illus. ads. $7.00.

Highpower motorboats are the thing here whether inboards or outboards. There are articles about regattas and other competitions, new boats and engines, and test reports (including skier appraisals). The same publisher

OUTDOOR RECREATION

also has *Powerboat Industry* (bimonthly, $8.00) and *Powerboat Performance Reports* (annual, $1.00), the latter title being a compilation of test reports from *Powerboat*.

850. **Rudder.** Fawcett Building, Greenwich, CT 06830. monthly. illus. ads. $7.00.

Calling itself the "first magazine for boatmen," this contains well-illustrated articles on all aspects of boating: travel and cruising, design and construction, supplies, equipment, engines, racing, and new boats and products.

851. **Sail.** 126 Blaine Ave., Marion, OH 43302. monthly. illus. ads. $7.50.

Published by the Institute for Advancement of Sailing, this contains articles on techniques of sailing and racing, technical material on design, electronics, travel suggestions, history of sailing, anything of interest to sailboat sailors. An annual publication called *Sailboat & Sailboat Equipment Directory* ($2.00pa.) contains specifications on boats and information about equipment of all kinds. Its many color photographs may make it preferable to *Sailing*.

852. **Sailing.** 125 East Main St., Port Washington, WI 53074. monthly. illus. ads. $5.00.

This large-format magazine (16½" high x 11" wide) is devoted to the "beauty of sail." It contains information on racing, travel, and boat plans. It is about all boats, from homebuilts to ocean racers. Illustrated with black and white photographs.

853. **Sea Magazine.** 550 Channel St., Marion, OH 43302. monthly. illus. ads. $7.00.

This California-based publication is issued in Northwest and Southwest editions. They are essentially the same but there are regional news items that account for several differing pages. Contains general articles on boating for West Coast readers plus an extensive "boats for sale" section. A very nicely done magazine.

854. **Skin Diver.** 8490 Sunset Blvd., Los Angeles, CA 90069. monthly. illus. ads. $7.50.

This is all about skin and scuba diving with articles on places to go, equipment, photography, medical problems, industry news, and notes about personalities in the sport. Many color photographs.

PERIODICALS

855. **Surfer.** P.O. Box 1028, Dana Point, CA 92629. bimonthly. illus. ads. $5.00.

Worldwide coverage of surfing with articles on personalities, photography, and equipment. Nicely illustrated, including many color photographs. Of the surfing magazines I've seen, this one seems best in both content and pictorial quality.

856. **Tracks.** 27635 Forbes Rd., Laguna Naguel, CA 92677. bimonthly. illus. ads. $3.00.

This is the American edition of an Australian magazine that is published as a companion to *International Surfing* magazine. In newspaper format, it has articles on personalities (with interviews), many photographs, and other items of interest to surfers, including recipes! Alternates with ISM.

857. **Underwater Reporter.** Underwater Society of America, Ambler, PA 19002. monthly (?). illus. ads. $5.00.

This small newspaper acts as the "Bulletin of the Underwater Society of America" and carries news of competitions, training courses, and other things of interest to amateur and professional divers.

858. **The Water Skier.** P.O. Box 191, Winter Haven, FL 33880. 7x/yr. illus. ads. $3.00.

This is the official publication of the American Water Ski Association. It contains information about techniques and events. Mostly of interest to competitive skiers.

859. **Water Sport.** 534 North Broadway, Milwaukee, WI 53202. quarterly. illus. $5.00 (membership required).

This is the publication of the Boat Owners Council of America; it contains no advertisements. There are general articles of interest to boaters: racing, places to visit, fishing. Nice color photographs.

860. **Yachting.** 50 West 44th St., New York, NY 10003. monthly. illus. ads. $10.00.

The thickest of the several boating journals calls itself "The world's foremost boating magazine." Covering both sail and power boats, the content ranges from articles on history of boats and of sailing to sailing techniques, racing, accessories, and new boat plans. Many advertisements for used boats.

OUTDOOR RECREATION

AERIAL ACTIVITIES

There are many more periodicals devoted to some aspect of aviation than we will list here. We have chosen several that are designed for the amateur or prospective pilot.

861. **The AOPA Pilot.** P.O.Box 5800, Washington, DC 20014. monthly. illus. ads. $18.50.

This is the official magazine of the Aircraft Owners and Pilots Association, and it comes only with membership. The AOPA calls itself the "voice of general aviation." The magazine carries articles about news events, legislative proposals, new and old airplanes, flying techniques, travel, and general topics.

862. **APM Bulletin.** P.O. Box H, Ottumwa, IA 52501. quarterly.

A small newsletter about old planes, especially those housed in the Airpower Museum (APM). Available with membership in the Antique Airplane Association. See also *International Antique Airplane News*.

863. **Aero Magazine.** P.O. Box 1184, Ramona, CA 92065. bimonthly. illus. ads. $4.00.

This publication calls itself the "World's Largest Aircraft Owners Circulation" magazine. It is sent to all registered owners of aircraft in the United States and carries news about new products and planes, regulations, techniques, and travel.

864. **Air Facts.** 110 East 42nd St., New York, NY 10017. monthly. illus. ads. $7.00.

"The Magazine for Pilots." A pocket-sized journal with articles on piloting techniques, equipment, and items of general interest.

865. **Aviation Times.** 6045 Wilson Blvd., Arlington, VA 22205. 18x/yr. illus. ads. $3.95.

A small newspaper first issued, I believe, on May 1, 1974. It carries news of personalities, exhibitions and "fly-ins," travel, the aircraft industry, and some technical material.

866. **Aviation Travel.** 6045 Wilson Blvd., Arlington, VA 22205. 6x/yr. illus. ads. price not reported.

"The Sports and Leisure Magazine for People Who Fly." Mostly about travel and places to visit by plane. Little technical information. A small magazine of some 34 pages.

867. **Ballooning.** Balloon Federation of America, Suite 610, 806 15th St., N.W., Washington, DC 20005. quarterly. illus. ads. $5.00.

Devoted to the promotion of ballooning as a sport. Includes information on safety, competitions, personalities, club news, technical and handling hints, and news of new equipment.

868. **Buoyant Flight.** 1800 Triplett Blvd., Akron, OH 44306. frequency unknown. illus. $2.00.

Published by the Lighter-than-Air Society to "further knowledge pertaining to the history, science, and techniques of buoyant flight." A mimeographed newsletter about ballooning and airships.

869. **Canadian Parachutist.** P.O. Box 848, Burlington, Ontario. bimonthly. $4.00.

Official publication of the Canadian Sport Parachuting Association, with news of interest to sky divers.

870. **Canadian Wings.** P.O. Box 3278, Station B, Calgary, Alberta T2M 4L8. monthly. illus. ads. $5.00.

A small publication giving news of Canadian aviation: conventions, fly-ins, regulations, safety, personalities, etc. A good bet for anyone who regularly flies in Canada.

871. **Cross Country News.** Meacham Field, Fort Worth, TX 76106. every 3rd Thursday. illus. ads. $3.50.

A small newspaper about events and rallies, general aviation items, and new regulations.

872. **Ground Skimmer.** P.O. Box 66306, Los Angeles, CA 90066. monthly. illus. ads. $5.00.

The official publication of the United States Hang Gliding Association, Inc. Contains news of personalities, competitions, new products, safety, and flying techniques.

873. **International Antique Airplane News.** P.O. Box H, Ottumwa, IA 52501. bimonthly. illus. ads. $15.00 (includes the APM Bulletin).

Formerly called the *Antique Airplane News*, this contains articles and news items about "old planes and the people who fly them." It is published by the Antique Airplane Association.

874. **International Flying Farmer.** Municipal Airport, Wichita, KS 67209. monthly. illus. ads. $4.00.

News of interest to members of the International Flying Farmers, Inc. Covers legislation, meetings, agriculture, and safety.

875. **Low and Slow.** 59 Dudley Ave., Venice, CA 90291. monthly. illus. ads. $6.00.

Published by the Self-Soar Association. Devoted to the sport of hang gliding, this publication provides news of new craft, safety, meets, etc.

876. **Motorgliding.** P.O. Box 66071, Los Angeles, CA 90066. monthly. illus. ads. $5.00.

Published by the Soaring Society of America, this is concerned with motorized sailplanes, those which have small engines to get them into the air.

877. **National Aeronautics.** 806 15th St., N.W., Suite 610, Washington, DC 20005. quarterly. illus. ads. $5.00.

The "Official Publication of the National Aeronautic Association." Devoted to sport aviation, this quarterly provides news of racing, soaring, ballooning, antique planes, parachuting, history of aviation, models, home-built aircraft, and aerobatics. Apparently trying to be general rather than technical.

878. **NEWS-National Pilots Association.** 806 15th St., N.W., Washington, DC 20005.

An eight-page newsletter about activities of the association.

879. **Parachutist.** P.O. Box 109, Monterey, CA 93940. monthly. illus. ads. $7.00.

This is the official publication of the United States Parachute Association. Covers events and competition, techniques and equipment, safety, legislation, and government regulations.

880. **Plane & Pilot.** P.O. Box 1136, Santa Monica, CA 90406. monthly. illus. ads. $7.00.

Contains pilot reports of new and old planes and articles on equipment and flying techniques. Appeals to the sport flyer.

881. **Private Pilot.** 1255 Portland Place, Boulder, CO 80302. monthly. illus. ads. $7.95.

A general magazine that provides news of planes and products, piloting techniques, technical articles, and pilot reports.

PERIODICALS

882. **Rotor & Wing.** News Plaza, Peoria, IL 61601. bimonthly. illus. ads. $6.00.

Gives news of helicopters, but it is mostly for business users. Included here only because the title may mislead the newcomer.

883. **Service Bulletin-National Pilots Association.** 806 15th St., N.W., Washington, DC 20005. monthly. illus. membership.

A two-page bulletin of information on safety and techniques for members of the Association.

884. **Sky Diver Magazine.** 15206 Raymond, Gardena, CA 90247. monthly. illus. ads. $5.00.

"The International Magazine of Parachuting" carries articles on the sport: safety, techniques, new products, competition, and records.

885. **Skysurfer Magazine.** P.O. Box 375, Marlboro, MA 01752. frequency unknown. illus. ads. $6.00.

"The magazine of hang gliding and man-powered flight" contains news of available craft, safety and competition, history, and general information.

886. **Soaring.** P.O. Box 66071, Los Angeles, CA 90066. monthly. illus. ads. $15.00.

Official publication of the Soaring Society of America. It publishes articles on techniques, equipment, safety, events, and the fun of soaring.

887. **Sport Aviation.** P.O. Box 229, Hales Corners, WI 53130. monthly. illus. ads. $15.00 (includes membership).

The official publication of the Experimental Aircraft Association is concerned with aviation education, the design and safe construction of homebuilt planes, the restoration of old planes, and the events and rallies that are regularly scheduled.

888. **Sport Flying.** 7950 Deering Ave., Canoga Park, CA 91304. bimonthly. illus. ads. $7.50.

"The Magazine of Fun Flying." It contains articles about old and new planes, homebuilt aircraft, piloting, personalities, races, exhibitions, ballooning, and other general aviation topics. It is also the official magazine of the Professional Race Pilots Association and of the Can-Am Amphibian Association.

889. **Sports Planes.** 631 Wilshire Blvd., Santa Monica, CA 90401. bimonthly. illus. ads. $4.50.

OUTDOOR RECREATION

Intended for private pilots, this contains articles on safety, good flying skills, equipment, homebuilt and other planes, and general news items.

890. **Trade-A-Plane.** Crossville, TN 38555. 3x/mo. illus. ads. $5.00.

A newspaper filled with advertisements for aircraft and equipment of all kinds. If it concerns aviation, you'll find it for sale here.

COUNTRY LIVING

891. **Backwoods Journal.** Paradox, NY 12858. bimonthly. illus. ads. $3.00.

A small mimeographed magazine with short notes on bird watching, country philosophy, etc. There may be a few hints on "country living" but not enough to matter. The title does not convey the content. Not for our purpose.

892. **Briarpatch Review.** 558 Santa Cruz Ave., Menlo Park, CA 94025. irreg. illus. $1.00 per issue.

This is sort of a sequel to the philosophical content of the *Last Whole Earth Catalog*, if you can stand that. It calls itself "A Journal of Right Livelihood and Caring-Based Economics."

893. **Canadian Whole Earth Almanac.** 341 Bloor St., West, Toronto 181, Ontario.

I've listed this only because inquiry gets no response. I have read that this publication is defunct.

894. **Coevolution Quarterly.** 558 Santa Cruz Ave., Menlo Park, CA 94025. quarterly. illus. $6.00.

This is called a "Supplement to the Whole Earth Catalogue" and it follows a similar format. I found notes on land use, shelter, food, ecology, "soft technology," communes, and Buddhism. There is enough practical information to make a trial worthwhile.

895. **Country Place.** 733 North Van Buren, Milwaukee, WI 53202. bimonthly. illus. ads. $5.00.

The premier issue states that this new magazine is "A new national publication for mini-farmers and 'two acre Edens'." A very neatly produced and well-illustrated (many color photos) effort, the first issue has articles on the philosophy of "homesteading," examples of back-to-the-land moves, training horses, knowing wildflowers, gardening and foods, clay sculpture, clothing, and other tidbits. More elaborate than most such journals, this one looks very good.

896. **Country Women.** P.O. Box 51, Albion, CA 95410. every 6 weeks. illus. ads. $7.00 per 12 issues.

Calling itself a magazine for feminists and back-to-the-land types, this does have a few items on practical subjects (water systems, pregnant goats, tools) but probably not enough to matter.

897. **Countryside & Small Stock Journal.** 318 Waterloo Rd., Marshall, WI 53559. monthly (except Dec. and June). illus. ads. $5.00.

This is an excellent little magazine for country people. It has articles on country living, rabbit raising, making cheese and honey, all kinds of suggestions for raising all kinds of small stock. Highly recommended for all homesteaders.

898. **Fur-Fish-Game.** 2878 East Main St., Columbus, OH 43209. monthly. illus. ads. $4.00.

This is what old-timers called "Hardings Magazine." It contains articles on hunting, fishing, firearms, dogs, camping, conservation, and trapping. For anyone planning to trap animals for even a partial living, this magazine is recommended as a good source of information.

899. **The Green Revolution.** Freeland, MD 21053. monthly (except July and Dec.). illus. ads. $6.00.

Apparently the oldest "alternative living" publication (issued since 1943), this eight-page newspaper carries news of homesteading movements but seems mostly concerned with economic and political problems such as decentralization of production and anti-Keynsian methods (for which we should all be grateful!). For actual instruction in homesteading and other such stuff, see the *Mother Earth News*.

Homesteaders and Landcrafters Newsletter. *See* **The Wildcrafters World.**

900. **Landward Ho!** Wilkinson Press, Route 1, Scio, OR 97374. monthly. illus. ads. $4.00.

This mimeographed newsletter contains various kinds of information for country dwellers: recipes, finding land, new books and magazines, how-to hints, etc. Lots of classified ads. Short, concise, interesting, and not the anti-everything nonsense that characterizes some of the "homesteading" papers.

OUTDOOR RECREATION

901. **Living in the Ozarks Newsletter.** LION, J. & S. Davidson, Pettigrew, AR 72752. monthly. mimeo. illus. ads. $5.00.

This interesting newsletter is devoted to those folks who live in (or wish to live in) the Ozarks. The February 1975 issue is about "gardens for self-sufficiency" but there is all kinds of information for country dwellers. Looks like a good, little paper.

902. **Mother Earth News.** P.O. Box 70, Hendersonville, NC 28739. bimonthly. illus. ads. $6.00.

This is the BIG back-to-the-land magazine. It has articles on growing things, country living, organic foods, methane engines, using windmills, etc. It is a good source of information about tools and equipment, books, and other supplies. "Mother's Bookshelf" will keep you abreast of new titles of interest and "Mother's General Store Catalogue" ($0.25) will lead you to boots, barber supplies, wooden toys, and a host of other such things. Great magazine for country folk.

903. **Natural Life Styles.** Gordon & Breach, 440 Park Ave., New York, NY 10016. bimonthly. illus. $9.00.

This was another magazine about country living, with material on cooking, natural foods, childbirth, beekeeping, building shelters, poetry, wild foods, philosophy, etc. It ceased publication in mid-1975.

904. **The Old-House Journal.** 199 Berkeley Place, Brooklyn, NY 11217. monthly. illus. $12.00.

This is concerned mostly with the mechanical aspects of restoring old homes. There are hints on proper supplies and equipment, sources of supply. Rather expensive, but it is included for the benefit of people who may need specialized information.

905. **Organic Gardening & Farming.** Emmaus, PA 18049. monthly. illus. ads. $6.85.

This is the one best source for continuing information on organic farming methods. Articles on all aspects of the subject from using compost to choosing lettuce seed.

906. **The Provoker.** St. Catherines, Ontario. bimonthly (?). illus. ads. $3.50.

A small newspaper with articles on natural living. The issue I've seen did not have enough information on practical matters to make it worthwhile, but the content is otherwise interesting. Contains many advertisements for books on country living, natural health, etc.

PERIODICALS

907. **Voice of the Trapper.** c/o George Wacha, 529 Spring St., Teaneck, NJ 07666. quarterly. illus. ads. $2.50 (included in a $5.00 membership).

This is the "Official Publication of the National Trappers Association, Inc." and carries news of the Association, articles on the history of trapping, legislation alerts, trapping methods, etc. Many book and supply advertisements. A very good magazine for the serious trapper.

908. **The Wildcrafters World.** R.R. 3, P.O. Box 118, Rockville, IN 47872. annual. price varies.

This is devoted to advancing the movement to live off the land in a natural way. Each issue is a compilation of articles on all aspects of country living: turtle trapping, gardening, homesteading, beekeeping, gathering ginseng, etc. Lots of interesting reading for country folks. Send a couple of first-class-mail stamps for a list of available publications. The same publisher apparently also offered the *Homesteaders and Landcrafters Newsletter*, but I don't find it listed in the complete catalog so I assume that it is defunct.

ANIMAL-RELATED ACTIVITIES

907. **American Cooner.** Sesser, IL 62884. monthly. illus. ads. $5.00.

"The national tree hound magazine." This contains articles on hunting, field trials, club activities, and other items of interest. Many advertisements for equipment and dogs.

908. **American Horseman.** Countrywide Pub. Co., 222 Park Ave. South, New York, NY 10003. bimonthly. illus. ads. $6.00.

Feature articles and shorter items on all aspects of horse ownership and use: raising, feeding, health problems, buying and selling, training.

909. **American Pigeon Journal.** Warrenton, MO 63383. monthly. illus. ads. $5.00.

This magazine is "Devoted to All Branches of Pigeon Raising—Fancy, Utility, and Racing." News of breeds and breeders, conventions and shows, supplies and equipment.

910. **American Racing Pigeon News.** 2421 Old Arch Rd., Norristown, PA 19401. monthly (except Aug.). illus. ads. $7.00.

"World's Oldest Racing Pigeon Publication—Established in 1885." News of birds and breeders, competition, etc.

OUTDOOR RECREATION

911. **Dogs.** Countrywide Pub. Co., 222 Park Ave. South, New York, NY 10003. bimonthly. illus. ads. $6.00.

Articles and editorial items of interest to dog owners: raising, training, showing, and caring for dogs.

912. **Full Cry.** P.O. Box 190, Sedalia, MO 65301. monthly. illus. ads. $5.00.

"Published Monthly for the Coon Hound and Tree Hound Enthusiast." News of clubs, kennels, dogs, and trials. Many advertisements.

913. **Horse & Rider.** Gallant Publishing Co., 145 East Rowland Ave., Covina, CA 91723. monthly. illus. ads. $6.00.

Features and comments on all aspects of horse ownership from proper care to biographies of famous horses.

914. **Hounds and Hunting.** 146 West Washington St., Bradford, PA 16701. monthly. illus. ads. $5.00.

This one seems to be the beagler's delight, with news of seminars, club activities, canine health, trial results and advertisements galore. It calls itself, "Beagles in Print."

915. **Hunter's Horn.** P.O. Box 426, Sand Springs, OK 74063. monthly. illus. ads. $6.50.

Devoted to foxhounds, this title contains notes on shows and other competitions, health problems, hunting techniques. Many advertisements.

916. **Hunting Dog.** P.O. Box 330, Greenfield, OH 45123. monthly. illus. ads. $7.00.

"The Monthly Authority on Sporting Dogs and the Outdoors." Contains articles about all kinds of sporting dogs: big game hounds, rabbit and coon hounds, bird dogs. Articles on training, field trials, guns, and taxidermy. This is probably the best choice for general information on the subject.

917. **Team & Trail.** Center Harbor, NH 03226. monthly. illus. ads. $5.00.

This magazine is concerned with all aspects of sled dog racing.

918. **The Western Horseman.** 3850 North Nevada Ave., Colorado Springs, CO 80901. monthly. illus. ads. $5.00.

"The Magazine for Admirers of Stock Horses." Contains articles on everything of interest to horsemen. Some recent articles have been about: building a chuck wagon, Western art, care of horses and equipment, horse breeds, club activities, and just plain stories.

MISCELLANEOUS

919. **The American Rifleman.** 1600 Rhode Island Ave., N.W., Washington, DC 20036. monthly. illus. ads. $7.50.

This is the journal of the National Rifle Association. It contains articles on most aspects of shooting, legislation, and hunting. Technical and practical material of many types.

920. **American Single Shot Rifle News.** Mount Prospect, IL 60056. bimonthly. $5.00 membership.

This is the organ of the American Single Shot Rifle Association. It carries news of the Association, histories of shooting clubs, and stories of guns and shooters. For the specialist target shooter.

921. **Archery.** Route 2, P.O. Box 514, Redlands, CA 92373. monthly. illus. ads. $5.00.

This is the official publication of the National Field Archery Association. It has articles on hunting and field shooting (especially the latter) and stories about personalities, matches, and new equipment.

922. **Archery World.** 534 North Broadway, Milwaukee, WI 53202. bimonthly. illus. ads. $4.00.

This is the publication of the National Archery Association. It includes material on hunting, tournament shooting, and equipment.

923. **The Black Powder News.** P.O. Box 6765, Burbank, CA 91510. monthly. illus. ads. $5.00.

As of mid-1975 there were numerous complaints of non-delivery; not recommended because of that.

924. **Bow & Arrow.** P.O. Box HH, Capistrano Beach, CA 92624. bimonthly. illus. ads. $3.50.

Contains both general information of interest to archers and much about hunting. Includes articles on target shooting and news of personalities and new equipment.

925. **Bowhunter Magazine.** 9715 King James Court, Fort Wayne, IN 46804. bimonthly. illus. ads. $3.50.

This is primarily for the archer who hunts. The articles are about hunting, new equipment and techniques, and other news of interest. A very good magazine.

OUTDOOR RECREATION

926. **The Buckskin Report.** Big Timber, MT 59011. monthly. illus. ads. $10.00.

This is a rather new (1973) magazine devoted to the shooting of muzzle-loading guns. It is the organ of the National Association of Primitive Riflemen, which one joins when one subscribes! The articles are about guns and shooters, modern shooting events, and the preservation of old-time methods and materials. The editor insists on using authentic weapons and clothing when engaging in the "rendezvous" that buckskinners enjoy. An excellent magazine for all muzzle-loader shooters.

927. **Celestial Observer.** 10444 El Comal Dr., San Diego, CA 92124. quarterly. illus. $2.40.

In newspaper format, this carries articles of interest to amateur stargazers: about eclipses, comets, stars, sky watching, photography, etc. Good information.

928. **Gun Week.** 119 East Court St., Sidney, OH 45365. weekly. illus. ads. $5.00.

This is the only weekly paper for shooters. It carries news of legislation, shooting, hunting, muzzle-loading shooting, and other aspects of the shooting sports. A very good source of current information.

929. **Gun World.** P.O. Box HH, Capistrano Beach, CA 92624. monthly. illus. ads. $7.50.

A general magazine for gun buffs, with articles on all aspects of the sport: hunting, reloading, collecting, history, etc.

930. **Guns & Ammo.** 8490 Sunset Blvd., Los Angeles, CA 90069. monthly. illus. ads. $7.50.

Intended to cover all aspects of the shooting sports, this is a general interest publication with articles on firearm history, handguns, shotguns, rifles, and other facets of the game. Always well illustrated.

931. **Guns Magazine.** 8150 North Central Park Ave., Skokie, IL 60076. monthly. illus. ads. $7.50.

This is a general magazine for gun fanciers and shooters. It has articles on all aspects of the shooting sports, including gun identification, collecting, repairing, etc.

932. **Gunsport & Gun Collector.** Leisure Pub. Co., 711 Penn Ave., Pittsburg, PA 15222. bimonthly. illus. ads. $9.95.

Although the title page lists this as a monthly magazine, don't you believe it. My issues arrive every two months or thereabouts. There are articles on guns and shooting accessories, hunting, repairing guns, modern and antique guns, etc. As of mid-1975, delivery of my subscription ceased; may be defunct.

933. **The Jogger.** 1910 K St., N.W., Suite 202, Washington, DC 20006. about 6x/yr. illus. ads. $10.00.

For the benefit of the jogging fraternity, we list this newsletter. It carries news of jogging, physiology, and other items of interest.

934. **Modern Photography.** 165 West 46th St., New York, NY 10036. monthly. illus. ads. $7.95.

One of the major photographic magazines. The serious amateur may wish to check this out.

935. **Muzzle Blasts.** Friendship, IN 47021. monthly. illus. ads. $6.00.

This is the official magazine of the National Muzzle Loading Rifle Association. It carries articles on all aspects of the old-time guns—shooting them, repairing them, identifying them, etc.

936. **The Muzzleloader.** P.O. Box 6072, Texarkana, TX 75501. bimonthly. illus. ads. $5.00.

A new publication (1974) with articles aimed at the muzzle-loader shooter and those interested in related fields: knives, hunting, etc. Contains tests of new guns and articles on history and personalities.

937. **Petersen's Photographic Magazine.** 8490 Sunset Blvd., Los Angeles, CA 90069. monthly. illus. ads. $9.00.

A general photography magazine for the amateur. Articles on cameras, techniques, etc. First issued in 1973.

938. **Popular Photography.** 1 Park Ave., New York, NY 10016. monthly. illus. ads. $7.98.

One of the "big" photographic magazines for amateurs.

939. **Precision Shooting.** P.O. Box 6, Athens, PA 18810. monthly. illus. ads. $5.00.

This is mostly about benchrest shooting with heavy rifles. It is the organ of the International Benchrest Shooters Association.

940. **Rifle.** P.O. Box 3030, Prescott, AZ 86301. bimonthly. illus. ads. $6.50.

Subtitled "The Magazine for Shooters," this is devoted to the use of

OUTDOOR RECREATION

accurate rifles. Many articles about guns, technical aspects of shooting, etc. An excellent magazine.

941. **Runner's World.** P.O. Box 366, Mountain View, CA 94040. monthly. illus. ads. $7.00.

Articles on all aspects of running and fitness, personalities, events, and equipment.

942. **Shooting Times.** News Plaza, Peoria, IL 61601. monthly. illus. ads. $5.00.

A general firearms magazine for the amateur. It carries articles on hunting, shooting, gun repair, rare guns, new equipment, etc. A very good magazine.

943. **Shooting Times & Country Magazine.** Burghley Hall, 809-813 High Rd., Leytonstone, London, E11 1HQ. weekly. illus. ads. £9.00.

This is the major British shooting journal. It carries articles on shooting, fishing, riding, conservation, etc.

944. **Skeet Shooting Review.** National Skeet Shooting Association, 2608 Inwood Rd., Dallas, TX 75235. monthly. illus. ads. $9.00.

News and information of interest to skeet shooters: events, scores, equipment, etc.

945. **Sky and Telescope.** 49 Bay State Rd., Cambridge, MA 02138. monthly. illus. ads. $9.00.

This is the magazine for amateur astronomers. It has news of expected phenomena, notes on astronomers and observatories, and a large monthly star chart. The best.

946. **Trap & Field.** 1100 Waterway Blvd., Indianapolis, IN 46202. 13x/yr. illus. ads. $8.00.

The official publication of the Amateur Trapshooting Association carries news of interest to trapshooters: events, scores, etc.

947. **Weatherwise.** 45 Beacon St., Boston, MA 02108. bimonthly. illus. ads. $5.00.

This is the principal magazine for amateur meteorologists. It has articles on all aspects of the weather: hurricanes, tornadoes, clouds, new equipment, etc.

ORGANIZATIONS AND ASSOCIATIONS

CAMPING, CAMPGROUNDS, AND TRAVEL

In addition to the several organizations listed here, there are many regional associations and commercial groups that have an interest in camping and travel.

American Camping Association, Bradford Woods, Martinsville, IN 46151.

Interested mostly in the organized or commercial areas of camping, the ACA published a resume of camping legislation.

Family Camping Federation of America, Bradford Woods, Martinsville, IN 46151.

This is apparently intended to serve the family camping set, but I have had no response to inquiries.

Family Motor Coach Association, P.O. Box 44144, Cincinnati, OH 45244.

Concerned with the problems of motor coach owners, this group offers insurance plans, chapter membership, tours, and other services.

International Travel and Trailer Clubs of America, Inc., 3001 N.E. Ainsworth St., Portland, OR 97211.

This organization is devoted to obtaining better, safer, and more enjoyable travel with trailers.

National Campers and Hikers Association, 7172 Transit Rd., Buffalo, NY 14221.

Intended for families, this organization stresses conservation programs, disaster assistance teams, programs for teens and retirees, and proper use of vehicles. They publish *Tent & Trail*, a newspaper, and are represented in *Camping and Trailering Guide*.

National Camping Association, 353 West 56th St., New York, NY 10019.

This is an association of camp directors and camp owners.

North American Family Campers Association, P.O. Box 552, Newburyport, MA 01950.

Individuals and families are included in this group, which seeks to improve campground numbers and quality, keep members informed on new campgrounds, and support appropriate legislation.

The Outdoor Nation, 4411 Grand Ave., Gurnee, IL 60031.

This is a new organization that hopes to be a "congress" of societies, organizations, and individuals interested in outdoor recreation. It plans to research problems and find solutions.

BACKPACKING, MOUNTAINEERING, AND SURVIVAL

The Adirondack Mountain Club, R.D. 1, Glens Falls, NY 12801.

Formed to promote conservation and recreational use of the New York State forest lands, especially in the Adirondack Mountains. Has local chapters and publishes trail guides and maps.

Alpine Club of Canada, P.O. Box 1026, Banff, Alberta.

This is "Canada's National Mountaineering Club." It coordinates climbing activity and publishes the annual record of Canadian mountaineering in *The Canadian Alpine Journal*.

American Alpine Club, 113 East 90th St., New York, NY 10028.

The publishers of the *American Alpine Journal* are interested in mountaineering safety, not recreational activities.

ORGANIZATIONS AND ASSOCIATIONS

American Youth Hostels, 20 West 17th St., New York, NY 10011.

Interested in sheltering hikers and bicyclists, this organization has many hostels scattered about the country. A card will bring membership information.

Appalachian Mountain Club, 5 Joy St., Boston, MA 02108.

Interested in all aspects of conserving and using the Appalachian Mountains, the Club publishes *Appalachia* and a number of maps and trail guides.

The Appalachian Trail Conference, P.O. Box 236, Harpers Ferry, WV 25425.

This group promotes interest in the Appalachian Trail and helps preserve it. Publishes guidebooks to the several sections of the Trail.

Canadian Orienteering Federation, P.O. Box 6206, Terminal Station, Toronto 1, Ontario.

Promotes interest in orienteering, sponsors meetings, etc.

Canadian Youth Hostels Association, 333 River Rd., Vanier City, Ottawa, Ontario, K1L 8B9.

The Colorado Mountain Club, 1723 East 16th Ave., Denver, CO 80218.

Interested specifically in mountaineering in Colorado, this Club publishes *Trail and Timberline* and guidebooks.

International Backpackers Association, P.O. Box 85, Lincoln Center, ME 04458.

This new organization publishes a quarterly newsletter, mostly on trail conditions.

Mountain Rescue Council, P.O. Box 696, Tacoma, WA 98401.

Interested in promoting safety among high altitude hikers and climbers.

The Mountaineers, 719 Pike St., Seattle, WA 98111.

Often called the "Seattle Mountaineers," this is a group of persons interested in hiking and conservation, especially in the Pacific Northwest. They organize climbing expeditions and climbing schools.

National Hiking & Ski Touring Association, P.O. Box 7421, Colorado Springs, CO 80907.

This group is devoted to rebuilding America's trails and to establishing new ones. They encourage hiking, ski touring, and similar outdoor activities. Their newsletter is called *Hiking & Ski Touring*.

OUTDOOR RECREATION

National Outdoor Leadership School, P.O. Box AA, Lander, WY 82520.

Organized to provide training for instructors in outdoor education work.

Sierra Club, 1050 Mills Tower, San Francisco, CA 94104.

This conservation society lobbies extensively for what it believes is best for Mother Nature. Not really concerned with outdoor recreation.

U.S. Orienteering Federation, 933 North Kenmore St., Suite 317, Arlington, VA 22201.

Promotes the international sport of orienteering throughout the United States.

IDENTIFYING AND COLLECTING

Associated Geographers of America, P.O. Box 188, Midway City, CA 92655.

Despite its name, this is an organization of treasure hunters. They publish *The Treasure Hunter.*

Circle of Companions, 1 Exanimo Bldg., Segundo, CO 81070.

This organization of treasure hunters seeks to keep the clan informed of better equipment and news of finds. They publish a monthly called *Adventure Bulletin* and a quarterly called *Exanimo Express*, but I have seen neither publication.

Mineral of the Month Club, P.O. Box 487, Yucaipa, CA 92399.

As the name implies, this Club sends a mineral specimen each month with information about it. The cost is about $2.00 per month for this, a book, and an identification service.

National Audubon Society, 950 Third Ave., New York, NY 10022.

I couldn't hope to list even a few of the many local and regional clubs devoted to birdwatching and other such activities. For interested persons, a card to the National Audubon Society will probably bring word of a club nearby.

ORGANIZATIONS AND ASSOCIATIONS

Prospectors Club International, P.O. Box 548, Midland, TX 79701.

This organization of treasure hunters publishes a monthly called *The Prospector*.

Prospectors and Treasure Hunters Guild, Segundo, CO 81070.

This large club publishes a monthly *Newsletter* and various technical bulletins.

Rocks & Minerals Association, P.O. Box 29, Peekskill, NY 10566.

Devoted to furthering the hobby of collecting and lapidary work.

VEHICLE ACTIVITIES

Amateur Bicycle League of America, P.O. Box 669, Wall Street Station, New York, NY 10005.

This is the governing body of amateur bicycle racing in the United States, supervising amateur competition, including the Olympics.

American Cycling Union, c/o H. C. Black, 192 Alexander St., Newark, NJ 07106.

This is for individuals interested in bicycling for sport or for racing.

American Land Sailing Organization, P.O. Box 4652, Irvine, CA 92664.

This is concerned with those weird looking "ice-boats on wheels."

American Motorcycle Association, P.O. Box 141, Westerville, OH 43081.

Since 1924, this has been the national association for motorcycle owners, riders, and dealers. It makes the rules for competitions and publishes the *AMA News*.

American Unicycling Society, c/o William Jenack, 67 Lion Lane, Westbury, NY 11590.

American Youth Hostels, 20 West 17th St., New York, NY 10011.

The AYH is concerned with bicycling and hiking. A card will bring full information about membership. They publish directories of hostels.

OUTDOOR RECREATION

L'Association Motorcycliste Canadienne. *See* Canadian Motorcycle Association.

Bicycle Club of America, 99 East Magnolia Blvd., Burbank, CA 91502.

A fairly new (1971) group for bicycle owners. They publish the *BCA Spokesman*, a bimonthly which I have not seen.

Bicycle Institute of America, 122 East 42nd St., New York, NY 10017.

This is a trade organization that publishes pamphlets on safety and other aspects of bicycling.

Canadian Cycling Association, 333 River Rd., Vanier City, Ontario, K1L 8B9.

Since 1882, this has been the leading Canadian bicycling organization.

Canadian Motorcycle Association, 20 Jarvis St., Hamilton, Ontario, L8R 1M2.

This is the national motorcycle organization for Canada. They publish *Cycle CMA* and are expanding their services to cyclists.

Canadian Youth Hostels Association, 268 First Ave., Ottawa, Ontario.

Family Motor Coach Association, 5200 Beechmont Ave., Cincinnati, OH 45230.

Publishers of two magazines for motor coach owners, they offer several services to members.

The League of American Wheelmen, 3582 Sunnyview Ave., N.E., Salem, OR 97303.

Since 1880, this group has been a leader in seeking favorable legislation for bicyclists. They offer insurance programs for members, organize tours, etc. During the past year or so, I've found at least six addresses for this group. My letters have been returned as undeliverable. The address listed here is the latest one I've found but I gave up. Happy days!

International Bike Touring Society, 846 Prospect St., La Jolla, CA 92037.

Calling itself the "huff-and-puff society," these folks organize tours for bicyclists. They do not camp out, and members must be at least 21 years old.

ORGANIZATIONS AND ASSOCIATIONS

Mini Bike Association of America, P.O. Box 158, South Station, Warren, MI 48090.

This is for both riders and dealers. They seek favorable legislation and are interested in racing and safety programs.

Motormaids, Inc., 556 West 4th St., Chillicothe, OH 45601.

This is a society for female motorcyclists.

National All Terrain Vehicle Association, 342 Broad St., New Bethlehem, PA 16242.

National Association of Bicycle Owners, Inc., Suite 232-B, High Point Plaza, Hillside, IL 60162.

Apparently formed to offer insurance programs for bicycle owners.

National Association of Trailer Owners, 1325 Main St., Sarasota, FL 33578.

Publishers of *Mobile Living Magazine.*

National Minicycle Racing Association, 23301 Ostronic Dr., Woodland Hills, CA 91364.

National Sand Sailing Association, 7305 Van Nuys Blvd., Van Nuys, CA 91405.

Formed to promote the "family sport" of land sailing.

North American Land Sailing Association, P.O. Box 2283, Newport Beach, CA 92660.

Sports Car Club of America, 2186 South Holly, Denver, CO 80222.

This is the leading organization for sports car racers.

Tricycle Racing Club of America, 41752 Chiltern Dr., Fremont, CA 94538.

Good luck!

The Wheelmen, c/o R. E. McNair, 32 Dartmouth Circle, Swarthmore, PA 19081.

For those interested in old bicycles and the accessories and romance that go with them.

OUTDOOR RECREATION

WINTER ACTIVITIES

American Snowshoe Union, 138 Bartlett St., Lewistown, ME 04240.

Founded in 1924, this is an association of French snowshoers who are interested in amateur racing.

International DN Ice Yacht Racing Association, 83 White St., Shrewsbury, NJ 07701.

A group devoted to racing DN Class iceboats.

International Skeeter Association, 6615 North Sioux Ave., Chicago, IL 60646.

Since 1939 this organization has been interested in racing the "Skeeter Class" iceboats.

National Iceboat Authority, 6615 North Sioux Ave., Chicago, IL 60646.

An association of individuals and clubs interested in iceboat racing. The Authority is in charge of racing rules.

Ski Touring Association, P.O. Box 9, West Simsbury, CT 06092.

An information agency for enthusiasts, primarily in New England.

Ski Touring Council, c/o R. F. Mattesich, West Hill Rd., Troy, VT 05868.

Formed in 1962 to promote the sport of ski touring, it publishes an annual called the *Ski Touring Guide.*

United States Ski Association, 1726 Champa St., Denver, CO 80202.

Since 1904, this has been the country's major ski organization. Although primarily interested in downhill skiing, it maintains a section devoted to Nordic or cross-country skiing.

United States Snowmobile Association, 534 North Broadway, Milwaukee, WI 53202.

This is the national snowmobile association; it is devoted to promoting the recreational and competitive aspects of the sport. The Association sanctions races, assists local clubs, provides legislative advice and offers an insurance program.

ORGANIZATIONS AND ASSOCIATIONS

WATER ACTIVITIES

American Canoe Association, 4260 East Evans Ave., Denver, CO 80222.

Founded in 1880, this has been the leading proponent of canoeing as a sport. Their official journal is called *Canoe* and a note will bring a good list of canoeing booklets, guidebooks, etc.

American Power Boat Association, 22811 Greater Mack, St. Clair Shores, MI 48080.

This is the "National Authority for the United States" of the Union of International Motorboating. Founded in 1903, it is concerned with power boat racing.

American River Touring Association, 1916 Jackson, Oakland, CA 94607.

This is a non-professional educational association that organizes river raft tours.

American Rowing Association, 4 Boat House Row, Fairmont Park, Philadelphia, PA 19130.

What better address for a boating organization interested in racing?

American Water Ski Association, P.O. Box 191, Winter Haven, FL 33880.

The publishers of *The Water Skier* actively promote the sport both for individuals and for professional purposes.

American White Water Affiliation, P.O. Box 1584, San Bruno, CA 94066.

Devoted to the running of fast water streams, this group promotes river racing, for the most part. They publish *American Whitewater.*

Antique Boat and Yacht Club, c/o South Street Seaport Museum, 16 Fulton St., New York, NY 10038.

The name is self-explanatory and you can't miss them—they are hard by the Fulton Fish Market.

Antique Outboard Motor Club, 2316 West 110th St., Minneapolis, MN 55431.

Dedicated to the history and other aspects of outboard motors, this organization, founded in 1965, will lead you to spare parts for your oldie. They publish a quarterly called *The Antique Outboarder* and a monthly *Newsletter.*

OUTDOOR RECREATION

Boat Owners Association of the United States, 1028 Connecticut Ave., Washington, DC 20036.

This association provides information and various services for boat owners. A large and growing body.

Boat Owners Council of America, c/o Watersport, 534 North Broadway, Milwaukee, WI 53202.

Founded in 1966, this organization is concerned with the needs of individual boat owners. They publish *Watersport*.

Canadian Canoeing Association, 32 Sedgewick Crescent, Islington, Ontario.

As the name implies, this is the reigning body for canoeists in Canada.

Midget Ocean Racing Club, P.O. Box 1151, Darien, CT 06820.

I'll bet that you didn't know there were midget oceans. These folks will help you find one and have information about racing small ocean-going craft.

National Association of Amateur Oarsmen, 31552 Waltham Rd., Birmingham, MI 48009.

An association of amateur racing enthusiasts.

National Association of Underwater Instructors, 22809 Barton Rd., Grand Terrace, CA 92324.

A large, authoritative body devoted to safety in diving. They certify instructors and organize courses for beginners.

North American Multi-Hull Sailing Association, P.O. Box 974, Darien, CT 06820.

This group is concerned with promoting the use of catamarans and other multi-hull craft.

Outboard Boating Club of America, 401 North Michigan Ave., Chicago, IL 60611.

This organization is a good source for information on the legal aspects of boat ownership—registration, numbering, federal regulations, and equipment.

Professional Association of Diving Instructors, P.O. Box 177, Costa Mesa, CA 92627.

This association offers several training courses for divers.

ORGANIZATIONS AND ASSOCIATIONS

Underwater Society of America, Ambler, PA 19002.

This group offers information for divers, insurance programs, meetings, competitions, and training courses. Their bulletin is called the *Underwater Reporter.*

United States Canoe Association, 1818 Kensington Blvd., Fort Wayne, IN 46805.

Devoted to all aspects of canoeing, this organization publishes *Canoe News.*

United States Coast Guard Auxiliary, 400 7th St., S.W., Washington, DC 20590.

This highly respected body is devoted to boating safety. They offer training courses and have a program of boat inspections.

United States Power Squadrons, P.O. Box 345, Montvale, NJ 07645.

Boating safety is the prime concern of this body, which offers training courses for boat owners.

YMCA National Scuba Headquarters, 1611 Candler Blvd., Atlanta, GA 30303.

This office should be able to tell you where the nearest diving course is taught.

Yachting Club of America, 700 South Federal Highway, Pompano Beach, FL 33062.

Founded in 1964, this association offers information and assistance to boat owners.

AERIAL ACTIVITIES

Societies, clubs, and other organizations of interest to pilots are not rare. We list several that are general or national in character or that seem to be the obvious ones to contact. Almost every airport has a flying club, and local inquiry will bring quick results. Most pilots belong to one or more groups and they will be happy to suggest further sources of information. There are clubs composed of owners of old or classic planes; we do not list these, since beginners are generally not that interested. Most states, incidentally, have

OUTDOOR RECREATION

departments of aviation of one name or another. They will give you information about flying in your state, usually for a fee, and will probably demand that you pay for the privilege of flying in their skies. I regard all such departments as fraudulent leeches on the body icaric as they do nothing that is not done better by other agencies. It seems absurd to require a state pilot's license when one already has a federal one. If you address one of these state bodies, they will insist that they are not issuing you a pilot license, but the fee and the result are the same.

Aircraft Owners and Pilots Association, P.O. Box 5800, Washington, DC 20014.

A large association of persons who own or fly aircraft. In addition to *The AOPA Pilot*, they issue other publications and offer numerous services to members: insurance plans, legislative alerts, safety bulletins, etc.

Antique Airplane Association, P.O. Box H, Ottumwa, IA 52501.

Since 1953, this organization has devoted itself to preserving the history and the actual aircraft of the past. They publish *International Antique Airplane News* and the *APM Bulletin*.

Balloon Platoon of America, P.O. Box 272, Bloomfield Hills, MI 48013.

I have seen this group listed as the publishers of a magazine called *Uprising*, but I have not been able to find a copy or other information.

Balloon Federation of America, c/o National Aeronautic Association, Suite 610, 806 15th St., N.W., Washington, DC 20005.

This is the official United States representative for ballooning. They seek to promote the sport, assist clubs, and supply legislative aid; they also publish a quarterly called *Ballooning*.

Canadian Sport Parachuting Association, P.O. Box 848, Burlington, Ontario.

The chief Canadian organization for sky divers, this group publishes the *Canadian Parachutist* and serves as a source for information on the sport.

Experimental Aircraft Association, Inc., P.O. Box 229, Hales Corners, WI 53130.

Founded in 1953, the EAA is devoted to furthering the hobby of home built aircraft and the restoration of other planes. They publish *Sport Aviation*, organize rallies, and promote safety and aviation education.

ORGANIZATIONS AND ASSOCIATIONS

International Freefall Association, P.O. Box 30147, Los Angeles, CA 90030.

I am unable to find any information about this group. It seems to be concerned with parachuting.

The Lighter-Than-Air Society, 1800 Triplett Blvd., Akron, OH 44306.

Organized to promote interest in the history and use of balloons and airships, this group publishes *Buoyant Flight*.

National Aeronautic Association, Suite 610, 806 15th St., N.W., Washington, DC 20005.

This is the official United States representative to the Fédération Aéronautique Internationale, the world body that certifies aviation and space records. It has numerous divisions, some listed in this section (the others are not aimed at the novice in aviation).

National Association for Air Cushion Vehicle Enthusiasts, 801 Poplar St., Terre Haute, IN 47807.

Several years ago, air cushion vehicles were fairly easy to come by, but I've not seen one lately. Perhaps I'm in the wrong place. In any event, this group apparently publishes a magazine called *Kestrel* and a *Guide to Small Hovercraft*.

National Collegiate Parachuting League, P.O. Box 109, Monterey, CA 93940.

This is the division of the United States Parachuting Association that supervises the sport on campuses.

National Pilots Association, 806 15th St., N.W., Washington, DC 20005.

This organization for pilots publishes newsletters concerning safety, legislation, and regulations, and information about the association and its members.

Popular Rotorcraft Association, P.O. Box 3896, South El Monte, CA 91733.

Founded in 1962 to promote interest in small rotorcraft, generally built from kits, this society publishes *Popular Rotorcraft Flying*.

Self-Soar Association, 59 Dudley Ave., Venice, CA 90291.

Devoted to the rising (?) sport of hang gliding, this association sponsors flying meets, assists local clubs, and publishes a monthly called *Low and Slow*.

OUTDOOR RECREATION

Soaring Society of America, P.O. Box 66071, Los Angeles, CA 90066.

Since 1932, this organization has promoted interest in sailplanes and soaring. They publish technical, legislative, and general information in a number of booklets and in the magazines *Soaring* and *Motorgliding.*

Sport Balloon Society of the United States of America, Menlo Oaks Balloon Field, Menlo Park, CA 94025.

Founded in 1965, this organization sponsors balloon rallies and publishes an irregular series of bulletins. Membership by invitation.

United States Hang Gliding Association, P.O. Box 66360, Los Angeles, CA 90066.

This group seeks to promote interest in the sport of hang gliding, organizing flying meets, assisting members, etc. They publish a monthly magazine called *Ground Skimmer.*

United States Parachute Association, P.O. Box 109, Monterey, CA 93940.

The publishers of *Parachutist* are devoted to promoting the sport of parachuting or sky diving. They are involved in safety, training, and legislative programs. As a division of the National Aeronautic Association, they are the official United States representatives for this sport.

Wind Drifters Balloon Club, 2814 Empire Ave., Burbank, CA 91503.

Membership in this group is expensive (some hundreds of dollars), but it includes expert training and numerous manuals. I presume that one must live fairly close to Burbank to participate.

COUNTRY LIVING

I have not heard of very many organizations concerned with country living, so I have only two to list. Several other "names" have come my way but I have had no replies to inquiries.

Christian Homesteading Movement, Oxford, NY 13830.

This group tries to help people become self-sufficient on the land. They have no regular publications at this time (late 1974) but formerly published *The Homesteader.* Most of the effort is now devoted to having Homesteading

Weeks, which feature instruction and demonstrations. Some titles: Home Childbirth Week, Herbalism Week, Log Cabin Week, etc. Send two first-class stamps for information on these workshops. Interestingly enough, the founder tried to keep this a general "Christian" movement but found that only Roman Catholics have enough interest in homesteading to keep going.

The New Alchemists.

This is a fairly small organization devoted to research and education in the field of living more naturally on the earth. They seem to have two branches: P.O. Box 432, Woods Hole, MA 02543 and P.O. Box 376, Pescadero, CA 94060. An associate membership costs $25.00. The group publishes quite a few things: books on windmills, aquaculture, methane digesters, etc. The serious "back-to-the-land" farmer should get a copy of the book list.

ANIMAL-RELATED ACTIVITIES

Animal lovers form a great number of clubs and societies to further their interests. Most of these are of no interest to the sporting fraternity but there are a few that should be listed for the benefit of beginners. There are, for example, clubs interested only in specific breeds of dogs. The owner of a dog of sufficient class to belong to such a club already knows about the organization. We are going to mention a few groups that may have something for beginners in one of the outdoor activities in which animals are used. I think that, in most cases, the name of the organization will explain the purpose well enough to obviate the need for a description.

I know of no club devoted to the use of burros on hiking trips or to the training of brown bears as backpacking companions, but I'm sure these will come with sufficient demand.

American Association of Sheriff's Posses & Riding Clubs, 1318 West Euless Blvd., Euless, TX 76039.

Although this kind of posse has been used to assist in a law enforcement problem, they are mostly concerned with doing displays, parades, and the like.

American Coon Hunters Association, c/o Mr. Raymond McClure, Eshman Ave., West Point, MS 39773.

For the owners of coon hounds.

American Quarter Horse Association, P.O. Box 200, Amarillo, TX 79105.

This group has several booklets that are valuable to owners of any breed of horse.

American Racing Pigeon Union, 34 South Bryant Ave., Pittsburgh, PA 15205.

Amateur Field Trial Clubs of America, Hernando, MS 38632.

California Hawking Club, P.O. Box 4718, Walnut Creek, CA 94523.

One of the very few clubs devoted to this sport.

International Federation of American Homing Pigeon Fanciers, 54 Revere Ave., Maplewood, NJ 07040.

Founded in 1881, this is one of the oldest extant "interest" groups of any kind.

International Sled Dog Racing Association, P.O. Box 144, Ontario, NY 14519.

National Fox Hunters Association, P.O. Box 1806, Jackson, TN 38301.

For the owners of foxhounds.

National High School Rodeo Association, Route 4, P.O. Box 87, Rapid City, SD 57701.

National Intercollegiate Rodeo Association, P.O. Box 2088, Huntsville, TX 77340.

National Pigeon Association, P.O. Box 83, Watertown, WI 53094.

National Retriever Field Trial Club, 46 William St., New York, NY 10005.

North American Falconers Association, 86 West Como Ave., Columbus, OH 43202.

ORGANIZATIONS AND ASSOCIATIONS

Trail Riders of the Wilderness, American Forestry Association, 1319 18th St., N.W., Washington, DC 20036.

This group organizes trail rides and may have just the information a novice will need to plan a summer vacation.

United States Racing Pigeon Association, 5014 Nevada Court, Portland, OR 97219.

MISCELLANEOUS

Amateur Astronomers Association, 212 West 79th St., New York, NY 10024.

This is the largest association for amateurs. It sponsors classes, field trips, and the magazine *Sky & Telescope*. Encourages telescope-making.

Amateur Trapshooting Association, P.O. Box 246, West National Rd., Vandalia, IN 45377.

This is the national trapshooting representative. It keeps records and sponsors the large annual events.

American Knife Throwers Alliance, 2155 Tremont Blvd., N.W., Grand Rapids, MI 49504.

This is the only national association of knife throwers. A card to them will bring you news of a club close to you.

American Single-Shot Rifle Association, 11439 Wicker Ave., Cedar Lake, IN 46303.

The association is devoted to shooting single-shot rifles, principally the older styles.

National Archery Association of the USA, P.O. Box 48, Ronks, PA 17572.

This is the official representative for archery in international events.

National Association for Cave Diving, 3001 West Tennessee, Tallahassee, FL 32304.

Devoted to exploring caves and promoting safety in the activity.

National Association of Primitive Riflemen, Big Timber, MT 59011.

This consists of the subscribers to *The Buckskin Report*. The group is concerned with authenticity of weapons and accessories for its members' activities. Several "rendezvous" have been held with great success.

National Bench Rest Shooters Association, 607 West Line St., Minerva, OH 44657.

This group is devoted to the shooting of heavy precision rifles. Some of the scores are unbelievable to a plinker like me. The *Rifle* is their official magazine.

National Field Archery Association, Route 2, P.O. Box 514, Redlands, CA 92373.

The Association promotes field archery, including bowhunting. Its journal is *Archery*.

National Muzzle Loading Rifle Association, Friendship, IN 47021.

The association is devoted to the history and preservation of muzzle-loading shooting. It sponsors large national events and publishes *Muzzle Blasts*.

National Rifle Association, 1600 Rhode Island Ave., N.W., Washington, DC 20036.

This is the largest national organization for gun owners. It keeps track of legislation, sponsors technical studies, publishes *The American Rifleman*, and is the principal information source for gun owners. Several Presidents of the United States have been members, and a couple of them have been presidents of the NRA.

National Shooting Sports Foundation, 1075 Post Rd., Riverside, CT 06878.

This is an organization concerned with publicizing the shooting sports. It issues news bulletins and has sponsored many studies on the technical aspects of gun ownership.

National Skeet Shooting Association, 2608 Inwood Rd., Dallas, TX 75235.

This is the chief national organization for American skeet shooters. It sponsors the large national events and records all official scores.

National Speleological Society, Cave Ave., Huntsville, AL 35810.

Since 1941, this has been the largest of the cave-exploring groups. It is concerned with safety and proper exploration methods.

ORGANIZATIONS AND ASSOCIATIONS

North/South Skirmish Association, c/o Richard L. Corrigan, P.O. Box 358, Fort Knox, KY 40121.

This group sponsors the annual North/South Skirmish, a meeting of muzzle-loader shooters who try to keep alive the color and the history of Civil War weaponry.

The Pope & Young Club, P.O. Box 887, Des Moines, WA 98016.

This is the recording agency for trophies taken with the bow and arrow. Bowhunters may wish to have this address handy.

Shooters Club of America, 8150 North Central Park Ave., Skokie, IL 60076.

This is for anyone interested in the sport of shooting. The club alerts members to impending legislation and is concerned with the rights of citizens to own firearms.

U.S. Revolver Association, 59 Alvin St., Springfield, MA 01104.

For many years, this has been the principal organization for handgun match shooters.

PUBLISHERS

Abingdon Press
201 8th Ave. South
Nashville, TN 37202

Adirondack Mountain Club
R.D. 1, Ridge Road
Glens Falls, NY 12801

Adventure Guides, Inc.
36 East 57th St.
New York, NY 10022
(distr.: Berkshire Traveller)

Aero Products Research, Inc.
11811 Teale St.
Culver City, CA 90230

Aero Publishers, Inc.
329 Aviation Rd.
Fallbrook, CA 92028

Alaska Northwest Pub. Co.
P.O. Box 4-EEE
Anchorage, AK 99509

Alaskabooks
P.O. Box 1494
Juneau, AK 99801

Allegheny Press
221 Wood St.
California, PA 15419

American Camping Association
Bradford Woods
Martinsville, IN 46151

American Orienteering Service
P.O. Box 547
LaPorte, IN 46350

American Youth Hostels
(distr.: Crown Publishers)

American Water Ski Association
P.O. Box 191
Winter Haven, FL 33880

Appalachian Books
P.O. Box 11
Oakton, VA 22124

Arco Publishing Co., Inc.
219 Park Ave. South
New York, NY 10003

Arctic Enterprises
Thief River Falls, MN 56701

Argus Publishers Corp.
131 South Barrington Pl.
Los Angeles, CA 90049

Association Press
291 Broadway
New York, NY 10007

PUBLISHERS

Astrographics
P.O. Box 2411
San Francisco, CA 94126

Auerbach Publishers, Inc.
121 North Broad St.
Philadelphia, PA 19107

Automobile Almanac
P.O. Box 32
Nyack, NY 10960

Aviation Book Co.
P.O. Box 4187
Glendale, CA 91202

Avon Books
959 Eighth Ave.
New York, NY 10019

BUC International Corp.
2455 East Sunrise Blvd.
Fort Lauderdale, FL 33304

Backcountry Horsemen
P.O. Box 1192
Columbia Falls, MT 59912

Bagnall Publishing Co.
P.O. Box 507
Lake Arrowhead, CA 92353

Ballantine Books
201 East 50th St.
New York, NY 10022

Bantam Books
666 Fifth Ave.
New York, NY 10019

Barnard Publications
P.O. Box 158
Saugus, CA 91350

A. S. Barnes & Co.
Forsgate Dr.
Cranbury, NJ 08512

Barre Publishers
South St.
Barre, MA 01005

Benjamin Co., Inc.
485 Madison Ave.
New York, NY 10022

Berkshire Traveller Press
P.O. Box 978
Stockbridge, MA 01262

Bond/Parkhurst
1499 Monrovia Ave.
Newport Beach, CA 92663

Book People, Inc.
2940 7th St.
Berkeley, CA 94710

The Book Publishing Co.
The Farm
Summertown, TN 38483

Bookworks
1409 5th St.
Berkeley, CA 94710

Bowmar
P.O. Box 3623
Glendale, CA 91201

Boy Scouts of America
Route 1
New Brunswick, NJ 08902

Charles T. Branford Co.
Newton Centre, MA 02159

OUTDOOR RECREATION

Brigham Young University Press
205 University Press Building
Provo, UT 84602

Brown Burro Press
P.O. Box 2863-D
Pasadena, CA 91105

The Buckskin Press
Big Timber, MT 59011

Buffalo Bull Press
335 18th St., S.E.
Cedar Rapids, IA 52403

Burgess Publishing Co.
7108 Olms Lane
Minneapolis, MN 55435

Campgrounds Unlimited
P.O. Box 248
Wakefield, KS 67487

Capra Press
631 State St.
Santa Barbara, CA 93101
(distr.: Book People)

H. Glenn Carson Enterprises
801 Juniper Ave.
Boulder, CO 80302

Caxton Printers Ltd.
312 Main St.
Caldwell, ID 83605

Cellar Book Shop
18090 Wyoming
Detroit, MI 48221

Wavie J. Charlton
P.O. Box 620
Hot Springs, MT 59845

Chatham Press
15 Wilmot Lane
Riverside, CT 06878

Chilton Book Co.
Chilton Way
Radnor, PA 19089

Chronicle Books
54 Mint St.
San Francisco, CA 94103

Cloudburst Press
P.O. Box 79
Brackendale, B.C.
(distr.: Book People)

Clymer Publications
222 North Virgil Ave.
Los Angeles, CA 90004

Collier Books. *See* Macmillan
  Publishing Company.

Condor Books
P.O. Box 7141
Berkeley, CA 94707

Cornerstone Library
630 Fifth Ave.
New York, NY 10020

Coronado Book Corp.
131 South Barrington Place
Los Angeles, CA 90049

Coward, McCann & Geoghegan, Inc.
200 Madison Ave.
New York, NY 10016

T. Y. Crowell Co.
665 Fifth Ave.
New York, NY 10019

PUBLISHERS

Crown Publishers
419 Park Ave. South
New York, NY 10016

Cycle Guide Publications
P.O. Box 267
Mount Morris, IL 61054

Darvill Outdoor Publications
P.O. Box 636
Mount Vernon, WA 98273

John DeGraff
34 Oak Ave.
Tuckahoe, NY 10707

Digest Books, Inc.
540 Frontage Rd.
Northfield, IL 60093

Dodd, Mead & Co.
79 Madison Ave.
New York, NY 10016

Doubleday & Co.
277 Park Ave.
New York, NY 10017

Dover Publications
180 Varick St.
New York, NY 10014

Driscoll/Hough Publications
P.O. Box 483
San Leandro, CA 94577
(distr.: Ten Speed)

E. P. Dutton & Co., Inc.
201 Park Ave. South
New York, NY 10003

ERCO, Inc.
P.O. Box 91648
Tacoma, WA 98491

Ernest P. Edwards
P.O. Box AQ
Sweet Briar, VA 24595

Emerson Books
Reynolds Lane
Buchanan, NY 10511

Emporium Publications
P.O. Box 539
Newton, MA 02158

Enderes Tool Co.
Labert Lea, MN 56007

Erving Publishing Company
P.O. Box 1899
Winter Park, FL 32789

M. Evans Co.
Orders to J. B. Lippincott

Exposition Press
50 Jericho Turnpike
Jericho, NY 11753

Farm and Ranch Vacations. *See* Berkshire Traveller.

Farnam Horse Library
8701 North 29th St.
Omaha, NB 68112

Frederick Fell, Inc.
386 Park Ave. South
New York, NY 10016

Filter Press
P.O. Box 5
Palmer Lake, CO 80133

247

OUTDOOR RECREATION

Fleet Press Corp.
156 Fifth Ave.
New York, NY 10010

Follett Publishing Co.
1010 West Washington Blvd.
Chicago, IL 60607

Funk & Wagnalls. Send orders to
 T. Y. Crowell Co.

Gala Books
444 Vineland Ave.
North Hollywood, CA 91603

Gembooks
Mentone, CA 92359

Golden Press. *See* Western
 Publishing Co.

Gousha Publications
P.O. Box 6227
San Jose, CA 95150
(distr.: Crown Publishers)

Government Printing Office
Washington, DC 20402

Great Outdoors Publishing Company
4747 28th St. North
St. Petersburg, FL 33714

Stephen Greene Press
Fessenden Road
P.O. Box 1000
Brattleboro, VT 05301

Grosset & Dunlap, Inc.
51 Madison Ave.
New York, NY 10010

The Gun Room Press
127 Raritan Ave.
Highland Park, NJ 08904

H. P. Books
P.O. Box 5367
Tucson, AZ 85703

A. R. Harding Publishing Company
2878 East Main St.
Columbus, OH 43209

Harper & Row, Publishers
10 East 53rd St.
New York, NY 10022

Hart Publishing Company
719 Broadway
New York, NY 10003

Hastings House Publishers
10 East 40th St.
New York, NY 10016

Hawthorn Books
260 Madison Ave.
New York, NY 10016

Hearst Books
250 West 55th St.
New York, NY 10019

Heidelberg Publishers
3707 Kerbey Lane
Austin, TX 78731

Herter's, Inc.
R.R. 1
Waseca, MN 56093

Hippocrene Books, Inc.
171 Madison Ave.
New York, NY 10016

PUBLISHERS

Holt, Rinehart & Winston
383 Madison Ave.
New York, NY 10017

Information Canada
Ottawa, Ontario K1A 0S9
(formerly The Queen's Printer)

International Marine Pub. Co.
21 Elm St.
Camden, ME 04843

Rich Israel
c/o Grace
P.O. Box 416
Keddie, CA 95952

E. W. Jameson, Jr.
P.O. Box 580
Davis, CA 95616

The Janus Press, Inc.
P.O. Box 75455
Los Angeles, CA 90075

Jeppesen & Co.
P.O. Box 5645 B
Denver, CO 80217

Ken Kern Drafting
Sierra Route
Oakhurst, CA 93644

Knife Digest Publishing Company.
See Ten Speed Press.

Alfred A. Knopf
201 East 50th St.
New York, NY 10022

Lane Books
Menlo Park, CA 94025

Laurida Books Publishing
Company
P.O. Box 2061
Hollywood, CA 90028

LeVoyageur
1319 Wentworth Dr.
Irving, TX 75061

Life Support Technology, Inc.
P.O. Box 13
Manning, OR 97125

Limbo Library
P.O. Box 405
Taos, NM 87571

Links Books
33 West 60th St.
New York, NY 10023
(distr.: Quick Fox)

J. B. Lippincott Co.
East Washington Square
Philadelphia, PA 19105

Little, Brown & Co.
34 Beacon St.
Boston, MA 02106

Lyman Products for Shooters
Route 147
Middlefield, CT 06445

Living Foods Dehydrators
P.O. Box 546
Fall City, WA 98024

OUTDOOR RECREATION

MIT Outing Club
Room 461, Student Center
Cambridge, MA 02139

R. H. McCrory
P.O. Box 13
Bellmore, NY 11710

McGraw-Hill Book Company
1221 Avenue of the Americas
New York, NY 10020

David McKay Company, Inc.
750 Third Ave.
New York, NY 10017

Mackinlay-Winnacker-McNeil,
AIA Associates, Inc.
5238 Claremont Ave.
Oakland, CA 94618

Macmillan Publishing Company
866 Third Ave.
New York, NY 10022

Macrae Smith Company
225 South 15th St.
Philadelphia, PA 19102

Manor Books
329 Fifth Ave.
New York, NY 10016

Maricopa County, Dept. of Civil
Defense & Emergency Services
2035 North 52nd St.
Phoenix, AZ 85008

Media House
P.O. Box 1770
Portland, ME 04104

Modern Canadian
(distr.: Hippocrene Books)

Mother Earth News, Inc.
P.O. Box 70
Hendersonville, NC 28739

Motor Boating & Sailing
P.O. Box 2319
FDR Station
New York, NY 10022

Motorbooks International
3501 Hennepin Ave.
South Minneapolis, MN 55408

Nash Publishing Company
9255 Sunset Blvd.
Los Angeles, CA 90069

National Muzzle Loading Rifle
Association
P.O. Box 67
Friendship, IN 47021

Nature Study Guild
P.O. Box 972
Berkeley, CA 94701

Naturegraph Publishers
8339 Dry Creek Rd.
Healdsburg, CA 95448

Naval Institute Press
Annapolis, MD 21402

Naylor Company
1015 Culebra Ave.
San Antonio, TX 78201

New American Library
1301 Avenue of the Americas
New York, NY 10019

PUBLISHERS

New Hampshire Publishing
  Company
1 Market St.
Somersworth, NH 03878

North American Falconry and
  Hunting Hawks
P.O. Box 1484
Denver, CO 80201

North Star Press
P.O. Box 451
St. Cloud, MN 56301

Northland Press
P.O. Box N
Flagstaff, AZ 86001

W. W. Norton & Company, Inc.
55 Fifth Ave.
New York, NY 10003

Ohio Canoe Adventures, Inc.
P.O. Box 2092
Sheffield Lake, OH 44054

The Old Farmer's Almanac
Dublin, NH 03444

Oliver Press
1400 Ryan Creek Rd.
Willits, CA 95490

101 Productions
834 Mission St.
San Francisco, CA 94103

Outdoor Education Association
P.O. Box 696
Tacoma, WA 98401

The Outpost
P.O. Box 423
Tofield, Alberta T0B 4J0

Oxmoor House
P.O. Box 2463
Birmingham, AL 35302

Paladin Press
P.O. Box 1307
Boulder, CO 80302

Pantheon Books, Inc.
201 East 50th St.
New York, NY 10022
(distr.: Random House)

Jack Park
15237 Lakeside
Sylmar, CA 91342

Penguin Books, Inc.
7110 Ambassador Rd.
Baltimore, MD 21207

Pequot Press
Old Chester Rd.
Chester, CT 06412

Petersen Publishing Company
8490 Sunset Blvd.
Los Angeles, CA 90069

Plant Deck, Inc.
2134 S.W. Wembley Park Rd.
Lake Oswego, OR 97034

Pocket Books, Inc.
630 Fifth Ave.
New York, NY 10020

Popular Library
355 Lexington Ave.
New York, NY 10017

Popular Science Books
355 Lexington Ave.
New York, NY 10017

OUTDOOR RECREATION

Potomac Books, Inc.
4832 Macarthur Blvd., N.W.
Washington, DC 20017

Clarkson Potter. Division of
 Crown Publishers.

Powder, Patch & Ball Publications
P.O. Box 37
Friendship, IN 47021

The Powell Company
Drawer 5975
Biltmore Station
Asheville, NC 28803

Power Rider Co.
P.O. Box 158
Saugus, CA 91350

Dan Poynter
P.O. Box 4232
Santa Barbara, CA 93103

Praeger Publishers, Inc.
111 Fourth Ave.
New York, NY 10003

Prentice-Hall, Inc.
Englewood Cliffs, NJ 07632

G. P. Putnam's Sons
200 Madison Ave.
New York, NY 10016

Pyramid Communications, Inc.
919 Third Ave.
New York, NY 10022

Quadrangle/The New York
 Times Book Company
10 East 53rd St.
New York, NY 10022

The Queen's Printer. Now called
 Information Canada.

Quick Fox, Inc.
33 West 60th St.
New York, NY 10023

Rajo Book Division
P.O. Box 1014
Grass Valley, CA 95945

Ram Publishing Company
P.O. Box 38464
Dallas, TX 75238

Rand McNally & Company
8255 Central Park Ave.
Skokie, IL 60076

Random House, Inc.
201 East 50th St.
New York, NY 10022

Real Enterprises, Inc.
P.O. Box 34376
Dallas, TX 75234

Recreation Consultants
P.O. Box 842
Seattle, WA 98111

Henry Regnery Company
114 West Illinois St.
Chicago, IL 60610

Remington Outdoor Tips
P.O. Box 432
Bridgeport, CT 06601

Review & Herald Publishing
 Company
Takoma Park
Washington, DC 20012

PUBLISHERS

Ward Ritchie Press
3044 Riverside Dr.
Los Angeles, CA 90039

Running Press
38 South 19th St.
Philadelphia, PA 19103

Rutgers University Press
30 College Ave.
New Brunswick, NJ 08903

Sage Books. *See* Swallow Press.

Sail Books
c/o W. W. Norton & Co.
55 Fifth Ave.
New York, NY 10003

Saturday Review Press. *See*
    E. P. Dutton.

Schocken Books, Inc.
200 Madison Ave.
New York, NY 10016

Schweizer Aircraft Corp.
821 Airport Rd.
Elmira, NY 14902

Schwinn Bicycle Company
1856 North Kostner Ave.
Chicago, IL 60639

Charles Scribner's Sons
597 Fifth Ave.
New York, NY 10017

Scrimshaw Press
149 Ninth St.
San Francisco, CA 94103

Sea Magazine
2706 Harbor Blvd., No. 200
Costa Mesa, CA 92626

Shambhala Publications, Inc.
2045 Francisco St.
Berkeley, CA 94709.
    Send orders to Random House,
    400 Hahn Rd., Westminster,
    MD 21157.

Sheed & Ward
475 Fifth Ave.
New York, NY 10017

Michael Sheridan
2526 North 56th St.
Phoenix, AZ 85008

G. Shumway Publisher
R.D. 7
York, PA 17402

Sierra Club
San Diego Chapter
P.O. Box 525
San Diego, CA 92418

Sierra Club Books
597 Fifth Ave.
New York, NY 10017

Signpost Publications, Inc.
16812 36th Ave. West
Lynnwood, WA 98036

Simon & Schuster, Inc.
630 Fifth Ave.
New York, NY 10020

Sincere Press
P.O. Box 17599
Tucso, AZ 85731

Soaring Society of America
P.O. Box 66071
Los Angeles, CA 90066

OUTDOOR RECREATION

Southern Publishing Association
P.O. Box 59
Nashville, TN 37202

Sports Car Press. *See* Crown
  Publishers.

Stackpole Books
Cameron and Kelker Streets
Harrisburg, PA 17105

Stark Research Corp.
Cedarsburg, WI 53021

Sterling Publishing Company
419 Park Ave. South
New York, NY 10016

Wilson Stone
241 Santa Isabel
Costa Mesa, CA 92627

Straight Arrow Books
625 3rd St.
San Francisco, CA 94107
(distr.: Simon & Schuster)

Sunflower Farm
R.R. 2
Shevlin, MN 56676

Survival Education Association
9035 Golden Given Rd.
Tacoma, WA 98445

Swallow Press
1139 South Wabash
Chicago, IL 60605

Swanson Publishing Company
P.O. Box 334
Moline, IL 61265

TAB Books
Monterey and Pinola
Blue Ridge Summit, PA 17214

Tacoma Mountain Rescue Unit
P.O. Box 696
Tacoma, WA 98401

Tafnews Press
P.O. Box 296
Los Altos, CA 94022

Ten Speed Press
2510 Bancroft Way
Berkeley, CA 94704

Raymond Thompson Company
15815 2nd Pl. West
Lynnwood, WA 98036

Touchstone Press
P.O. Box 81
Beaverton, OR 97005

Trailer Life Publishing Company
23945 Craftsman Rd.
Calabasas, CA 91302

Trail-R-Club of America
3211 Pico Blvd.
Santa Monica, CA 90405

Transatlantic Arts, Inc.
North Village Green
Levittown, NY 11756

Transmedia
P.O. Box 2847
La Mesa, CA 92041

Charles E. Tuttle Company
Rutland, VT 05701

PUBLISHERS

United Prospectors, Inc.
5665 Park Crest Dr.
San Jose, CA 95118

University of Arizona Press
P.O. Box 3398
Tucson, AZ 85722

University of Chicago Press
5801 Ellis Ave.
Chicago, IL 60637

University of Michigan Press
Ann Arbor, MI 48106

University of Minnesota Press
2037 University Ave. S.E.
Minneapolis, MN 55455

University of New Mexico Press
Albuquerque, NM 87106

University of Oklahoma Press
1005 Asp Ave.
Norman, OK 73069

University of Texas Press
P.O. Box 7819
Austin, TX 78712

University of Washington Press
Seattle, WA 98105

VITA
3706 Rhode Island Ave.
Mt. Rainier, MD 20822

M. Van Atta
P.O. Box 2131
Melbourne, FL 32901

Van Nostrand Reinhold Company
450 West 33rd St.
New York, NY 10001

Walker & Company
720 Fifth Ave.
New York, NY 10019

Western Publishing Co.
1220 Mound Ave.
Racine, WI 53404

Wildcrafters Publications
R.R. 3, P.O. Box 118
Rockville, IN 47872

Wilderness Press
2440 Bancroft Way
Berkeley, CA 94704

Wilshire Book Co.
12015 Sherman Rd.
North Hollywood, CA 91605

Winchester Press
460 Park Ave.
New York, NY 10022

Woodall Publishing Co.
500 Hyacinth Pl.
Highland Park, IL 60035

Xyzyx Information Corp.
(distr.: Crown Publishers)

INDEX

References are to entry numbers, not page numbers.
Subject entries are in boldface type.

AMA News, 790
AOPA Pilot, 861
APM Bulletin, 862
Abbott, R. Tucker, 235-36
Abel, Michael, 90
Abler, Bill, 579
Ackerman, R. O., 673
Adams, George F., 288
Adkins, Jan, 472
Adventure Trip Guide: 1000 Selected Vacation Ideas, 1
Aero Magazine, 863
Aeroscience: Basic Textbook for Aeroscience Courses, 568
After Solo, 559
Aigner, Hal, 333
Air Facts, 864
Air Progress Sport Aircraft 1973, 555
Alaska, 48, 51, 428-29, 439, 484
Alaska! By Pickup Camper, 439
Albano, Charles M., 289-90
Albright, Priscilla, 2
Albright, Rodney, 2
Ald, Roy, 334, 674
Alden, Peter, 237
Alexander, Taylor R., 238
Alferd Packer's Wilderness Cookbook, 185
All About . . .
   Bicycling, 335
   Bikes and Bicycling: Care, Repair and Safety, 336
   Camping, 50
   Camping in Alaska and the Yukon, 48
   Camping in Europe, 71
   Houseboats . . . , 530
   Minibikes, 387
   Pickup Campers, Van Conversions and Motor Homes, 416
   Snowmobiles, 444

Allen, Jana, 182
Allen, Peter, 688
Allen, William H., 149
Allen, William H., Jr., 654
Alth, Max, 336
Amateur Archaeologist's Handbook, 317
Amateur Boat Building, 835
Amateur Navigator's Handbook, 549
Amateur Photographer's Handbook, 732
Amateur's Guide to Caves & Caving, 712
Amber, John T., 675
American Bicyclist & Motorcyclist, 791
American Boating, 836
American Boy's Handy Book: What to Do and How to Do It, 584
American Canoeist, 842
American Cooner, 907
American Girl's Handy Book: How to Amuse Yourself and Others, 586
American Hiker, 757
American Horseman, 908
American Pigeon Journal, 909
American Racing Pigeon News, 910
American Rifleman, 919
American Single Shot Rifle News, 920
American Trail Hound, 669
American Whitewater, 837
American Wilderness: Where to Go in the Nation's Wilderness . . . , 39
American Youth Hostels' North American Bicycle Atlas, 337
America's Backpacking Book, 99
America's Camping Book, 14
America's Flying Book, 561
Anderson, A. J., 15
Anderson, L. O., 580
Anderson, Robert R., 496
Angier, Bradford, 3, 15, 91-93, 131, 183, 581-82

257

Animal/Plant Identification, 235-87
(*See also* **Food Plants**; **Poisonous Plants**.)
Animal Tracks and Hunter Signs, 266
Antique Airplane News, 873
Anybody's Bike Book: An Original Manual of Bicycle Repairs, 344
Apache Jim: Stories from His Private Files, 330
Appalachia, 758
Appalachian Hiker: Adventure of a Lifetime, 117
Appalachian Waters—The Delaware River and Its Tributaries, 481
Appalachian Waters—The Hudson River and Its Tributaries, 482
Aquatic World, 838
Archaeology, 317, 783
Archery, 921
Archery and Bow Hunting, 9, 38, 76, 691, 696, 705-706, 708, 735, 921-22, 924-25
Archery World, 922
Arctander, Erik, 366-67
Arctic Enterprises, Inc., 445
Arem, Joel, 291
Arighi, Margaret S., 473
Arighi, Scott, 473
Art and Practice of Hawking, 666
Art and Science of Taking to the Woods, 15
Art and Technique of Soaring, 578
Art of Blacksmithing, 583
Art of Survival, 169
Asa, Warren, 337
Ash, David, 401
Ashbrook, Frank G., 184
Astronomy, 686, 739, 927, 945
At Home in the Wilderness, 640
Auran, John Henry, 446
Austin, Oliver L., Jr., 239
Automobile Almanac, 401
Automobile Operation and Maintenance, 646
Aviation, 112, 555-78, 861-90
Aviation Times, 865
Aviation Travel, 866
Away We Go! A Guidebook of Family Trips to Places of Interest in New Jersey, Nearby Pennsylvania, and New York, 54
Aymar, Gordon C., 474
Azarian, Mary, 216

BEAM, 596
BUC Book: A Statistically Authenticated Used Boat Directory . . . , 475
BUC'S 1974 New Boat Directory . . . , 476
Back, Joe, 655
Back Country, 759
Back Country Horsemen's Guidebook, 656
Back Roads of New England, 84
Back to the Bike, 354
Backpacker, 160, 760
Backpacker's Cookbook, 198
Backpacker's Digest, 134
Backpacking, 14, 23, 59, 69, 90-91, 93, 98-101, 103-104, 107, 112, 116-17, 124, 126-28, 133-34, 138, 143, 145, 152, 154, 160, 171, 174-75, 177-79, 181, 757-79, 181, 757-61, 764, 768-70, 772-73, 795
Backpacking, 154
Backpacking for Fun: A Beginner's How-to-do-it with Special Suggestions for Families, 177
Backpacking Made Easy, 90
Backpacking One Step at a Time, 138
Backpacking, Tenting & Trailering, 23
Backwoods Journal, 891
Bacon, Thorn, 477
Bailey, Gary, 368
Baja, 434
Baja California, 81
Baker, Robert H., 739
Baldwin, Edward R., 447
Ballantine, Richard, 338
Ballistics and the Muzzle Loading Rifle, 694
Ballooning, 558, 577, 867-68, 877
Ballooning, 558, 867
Banks, James E., 185-86
Barlowe, Dorothea, 285-86
Barlowe, Sy, 285-86
Bartmess, Marilyn A., 187
Barton, Kent O., 4
Basic Auto Repair Manual, 425
Basic Automotive Troubleshooting, 403
Basic Book of Organic Gardening, 635
Basic Guide to Photography, 699
Basic Manual: A Standardized Guide to Training and Advanced Soaring, 573
Basic Mountaineering, 137
Basic River Canoeing, 519
Basic Sailing, 498
Batchelor, John, 338

INDEX

Bauer, Erwin, 5, 402, 676-77, 705
Bauer, Peggy, 5
Be Expert with Map and Compass: The Orienteering Handbook, 129
Beach Strollers Handbook from Maine to Cape Hatteras, 287
Beachcombing for Treasure, 289
Bealer, Alex, 583
Bean, Richard, 403
Bear, Fred, 706
Beard, Adelia B., 586
Beard, Daniel Carter, 584-85
Beard, Lina, 586
Bearse, Ray, 478
Beebe, Frank L., 657
Beginner's Guide to Flying, 562
Behme, Bob, 369
Being Your Own Wilderness Doctor: The Outdoorsman's Emergency Manual, 131
Belanger, Jerome D., 587
Bennett, Linda, 198
Bennett, Margaret, 448
Benoliel, Doug, 188
Bentley, W. A., 678
Berglund, Berndt, 94, 189
Bergman, Joe G., 355
Bernewitz, Max von, 310
Bernstein, Susan, 658
Best about Backpacking, 171
Best of Europe, 404
Better Camping & Hiking, 761
Bicentennial Bike Tours: Recycle the Past . . . , 339
Bicentennial Tourguide Celebrating Our Country's 200th Birthday, 6
Bicycle Book (Bike-Ways), 350
Bicycle Digest, 363
Bicycle Manual on Maintenance and Repair, 365
Bicycle Paper, 792
Bicycle Spokesman, 793
Bicycle Touring in Europe, 352
Bicycling (incl. Repairing), 14, 59, 112, 175, 333-65, 791-96, 798, 805, 816
Bicycling, 349
Bicycling!, 794
Bicycling for Fun and Good Health, 356
Bicycling in Seattle, 362
Biermann, June, 448
Bike Fever, 378
Bike Tripping, 345
Bike World, 796
biker/hiker, 795

Bikes: A How-to-Do-It Guide to Selection, Care, Repair . . . , 353
Bikes and Riders, 364
Bike-Ways (101 Things to Do with a Bike), 351
Bill Kaysing's the Ex-Urbanite's Complete & Illustrated Easy-Does-It First Time Farmer's Guide, 616
Birds: A Guide to the Most Familiar American Birds, 279
Birds of North America: A Guide to Field Identification, 264
Black and White Photography: A Basic Manual, 697
Black Powder Basics, 679
Black Powder Gun Digest, 681
Black Powder News, 923
Blackshaw, Alan, 95
Blandford, Percy W., 588-89
Blevins, Winfred, 680
Bleything, Dennis, 176
Blish, Jeffrey, 340
Blue Ridge Voyages, Vol. 1 . . . , 490
Boat Carpentry, 539
Boat Maintenance by the Amateur, 551
Boat Owners Buyers Guide, 839
Boat Owner's Maintenance Manual, 548
Boatbuilding Manual, 543
Boating, 840
Boating and Boats, 9, 24, 76, 474-76, 479-80, 483, 487-88, 495, 503, 510-11, 513-16, 521, 524, 530-31, 533, 535, 538-41, 543, 547-48, 550-51, 553-54, 835-60 (*See also* **Sailing; Weather**.)
Boatman's Handbook: The Keep-Aboard Almanac of Useful Boating Information, 479
Boatowner's Sheet Anchor: A Practical Guide to Fitting Out . . . , 513
Boericke, Art, 590
Bolsby, Clare E., 189
Book of Country Things, 632
Book of Motorcycles, Trail Bikes & Scooters, 366
Book of Survival . . . , 120
Boonie Book, 385
Borror, Donald J., 260
Boswell, Cliff, 370
Bottomly, Tom, 479
Boudreau, Eugene, 97
Boughton, Warren, 688
Bow & Arrow, 924
Bow & Arrow Archer's Digest, 708
Bowers, Peter M., 556

OUTDOOR RECREATION

Bowhunter Magazine, 925
Bowhunter's Digest, 706
Bowhunting for Deer, 735
Boy's Book of Biking, 357
Boys Life, 740
Boy Scouts of America, 7
Bradner, Gary, 98
Briarpatch Review, 892
Bridge, Raymond, 99, 171, 449
Bridges, Toby, 681
Brittan, Nick, 405
Brockman, C. Frank, 240
Bromfield, Louis, 591
Brower, David, 100-101
Brown, Edward Espe, 190-91
Brown, Vinson, 241-43
Browning, Peter, 406
Brummitt, Wyatt B., 682
Brunner, Hans, 450
Bruun, Bertel, 264
Bryan, Caralie, 593
Buchele, William, 683
Buckskin Report, 926
Buckskinning. *See* **Muzzle Loader Shooting.**
Build Your Own Low-Cost Home, 580
Bull Cook and Authentic Historical Recipes and Practices, 210
Bunker, Moss, 480
Bunnelle, Hasse, 192
Buoyant Flight, 868
Burch, Monte, 8, 121, 606
Burmeister, Walter F., 481-82
Burnett, R. Will, 682, 707
Burt, Calvin P., 176, 194-95
Burt, W. H., 260
Burton, Bill, 9
Buryn, Ed, 10-11
Bushcraft: A Serious Guide to Survival and Camping, 119
Bushcraft Handbooks, 119
Butcher, Bob, 688
Butchering, Processing and Preservation of Meat, 184
Butterflies and Moths: A Guide to the More Common American Species, 257
Buyer's & User's Guide to Recreational Vehicles, 417
Buying Country Property, 629

Cabin/House Building, 580-81, 585, 590-614, 618, 621, 623, 626, 634, 641, 645, 647, 727, 904

Cache Lake Country: Life in the North Woods, 726
Caldwell, John, 451
California National Parks, 78
California State Parks, 79
California Trail Bike Guide, 374
Cameron, Ben, 12
Camp and Trail Methods . . . , 132
Camper Coachman, 797
Camper's and Hiker's Guide to the Blue Ridge Parkway, 155
Camper's Cookbook, 226
Camper's Cookbook: Equipment, Recipes, Menus, 225
Camper's Digest, 5
Camper's Guide to Woodcraft and Outdoor Life, 122
Camper's Handbook . . . , 61
Campground & RV Park Management, 741
Campground Guide for Tent & Trailer Tourists, 58
Campground Guides, 12-13, 17-19, 28, 32, 58, 62, 65, 86, 89
Camping, 5, 7, 14-15, 23-24, 30-31, 35, 37-38, 49-50, 52, 56-57, 59, 61, 72, 75-77, 80, 87, 122, 128, 130, 133, 140-41, 162, 175, 370, 465, 740-45, 748, 751-56
Camping, 49, 742
Camping and Caravanning Handbook, 13
Camping and Trailering Guide: The Magazine of the Friendly Campers, 743
Camping and Trailering in Alaska: The Complete Guide, 429
Camping and Woodcraft . . . , 128
Camping Around California: The North, 17
Camping Around California: The South, 18
Camping Around New England, 19
Camping by Backpack and Canoe, 103
Camping in Comfort: A Guide to Modern Outdoor Vacations, 77
Camping Journal, 744
Camping Magazine, 745
Camping Today, 23
Canada, 21, 34, 48, 64, 67, 428, 484, 507
Canadian Alpine Journal, 762
Canadian Boating, 841
Canadian Frontier, 746
Canadian Parachutist, 869
Canadian Rockhound, 774
Canadian Treasure, 775

260

INDEX

Canadian Whole Earth Almanac, 893
Canadian Wings, 870
Canfield, D. M., 592
Canoe, 842
Canoe and You, 529
Canoe Camper's Handbook, 478
Canoeing/Rafting/Kayaking, 9, 14, 24, 69, 103, 130, 132-33, 151, 473, 478, 481-82, 484, 486, 490, 496-97, 501, 507, 517, 519-20, 529, 532, 536-37, 837, 842, 844
Canoeing and Kayaking, 536
Canoeing for Beginners, 529
Canoeing Whitewater, 486
Cantin, Donald, 483
Cantin, Eugene, 484
Cardwell, Paul, Jr., 14
Care & Maintenance of Small Boats, 483
Care and Repair of Muzzle Loaders, 673
Carlisle, Norman, 292
Carmichael, Bill, 688
Carrell, Al, 341
Carrier, Barbara, 485
Carrier, Rick, 485, 557
Carson, H. Glenn, 293-94
Cart and Sled Dog Training Manual, 670
Carter, Randy, 486
Casanova, Richard, 295
Case, Marshal T., 244
Cassidy, William L., 684
Castle, Bryan, 593
Castrol Rally Manual, 2, 406
Catalogue of the South, 685
Caving. *See* **Spelunking.**
Celestial Observer, 927
Celestial Wall Map, 686
Central America: How to Get There and Back in One Piece with a Minimum of Hassle, 66
Centre Nautique des Glénans, 500
Charlton, Wavie J., 598
Cheney, Theodore A., 103
Chilton's Complete Guide to Motorcycles and Motorcycling, 381
Chilton's More Miles Per Gallon Guide, 442
Chilton's Repair and Tune-Up Guide for Snowmobiles, 452
Chilton's Repair and Tune-Up Guide: Outboard Motors 30 Horsepower & Over, 487
Chilton's Repair and Tune-Up Guide: Outboard Motors Under 30 Horsepower, 488

Christensen, Clyde M., 196
Churchill, James E., 594
Cities, 25
Clear Creek Bike Book, 333
Clifford, Bill, 502
Climbing, 763
Cloudburst: A Handbook of Rural Skills & Technology, 595
Clouds of the World: A Complete Colour Encyclopedia, 728
Coast, 25
Coaster & 3-Speed Bicycle Repair, 342
Cobb, Boughton, 260
Coevolution Quarterly, 894
Coinshooting: How and Where to Do It, 293
Colby, Carroll B., 15
Cold Steel, 731
Coles, Clarence W., 343
Coles, K. Adlard, 489
Collecting, 82, 235-332
Collins, Leighton, 566
Colwell, Robert, 16, 104, 453
Common Edible and Useful Plants of the West, 229
Common Edible Mushrooms, 196
Common Weeds of the United States, 269
Competitive Cycling, 798
Compleat Backpacker, 124
Complete Archery Book, 696
Complete Bicycle Book, 347
Complete Book of . . .
    Boating . . . , 554
    Camping and Backpacking, 59
    Cross-Country Skiing and Ski Touring, 458
    High Altitude Baking, 206
    Karting, 410
    Mobile Home Living, 413
    Moto-Cross, 371
    Motor Camping, 414
    Powerboats, 541
    Practical Camping, 37
    the Bow and Arrow, 691
    Trailering, 415
    Trick & Fancy Shooting, 709
    Water Sports: Completely Illustrated, 517
    Winter Sports, 459
Complete Cross-Country Skiing and Ski Touring, 457
Complete Guide to . . .
    Cross-Country Skiing and Touring, 469
    Home Canning, Preserving and Freezing, 232

261

OUTDOOR RECREATION

Complete Guide to . . . (cont'd)
  Houseboating, 521
  Rocks, Gems & Minerals, 324
  Treasure Hunting, 292
Complete Horseshoeing Guide, 672
Complete Mini-Bike Handbook, 373
Complete Motorcycle Nomad: A Guide to Machines, Equipment, People and Places, 382
Complete Outdoors Encyclopedia, 76
Complete Outdoorsman's Handbook . . . , 130
Complete Rehabilitation of the Flintlock Rifle & Other Works, 734
Complete Snow Campers Guide, 449
Complete Snowmobiler, 470
Comstock Backpacking Guide to California, 178
Comstock Backpacking Guide to the Pacific Northwest, 179
Conant, Roger, 260
Conrotto, Eugene L., 197
Cookery, 182-234, 649-50, 690. (*See also* most camping books.)
Cooking for Camp and Trail, 192
Cooper, Jeff, 687
Cooper on Handguns, 687
Copans, Stu, 596
Corbett, H. Roger, Jr., 490
Cottam, Clarence, 282
Cotter, Edward F., 491
Country Commune Cookbook, 212
Country Craft Tools, 588
Country Inns and Back Roads, 74
Country Life and Skills, 579-653, 891-908
Country Place, 895
Country Women, 896
Countryside & Small Stock Journal, 897
Cox, Jack R., 296-97
Craft of Sail, 472
Crafts and Repairs, 3, 7-8, 36, 47, 88, 93, 106, 122, 140, 167, 173, 540, 553, 579-81, 583-86, 588, 599, 602-606, 612, 625, 628, 642, 648, 700, 713-17, 725, 730, 734, 736-45
Craighead, Frank C., Jr., 105
Craighead, John J., 105, 260
Crain, Jim, 17-19
Creagh-Osborne, Richard, 492
Cross, Margaret, 198
Cross Country News, 871
Cross-Country Skiing, 450

Cross-Country Skiing for the Fun of It, 448
Cross-Country Skiing Handbook . . . , 447
Crow, James T., 407-408
Cruiser's Compendium: A Complete Guide to Coastal, Inland and Gunkhole Cruising, 505
Cruiser's Manual: A Complete Handbook of Yacht Cruising Under Sail and Power, 514
Cruising Guide to the New England Coast . . . , 495
Cruising: Sail or Power, 503
Cuddy, Dore, 597
Cuddy, John, 597
Cummings, Elsie J., 598
Cunningham, Gerry, 106
Cuthbertson, Tom, 344-45
Cutter, Robert K., 107
Cycle, 799
Cycle CMA, 800
Cycle Guide, 801
Cycle Illustrated, 802
Cycle News West, 803
Cycle World, 804
Cyclenews: A Journal of Bicycle Racing, 805
Cycling, 334, 360

Dahlem, Ted, 199, 599
D'Alpuget, Lou, 493
Dalrymple, Byron, 108
Damn the Garbage, Full Speed Ahead: A Handbook on the Joys and Sorrows of Pleasure Boating, 480
Dangers of the Air, 566
Danielsen, John A., 454
Darvill, Fred T., Jr., 20
Davidson, Gary, 409
Davidson, Sharon, 409
Davis, Cindy, 600
Davis, Don, 688
Davis, Jim, 371
Davis, Pedr, 372
Dawson, Ronald L., 176
Day, Dick, 410
Deadly Harvest: A Guide to Common Poisonous Plants, 214
Dempsey, Paul, 373
Derailleur 5, 10 & 15-Speed Bicycle Repair, 346

Desert Gem Trails: A Field Guide to Localities of the Mojave and Colorado Deserts in California and Adjacent Areas of Nevada, 323
Desert Magazine, 747
Desert Survival: Information for Anyone Traveling in the Desert Southwest, 139
Desert Tree Finder, 272
Deserts, 25
Detector How to Test Field Guide, 304
Detector How to Use Field Guide, 305
Devereaux, Frederick L., Jr., 494
Dickey, Esther, 200
Dickson, Lew, 21
Diet for a Small Planet, 218
Dig Here!, 312
Dirt Bike, 806
Dirt Cycle, 807
Disley, John, 109
Dive: The Complete Book of Skin Diving, 485
Dive: The Prestige Magazine of Sport Diving and Oceanology, 843
Diving (Skin or Scuba), 9, 24, 485, 517, 522, 526-28, 545, 843, 854, 857
Dixon, Peter L., 558
Doan, Daniel, 110
Dog Digest: The Total Guide to Dog Ownership, 658
Dogs, 69, 76, 88, 112, 459, 658-59, 661, 668-71, 907, 911-12, 914-17
Dogs, 911
Doherty, William E., 559
Dohme, Alvin R. L., 22
Dolen, Tom, 261
Dome Builder's Handbook, 634
Doodlebug Edition of Treasure Trails with Extracts from Mysteries of Treasure Hunting, 320
Doodlebugs and Mysteries of Treasure Hunting, 321
Down But Not Out, 111
Down River, 844
Down the Wild Rivers: A Guide to the Streams of California, 501
Draughton, Guy, 347
Drawing, 729
Drawings of Locks and Pistols, 713
Driscoll, Joe, 374
Dry It—You'll Like It!, 221
Duncan, Roger F., 495
Duncan, S. Blackwell, 23
Dune Buggies & Hot VWs, 808
Dunlop, Richard, 24

Dunn, William J., 411
Dunne, Jim, 412
Durenceau, André, 257
Dwyer, John N., 298

Earth Science, 776
Eastern Gem Trails, 309
Easy Crafts, 700
Easy Motorcycle Riding, 394
Ecology, 238
Edible and Poisonous Plants of the Eastern States, 194
Edible and Poisonous Plants of the Western States, 195
Edible? Incredible!, 202
Edible Native Plants of the Rocky Mountains, 207
Edible, Ornamental Garden, 593
Edible Plants in the Wilderness, 176
Edible Wild Plants of Pennsylvania, 231
Edmonds, I. G., 375
Edwards, Ernest P., 245
Eisentraut, Albert, 345
Elder, Leon, 601
Elements of Farrier Science, 592
Elliott, Charles, 249
Enduro, 380
Engel, Lyle Kenyon, 413-15, 430
Enjoy Europe by Car, 411
Epstein, Ed, 336
Ericson, Virginia, 549
Ervin, Jonathan, 602
Erving's World Wide Skindiver's Guide, 528
Europe (and Western Hemisphere), 13, 63, 71, 83, 87, 404-405, 409, 411, 531
Europe with Two Kids and a Van, 409
Evans, Jay, 496
Ewald, Ellen Buchman, 201
Ewers, William, 348
Explore Canada, 34
Explorer's Guide to the West, 25
Explorers Ltd., 112
Explorers Ltd. Source Book, 112
Exploring and Mining for Gems and Gold in the West . . . , 318
Exploring Canada by Recreational Vehicle, 21
Exploring Mount Rainier, 44
Exploring the Olympic Peninsula, 45
Exploring Yellowstone, 46
Extraction of Free Gold, 307

OUTDOOR RECREATION

Falconry, 112, 657, 664-66
Falk, John R., 659
Families of Birds, 239
Family Camping Guide, 56
Family Fun with Rocks . . . , 299
Family Houseboating, 845
Family Motor Coaching, 809
Family Wilderness Book, 175
Farm, Ranch & Countryside Guide: 500 Selected Vacation Ideas, 26
Farming. *See* **Country Life and Skills.**
Farnam Horse Library, 660
Farnham, Albert B., 603
Fatigue and Exhaustion, 165
Faulk, Terry R., 301
Fay, Gordon S., 300
Fear, Daniel E., 113
Fear, Eugene H., 113-15
Federal Aviation Regulations for Pilots 1974, 560
Fell's Teen-Age Guide to Skin and Scuba Diving, 545
Fences, Gates and Bridges: A Practical Manual, 627
Fichter, George S., 238, 250, 349
Field and Stream, 748
Field & Stream Guide to Family Camping, 31
Field Guide to . . .
    Animal Tracks, 258, 260
    Mexican Birds, 260
    Reptiles and Amphibians, 260
    Rocks and Minerals, 260
    Rocky Mountain Wildflowers, 260
    Shells of the Pacific Coast and Hawaii, 260
    Snow Crystals, 701
    the Birds, 260
    the Birds of Mexico . . . , 245
    the Birds of Texas and Adjacent States, 260
    the Butterflies, 260
    the Ferns and Their Related Families, 260
    the Insects of America North of Mexico, 260
    the Mammals, 260
    the Shells of Our Atlantic and Gulf Coasts, 260
    the Stars and Planets, 260
    Trees and Shrubs, 260
    Western Reptiles and Amphibians, 260
    Western Birds, 260

Field Guide to . . . (cont'd)
    Wilderness Living, 118
    Wildflowers of Northeastern and North-Central North America, 260
Fieldbook for Scouts, Explorers, Scouters, Educators, Outdoorsmen, 7
Fifty Hikes: Walks, Day Hikes . . . in New Hampshire's White Mountains, 110
Finding the Birds in Western Mexico . . . , 237
Finding Your Way in the Outdoors: Compass Navigation, Map Reading, Route Finding, Weather Forecasting, 146
Fionella, Jay, 558
Firearms Encyclopedia, 719
First Aid, 131, 176, 596 (*See also* most camping books.)
First Horse: Basic Horse Care Illustrated, 663
First New England Catalogue, 689
Fishback, Mel, 661
Fishes: A Guide to Fresh- and Salt-Water Species, 280
Fishing. *See* **Hunting and Fishing.**
Fiske, Jean, 198
Five Acres and Independence . . . , 615
Fix Your Bicycle: All Speeds—All Major Makes—Simplified—Step-by-Step, 355
Fixing Up Motorcycles, 392
Fletcher, Colin, 116, 171
Florida Marine Shells . . . , 270
Flower Finder: A Key to Spring Wild Flowers and Flower Families East of the Rockies and North of the Smokies, Exclusive of Trees and Shrubs, 273
Flowers: A Guide to Familiar American Wildflowers, 281
Fly: The Complete Book of Sky Sailing, 557
Flying Magazine, Editors of, 561
Foam Sandwich Boatbuilding: A Practical Guide to Home Construction, 553
Food Conspiracy Cookbook: How to Start a Neighborhood Buying Club and Eat Cheaply, 234
Food for Knapsackers and Other Trail Travellers, 193
Food Plants, 176, 183, 188, 194-96, 204-205, 207-208, 215-17, 220, 227, 229, 231, 233, 593 (*See also* **Poisonous Plants.**)
Foods. *See* **Cookery.**
Foods-from-the-Woods Cooking, 183

264

INDEX

Foraging for Edible Wild Mushrooms, 204
Formula Manual, 638
Formulas, 603-604, 638, 644
42 More Short Walks in Connecticut, 42
Four Season Trails, 749
Four Wheel Drive Handbook, 407
Four Wheeler, 810
Fossils, 295, 306, 316
Fossils: A Guide to Prehistoric Life, 316
Fossils for Amateurs: A Handbook for Collectors, 306
Foxfire Book, 649
Foxfire 2, 650
Foy, Charles, 662
Francis, Mary, 562
Frankel, Godfrey, 350-51
Frankel, Lillian, 350-51
Freund, Rudolf, 281
Fries, Gene E., 604, 690
Frome, Michael, 27
Full Cry, 912
Fun Flying Guide, 576
Fun on Horseback, 667
Fundamental Rock Climbing, 153
Fur-Fish-Game, 898
Furlong, Marjorie, 202, 251
Furred and Feathered Wild Game from Bullet to Table, 219
Furrer, Werner, 497

Gabrielson, Ira N., 279
Game Cookery, 228
Game Cookery: 96 XIXth Century Recipes, 197
Gamebirds: A Guide to North American Species and Their Habits, 268
Gann, Ernest K., 561
Gardening. *See* **Country Life and Skills.**
Gartner, John, 416
Garvey, Edward B., 117
Gearing, Catherine, 118
Gem Cutter's Handbook: Cabochon Cutting, 296
Gem Cutter's Handbook: Specialized Gem Cutting, 297
Gems & Gemology, 777
Gems and Minerals, 778
Geology. *See* **Rockhounding.**
Geology, 315
George, M. B., 498
Getting in Shape to Ski, 464
Gibbs, Tony, 499
Gibson, Charles E., 605

Gillelan, G. Howard, 691
Gin, Margaret, 182
Give Your Heart to the Hawks: A Tribute to the Mountain Men, 680
Gjersvik, Maryanne, 252
Gladson, Deek, 302
Glénans Sailing Manual, 500
Glenn, Harold T., 343
Glenn's Complete Bicycle Manual: Selection, Maintenance, Repair, 343
Going Camping: A Complete Guide for the Uncertain Beginner in Family Camping, 72
Going Light with Backpack or Burro, 100
Gold Dredger's Handbook, 325
Gold Hex, 308
Golden Book of Camping . . . , 35
Golden Guide to Camping, 75
Golden Guide to Scuba Diving: Handbook of Underwater Activities, 527
Good Earth Almanac, 606
Good Earth Almanac Survival Handbook, 121
Good Sam Club's 1973 Recreational Vehicle Owner's Directory, 28
Gorton, Audrey Alley, 203
Gourmet Cooking for Free, 183
Graves, Richard, 119
Great Bicycle Conspiracy, 792
Green Fun, 252
Green Revolution, 899
Greenbank, Anthony, 120
Greene, Bob, 376
Greene, Janet, 211
Gregg, James R., 29
Gregory, Mark, 121, 606
Gresham, Grits, 30
Grey, Hugh, 31
Griffin, Al, 377, 417
Grossenheider, R. P., 260
Grote, Walter, 688
Ground Skimmer, 872
Guerny, Gene, 563
Guide to . . .
    Competition Driving, 431
    Family Camping, 87
    Movie Making, 711
    Spiders and Their Kin, 247
Guidebook to the Colorado Desert of California, 60
Gun Digest, 675
Gun Digest Book of Knives, 698
Gun Week, 928
Gun World, 929
Gunby, R. A., 564

Guns & Ammo, 930
Guns & Ammo Complete Guide to Blackpowder, 737
Guns & Ammo Guidebook to Knives & Edged Weapons, 738
Guns & Ammo 1974 Annual, 692
Guns Magazine, 931
Gunsmith's Manual, 730
Gunsport & Gun Collector, 932
Gutkind, Lee, 378

Haard, Karen, 204
Haard, Richard, 204
Habitat Guide to Birding, 248
Hall, Alan, 205
Halonen, Keith, 354
Hamilton, Donna Miller, 206
Hand, Reef and Steer, 506
Handbook and Directory for Campers, 32
Handbook for Prospectors, 310
Handbook of Gemstone Carving . . . , 329
Handbook of Knots and Splices and Other Work with Hempen and Wire Ropes, 605
Handmade Houses: A Guide to the Woodbutcher's Art, 590
Hanenkrat, Frank T., 722
Hang Gliding, 557, 569-71, 872, 875, 877, 885
Hang Gliding: The Basic Handbook of Skysurfing, 570
Hannson, Margaret, 106
Hapgood, Ruth, 663
Hardman, Tom, 502
Harlé, Philippe, 500
Harrington, H. D., 207-208
Harris, Gertrude, 209
Harris, Thomas, 501
Harrison, William B., 730
Hartline, Ben, 161
Hartline, Fred, 161
Havens, David, 607
Hawk for the Bush . . . , 665
Hawking. *See* **Falconry.**
Hawkins, Gary, 352
Hawkins, Karen, 352
Hayes, Richard L., 33
Hays, George, 370
Heaton, Peter, 503-504
Heavy Weather Sailing, 489
Helmker, Judith, 455
Henderson, Joe, 693

Henderson, Luis M., 122
Henderson, Richard, 505-506
Henkel, Stephen C., 353
Hennessey, James, 608-609
Henrichsen, Harold, 303
Henrichsen, Winifred, 303
Herbster, Mary Lee, 244
Here Is Your Hobby . . . Motorcycling, 400
Herring, William C., 694
Herter, Berthe E., 210, 610
Herter, George Leonard, 123, 210, 610
Herter, Jacques P., 123
Hertzberg, Ruth, 211
Herz, Jerry, 124
Hey Beatnik! This Is the Farm Book, 611
Heyl, Frank G., 176
Hidden Riches (Searching Old Abandoned and Deserted Houses for Treasures and Antiques), 290
High Country Safety, 165
High Sierra Hiking Guides, 125
High Trails West, 135
Hiker's and Backpacker's Handbook, 143
Hiker's Guide to the Smokies, 147
Hiking: A Teaching Guide, 145
Hiking & Ski Touring, 764
Hiking Guides, 2, 16, 20, 41-43, 110, 117, 125, 134, 147, 151, 156-57, 161, 163-64, 172, 178-80, 453, 767
Hillcourt, William, 35
Hilts, Len, 34
History and Racing Rules, 668
History of the Tipi, 621
Hoagland, Clayton, 695
Hochman, Louis, 696
Hoffmeister, Donald F., 283
Holdgate, Charles, 612
Hollatz, Thomas, 456
Home Comfort: Stories and Scenes of Life on Total Loss Farm, 652
Home Guide to Muzzle-Loading, 720
Home Health Handbook, 596
Home in Your Pack: The Modern Handbook of Backpacking, 91
Home Tanning and Leather Making Guide, 603
Homemade Beer Book, 224
Homesteaders and Landcrafters Newsletter, 908
Homesteader's Handbook, 594, 613
Homesteader's Handbook to Raising Small Livestock, 587
Homesteading: How to Find New Independence on the Land, 624

INDEX

Horenstein, Henry, 697
Horse & Rider, 913
Horses and Horseback Riding, 9, 14, 24, 50, 52, 69, 112, 592, 655-56, 660, 663, 667, 672, 908, 913, 918
Horses, Hitches and Rocky Trails, 655
Horseshoeing, 592, 660, 672
Horton, Lucy, 212
Hot Tubs: How to Build, Maintain & Enjoy Your Own, 601
Hounds and Hunting, 914
How to . . .
    Become a Better Rider, 660
    Break and Train the Western Horse, 660
    Build Your Home in the Woods, 581
    Buy a Used Motorcycle, 395
    Buy Recreational Vehicles, 423
    Buy the Right Horse, 660
    Correct the Problem Horse, 600
    Get Out of the Rat Race and Live on $10 a Month, 610
    Get Started in Soaring: Guide to Sky Sailing, 565
    Grow Almost Everything, 636
    Identify 101 Popular Sailboats Under 30 Feet, 511
    Know the Minerals and Rocks, 311
    Make and Mend Cast Nets, 599
    Raise and Train Pigeons, 654
    Recognize Horse Health Problems, 660
    Ride in Sand, 396
    Ride Motorcycles, 379
    Ride Observed Trials for Fun, 391
    Select a Car or Truck for Trailer Towing, 424
    Select, Ride and Maintain Your Trail Bike, 388
    Shoe Your Horse, 660
    Show Your Horse and Win, 660
    Smoke Seafood Florida Cracker Style, 199
    Stay Alive in the Woods, 92
    Survive on Land and Sea, 105
    Use the Front Brake, 397
    Win Motocross, 368
Howes, Connie B., 418
Hudson-Evans, Richard, 419
Hughes, B. R., 698
Hull, Clinton R., 420-21
Humphrey, Clifford C., 354
Humphreys, W. D., 678
Hunt, the Quarry, and the Skillet, 220
Hunter's Cookbook, 223

Hunter's Digest, 676
Hunter's Horn, 915
Hunters of the Northern Forest . . . , 148
Hunting and Fishing, 30, 38, 57, 69, 76, 88, 123, 148, 173, 676, 705-706, 735, 748, 898
Hunting Dog, 916
Hunting With a Camera: A World Guide to Wildlife Photography, 677
Hunting With Bow and Arrow, 705
Hurley, Leslie J., 462-63

Ice Skating, 9, 459
Illustrated Guide to Fossil Collecting, 295
Indian, Pioneer and Home Tanning Methods, 604
Indian Tipi: Its History, Construction, and Use, 621
Innards and Other Variety Meats, 182
Insect Pests, 250
Insects: A Guide to Familiar American Species, 282
International Antique Airplane News, 873
International Flying Farmer, 874
International Surfing, 846
Introduction to . . .
    Backpacking, 104
    Foot Trails in America, 16
    Hawking, 664
    Muzzle Loading, 673
    Rock & Mountain Climbing, 142
    Sailing, 523
    Treasure Hunting, 322
Irving, James G., 268, 279, 280, 282-84
Irving, Mary B., 317
Israel, Rich, 613
It's Easy to Fix Your Bike, 358

Jackson, Bob, 371
Jacobs, Lou, Jr., 699
Jaderquist, Malcolm, 369
Jaeger, Ellsworth, 36, 253, 700
Jameson, E. W., Jr., 664
Jansen, Charles L., 126
Jenkinson, Michael, 507
Jobson, John, 37
Jogger, 933
Jogging, Aerobics & Diet: One Is Not Enough—You Need All Three, 674
Jonathan Ervin's Leather Notebook, 602
Jones, Charles, 39
Jones, Theodore A., 508
Jones, Thomas Firth, 380

OUTDOOR RECREATION

Johnson, L. W., 38, 213
Jorgensen, Eric, 355
Joy of Camping . . . , 133
Jungle Handbook, 170
Jusem, Pearl, 153

Kahn, Lloyd, 614
Kaicher, Sally D., 261
Kains, Maurice, 615
Kalin, Alois, 450
Kalmenoff, Matthew, 248
Kane, Henry B., 726
Karting, 437
Kayaking. *See* **Canoeing.**
Kayaking: The New Whitewater Sport for Everyone, 496
Kaysing, William, 616-17
Kelsey, Robert J., 127
Kendall, Arthur I., 690
Kennedy, Mopsy Strange, 40
Kephart, Horace, 128
Kern, Ken, 618-19
Keyarts, Eugene, 41-43
Kingbay, Keith, 349
Kings of the Open Road, 422
Kingsbury, John M., 214
Kirk, Donald R., 215
Kirk, Ruth, 44-46
Kite Flying, 9
Kits & Plans, 725
Kittredge, Robert Y., 509
Kjellstrom, Bjorn, 129, 171
Klots, Alexander B., 260
Kluger, Marilyn, 216
Knab, Klaus, 39
Knap, Jerome J., 130
Knapsacking Equipment, 174
Kneass, Jack, 423-24
Knife Digest, 684
Knife Throwing: A Practical Guide, 718
Knight, Austin M., 510
Knight, David C., 511
Knights, Jack, 512
Knight's Modern Seamanship, 510
Knives & Knifemakers, 704
Knives, 625, 684, 698, 704, 718, 731, 738
Knobel, Bruno, 47
Knots and Ropework, 589, 599, 605, 612, 637
Knots & Splices, 589
Know All About Tack, 660

Know English Equitation and Training, 660
Know First Aid for Your Horse, 660
Know Practical Horse Breeding, 660
Know Practical Horse Feeding, 660
Know the American Quarter Horse, 660
Know the Anatomy of the Horse, 660
Know the Arabian Horse, 660
Knowing the Outdoors in the Dark, 241
Knox, Bob, 48
Knox, Wilma, 48
Koch, Don, 381
Kodet, E. Russell, 131
Kotschnig, Enid, 288
Kouba, Les, 159, 537, 727
Kreps, Harry Elmer, 132, 620
Krieger, Louis C. C., 217

LION, 901
LaChapelle, Edward R., 701
Lachuck, John, 702
Lagal, Roy, 304-305
Lahue, Kalton C., 425, 703
Land Cruising and Prospecting, 173
Landforms, 288
Landsailing, 436, 824
Landsailing: From RC Models to the Big Ones, 436
Landward Ho!, 900
Lane, Carl D., 513-15
Langer, Richard W., 133, 171
Langewiesche, Wolfgang, 566
Lapidary Journal, 779
Lappé, Frances Moore, 218
Latest Aztec Discoveries: Origin and Untold Riches, 313
Latham, Sid, 704
Laubin, Gladys, 621
Laubin, Reginald, 621
Laurel, Alicia Bay, 622
Laycock, George, 705
Learn, C. R., 134, 706
Learn to Hill Climb!, 398
Learn to Sail, 508
Learn to Wheelie!, 399
Lederer, William J., 457
Lee, Eric C. B., 516
Lee, Kenneth, 516
Lehr, Paul E., 707
Leisure Trails, 750
Lempfert, O. C., 246
Leslie, Robert Franklin, 135

Let's Go Shelling: A Handbook on How, When and Where to Find Florida Shells, 254
Let's Go: The Student Guide to the United States and Canada, 40
Let's Go Water Skiing, 502
Levi, Hubert W., 247
Levi, Lorna R., 247
Lewis, Jack, 698, 708
Liebers, Arthur, 458-59, 517
Light Weight Camping Equipment and How to Make It, 106
Light Weight Outing Equipment with Check List, 107
Lightweight Backpacking: 2 Cups, 2 Spoons, 2 Pots, 126
Lincoln, Joseph Colville, 567
Lind, Ernie, 709
Lindblad, Robert L., 136
Line Breeding and Racing Notes, 668
Living in the Ozarks Newsletter, 901
Living Off the Country: How to Stay Alive in the Woods, 92
Living Off the Land, 98
Living Off the Land: A Handbook for Living in the Subtropics, 233
Living on the Earth . . . , 622
Living on Wheels, 443
Living with Your Land, 271
Locating Gold, Gems & Minerals, 780
Locating Low Cost Land, 597
Lock, Stock and Barrel: Antique Gun Repair, 714
Lockwood, Tim, 426
Log Cabin Manual, 623
Logsden, Gene, 624
Long, Sam, 625
Long Slow Distance: The Humane Way to Train, 693
Look What I Found!, 244
Lovin, Roger, 382
Low and Slow, 875
Lund, Morten, 460
Luray, Martin, 469
Luther, Kenneth E., 356
Lyman Black Powder Handbook, 723
Lyman Cast Bullet Handbook, 710

MV Pathfinder Field Guide, 141
Mabe, Elizabeth, 600
McCarthy, Mike, 372
McClurg, David R., 712
McCollam, Jim, 518
McCready, Jack, 219

McCrory, Robert H., 713-17
McElroy, Thomas P., Jr., 248
McEvoy, Harry K., 718
MacFall, Russell P., 306
Macfarlan, Allan A., 357
McFarland, Kenton D., 427
McFarlane, John W., 358
McGowen, Al, 307
McKay, Frances Peabody, 254
McKenny, Margaret, 220, 260
Mackinley, Ian, 626
MacLachlan, Don, 324
MacLoud, David, 711
MacManiman, Gen, 221
MacMillan, Diane D., 222
McNair, Robert E., 519
McNally, Tom, 49
Maine Catalog, 733
Make Muzzle Loader Accessories, 715
Makens, James C., 520
Makens' Guide to U.S. Canoe Trails, 520
Making of Tools, 648
Malabar Farm, 591
Malo, John W., 521
Mammals: A Guide to Familiar American Species, 283
Mandolf, Henry J., 137
Manna: Foods of the Frontier, 209
Manned Kiting: The Basic Handbook of Tow Launched Hang Gliding, 571
Manning, Harvey, 138, 171
Manual for Neanderthals, 628
Manual of Snowmobiling, 455
Maricopa County (Arizona), 139
Marine & Outdoor Trades, 841
Marine Shells of the Pacific Coast, 262
Marlinspike Sailor, 540
Marquiss, Ken, 308
Martin, Alexander C., 255, 281, 286
Martin, George A., 627
Mason, Bernard S., 140
Mason, Otis T., 604
Master Hunter Manual, 326
Master Tree Finder: A Manual for the Identification of Trees by Their Leaves, 274
Matacia, Louis J., Jr., 490
Mavrogordato, Jack, 665
Maxwell, Lawrence, 141
May, Judy Gail, 522
Melville, Betty, 223
Melvin, A. Gordon, 256
Mendenhall, John, 142
Mendenhall, Ruth, 142
Menzel, Donald H., 260

OUTDOOR RECREATION

Merrilees, Rebecca, 240
Merrill, William K., 50, 143-44
Meteorology of Depressions, 489
Mewhinney, H., 628
Mexico/Latin America, 64, 66, 81, 97, 507
Michell, E. B., 666
Michelsohn, David, 292
Midwest Gem Trails: A Field Guide..., 331
Midwest Outdoors, 751
Midget Motoring and Karting, 427
Milepost: All-the-North-Travel Guide, 428
Miller, Mike, 51, 429
Milne, Peter, 492
Milne, Terry, 17-19
Mineral Recognition by the Five-Digit System, 324
Mineralogical Record, 781
Minerals. *See* **Rockhounding.**
Mines, Stephanie, 10
Mini-Cycle, 811
Miracle, Leonard, 52
Misenhimer, Ted G., 568
Mitchell, Jim, 145
Mitchell, Leeds, Jr., 523
Mitchell, Robert T., 257
Mobil Travel Guides, 53
Mobile Home Owner Magazine, 812
Mobile Living: The Magazine of Recreational Living, 812
Modern ABC's of Family Camping, 87
Modern Blacksmith, 736
Modern Kentucky Rifle: How to Build Your Own, 716
Modern Photography, 934
Modern Seamanship, 510
Mole, Michaela M., 54
Mooers, Robert L., Jr., 146, 171
Moral, Herbert R., 629
Morgan, Lael, 524
Morrall, Rick, 344-45
Morris, Percy A., 260
Mother Earth News, 902
Mother Earth News Almanac: A Guide Through the Seasons, 630
Mother Earth News Handbook of Homemade Power, 631
Motor and Other Vehicles (excluding Motorcycles), 401-443, 646, 797, 808-810, 812, 815, 817-20, 822, 825, 827-29 (*See also* **Motorcycles**.)
Motor Boating & Sailing, 847
Motor Home Manual, 420
Motor Racing Year, 432
Motor Trend, 828
Motorcamping Handbook 1973, 412
Motorcycle & Trail Bike Handbook, 369
Motorcycle Repair Manual, 376
Motorcycle World, 813
Motorcycles, 366-400, 790-91, 799-804, 806-807, 811, 813-14, 817, 821, 823, 826
Motorcycles: A Buyer's and Rider's Guide, 377
Motorcycling and the New Enthusiast, 389
Motorcycling for Beginners: A Manual for Safe Riding, 375
Motorcyclist, 814
Motorcyclopedia, 386
Motorgliding, 876
Motorhome Life, 815
Mountain Climbing, 50, 59, 95, 137, 142, 153, 465, 762-63, 765-66, 771
Mountain Gazette, 765
Mountain Men, 680
Mountain Safety Research Newsletter, 766
Mountaineering: From Hill Walking to Alpine Climbing, 95
Mountaineer's Guide to the High Sierra, 172
Multi-Hull Sailboats: Sailing, Cruising, Racing, 491
Multihull Sailing, 848
Murie, Olaus J., 258, 260
Murlless, Dick, 147
Murray, Sonia Bennett, 259
Murray, Spencer, 425
Mushroom Handbook, 217
Mushroom Hunter's Field Guide, 227
Muzzle Blasts, 935
Muzzle Loader Shooting, 673, 679-81, 683, 688, 690, 694, 710, 713-17, 720-21, 723-25, 730, 734, 737, 923, 926, 928, 935-36
Muzzle Loaders Almanac, 690
Muzzle Loader's Little Library, 673
Muzzle-Loading Cap Lock Rifle, 724
Muzzle-Loading Pistol You Can Build for Under $10, 717
Muzzle Loading Shooting and Winning with the Champions, 688
Muzzleloader, 936

National Aeronautics, 877
National Park Guide, 27
National Trails Council Newsletter, 767

INDEX

National Treasure Hunters League, 782
Natural Life Styles, 903
Nature Crafts, 700
Navigation, 494, 509, 549 (*See also* many of the boating books.)
Needham, Walter, 632
Nelson, Richard K., 148
Nelson, William D., 525
Nemiro, Beverly Anderson, 206
Nesbitt, Paul H., 149
Nessmuk, 162
Net Making, 612
New Baja Handbook for the Off-Pavement Motorist in Lower California, 408
New Boatman's Manual: A Complete Manual of Boat Handling . . . , 515
New Book of Motorcycles, 367
New Complete Book of Bicycling, 361
New Complete Walker . . . , 116
New Cross-Country Ski Book, 451
New Directions in Bicycle Safety, 816
New Science of Skin and Scuba Diving, 526
New Way of the Wilderness, 69
New York Times Guide to Outdoors, U.S.A., 12
Newberry, Lida, 55
NEWS-National Pilots Association, 878
Newman, Barbara, 56
Newman, Doug, 461
Newman, James, 56
1973-1977 Yacht Racing Rules and Tactics, 474
Nomadic Furniture, 608
Nomadic Furniture 2, 609
Non-Flowering Plants: Over 400 Species in Full Color, 267
Nonte, George C., Jr., 719-20
Nordic World, 830
Norris, Monty, 430
North, Wheeler J., 527
North American Canoe Country, 537
North American Falconry and Hunting Hawks, 657
North Cascades Highway Guide, 20
Northeast Outdoors, 752
Northern Mountains, 25
Northwest Foraging, 188
Nourse, Alan E., 171
Novice Sled Dog Training, 661

ORV Monitor, 817
Ocean Sailing Yacht, 544
Oetinger, Bill, 409

Off Road Handbook with Back Country Travel Tips, 441
Off Road Racing, 383
Off Road Vehicles, 819
Off the Beaten Path in Alaska, 51
Off-Road Advertiser, 818
Off-Road Racing, 430
O'Keefe, M. Timothy, 528
Old Farmer's Almanac, 633
Old-House Journal, 904
Oles, Floyd, 309
Oles, Helga, 309
Olsen, Larry Dean, 150
Olsen, Mark, 188
On Quiet Wings: A Soaring Anthology, 567
Once Upon a Wilderness, 158
101 Camping-Out Ideas & Activities, 47
101 Wals to Go Boating for Under $1000, 547
1,000,000 Miles of Canoe and Hiking Routes, 151
One-Day Adventures by Car with Full Road Directions for Drivers Out of New York City, 55
O'Neill, John, 237
Oregon Ski Tours (65 Cross Country Ski Trails), 461
Organic Gardening & Farming, 905
Orienteering, 109
Orienteering and Route Finding, 109, 129, 146, 159
Ormond, Clyde, 57
Orton, Vrest, 224
Osgood, David, 596
Osgood, William E., 462-63
O'Shea, Paul, 431
Ottenheimer, Inc., 9
Out of the Molasses Jug, 600
Outdoor Adventure, 88
Outdoor Guide, 122
Outdoor Life, 753
Outdoor Living: Problems, Solutions, Guidelines, 114
Outdoor Lore, 122, 128, 130, 132, 140-41, 158, 162, 173, 235-87, 726, 908
Outdoor Observer: How to See, Hear and Interpret in the Natural World, 249
Outdoor Recreation Guide, 24
Outdoor Survival Skills, 150
Outdoor Tips, 38
Outdoorsman's FIX-IT Book, 8
Outdoorsman's Handbook, 57
Owner-Built Home, 618
Owner-Built Homestead, 619

271

PV4, Pickup, Van & 4WD, 820
Pacific Crest Trail, Vol. 1: California, 180
Pacific Crest Trail, Vol. 2: Oregon and Washington, 161
Pacific Coast Tree Finder: A Pocket Manual for Identifying Pacific Coast Trees, 277
Pacific Wilderness Journal, 768
Packing Dogs, 668
Palmer, Heidi, 209
Parachutes and Parachuting: A Modern Guide to the Sport, 574
Parachuting, 564, 574, 869, 877, 884
Parachutist, 879
Paradise Below Zero, 466
Park, Jack, 569
Passport to Survival: Four Foods and More to Use and Store, 200
Patterson, Frank, 360
Patterson, Jerry G., 58
Patty, Thomas F., 59
Paw Prints: How to Identify Rare and Common Mammals by Their Tracks, 246
Pearl, Richard M., 310-11
Pedaler's Handbook: A Guide for Bicyclists, 340
Pedersen, Tage, 464
Peeters, Hans J., 664
Pellegrini, A. M., 220
Penfield, Thomas, 312
People's Guide to Country Real Estate, 653
Pepper, Choral, 60
Pearlman, Raymond, 315-16
Pearlman, Richard, 238
Perry, Robin, 383-85
Perry, Ronald H., 529
Petersen's Guide to Pocket Camera Photography, 703
Petersen's Photographic Magazine, 937
Peterson Field Guide Series, 260
Peterson, Roger Tory, 260
Petrides, George A., 260
Petzoldt, Paul, 152
Phillips, Norman, 530
Photography, 14, 30, 57, 112, 517, 677, 682, 697, 699, 703, 711, 732, 934, 937-38
Photography: The Amateur's Guide to Better Pictures, 682
Phydeaux, Djaugh, 721
Physical Fitness, 674, 693, 933, 941
Pickup Camper Manual, 421
Pigeons, 654, 662, 909-910

Pigeons for Pleasure and Profit, 662
Pilkington, Roger, 531
Pill, Virginia, 202, 251
Pilot's Handbook of Weather, 563
Pioneer & Game Recipes, 690
Plane & Pilot, 880
Plant/Animal Identification, 235-87 (*See also* **Food Plants**; **Poisonous Plants**.)
Plant Decks, 194-95
Pleasure Packing: How to Backpack in Comfort, 181
Pleasures of Cross-Country Skiing, 460
Pleasures of Sketching Outdoors, 695
Poisonous Plants, 176, 188, 194-95, 214
Poisonous Plants in the Wilderness, 176
Pole, Paddle & Portage, 532
Pond, Alonzo W., 149
Pond Life: A Guide to Common Plants and Animals of North American Ponds and Lakes, 261
Popular Archaeology, 783
Popular Cycling, 821
Popular Photography, 938
Popular Snowmobiling, 831
Portable Feast, 222
Position Rifle Shooting: A How-To Text for Shooters and Coaches, 722
Potomac Trail Book, 164
Pough, Frederick H., 260
Powell, Guy E., 313
Power, John, 61
Power, 631, 639, 647
Powerboat Industry, 849
Powerboat Performance Reports, 849
Powerboat: The World's Leading Performance Boating Magazine, 849
Poynter, Dan, 570-71
Practical Hunter's Dog Book, 659
Practical Navigation for the Yachtsman, 494
Practical Sailing, 499
Precision Shooting, 939
Prenis, John, 634
Primitive Medical Aid in the Wilderness, 176
Pritchard, Anthony, 432
Private Pilot, 881
Private Pilot Study Guide, 575
Private Pilot's Guide, 572
Proceedings of the Company of Amateur Brewers, 224
Producing Your Own Power: How to Make Nature's Energy Sources Work for You, 639

Professional Guides Manual, 123
Prospecting Hints, Vol. 1, 314
Provoker, 906
Public Works, 641
Pullam, William C., 722
Putting Food By, 211

RV World, 822
Radlauer, Ed, 386
Rafting. *See* **Canoeing.**
Rally Handbook, 419
Rallying, 405-406, 440
Rallying: Preparation–Navigation–Organisation, 440
Ramage, C. Kenneth, 723
Rand McNally Guide to European Campgrounds, 63
Rand McNally Road Atlas of Europe, 63
Rand McNally Road Atlas, United States, Canada, Mexico, 64
Rand McNally Western Campgrounds & Trailer Parks 1974, 65
Raup, Lucy G., 225
Reading the Woods, 242
Recipes for a Small Planet: The Art and Science of High Protein Vegetarian Cookery, 201
Recreating the American Longrifle, 683
Recreational Rental Guide, 433
Recreational Vehicle Handbook, 418
Recreational Vehicle Maintenance: All Sizes of Campers, Trailers, Motor Homes, 426
Regional Catalogs, 685, 689, 733
Reid, George K., 261
Reidel, Arthur, 153
Reithmaier, L. W., 563, 572
Reptiles and Amphibians: A Guide to Familiar American Species, 284
Reptiles & Amphibians of the West, 243
Rethmel, R. C., 154
Rhodes, Frank H. T., 315
Rice, Tom, 262-63
Richard's Bicycle Book, 338
Richmond, Doug, 66, 387-88, 434
Ride . . . and Stay Alive, 372
Riding the Dirt, 390
Riding the Gymkhana Winner, 660
Riding the Show-Ring Hunter, 660
Rifle, 940
Rifle & Shotgun Shooting, 722

Rifle Making in the Great Smokey Mountains, 690
Right Boat for You, 533
Rivers and Lakes, 25
Riviere, Bill, 532
Road Atlas Canada, 67
Road Atlases, 63-64, 67
Road Rider, 823
Road Rider: A Guide to On-the-Road Motorcycling, 384
Robbins, Chandler S., 264
Robbins, Maurice, 317
Robert Colwell's Guide to Snow Trails, 453
Roberts, Ned H., 724
Robin Hood Handbook, 617
Robinson, Donald H., 155
Robinson, Ellis H., 265
Robinson, Gayle D., 265
Robinson, John W., 156-57
Robinson, William W., 533-34
Rock and Gem, 784
Rock Hound's Guide to Connecticut, 319
Rockhound, 785
Rockhounding, 24, 57, 288, 291, 296-301, 303, 307-312, 314-15, 318-21, 323-25, 329, 331-32, 747, 774, 776-81, 784-86
Rockhound's Manual, 300
Rocks and Minerals, 291, 786
Rocks and Minerals: A Guide to Familiar Minerals, Gems, Ores and Rocks, 332
Rocks and What to Do with Them, 303
Rocky Mountain Tree Finder: A Pocket Manual for Identifying Rocky Mountain Trees, 278
Rodale, Robert, 635
Rope Roundup: The Lore and Craft of Rope and Roping, 637
Ropework. *See* **Knots and Ropework.**
Rosenbloom, Joseph, 725
Rossit, Edward A., 465
Rothrock, Bill, 535
Rotor & Wing, 882
Roughing It Easy: A Unique Ideabook for Camping and Cooking, 230
Rowlands, John J., 726
Ruck, Wolfgang E., 536
Rudder, 850
Runner's World, 941
Ruth, Kent, 68
Rutstrum, Calvin, 69, 158-59, 466, 537, 727
Ryerson, Kathleen H., 319
Rynerson, Fred, 318

OUTDOOR RECREATION

Safari Fever: The Story of a Car Rally They Said No European Could Win, 405
Safe Snowmobiling: Fun without Damage, 468
Safety and Survival at Sea, 516
Safran, Rose, 70
Saijo, Albert, 160, 171
Sail, 851
Sailboat & Sailboat Equipment Directory, 851
Sailing, 472, 489, 491-93, 498-500, 503-506, 508, 512, 514, 523, 534-35, 544, 552, 554, 847-48, 851-52
Sailing, 504, 852
Sailing: A Guide to Handling, Equipping, Maintaining, and Buying the Small Sailboat, 552
Sailing Life and How to Enjoy It, 534
Sailing Step By Step, 512
Sailing Wheels, 824
Salinger, Peter H., 389
San Bernardino Mountain Trails: 100 Hikes in Southern California, 156
Sanders, E. B., 189
Sandstrom, George F., 235-36
Sandstrom, Marita, 236
Sanford, Robert, 390
Santschi, Roy J., 320-21
Sarvis, Shirley, 192
Sauna: The Finnish Bath, 645
Savory Wild Mushroom, 220
Schaffer, Jeff, 161
Schell, Hal, 71
Schubert, Ruth L., 226
Schuler, Stanley, 636
Schwartz, Alvin, 72
Schweizer Aircraft Corp., 573
Schwinn Bicycle Service Manual, 359
Science of Trapping, 620
Scissors Sam Says Be Sharp . . . , 625
Scorer, Richard Segar, 728
Scuba Diver's Guide to Underwater Ventures, 522
Sea Boating Almanac, 538
Sea Magazine, 853
Sea Shells of the World, 256
Sears, George Washington, 162
Seashells of North America: A Guide to Field Identification, 235
Seashells of the World: A Guide to the Better-Known Species, 236
Seashores: A Guide to Animals and Plants Along the Beaches, 285
Self, Margaret Cabel, 667

Self-Taught Navigation: Ten Easy Steps to Master Celestial Navigation, 509
Sellick, Bud, 574
Sensuous Gadgeteer: Bringing Tools and Materials to Life, 579
Service Bulletin—National Pilots Association, 883
Seton, Ernest Thompson, 266
Severn, Bill, 637
Shaffer, Paul R., 316, 332
Shaffer, R. L., 217
Shapiro, Barry, 590
Sharrard, Sally, 461
Shaw, Reginald C., 360
Shedenhelm, W. R. C., 59
Shelter, 614
Shelters, Shacks, and Shanties, 585
Shenendoah: The Valley Story, 22
Sheridan, Michael F., 163
Shipman, Carl, 368, 385, 391
Shoemaker, Hurst H., 280
Shooting and Firearms (General), 9, 30, 38, 52, 76, 132, 165, 675, 687, 692, 702, 709-710, 719, 722, 919-20, 928-32, 939-40, 942-44, 946 (*See also* **Muzzle Loader Shooting**.)
Shooting the Percussion Rifle, 673
Shooting Times, 942
Shooting Times & Country Magazine, 943
Short Walks in Connecticut, 41-43
Short Walks on Long Island, 2
Shosteck, Robert, 73, 164
Shumway, George, 683
Shuttleworth, Floyd S., 267
Siebert, Alan H., 435
Sierra Club Bulletin, 769
Sierra Club Wilderness Handbook, 101
Signpost, 770
Simonson, Leroy, 575
Simple Methods of Mining Gold, 301
Simplified Performance Testing for Hang Gliders, 569
Simpson, Norman T., 74
Sincere's Bicycle Service Book, 348
Singer, Arthur, 239, 264
Siposs, George, 436
Skeet Shooting Review, 944
Sketching, 695, 729
Ski Touring: An Introductory Guide, 462
Skiera, Joseph A., 563
Skiing, 446-48, 450-51, 453, 457-58, 460-62, 464, 467, 469, 764, 830
Skiing Is a Family Sport, 446

INDEX

Skijoring with Dogs, 668
Skills for Taming the Wilds: A Handbook of Woodcraft Wisdom, 93
Skin Diver, 854
Skipper's Course, 550
Sky and Telescope, 945
Sky Diver Magazine, 884
Skysurfer Magazine, 885
Slay, Reny, 613
Sled and Harness Styles, 668
Sled Building Plans, 668
Sled Dog Bulletin, 668
Sled Dog Encyclopedia, 671
Sloane, Eugene A., 361
Smallman, Robert E., 75
Smatko, A. J., 172
Smith, Alan, 322
Smith, Alexander H., 227
Smith, Hervey Garnett, 539-40
Smith, Hobart M., 284
Smith, Leroi, 392, 437
Smith, Ronald, 729
Sno Mobile Times, 832
Snotrack, 834
Snow Camping and Mountaineering, 465
Snow Country Design, 626
Snow Crystals, 678
Snow Goer, 833
Snowmobile Operator Responsibility Training: Student Manual, 445
Snowmobiler's Companion, 471
Snowmobiling and Snowmobiles, 30, 38, 444-45, 452, 455, 459, 468, 470-71, 831-34
Snowshoe Book, 463
Snowshoeing, 456, 459, 463
Soaring, 556, 559, 565, 567, 573, 578, 876-77, 886
Soaring, 886
Soaring in America, 556
Soaring School Manuals, 565
Somewhat Irreverent Look at the Design of the Long Distance Cruiser, 535
Southern Mountains, 25
Southern Outdoors, 754
Sparano, Vin T., 76
Sparks, James C., Jr., 427
Spelunking, 14, 24, 59, 112, 712
Sport Aviation, 887
Sport Car, 825
Sport Flying, 888
Sport Parachuting Handbook: The 1970's Textbook of Sport Parachuting, 564
Sport Planes, 889
Sports Afield, 755

Sportsman and His Family Outdoors, 30
Sportsman on Wheels, 402
Sportsman's Camping Guide, 52
Sportsman's Encyclopedia, 9
Sportsman's Eye: How to Make Better Use of Your Eyes in the Outdoors, 29
Sprunt, Alexander, IV, 268
Stallings, Constance, 147
Starfish: Guides to Identification and Methods of Preserving, 251
Stark, Norman H., 638
Stark, Steven D., 40
Stars: A Guide to the Constellations, Sun, Moon, Planets, and Other Features of the Heavens, 739
Stebbins, Robert C., 260
Steck, Allen, 467
Stelle, James Parish, 730
Stensvold, Mike, 541
Stephens, Kenneth, 542
Steward, Chuck, 362
Steward, Robert M., 543
Stick and Rudder: An Explanation of the Art of Flying, 566
Stoner, Carol Hupping, 639
Streano, Vince, 393
Street, Donald, 544
Streever, Fred, 669
Strekalovsky, Nicholas, 248, 250
Strong, Mary Frances, 323
Strung, Norman, 77
Strung, Sil, 77
Stuntz, Daniel E., 220
Sturdivant, E. N., 228
Sturdivant, Edith, 228
Styers, John, 731
Successful Sailing, 493
Sudden Wealth: An Introduction to Successful Treasure Hunting, 302
Sullivan, George, 545
Summer Gold: A Camper's Guide to Amateur Metal Prospecting, 298
Summit, 771
Sun Bear, 640
Sunset Beachcomber's Guide to the Pacific Coast, 82
Sunset Books/Magazine, Editors of, 78-82
Sunset Camping Handbook, 80
Super Handyman's Big Bike Book, 341
Superstition Wilderness Guidebook, 163
Surfboard Builder's Yearbook, 546
Surfer, 855
Surfing, 9, 517, 525, 546, 846, 855-956
Surfing: A Handbook, 525

275

Survival, 59, 69, 91, 93-94, 98, 105, 108, 111-15, 118-21, 130, 136, 139, 144, 148-50, 152, 165-70, 176, 408, 434-35, 441, 454, 466, 516, 598, 606, 641
Survival Book, 149
Survival Education Association, 165
Survival Guns, 166
Survival Handbook, 144
Survival in the Outdoors, 108
Survival in the Wilderness, 176
Survival: Pioneer, Indian and Wilderness Lore, 598
Survive!, 168
Surviving the Unexpected: A Curriculum Guide for Wilderness Survival and Survival from Natural and Man-Made Disasters, 113
Surviving the Unexpected Wilderness Emergency, 115
Sussman, Aaron, 732
Sweet, Muriel, 229
Szykitka, Walter, 641

THing, a Modern Search for Adventure, 294
Tallman, Annie S., 134
Tangerman, E. J., 642
Tanguay, Margaret Fife, 83
Tanguay, Peter E., 83
Tanner, Hans, 324, 576
Tappan, Mel, 166-67
Tassajara Bread Book, 190
Tassajara Cooking, 191
Tate, Grover Ted, 168
Taylor, Zack, 547
Team & Trail, 917
Tejada-Flores, Lito, 467
Terry, Webb, 688
Thiffault, Mark, 363
This Is Sailing: A Complete Course, 492
Thollander, Earl, 84
Thomas, Bill, 85
Thomas, Dian, 230
Thomas, James L., 468
Thompson, Raymond, 670-71
To Hell on Wheels: The Illustrated Manual of Desert Survival, 435
Toghill, Jeff, 548
Tokle, Art, 469
Tomikell, John, 231
Toohey, Barbara, 448
Tools for Survival and Self-Sufficient Living, 167
Touching America with Two Wheels, 393

Touring the Old West, 68
Tourist Tips and Hints, 4
Townsend, Philip, 733
Townsend, Sallie, 549
Tracks, 856
Tracks and Trailcraft, 253
Trade-A-Plane, 890
Trail Bike Quarterly, 826
Trail Camping, 772
Trailer Life, 827
Trailer Life's 1974 Recreational Vehicle Campground and Service Guide: The Official Directory for the Good Sam Club, 86
Trailer Travel, 829
Trailering America's Highways and Byways: Vol. 1, The West; Vol. 2, The East, 33
Trail-R-Club of America, 438
Trails of the Angeles: 100 Hikes in the San Gabriels, 157
Trails of the Sierra Madre, 97
Trap & Field, 946
Trapper's Companion, 643
Trapper's Guide, 721
Trapping, 620, 643, 651, 721, 898, 907-908
Travel Adventure in Europe with Tent, Van or Motorhome, 83
Travel Hints, 4, 10-11, 14, 21-22, 33-34, 40, 53-55, 60, 66, 97, 163, 749-50
Treasure Hunter, 787
Treasure Hunter's Manual #6, 327
Treasure Hunter's Manual #7, 328
Treasure Hunting, 289-90, 292-94, 302, 304-305, 313, 320-22, 326-28, 330, 746, 775, 782, 787-89
Treasure Hunting Unlimited, 788
Tree Finder: A Pocket Manual for Identification of Trees by Their Leaves, 275
Trees: A Guide to Familiar American Trees, 286
Trees of North America: A Field Guide to the Major Native and Introduced Species North of Mexico, 240
Tripping in America: Off the Beaten Track, 85
Troebst, Cord Christian, 169
Trout, Perry, 439
True Treasure, 789
Tryon, T. B., 734
Tucker, John, 170
Turner, Stuart, 440
Tyler, V. E., 220
2,000 Down Home Skills & Secret Formulas for Practically Everything, 644

INDEX

Two Wheel Trip, 794
Two-Wheel Touring & Camping, 370

USSA Snotrack, 834
Uncle Jim's Book of Pancakes, 186
Understanding Horse Psychology, 660
Underwater Reporter, 857
U.S. Coast Guard, 550
U.S. Dept. of Agriculture, 232, 269

Vacation Ideas, 1, 6, 25-27, 39, 44-46, 53-55, 68, 70, 73-74, 78-79, 84-85
Vagabonding in America: A Guidebook about Energy, 10
Vagabonding in Europe and North Africa, 11
Van Atta, Marian, 233
Van Lear, Denise, 171
Vaughn, Beatrice, 211
Venison Book: How to Dress, Cut Up and Cook Your Deer, 203
Verney, Michael, 551
Very Special Resorts, 70
Vestal, Stanley, 621
Vickery, Max, 688
Viherjuuri, H. J., 645
Vilas, Curtis N., 270
Vilas, Naomi R., 270
Village Technology Handbook, 647
Vision, 29, 242, 249
Voge, Hervey H., 172
Voice of the Trapper, 907
Volunteers in Technical Assistance, 646-47
Von Mueller, Karl, 325-28
Vosburgh, John, 271

Waar, Robert, 441
Wagenvoord, James, 364
Walking in the Wild: The Complete Guide to Hiking and Backpacking, 127
Wallace, Arthur Fuller, 173
Wallace, Bill, 552
Wallace, Clarke, 470
Wallach, Theresa, 394
Wambold, H. R., 735
Ware, John P., 495
Warren, Cameron A., 407
Water Skier, 858
Water Skiing, 9, 502, 517, 542, 858
Water Sport, 859
Water Trails of Washington, 497

Waterskiing, 542
Waterways in Europe: A Guide to Inland Cruising, 531
Watson, Jack B., 395-99
Watters, Jim, 174
Watts, Alan, 489
Watts, May, 272-76
Watts, Tom, 276-78
We Like It Wild, 582
Weather, 477, 489, 518, 563, 678, 701, 707, 728, 947
Weather: Air Masses–Clouds–Rainfall–Storms–Weather Maps–Climate, 707
Weather for Sportsmen: A New Kind of Book for Sailors and All Outdoorsmen, 477
Weatherwise, 947
Webster, Harold M., 657
Weeds, 255
Weekender's Guide: Places of Historic, Scenic and Recreational Interest within 200 Miles of the Washington-Baltimore Area, 73
Weiers, Ronald M., 442
Welch, Mary Scott, 175
Wells, George S., 87
Wertz, Ed, 329
Wertz, Leola, 329
Western Edible Wild Plants, 208
Western Horseman, 918
Western Outdoors, 756
Weygers, Alexander G., 648, 736
What Is a Shell?, 263
Wheels Afield, 828
White, Richard E., 260
White Earth Snowshoe Guide Book, 456
Whiter, Robert, 365
Whittling and Woodcarving, 642
Wickstrom, Lois, 234
Wigginton, Brooks Eliot, 649-50
Wild Country, 759
Wild Edible Plants of the Western United States . . . , 215
Wild Flavor, 216
Wild Flowers of the Pacific Northwest Photographed in Their Natural Environment, 265
Wild Game Cookbook, 213
Wild Game Trailguide, 205
Wild Rivers of North America, 507
Wildcrafter Manuals, 651
Wildcrafter Publications, 651
Wildcrafters World, 908
Wilderness Cabin, 727
Wilderness Camping, 773

OUTDOOR RECREATION

Wilderness Cooking: A Unique Illustrated Cookbook and Guide for Outdoor Enthusiasts, 189
Wilderness Gear You Can Make Yourself, 3
Wilderness Handbook, 152
Wilderness Pocket n' Pak Library, 176
Wilderness Route Finder, 159
Wilderness Skiing, 467
Wilderness Survival: A Complete Handbook and Guide for Survival in the North American Wilds, 94
Wilderness Travel-Summer, 165
Wildwater Touring: Techniques and Tours, 473
Wildwood Wisdom, 36
Williams, Herb, 88
Willis, W. E., 626
Wilson, James, 330
Wilson, Joe Pete, 457
Wimer, Sally, 471
Wind Drifters Balloon Club, 577
Winnett, Thomas, 177-80
Winter Camping and Travel, 50, 69, 99, 112, 123, 130, 132-33, 138, 141, 449, 454, 459, 465-66
Winter Hiking and Camping, 454
Winter Tree Finder: A Manual for Identifying Trees in Winter, 276
Wiseman, Robert F., 672
Wizansky, Richard, 652
Wollin, Jay C., 306
Wolters, Richard A., 443, 578
Woman's Guide to Boating & Cooking, 524

Wonderful World of the .22, 702
Wood, Robert S., 17, 181
Woodall's Better Camping, 761
Woodall's Campsite Cookbook, 187
Woodall's Trailer Travel, 829
Woodall's Trailering Parks and Campgrounds, 89
Woodburner's Handbook, 607
Woodcraft, 140
Woodcraft and Camping, 140, 162
Woods, Jim, 737-38
Woods Rider: A Guide to Off-the-Road Motorcycling, 385
Wyckoff, Jerome, 288
Wynn, Peter, 553

Yachting, 860
Yachtsman's Weather Manual, 518
Yerkow, Charles, 400
You Can Survive: A Guide to Survival, 136
Young, Erni, 222
Young, Jean, 653
Young, Jim, 653
Yukon Summer, 484

Zadig, Ernest A., 554
Zallinger, Jean, 255
Zeitner, June Culp, 331
Zim, Herbert S., 257, 264, 267-68, 279-86, 316, 332, 682, 707, 739
Zinn, Donald J., 287
Zornig, Harold F., 580